EXECUTIVE POWER AND SOVIET POLITICS

Contemporary Soviet/Post-Soviet Politics

PERESTROIKA-ERA POLITICS
THE NEW SOVIET LEGISLATURE
AND GORBACHEV'S POLITICAL REFORMS
Robert T. Huber and Donald R. Kelley, eds.

SOVIET CONSTITUTIONAL CRISIS
FROM DE-STALINIZATION TO DISINTEGRATION
Robert Sharlet

EXECUTIVE POWER AND SOVIET POLITICS
THE RISE AND FALL OF THE SOVIET STATE
Eugene Huskey, editor

CRACKS IN THE MONOLITH
PARTY POWER IN THE BREZHNEV ERA
James R. Millar, ed.

CRIME AND PUNISHMENT IN SOVIET OFFICIALDOM
COMBATING CORRUPTION IN THE SOVIET ELITE, 1965–1990
William Clark

EXECUTIVE POWER AND SOVIET POLITICS

The Rise and Decline of the Soviet State

EDITED BY **Eugene Huskey**

M.E. Sharpe Inc. • Armonk, New York • London, England

Available in the United Kingdom and Europe from M. E. Sharpe,
Publishers, 3 Henrietta Street, London WC2E 8LU.

Library of Congress Cataloging-in-Publication Data

Executive power and Soviet politics:
the rise and fall of the Soviet state/
Eugene Huskey, editor
p.   cm. — (Contemporary Soviet/post Soviet politics)
Includes bibliographical references and index.
ISBN 1-56324-059-9 (cloth)
ISBN 1-56324-060-2 (pbk.)
1. Executive power—Soviet Union.
2. Soviet Union—Politics and government—1945–1991.
I. Huskey, Eugene, 1952– .
II. Series.
JN6540.E94   1992
354.4703′22—dc20
92-8452CIP

Printed in the United States of America

The paper used in this publication meets the minimum requirements of
American National Standard for Information Sciences—
Permanence of Paper for Printed Library Materials,
ANSI Z39.48–1984.

⊗

BB (c)   10   9   8   7   6   5   4   3   2   1
BB (p)   10   9   8   7   6   5   4   3   2   1

CONTENTS

List of Tables   vii

Acknowledgements   ix

Introduction
  Eugene Huskey   xi

The State in Imperial Russia and the USSR

1 The Government in the Soviet Political System
   T.H. Rigby   3

2 Party-State Relations
   Cameron Ross   49

3 Executive-Legislative Relations
   Eugene Huskey   83

4 The Rise of Presidential Power under Gorbachev
   Brenda L. Horrigan and Theodore Karasik   106

The State and the Economy

5 The Ministry of Finance
   Peter B. Maggs   129

6 The Industrial Ministries
   Stephen Fortescue   143

7 The Agricultural Ministries
   Barbara Ann Chotiner   161

The State and Security

8 The Ministry of Defense
   Ellen Jones and James Brusstar   181

9 The Ministry of Internal Affairs
   Louise Shelley   202

10 The Administration of Justice:
   Courts, Procuracy, and Ministry of Justice
   Eugene Huskey   221

The State and the Future

11 The Rebirth of the Russian State
   Eugene Huskey   249

Index   271

Contributors   281

LIST OF TABLES

Table   1.1   People's Commissariats, November 1923   16
Table   1.2   Membership of Key Executive Bodies, 14 March 1953   28
Table   1.3   Membership of Key Executive Bodies, January 1982   37
Table   2.1   The Communist Party and the Soviet State, 1986   50
Table   2.2   The Central Committee Secretariat and Its
                   Departments, 1986   51
Table   2.3   The Politburo, 1986   53
Table   2.4   Government Institutions and Their Representation
                   in the Central Committee, 1986   54
Table   2.5   The Central Party Apparatus, September 1988   63
Table   2.6   USSR Presidential Council, October 1990   65
Table   2.7   The Politburo, October 1990   66
Table   2.8   The CPSU Secretariat and Its Apparatus, October 1990   67
Table   2.9   Central Committee Members in State Institutions, 1990   69
Table   2.10   The Communist Party and the Soviet State, January 1991   72
Table   8.1   Structure of the Armed Forces   184
Table   11.1   Structure of Regional Government in Russia,
                   January 1992   252
Table   11.2   Ethnic Republics in the Russian Federation, 1989   255
Table   11.3   Ministries and State Committees in the Russian
                   Federation, December 1991   260

ACKNOWLEDGEMENTS

Like other projects conceived at the end of the Soviet era, this book had a long and difficult gestation. Its appearance is a tribute to the patience and flexibility of the contributors, whose topics underwent a dizzying transformation in the final months of 1991.

In editing and preparing the manuscript for publication, I was assisted at Stetson University by the staff of the DuPont-Ball Library and by Michael Connelly, Don Gast, Kim Simonds, and Judy Usher in the Department of Political Science. It is a pleasure to acknowledge their work. I am also grateful to the Knight Foundation and the Jessie Ball duPont Fund for financial support.

DeLand, Florida
May 1992

Note on Transliteration and Usage. The transliteration system used here is that of the Library of Congress. Exceptions to that system have been made in the case of surnames widely used in the Western press (thus, Yeltsin rather than El'tsin). The term 'government' has several meanings in English. Government is capitalized here when it refers to the institution (*pravitel'stvo, Sovet ministrov, Kabinet ministrov*) that sits atop the state's executive agencies.

INTRODUCTION

Eugene Huskey

By the summer of 1991, Gorbachev's policies of *glasnost'* and *demokratizatsiia* had fundamentally transformed the central institutions of the Communist Party and the Soviet legislative system. But the central executive institutions of state, known collectively as the Government (*pravitel'stvo*), remained largely unreconstructed. The Government's vast network of ministries and state committees, which had always functioned as the institutional core of the Soviet political and economic system, continued to employ the population, to administer the economy and society, and to function as a key source of information and influence in the shaping of policy. The reforms of the Gorbachev era revealed that remaking the party's "power over words" was easier than remaking the Government's "power over things."[1]

The Government became, in effect, the last line of defense against a new order. In August 1991, leading members of the Government launched a coup to reassert executive authority amid the decline of the Communist Party and the rise of social movements and independent-minded legislatures. Although support for the coup came from conservative elements in party and legislative bodies as well as officials in the machinery of Government, it was the Government's Cabinet of Ministers that served as the coup's "general staff." Ranking members of the Government emerged as the central figures in the short-lived junta, the State Committee for Extraordinary Events. Standing behind the junta's constitutional prop, Vice-President Gennadii Yanaev, were the prime minister, Valentin Pavlov, the minister of defense, Dmitrii Yazov, the minister of internal affairs (MVD), Boris Pugo, and the head of the Committee on State Security (KGB), Vladimir Kriuchkov. The failure of the coup crippled the Government's economic and repressive institutions, which had given cohesion to the Soviet

Union. Without respected or effective institutions of state in the center, the Union soon became ungovernable, and, in December 1991, 11 of the former republics of the USSR regrouped into a loose confederation known as the Commonwealth of Independent States. For the moment, the Commonwealth has eschewed the formation of its own Government, leaving the development of state executive institutions to the constituent states.

The August 1991 coup is only the latest illustration of the centrality of the Government to an understanding of Soviet politics and society.   Yet the scholarly literature (and much journalism) on the Soviet Union in the last quarter century has neglected the state's executive institutions, leaving a legacy focused on the party, parliament, and political movements to the virtual exclusion of what in American political science would be called public administration.[2] How does one make sense of the neglect of the Government in such a state-centered political system? Three explanations seem to be in order.

First, executive institutions of state were more inscrutable than the Communist Party and the parliament. Put starkly, information was an instrument of legitimation for the party and parliament and was therefore more widely disseminated; for the Government, it was largely reserved for internal bureaucratic communication. Most Government information flowed within closed, vertical channels "for internal use only" (*dlia sluzhebnogo pol'zovaniia*).[3] When information on the structure and operation of Government institutions did seep out into the public realm, it was often found in little-known works on administrative law and in the heavily-censored decisions and circulars of the Government and its ministries. Information on the party Politburo, for example, was easier to come by than that on the presidium of the Council of Ministers, the collective body at the apex of the state's executive hierarchy.

If the obscurity and paucity of data on Soviet Government discouraged research on the subject, so did the traditional view of the Government as an administrative arm of the Communist Party. In this neat division of politics and administration, decisions were made by the party and implemented by the Government. From this perspective, studies of the Government were derivative and technical in comparison with research into the core political problems posed by party rule. Yet we know from the political history of the USSR that the relations between Government and Communist Party were far more nuanced than this convenient dichotomy of political and administrative functions admits. The Government served as a source of information, expertise, and personnel for the Communist Party, and at times it rivalled the party for institutional pre-eminence in the Soviet political system.   Party and Government rule were therefore interwoven, with influence flowing between both institutional hierarchies.

The neglect of the Government in Soviet studies is rooted finally in the behavioral revolution that gripped Western social science in the first two decades after World War II. The behavioral revolution shifted the focus of research from the state to society and from institutions to functions. Unfortunately, the pendulum swung so far as to lead to an abandonment, or at best a marginalization, of work that retained state institutions at the center of analysis. The result has been the rise of a generation of students and scholars who have little appreciation of the role of state executive institutions in Soviet politics. There has simply been nowhere to turn for an introductory, never mind a monograph-length, analysis of contemporary institutions such as the Ministry of Finance and the State Committee on Supply (*Gossnab*).

During the last decade, scholars in comparative politics with varied regional interests and political perspectives have been bringing the state back to the forefront of political inquiry. As Theda Skocpol argues, the movement is in some respects a Continental reaction to an Anglo-American paradigm that failed to account for the continuing centrality of the state to European, and often Latin American and Asian, politics.[4] The resulting research has not divorced the state from society but it has emphasized the relative autonomy of the state, and of the state's constituent institutions, in the formulation and implementation of policy.

The chapters that follow seek to revive an understanding of and interest in state institutions in the Soviet Union and its successor states. This is obviously a difficult time for such an enterprise. There is an understandable emphasis at present on groups and the rise of a civil society in Russia and on survey research that explores the linkages between individual attitudes and their social, cultural, and economic determinants. Further, the instability of the state and the crises of statehood in post-Soviet politics make institutions particularly slippery subjects for investigation. But both the Russian and Soviet heritages suggest that institutions of state will continue to propel and direct social change. In this period of state building--or perhaps more accurately state renovation--on the territories of the former USSR, it is essential to refocus attention on the development and behavior of state institutions as political actors. This volume, which examines the rise and fall of the Soviet Government and its leading ministries and state committees, is offered as a primer on state institutions and as an opening contribution to the debate on the state in the transition from Soviet to post-Soviet politics.

Notes

1. See the comments by K.G. Kholodkovskii of IMEMO in "Prospects for Democratization," *Soviet Review* (May-June 1991), pp. 11-15.

2. One only needs to compare the traditional state-centered textbooks on Soviet politics to more recent works (which often mirror American politics texts in format) to understand the effects of the behavioral revolution on the research agenda in Soviet studies. Compare, for example, J.N. Hazard, *The Soviet System of Government*, 4th revised edition (Chicago: University of Chicago Press, 1968), L.B. Schapiro, *The Government and Politics of the Soviet Union* (New York: Random House, 1965), and D.J.R. Scott, *Russia's Political Institutions* (New York: Frederick A. Praeger, Publishers, 1961), with the textbooks by J.F. Hough, *How the Soviet Union is Governed* (Cambridge, MA: Harvard University Press, 1979) and M. McAuley, *Politics and the Soviet Union* (Harmondsworth, UK: Penguin Books, 1977). While the textbooks of the last two decades are to be welcomed for bringing society into Soviet politics, they tended to push the state, and especially the Government, into a dimly lit corner of the field.

3. See D.A. Loeber, "Legal Rules 'For Internal Use Only'," *International and Comparative Law Quarterly* (January 1970), pp. 70-98, and E. Huskey, "Government Rulemaking as a Brake on Perestroika," *Law and Social Inquiry*, no. 3 (1990), pp. 419-432.

4. T. Skocpol, "Bringing the State Back In: Strategies of Analysis in Current Research," in *Bringing the State Back In*, ed. P. Evans, D. Rueschemeyer, and T. Skocpol (Cambridge: Cambridge University Press, 1985), pp. 3-37.

THE STATE IN IMPERIAL
RUSSIA AND THE USSR

1

THE GOVERNMENT IN THE SOVIET POLITICAL SYSTEM

T.H. Rigby

Before 1917

When the Bolsheviks took power in 1917 they were successors to a system of strong, centralized government whose origins went back to sixteenth–seventeenth century Muscovy. The princes of Moscow, having "gathered in" all the Russian lands under their primacy and fought free of the Tatar yoke, were now masters of the largest Christian state in the world and the only *Orthodox* state free of infidel domination. Small wonder, then, that they saw themselves as the proper heirs to the *imperium* of Byzantium (the second Rome) and beyond that the first Rome, and asserted the title and authority of Caesar (Tsar). This claim was brutally enforced by Ivan IV (1530–84) and consolidated in the following century by the first Romanov tsars. Meanwhile a ramshackle bureaucracy grew up, drawing partly on the legacy of Tatar administration, to help run this great empire now stretching from the Polish frontier to the Pacific.

While the essentials of this autocratic and increasingly bureaucratic system remained unchanged up to the early twentieth century, its details were progressively altered under the influence of Western ideas and models and of socio–economic changes. In the early eighteenth century Peter the Great sought to rationalize its administration along Prussian and Swedish lines, and the process was taken further a century later by Alexander I's reformist adviser Mikhail Speransky (1772–1839). By now the earlier "colleges" (*kollegii*), or boards, on the main branches of government had been supplanted by a group of ministries (initially for foreign affairs, war, navy, interior, justice, finance, commerce, and education), and the quasi–patrimonial pattern of regional administration had been replaced by a system of provincial governors coming under the Interior Ministry.[1]

The most significant development in the nineteenth century was the necessary recourse of the autocracy to instruments of policy consultation and administrative coordination, and the tendency of these to acquire a life of their own, which was suggestive of a possible evolution towards a parliamentary–cabinet system of government. Here Russia was following similar developments in the autocratic empires of Prussia–Germany and Austria–Hungary. Like them, it saw repeated conflicts between reformers influenced by Western ideas and examples and reactionaries anxious for their own privileges and the emperor's sacred prerogatives. The elements of such a parliamentary–cabinet system, albeit more oligarchical than democratic, were specifically envisaged in the reform plans worked out under Speransky in the early years of Alexander I's reign. There was to be a hierarchy of elective assemblies (*dumy*) capped by a State Duma, meeting annually to consider legislation and other measures introduced by ministers (although the appointment of ministers would remain the sole prerogative of the emperor). Meanwhile a proto–cabinet already existed in the form of the Committee of Ministers (*Komitet ministrov*) established in 1802.[2]

By now, however, the impetus for reform was running out. Speransky's proto–parliamentary State Duma was rejected and all that came of these institutional reform proposals was the creation, in 1810, of an appointive State Council (*Gosudarstvennyi sovet*) of elder statesmen to advise the emperor on current legislation. As for the Committee of Ministers, it gave early promise of evolving into a cabinet, especially while Alexander was preoccupied with the war with Napoleon, when under the chairmanship of Count N.I. Saltykov, it exercised something like full collective responsibility for domestic government. After 1815, however, falling under the influence of Alexander's reactionary adviser, Count A.A. Arakcheev, and lacking a wider institutional framework from which it might have gained support, it declined in importance and came to deal mainly with second–order administrative matters. Under Alexander II it was overshadowed for a time by a new body called the Council of Ministers (*Sovet ministrov*). Functioning unofficially from 1857 and given official standing in 1861, the Council of Ministers served initially to coordinate the work of various *ad hoc* commissions preparing proposals for reform in the confused, quasi–revolutionary atmosphere following the Crimean War; but it also involved itself in interministerial coordination and reviewed the annual reports of ministers and their proposals for major legislation. Its subsequent decline appears to have been set in train by the restoration of social order and discipline, and was accelerated by the weakness of its institutional autonomy and identity, due to Alexander's chairing its meetings and to the overlap of its functions and membership with those of the Committee of Ministers.

Moribund during the 1870s, the Council of Ministers was suddenly revived in 1881, in the wake of Alexander II's assassination. In order to ensure that the Government maintained a common front in the face of the "nihilist" threat, it was resolved that no minister should make recommendations to the emperor without the collective agreement of members of the Council. This ostensibly modest procedural innovation evidently had the initial approval of the new emperor, Alexander III, but its radical implications were soon perceived by at least some astute observers. For such a unified and collectively responsible ministry would be able to deal from a position of strength with the emperor, who would be constrained to give it a wide scope for independent action, so that gradually it would come to see itself as responsible to the public at large as much as to the emperor. As Anatole Leroy-Beaulieu put it, "the Tsar would find himself reduced almost to the role of a constitutional monarch, [even] without a constitution or parliament."[3]

While this development was laying the potential groundwork for the cabinet component of a cabinet-parliamentary system, there were changes in the State Council that opened new prospects for the parliamentary component. Shortly before Alexander II's death he had authorized a "Supreme Commission" chaired by the relatively liberal General M.T. Loris-Melikov to reorganize the administration and prepare proposals for overhauling the whole system of central government. The latter envisaged bringing under the State Council certain policy-formulating commissions composed of elective members and experts as well as government officials, and the adding of fifteen elected members to the State Council itself. Alexander approved the former, and the latter, which had the strong support of the majority of ministers, was about to be approved at the time of his death. It was at this point that K.P. Pobedonostsev, the reactionary adviser to the new emperor, Alexander III, struck the first of many severe blows against reform. He persuaded the tsar to issue a proclamation, without informing his ministers in advance, which asserted the full force of the autocratic principle, "against all encroachments." Loris-Melikov resigned, and for over 20 years no more was heard of a collectively responsible Council of Ministers or a partly elective State Council.[4]

On the face of it, the tsar's prerogatives remained as untrammeled and Russia as far from a system of responsible government at the end of the nineteenth century as it had been at its beginning. The repeated emergence and curtailment of proto-cabinet and proto-parliamentary institutions, however, followed a spiral rather than a circular pattern. At each stage new institutional experience was gained. The growing size and complexity of the bureaucracy, which reflected accelerating socio-economic and cultural change, heightened the need for effective institutions of administrative coordination, policy advice, and consultation. Thus, despite the reactionary animus of the *fin de siècle* court, the Committee of Ministers was reactivated as a partial substitute for the discredited Council of Ministers, while the State Council, far from fading into insignificance, subjected many governmental proposals to close scrutiny, delaying the enactment of quite a few measures and even causing some of them to be dropped.

The institutional changes following the 1905 Revolution brought Russia much closer to a cabinet-parliamentary system of government. A bicameral legislature was created, the partly reformed State Council constituting the upper house and a new fully elective assembly (Duma) constituting the lower. The Committee of Ministers was abolished and the Council of Ministers revived, now chaired by a "prime" minister. The change was seen by many as portending a genuine cabinet, exercising collective responsibility for the whole work of government.

These reforms marked the end of tsarist absolutism, but its legacy severely crippled both "parliament" and "cabinet." The amended Fundamental Laws of 1906 reasserted the autocratic powers of the emperor. Each minister was directly responsible to the emperor rather than to the Duma, which possessed only the power of interpellation. When the Duma and State Council were not sitting, laws could be enacted subject to the legislature's subsequent endorsement. The monarch's "sovereign commands" (*vysochaishie poveleniia*), countersigned by a single minister without submission to either State Council or Duma, served virtually as an alternative channel of legislation. Nicholas II made full use of these powerful vestiges of the autocratic system. The powers of the Council of Ministers were further curtailed by its division into so called "Council" and "non-Council" ministers. Under its statute the ministers responsible for defense and foreign affairs, as well as the imperial court and domains, were not required to refer matters to the Council except where this was stipulated by "sovereign command" or where other ministries were affected.

While both Russian and Western scholars differ over how radical the reforms of 1905-06 proved in practice, one can hardly rate the system of government they ushered in as better than semi-constitutional and semi-responsible. Yet the trajectory seemed plain, and its inexorability seemed confirmed by the collapse of the monarchy in March 1917 and the creation of a "Provisional Government" chosen by and collectively responsible to a multiparty legislature.[5]

But then, eight months later, came the dénouement; power passed to a revolutionary dictatorship committed to "smashing" and "sweeping away" the whole existing political and administrative order and constructing a new "proletarian" one on the resultant *tabula rasa*. Have I, then, spent the first pages of my chapter outlining the buildup to a mere might-have-been? The answer is no: the evolution of Russian government before 1917 is very pertinent to the topic of this book. The most obvious reason is that, whatever their intentions, the Bolsheviks ended by drawing heavily on structures and processes inherited from the Provisional Government and beyond that from the Imperial Government. Secondly, the "dictatorship of the proletariat" proved to be a formula for placing "power unlimited by any laws" in the hands of the Communist Party leadership, including absolute power over the formal origins of government, thus reviving in a new form the pre-1905 "untrammeled" prerogative of the tsar-autocrat. In both cases, moreover, the absolutist state claimed legitimacy in terms of a universal mission, the one dedicated to Orthodox Christianity and the other to the World Proletarian Revolution. And further, in both cases the complex and uneasy relationship between rulers and administrators underwent a painful evolution, in which institutional learning, against a background of socio-economic and cultural development, gradually mitigated arbitrariness. And finally, with the end of the Communist Party dictatorship, the relevant antecedents of contemporary politics and government, whether in a Commonwealth of Independent States or the reborn Russian Republic, will be found less and less in the last 70 years and more and more in the decades and centuries that went before.

Lenin's Government

Institutionally, one of the most remarkable consequences of the October Revolution of 1917 was the survival of the Council of Ministers and its emergence, under Lenin, as the key organ of government.[6] Granted, efforts were made to mask its continuity with the past and to make it more palatable, by calling ministers by the revolutionary-sounding title of "people's commissars" and by initially describing it as "temporary"; but there is abundant evidence that among themselves the Bolshevik leaders meant "ministers" when they said "people's commissars" and that Lenin, at least, had no intention of really treating it as transitional, "pending the convening of the Constituent Assembly."[7] The approval of this Council of People's Commissars (*Sovet narodnykh komissarov*) as the "Temporary Worker and Peasant Government" (*Pravitel'stvo*) of Russia, by resolution of the rump of the Second Congress of Soviets, was the prime institutional expression of the armed seizure of power by the Bolsheviks.

The people's commissars' portfolios corresponded almost completely with the existing ministries, and their first task was to take charge of these and get them working for the new Government. This took several weeks to accomplish, owing to the organized non-cooperation of most Government officials who saw Bolshevik rule as illegitimate. In the meantime improvised administration was in the hands of the Military Revolutionary Committee, which had played a major organizing role in the seizure of power.[8]

Lenin's lack of public candor about the character of his new Government is hardly surprising, since what he was now doing ran directly counter to what he had been advocating, most forcefully in his article "The State and Revolution," in the leadup to the seizure of power: namely to "smash" and "sweep away" the existing state machine and replace it with a non-bureaucratic, spontaneous, amateur regime of workers' soviets, modeled on the Paris commune of 1871. With the forceful dispersal of the Constituent Assembly in January 1918, all talk of the Sovnarkom (the acronym by which the Council of People's Commissars was beginning to be called) being temporary was dropped. By early 1918, it had clearly established itself as the fountainhead of executive authority in the new "Soviet" state.[9] The structural and operational characteristics it assumed in this earliest period were retained and developed after the seat of government moved to Moscow in March.

Throughout the Lenin years the Sovnarkom numbered 18 to 19 members. Apart from the brief period (November 1917–March 1918) when a handful of Left Socialist-Revolutionaries joined the Government, they were all Bolsheviks. In addition to such major figures as Lenin himself, Lev D. Trotsky, and Iosif V. Stalin, its original membership consisted mostly of leading Bolsheviks from the Petrograd and Moscow party committees. With time such veterans of the revolutionary underground were partially replaced by men of lesser party standing but better qualified by training and experience for senior administrative responsibilities. Very few were workers by background or occupation, and the preponderance of men from upper or middle-class families actually increased over the early years of the "worker-peasant Government."

The central importance of the Sovnarkom in Lenin's regime was largely due to his personal commitment to it. He held no executive office in the central bodies either of the Communist Party (as his Bolshevik faction of the Russian Social-Democratic Workers' Party renamed itself in 1918) or of the soviets. His apartment in the Moscow Kremlin opened onto the corridor of the Sovnarkom offices, where he spent most of his working day. There, ably assisted by his first chancellery head, Vladimir D. Bonch-Bruevich, he devoted much attention to establishing structures and procedures, such as rules for standing and ad hoc subcommittees, for participation in and conduct of Sovnarkom meetings, for the preparation of agendas and circulation of properly documented agenda papers, and for inter-agency consultations. In its earliest months, Sovnarkom met every evening, heavy agendas often keeping it in session until well after midnight. Thereafter meetings grew progressively shorter and less frequent, until by 1921 they were being held only once a week.

This reflected in part the better organization of meetings, but was due primarily to the devolution of much of its business to the Sovnarkom "commissions," and especially the Little Sovnarkom and the Defense Council.

The Little Sovnarkom, set up in late 1917 to deal with second-order business, especially financial matters requiring top-level resolution ("vermicelli" in the slang inherited from tsarist officialdom), was directly modeled on the prerevolutionary Little Council of Ministers, which operated informally from 1905 until its formalization by Stolypin in 1909.[10] A businesslike committee of relatively junior Bolshevik administrators, the Little Sovnarkom gradually expanded its scope and powers until by 1920–21 it was giving preliminary consideration to almost all matters referred for Sovnarkom decision.   In practice, moreover, its decisions were often final, even on matters of major importance, since they acquired legal force once signed by Lenin, unless quickly challenged by a member of the full Sovnarkom or the Defense Council.   The essential factor in the Little Sovnarkom's growing power and stature was again the high value placed on it by Lenin, who termed it his "first assistant." Although he did not attend its meetings, his power to endorse its decisions, return them for further consideration, or refer them to the Sovnarkom proper gave him unique leverage over the development and implementation of government policy.[11]

The Defense Council (*Sovet oborony*) was set up in November 1918 and was vested with virtually unlimited power to deal with the catastrophic economic and military crisis confronting the regime.   A small subcommittee of senior Sovnarkom members chaired by Lenin, it quickly became the key decisionmaking body for mobilizing the economy and the population for waging the Civil War.   It had no responsibility for the conduct of actual military operations, which was the province of a Revolutionary–Military Council, set up some months earlier under the chairmanship of Trotsky.   As the war drew to a close, it was decided to retain the Defense Council as an instrument for coordinating the national economy, and in March 1920 it was renamed the Labor and Defense Council (*Sovet truda i oborony*, or STO).

No account of the formative period of the Soviet Government would be complete without mentioning its chancellery (*upravlenie delami*), which serviced the meetings of Sovnarkom proper, the Little Sovnarkom and the Defense Council, and the numerous other standing and ad hoc commissions, prepared agenda papers, arranged intercommissariat consultations, and monitored the implementation of decisions.   Its able and devoted staff numbered over a hundred by 1921.   It included a small Sovnarkom secretariat, which also functioned as Lenin's personal secretariat.   Lenin involved himself closely in the operation of the chancellery and relied heavily on its senior officials, especially chancellery head Bonch-Bruevich and secretary (from 1918) Lidia Fotieva, both of whom had worked closely with him as early as 1904, when he was seeking to run his infant Bolshevik faction from Geneva.

Space will permit only a brief outline of the structural and personnel changes in the central government machine during these early years. Major structural changes were relatively few. The people's commissariats for internal affairs, foreign affairs, justice, state control, finance, labor, welfare, education, posts and telegraphs, agriculture, food supplies, trade and industry, and war were all based on existing ministries, some of which could boast a continuity going back beyond Speransky to the colleges of the eighteenth century. Bolsheviks and a few trusted socialist allies took over most of the key posts in these ministries, and in some cases, notably those for foreign affairs, justice, and labor, there were extensive personnel changes. Former officials continued to predominate in most parts of the central administration, however, and their predominance would have been greater had it not been for the civil servants' strike against the Bolshevik takeover. The task of dismantling those Government institutions which were integral to the tsarist autocracy, including the Ministry of the Court, the Procuracy of the Holy Synod, and the Governing Senate, had been begun by the Provisional Government and was now rapidly completed by the Bolsheviks. The agency for administering the properties of the imperial family was transformed into a short-lived People's Commissariat for Properties of the Republic.

Within the first weeks of Sovnarkom's existence three important new agencies were created. The People's Commissariat for Nationalities, headed throughout the period by Stalin, was responsible for consolidating Bolshevik power and promoting their policies among the non-Russian half of the population. The All-Russian Extraordinary Commission for Combating Counter-Revolution, Speculation and Sabotage (official acronym Vecheka, usually referred to as "the Cheka"), headed by Felix Dzerzhinsky, was assigned the task of "tracking down and liquidating all counter-revolutionary and sabotage attempts and actions throughout Russia, irrespective of from whom they stem," and given vast powers and resources for the purpose, which it deployed with legendary ruthlessness.[12] The All-Russian National Economic Council (VSNKh) integrated the organizing centers of the largely spontaneous but Bolshevik-promoted "workers' control" movement with the Government apparatus, and thus helped to ensure that the participation of workers' organizations in the running of industry would be exercised along lines conforming with the policies of the Sovnarkom. Of greater long-term importance, it also took on the main functions of the Chief Economic Council in the old Ministry of Trade and Industry, in whose offices VSNKh quickly established itself, incorporating several other sections of the Ministry as well as the apparatus of the state conferences and committees on various industries that had been established during the war.   Soon it was to assume a new importance as the authority responsible for taking over and administering nationalized industry.   However it never became the economic cabinet that some designed for it, STO soon replacing it as the regime's chief coordinating body for the economy.[13]

Shortly before his death, Lenin grew increasingly distressed by the ubiquitous "bureaucratism" of Soviet society, blaming it largely on the continuities of structures, processes, and personnel between the old state machine and the new. He was inclined to exaggerate these continuities, and his diagnosis of the system's ills was grossly incomplete.   Nevertheless, the tsarist administrative heritage, with its virtues as well as its vices, was indeed substantial,[14] and this again underlines the need for a long historical perspective in any general account of the Soviet Government.

While Sovnarkom was officially designated the "Government," it was not the only body involved in governing the infant Soviet republic.   Granted, its responsibility to the Congress of Soviets was quickly reduced to a mere formality, but the same cannot be said of its relationship with the latter's Central Executive Committee (CEC, official acronym VTsIK).   The CEC was eventually to evolve into a pseudo-parliamentary body, but originally it was endowed with both legislative *and* executive powers, and this was reflected in the first (July 1918) constitution of the Russian Soviet Federated Socialist Republic (RSFSR). Since Sovnarkom also enjoyed legislative powers (albeit under "emergency" regulations), conflict could hardly be avoided.   Although he clearly had no intention of allowing his Sovnarkom to play second fiddle to any other body, Lenin was initially on shaky ground owing to the greater legitimacy of the CEC in terms of his own "commune" model of government by soviets.   Moreover, he needed to concede the CEC some real power in order to maintain the support of the Left Communists and those Bolsheviks who were uneasy about the emergent one-party dictatorship.   However, his success in having his loyal and able colleague Iakov Sverdlov elected as CEC chairman minimized conflict and led to a highly valuable division of labor, in which the Sovnarkom made the decisions and the CEC legitimated them and got them implemented through the network of Bolshevik-led provincial and city soviets--Sverdlov also being secretary of the party Central Committee.   With Sverdlov's death and the intensification of the Civil War, other changes made this arrangement redundant, and by mid-1919 the CEC was no longer meeting.[15]

So long as the fate of the "Worker-Peasant Republic" hung in the balance, misgivings over the atrophy of the soviets, both locally and at the center, remained muted. But with the Bolshevik victory, demands for the revival of the soviets became irresistible. Moreover, the soviets had a vital new role to play in the entrenchment and legitimation of Bolshevik rule over the vast population "liberated" from the Whites. This was effected in the name of the CEC, and it was the CEC, and especially its newly activated presidium, that the party relied on to coordinate this process. However, there were many who thought it was not enough for the CEC to have a greatly expanded legitimating and mobilizing role—it should be assuming a more active and central role in the actual work of government. Some now saw the dominance of the Sovnarkom, like the arbitrary powers of the Cheka, the Food Ministry's procurement detachments, and the Revolutionary Military Council, as a temporary by-product of the Civil War. Indeed, by 1922, with the onset of the New Economic Policy (NEP), the curbing of the "extraordinary organs", and the move to "socialist legality", the CEC presidium seemed on the way to overshadowing the Sovnarkom, judging by the quality and content of its enactments. However, while some contemporary lawyers and propagandists built this into engaging fantasies of constitutionalization or democratization, the essential reality here was the passing of power from Sovnarkom not to the CEC and its presidium but to the party Central Committee and its Politburo and Orgburo.[16]

The assumption by the Communist Party executive of a direct role in the day-to-day work of government was due, in part, to certain functional defects that became entrenched in Sovnarkom itself, despite the best efforts of Lenin and his staff. Its agendas were overloaded with minor issues, notwithstanding the work of the Little Sovnarkom, STO, and various standing and ad hoc commissions.[17] The rules of attendance allowed numerous outsiders to take part in Sovnarkom meetings, as specialists or representatives of various departments, while at the same time the people's commissars themselves were permitted to depute proxies. Understandably, the more senior members, including Trotsky and Stalin, virtually stopped attending, concentrating their activities within their own executive machinery and relying on their right of appeal to the party Central Committee when the Sovnarkom failed to resolve matters to their satisfaction. Despite the general acknowledgement of the party's authority to determine the broad lines of policy, to take the most crucial decisions, and to settle major disputes, the occasional exercise of this right of appeal did not immediately threaten the dominant role of the Sovnarkom in day-to-day government, for the party Central Committee had at first no effective executive machinery. But this changed in March 1919, when the Political Bureau (Politburo) and Organization Bureau (Orgburo) were set up in the Central Committee, along with similar tight-knit executive bodies at subordinate levels.

These party executive institutions were supported by an "apparatus" of full-time party officials and exercised authority over all regime agencies in their area in order to counter widespread administrative chaos and inter-agency conflict and to ensure implementation of central policies and programs. Party channels now became as important as Government channels for the transmission of information and executive commands, and by 1921 this had brought about a substantial shift of top-level decisionmaking to the Politburo, imbuing it with the requisite experience and authority to function effectively as a court of appeal from the Sovnarkom.[18]

Even then, however, Lenin's personal authority, his energy, his strategic institutional location, and his skill in maneuvering between the various top decisionmaking bodies remained a formidable obstacle to any catastrophic decline in the Sovnarkom's role and standing. That obstacle collapsed with the rapid decline in Lenin's health from the middle of 1921. At first he sought to shore it up by improving procedural arrangements, especially relating to the distribution of business between the Sovnarkom proper, the Little Sovnarkom, and STO, and by the appointment of Deputy Chairmen: Alexei I. Rykov in May 1921, Alexander D. Tsiurupa in December 1921, and Lev B. Kamenev in September 1922 (Trotsky turned down Lenin's proposal that he became the fourth deputy). Without a single authoritative figure at the helm, however, policy disputes and administrative conflicts grew ever more difficult to resolve within the Sovnarkom system, and the locus of final decision shifted even faster to the party Central Committee and especially its Politburo.[19]

No one was more disturbed at this development than Lenin himself, who saw the body he had labored for five years to make the key instrument of Bolshevik rule being relegated to an inferior role. He strongly believed that party bodies could not effectively perform *their* proper role of determining the broad lines of policy and resolving the most contentious issues if they became bogged down in the day-to-day details of government. Accordingly, he sponsored a resolution at the Eleventh Party Congress in March–April 1922 aimed at reversing these developments. It was to have little effect, however, as Lenin was incapacitated by a stroke shortly thereafter. Eight months later he devoted his last brief outburst of work in his Sovnarkom office largely to ways of restoring the Sovnarkom's effectiveness and authority. His final stroke and his death in January 1924 completed the dethronement of Lenin's Government.[20] Henceforth, for nearly seven decades, the Soviet state was to be governed by a party oligarchy institutionalized in a body not even mentioned in the constitution, with the "Government" serving mainly as its instrument for dealing with second-order business channeled through the state bureaucracy.

Rykov's Government

Successor to the pre-1917 Council of Ministers in all but name, the Sovnarkom was the key instrument through which the Bolsheviks took over and adapted the government machine to serve their purposes of revolutionary transformation. Furthermore, in contrast to its predecessor, the Sovnarkom included in its number the most authoritative figure in the state, who worked in its offices, chaired its meetings, and directed it. However, while they thereby removed the old duality of "systematized" and arbitrary government on one level, the Bolsheviks reimposed it on another, in the form of the unlimited prerogative of the party. At the same time, the constitutional sovereignty of elected "soviet" assemblies was quickly reduced to a legitimating fiction, and then employed for purposes of mass mobilization and intra-elite politics. Well before Lenin's death the degraded status of both the Soviet "Government" and the Soviet "parliament" had reached the point where only a leader of exceptional vision, perspicacity, political skill, and authority would have been capable of bringing them again into center stage, and thus laying the groundwork of what might have evolved into a new system of responsible and representative government.

Aleksei Ivanovich Rykov was not such a man, and indeed if he had been he would not have been tolerated by his Politburo colleagues as Lenin's successor in the Sovnarkom chairmanship. To be sure, he was a relatively "soft" Bolshevik, with a record of opposing Lenin on such issues as breaking completely with the Mensheviks and, more recently, the formation of a one-party dictatorship. But there is no evidence that he ever came to reject the Leninist principle of the overriding authority of the party vis-à-vis the state, or that if he did he was of the mettle to actively combat it.[21] Despite earlier policy differences, Lenin trusted him, and his administrative performance, especially as the chief organizer of supplies to the army and as chairman of the National Economic Council, won him appointment as Lenin's first deputy, and effectively as acting chairman during Lenin's final months.[22] Given his proven capacity, his thorough knowledge of the government machine, his practical and cooperative style, his manifest lack of soaring ambition, and the reduced profile of the chairmanship, it is not surprising that his Politburo colleagues chose him to head the Sovnarkom after its founder's death in January 1924.

We have now mentioned several of the factors that helped determine the character of Soviet government under Rykov: the return to peacetime conditions, the reduced policymaking role of the Sovnarkom vis-à-vis the party Politburo, its reduced visibility vis-à-vis the Central Executive Committee of the Congress of Soviets, and the relatively modest leadership standing of its chairman. There were, however, two other factors of major importance. The first was the transition to the New Economic Policy (NEP), with its revival of peasant agriculture, private trade, and small-scale business enterprise, and such correlates as the emphasis on "socialist legality", the curbing of the Cheka, and relaxed controls over cultural and economic life. Under Lenin, Rykov had made a vital contribution to get the NEP under way, and he remained strongly committed to it throughout his chairmanship.

The second factor shaping Rykov's Government was the creation of a new federal level of government with the formation of the Union of Soviet Socialist Republics in December 1922.   The Bolsheviks' slogan of national self-determination had not prevented them from bringing as much of the old Russian Empire under their dominance as possible, and by the end of the Civil War they controlled several other successor states that were formally allied with the Russian Soviet Federated Socialist Republic (RSFSR) but in practice subordinated to it.[23]   The new Union consisted initially of four "union republics": the RSFSR (which itself included several non-Russian "autonomous republics"), the Ukrainian SSR, the Belorussian SSR, and the Transcaucasian Soviet Federated Socialist Republic (of Georgia, Armenia, and Azerbaijan). An Uzbek and a Turkmen SSR followed in 1925, and a Tadzhik SSR in 1929. Under the new federal constitution, each union republic, like the Union itself, formed its own congress of soviets with its central executive committee and its own people's commissariats and council of people's commissars, or sovnarkom. The formal distribution of powers, as determined in November 1923, was complicated by the fact that in addition to "all-union people's commissariats" and "republican people's commissariats" there was also a category of "unified people's commissariats," in which the central commissariat was supposed to determine policy and the republican ones to implement it (see Table 1.1). These arrangements provided some appearance of republic autonomy, but given the overriding authority of the highly centralized Communist Party of the Soviet Union, and such institutional devices as attendance of representatives of all-union commissariats at meetings of republic sovnarkoms, the latter "tended to become," in E.H. Carr's words, "the local executive organs of the central authority,"[24] even in fields which were their constitutional preserve.

There were few changes in the seven years of Rykov's chairmanship to the original collection of all-union and unified commissariats listed in Table 1.1. In May 1924, the Food Supplies Commissariat was abolished and a unified People's Commissariat for Domestic Trade was created, reflecting the progress in marketization of distribution. Six months later the two trade commissariats were combined into a single People's Commissariat of Foreign and Domestic Trade. The Central Statistical Directorate, which had operated since 1918 as a

Table 1.1
People's Commissariats
November 1923

■Under all-union sovnarkom■	■Under republic sovnarkoms■	
All-union commissariats	Unified commissariats	Republic commissariats
Foreign Affairs	Supreme Economic Council	Agriculture
Army and Navy	Food Supplies	Internal Affairs
Foreign Trade	Labor	Justice
Transport	Finance	Education
Posts and	Worker–Peasant Inspection	Health
Telegraphs		Social Welfare

body under (*pri*) the Sovnarkom, acquired the status of a unified people's commissariat in February 1926.

The People's Commissariat for Worker–Peasant Inspection (*Rabkrin*) had been established in 1920 for the purpose of debureaucratizing the work of the old State Control Commissariat by mobilizing thousands of purportedly elected inspection teams of ordinary working people. Under Stalin's direction it had become the focus of acute inter-leadership conflict and provoked Lenin's demands for its radical reform, which Stalin deftly turned to his advantage. In late 1923, now part of the USSR Sovnarkom, it was in effect merged with the party's Central Control Commission, and henceforth kept in the hands of Stalin's allies (Valerian V. Kuibyshev till August 1926, then Grigorii K. [Sergo] Ordzhonikidze).[25]   No appointment was made to the central Agriculture Commissariat until December 1929, when collectivization was under way. Before that, republic governments enjoyed a certain leeway in applying central party policies in the countryside.

The head of the OGPU, as the political police were now called, had the right to attend Sovnarkom meetings in an "advisory" (*soveshchatel'nyi*) capacity (his subordinates in the republics were full members of their sovnarkoms). The Cheka had been formally abolished in February 1922 against the background of widespread indignation at its ruthless and arbitrary conduct. In practice, however, it was now transformed into a "State Political Directorate" (*Gosudarstvennoe Politicheskoe Upravlenie*, or GPU) initially within the RSFSR

Internal Affairs Commissariat. Under the new Union constitution it became a free-standing Unified (*Ob "edinennoe*) State Political Directorate. While it could no longer engage in summary executions, its legal powers were actually enlarged and its activities broadened to target Communist Party opponents of the ruling oligarchy as well as non-communists deemed dangerous.[26] Felix Dzerzhinsky remained in charge throughout these transmogrifications, until his death in 1926.

The Council of Labor and Defense (STO), the *alter ego* of Lenin's Sovnarkom,[27] now became an integral part of the new all-union Government. So, too, did the State Planning Commission (Gosplan), which had been established in 1921 under Professor Gleb M. Krzhizhanovskii.[28] And along with the institutions came the key personnel, namely Rykov's two fellow deputy chairmen of Lenin's RSFSR Sovnarkom, Kamenev and Tsiurupa, who now became his deputies in the all-union Sovnarkom, the former also taking over the chairmanship of STO and the latter the chairmanship of Gosplan. Kamenev continued to combine his Government responsibilities with chairmanship of the Moscow soviet. Initially there were two additional deputy chairmen, the chairmen of the Ukrainian and Transcaucasian sovnarkoms, Vlas Ia. Chubar' and Ivan D. [Mamiia] Orakhelashvili, respectively, but they had no administrative roles in the central Government, and their membership ceased in May 1925. Tsiurupa, ostensibly an equivalent representative of the RSFSR, was in contrast a genuine working member of the USSR Government and remained a deputy chairman until his death in May 1928. Kamenev, however, was demoted in January 1926 following his break with Stalin, to be replaced by Ian E. Rudzutak. Kuibyshev also had a brief spell as deputy chairman from January until November 1926, when he was replaced by Ordzhonikidze. The three last-named all followed Stalin when he broke with Rykov and the "Right", but Vasilii V. Shmidt, the former labor commissar appointed deputy chairman in November 1928, was too close to Rykov and fell with him. As a rule deputy chairmen were also in direct charge of one or other commissariat or other Sovnarkom agency, but political and administrative exigencies evidently determined the changing pattern of job combination.

The USSR Sovnarkom began to meet immediately after the adoption of the Federal Constitution by the Central Executive Committee (all-union CEC, official acronym TsIK) of the Congress of Soviets on 6 July 1923, but it was to be some months before its structures were fully operational and the relevant central administrative functions transferred from those of the RSFSR Government. Indeed, Rykov continued to chair both the USSR and RSFSR sovnarkoms right up to May 1929.[29] Not surprisingly, there was a high level of continuity in almost all respects. Rykov's USSR Sovnarkom normally met at weekly intervals as had Lenin's Sovnarkom since 1921.[30] Its greatest number of meetings was 61 in 1925, after which it gradually declined, dropping to 39 in both 1929 and 1930.[31]

Although its formal membership was down to 14 or 15, a far larger number were entitled to attend and speak, though not to vote, as had been the case under Lenin. Apart from the already mentioned chairmen of the OGPU and the Central Statistical Directorate, these included members of the all–union CEC, and the Sovnarkom chairmen, CEC chairmen, and official Moscow representatives of the union republics, as well as a list of specifically designated office–holders. While some of these, especially the all–union CEC members, might rarely exercise their right to take part, enough did so to pack the meeting room, especially on days when there were numerous experts present as well.

A similar replication of earlier patterns was evident in the internal decisionmaking machinery of the new USSR Government. As already implied, in effect it simply took over the RSFSR Labor and Defence Council (STO). Late in 1925, as Kamenev moved into opposition to Stalin, Rykov took over from him the chairing of STO, thus ending what had been almost a duumviriate in the central government. Kamenev was removed from the deputy chairmanship a few weeks later. Joint meetings of STO and the (full) Sovnarkom now became common.[32] The division of labor between them had indeed always been blurred, with the full Sovnarkom devoting much of its time to areas within STO's purview,[33] as analyses of the matters dealt with at their meetings make clear.[34] Nor did the Sovnarkom necessarily reserve the more important items for its agenda. Nevertheless the leadership clearly found it advantageous throughout this period to syphon off into STO much of the central Government's work of administering the economy of the USSR, even if it never became a genuine economic inner cabinet.[35]

The body exercising the functions of Lenin's Little Sovnarkom in the new USSR Government was initially called the Administrative–Financial Commission. Like the former it was a small (eight members) body of relatively junior officials chosen by the Sovnarkom, and it was chaired by G.M. Leplevskii, who had been a vice–chairman of the Little Sovnarkom since 1921.[36] Its decisions had the force of a Sovnarkom or STO decree once signed by the chairman of the body concerned (i.e. by Rykov or Kamenev, respectively). Other Sovnarkom members had the right of appeal, but few appeals were upheld by Sovnarkom or STO, which tended to discourage the practice and to make the Administrative–Financial Commission, like the Little Sovnarkom, a very important institution.[37]

A five–member Legislative Proposals Commission was also set up in 1923, in order to vet, draft, and systematize Government decisions with legislative force.[38] The creation of a special Government body for this purpose reflected the current concern for "socialist legality," reinforced, as van den Berg suggests, by the lack of a central Justice Commissariat--this now being a republic prerogative. In 1926, however, the Legislative Proposals Commission was merged with the Administrative-Financial Commission to form a single Preparatory Commission, which also included as members the standing representatives of the union republics attached to the USSR Government.[39] The Preparatory Commission lasted until the end of Rykov's chairmanship, but its role, in contrast with Lenin's Little Sovnarkom, never seems to have gone beyond administrative coordination and processing "vermicelli".

Finally, the chancellery of the all-union Sovnarkom also drew on the key personnel and experience of its RSFSR predecessor. Its head was Nikolai P. Gorbunov, the first secretary of Lenin's Sovnarkom and later its head of chancellery. As approved in 1924, its staff of 163 comprised separate secretariats for the full Sovnarkom, STO, the Preparatory Commission, and the chancellery itself, in addition to six functional departments, and by 1929 six groups dealing with various branches of administration (industry, trade, etc.) had been added.[40]

Despite the high level of structural and procedural continuity from Lenin's Government to Rykov's that emerges from the above analysis, the changed political context not only sharply reduced its policy role but also affected its internal operation. The essential factors were, of course, Rykov's lack of Lenin's political authority and the leadership struggles of the post-Lenin years. The supreme authority of the party Politburo over both policy and personnel decisions had been fully established by 1921, but Lenin's personal authority within the Politburo and the full Central Committee helped him to bolster the Sovnarkom's role and to dominate the decisionmaking process by maneuvering between the Politburo, Central Committee, the CEC and its presidium, the full Sovnarkom, STO, and the Little Sovnarkom. During Lenin's illness and after his death there was no leader able or willing to attempt this role, and the decline of Sovnarkom to an essentially administrative mechanism was accelerated. It remained important for deciding second-order issues and resolving bureaucratic conflicts, but any matter of consequence was settled in the Politburo.

For the same reason, the manifest potential for conflict between the Sovnarkom and the Central Executive Committee of the All-Union Congress of Soviets and its presidium never came to much.[41] This was despite the fact that the presidium of the all-union CEC had the task of adjudicating conflicts between republic governments and central government agencies[42] and appeals against Sovnarkom decisions by individual people's commissars.[43] In general it was the Politburo that determined, on grounds of practical convenience or the significance of the issue, whether to have its decisions embodied in all-union CEC legislation or

Sovnarkom regulations, and the Sovnarkom or a particular commissariat could also welcome a desired decision being enacted with the authority of the all-union CEC. Van den Berg has shown that during Lenin's illness the percentage of Sovnarkom decisions formally endorsed by the all-union CEC jumped from 7.2 in 1921 to 28.2 in 1922 and 42.9 in 1923, and continued to rise under Rykov's chairmanship until it reached a maximum of 61.6 percent in 1927.

The Sovnarkom and its chairman, however, could enjoy this comfortable if secondary role only so long as the chairman retained a firm place in the dominant Politburo coalition, and this came to an end in 1928, when Rykov emerged as a leader, albeit irresolute at times, of the "Right Opposition" to Stalin's new and harshly radical economic policies. Since Stalin's adherents, including senior Sovnarkom members Kuibyshev, Rudzutak, and Kliment E. Voroshilov, dominated the Politburo, Rykov quickly lost all capacity to give direction to the Sovnarkom. Inter-agency conflicts over such issues as rural policy and planning now became fronts in the war between the Stalinists and the "Right", in which the decisive battles were fought out in party arenas.[44] Substantially before Rykov himself was removed, the men in charge of nearly all of the Sovnarkom's major economic bodies were changed, accompanied by a deep purge of senior officials and widespread arrests and trials of "wreckers."[45] The process also involved considerable infighting among such leading allies of Stalin as Ordzhonikidze, Kuibyshev and Rudzutak. In the two years before Rykov was finally removed from both the Politburo and the Sovnarkom chairmanship, Government structures and processes going back to Lenin's time and beyond went into a crucible from which they were soon to be remolded, as radically, in some respects, as in 1917.

Stalin's Government

Although Stalin did not personally take over the leadership of Sovnarkom until 1941, it was already manifestly *his* Government by the time his closest adherent Viacheslav M. Molotov was appointed chairman on 19 December 1930. The 22 years of Stalin's Government can be divided into three sub-periods, in each of which the internal arrangements and external relationships of the Sovnarkom reflected the ambient political realities. The first, which coincided with Molotov's premiership, saw the establishment and entrenchment of the "administrative-command system" and Stalin's personal dictatorship; the second covered the years of war against Nazi Germany; and the third brought the "high Stalinism" of 1946-53.

The ingredients of the administrative-command system and Stalin's dictatorship were of course very much in evidence by 1930. The cult of Stalin had been launched the previous year and NEP was virtually brought to an end with the launching of forced collectivization and the crash industrialization of the first five-year plan. Yet alternative policy positions were still being argued, albeit in ever more muted tones, within the network of formal party and Government bodies, so that one could still speak of a semi-public political process. From 1930 on, however, as the remnants of independent peasant farming and private trade were suppressed, public associations came under ever closer party direction, and as repression and fear became a growing factor in intra-party affairs, the competition of policy and interests was increasingly constrained within an intense but largely concealed sphere of bureaucratic politics. Central Committee plenums and party congresses were convened ever less frequently, and discordant voices were replaced by the unanimous acclamation of Stalin and his policies. The climax of this process, of course, was the terror of 1937–38, which also brought a massive turnover in the political elite, involving many of the first generation of Stalin supporters as well as former "oppositionists." In the three or four years that followed, a personal tyranny completely supplanted the party oligarchy and all permitted activities were run through a congeries of command hierarchies over whose leaders the tyrant enjoyed the power of life and death. This Stalinist "system" was to become the "normal" context of the day-to-day work of government as well as of life generally.

The key element of the Stalinist administrative-command system was the directing, controlling, and integrating role of the Communist Party apparatus. This meant that all other organizations were deprived of the power to choose their own goals, structures, rules, and personnel. These basic organizational functions were exercised on their behalf by Communist Party bodies, thus in effect *incorporating* them all into a single organizational whole. This system of "mono-organizational socialism" had been potential in the Bolshevik "dictatorship of the proletariat" from the outset, but it was only in the 1930s that it was fully realized.[46] Thus, for the Sovnarkom, the years of Molotov's chairmanship saw not only its complete subjection to Stalin's will but also its full integration into the party-run system of mono-organizational socialism.

Molotov was quintessentially the man for this twin task. He had had a vigorous apprenticeship to it during his years as Stalin's "second secretary" during the 1920s. At the Fourteenth Party Congress in 1925, for example, he proclaimed that one of the party's primary tasks was "to increase the influence and direction of the party over both the leading organs of the state apparatus and the entire body of the state apparatus as a whole."[47] In his first major speech as Sovnarkom chairman, he said: "I declare to you, comrades, that at my work in the Sovnarkom I shall continue to be a party worker, an instrument of the will of the party and of its Central Committee."[48]

Of course the legitimating fiction of the responsibility of the Government to elected soviet assemblies was maintained, and indeed refurbished in the 1936 "Stalin" constitution, which replaced the indirectly "elected" all-union Congress of Soviets and its CEC by the directly "elected" (though similarly unopposed) two-house Supreme Soviet of the USSR. The practice of solemnizing the more important Sovnarkom decisions by issuing them jointly with the all-union CEC persisted until the mid-1930s, although at a rapidly declining rate,[49] and it had no parallel under the new institutional arrangements after 1937. But the overriding subordination of Government to party was now given symbolic emphasis by the new practice of promulgating decisions of prime importance as joint decrees of the Sovnarkom and the CPSU Central Committee, signed by both Stalin and Molotov,[50] thus symbolizing the superordination of party leadership over Government leadership.

Simultaneously, the processes of decisionmaking showed a constant drift from a collective to a hierarchical and bureaucratic basis. The frequency of Sovnarkom meetings slipped to barely one every two weeks.[51] An unofficial "inner cabinet" comprising the chairman and deputy chairmen took to meeting in between full Sovnarkom meetings, disposing of some business on the spot, sharing out other matters to be dealt with executively, and leaving only a few items for the Sovnarkom agenda.[52] STO, no longer, in the view of van den Berg, a coordinating body but merely an auxiliary decision level for economic business, met with ever decreasing frequency (64 times in 1930, 30 in 1933, 16 in 1935) before being abolished in 1937.[53] Rykov's Preparatory Commission, the heir to Lenin's Little Sovnarkom, was discarded as soon as Molotov took over, its functions absorbed by sections of the Sovnarkom Chancellery.[54]

Sovnarkom now took a direct hand in the Worker-Peasant Inspection Commissariat's (*Rabkrin*) domain of "control," i.e. checking on efficiency and discipline in state institutions and enterprises. In December 1930, it set up an Execution Commission (*Komissiia ispolneniia*), whose job it was to follow up the actual carrying out of decisions, while Rabkrin was left with such tasks as improving structures and procedures. In 1934, when the apparatus "had been brought totally into accord with the tasks of building socialism,"[55] Rabkrin and the Execution Commission were merged in a new People's Commissariat of Soviet Control.

The abolition, also in 1934, of the commissariats' boards (*kollegii*) is a further example of the move from quasi-collective to more emphatically hierarchical patterns of decisionmaking, even if the boards had long since lost their original executive powers and been reduced to a consultative role. Commissariat boards were to be revived in 1938, but with limited powers that stressed control over the performance of subordinate bodies and executives.[56] Meanwhile the executive autonomy of people's commissariats further declined as the Sovnarkom sharply stepped up its vetting of their draft decrees and instructions.[57]

One of the most conspicuous features of the Sovnarkom in this period was its constantly accelerating growth: from 15 members in 1931 to 19 in 1936, 29 in 1938, and 38 in 1941. In the process it crossed the Rubicon beyond which a body is too large to function as a "cabinet," or indeed a committee of any kind (setting aside the question of non–members permitted to be present, and in some cases to speak, at Sovnarkom meetings).[58] The main engine of this process was the proliferation of industrial and other economic enterprises, which provoked the division and redivision of commissariats in a search for a more effective span of control. Thus, in 1932, the Supreme Economic Council (*Vesenkha*) split into the three commissariats for the heavy, light, and lumber industries. Two years later the Commissariat for Supply divided into commissariats for domestic trade and the food industry, and the Agriculture Commissariat spawned a separate Commissariat for Grain and Livestock State Farms. Between 1937 and 1939 the recently formed heavy and light industry commissariats each again split in two. And so on.[59] Between January 1939 and the German invasion in May 1941 a further 17 people's commissariats were formed, 11 of them from two waves of splits in the Heavy Industry Commissariat.[60]

This multiplication of agencies separately represented in the Sovnarkom obviously magnified the problems of the coordination of related agencies and of input overload in the full Sovnarkom. The first reaction to this was the creation in November 1937, following the demise of STO, of an Economic Council (*Ekonomicheskii sovet*), with very broad powers over the approval and implementation of planning targets, prices, wages, management structures, economic trouble–shooting, and commissariat decisions.[61] It clearly merited van den Berg's characterization of it as the "economic cabinet" of the USSR during this period. Comprising the chairman and deputy chairmen of the Sovnarkom and the chairman of the trades union council, it met every few days, with an agenda expanding from an average of 11 to one of 33 items per meeting between 1938 and 1940.[62] The Sovnarkom had four deputy chairmen at the time of the Economic Council's establishment, but how many were active in the Council during this period of arrests and turbulence it is difficult to say. The number rose to six during 1939 and to 11 during 1940. In April 1940 six industry councils (*Khoziaistvennye sovety*), each headed by one of the deputy premiers, were set up under the Economic Council to give "expeditious [*operativnoe*] leadership."[63] Thus, as far as the economic agencies were concerned, the hierarchy now ran from the Sovnarkom chairman through the Economic Council and the chairman of the appropriate industry council to the people's commissar.

In less than a year, on 21 March 1941, the whole system of councils was scrapped and a simplified structure based on a Bureau of the Sovnarkom replaced it.   This seems to have been intended, *inter alia*, to reinforce the hierarchical dimension in order to render decisionmaking more "expeditious"[64] and was evidently related to the appointment of Nikolai A. Voznesenskii, 11 days earlier, as the first deputy chairman of the Sovnarkom, with responsibility for general oversight of the economy.   Finally, on May 6, the hierarchy was capped by Stalin's assumption of the Sovnarkom chairmanship.[65]   Molotov, who in 1939 had added the foreign affairs portfolio to his duties as chairman, became one of the deputy chairmen.   There was now a direct line of personal responsibility, in form as well as fact, that ran all the way from workshop foreman to the top man in party and state, the "Boss" (*Khoziain*), Stalin.   And of course similar lines of responsibility converged on Stalin's office from all other sectors of the mono–organizational system––armed forces, police, culture and ideology, foreign relations, and so on.

Six weeks later Hitler launched his "treacherous" attack, and the four years of war that followed profoundly affected the operations of government.   On 30 June 1941, by a decision promulgated in the name of the presidium of the Supreme Soviet, the Central Committee of the CPSU, and the Sovnarkom, a State Defense Committee (*Gosudarstvennyi Komitet oborony*––GKO) was established and entrusted with "the full entirety (*vsia polnota*) of power in the State.   All citizens and all party, soviet, Komsomol, and military organs are obliged to carry out without question the decisions and orders of the State Defense Committee."[66]   Initially GKO comprised Stalin, Molotov, Voroshilov, Georgii M. Malenkov and Lavrentii P. Beria––the last three representing the armed forces, party apparatus, and security organs, respectively.   In February 1942, deputy premiers Anastas I. Mikoian (foreign trade), Voznesenskii (planning and industry), and Lazar M. Kaganovich (transport) were added.[67]

GKO depended for its effectiveness on its combination of extraordinary powers, fluidity of structures, and flexibility of operation.   Rather than build a large bureaucratic apparatus of its own, it operated by commandeering and combining the resources of existing organizations, creating and disbanding various task–oriented committees, bureaus, and councils in response to rapidly changing priorities.   It enforced these priorities by assigning selected officials and executives the status of GKO "plenipotentiaries" (*upolnomochennye*) in particular sectors or areas (area plenipotentiaries were usually the regional party first secretaries).   GKO's numerous but irregular meetings lacked formal agendas and went unminuted, the watchword being speed and decisiveness in resolving issues as they arose.[68]

Every effort was made to extend this flexibility and "expeditiousness" of administration down the line. For example, although of course the establishment of GKO drastically reduced the role of the peoples commissariats, within their new limits the powers of both peoples commissars and industrial executives to reassign resources without higher–level approval were substantially broadened.[69] Meanwhile, the general administration of civilian life had to go on, demanding much of the attention of certain Sovnarkom members, notably, to judge by the regulations and ordinances issued over his name, Deputy Premier Alexei N. Kosygin.

Although GKO and much else in Stalin's wartime government left little or no specific legacy, in an indirect way the experience of these years of travail and triumph proved very important for the future. The sense of the continuity of the Soviet state with imperial Russia, and of Stalin with past nation–building rulers, which had been an emergent theme in the prewar years, was now massively reinforced, evidently reflecting not only its instrumental value to the regime, but also Stalin's self–identification. While the temporarily muted pressure of communist ideology was vigorously reinforced once victory was assured, it henceforth shared the stage in legitimating the regime with appeal to a patriotism centering on the centuries–old Russian–Soviet state. One important symbolic reflection of this came in 1946, with the revival of the old term "ministers" and the consequent renaming of the Council of People's Commissars (Sovnarkom) as the Council of Ministers.[70]

A related factor was the party–state relationship at the summit of power, and the nexus between its structural, procedural, and personal aspects. On the one hand, there was a substantial operational merging of the party and Government leadership, while on the other most of the leaders with whom Stalin was closely working, especially in GKO, were deputy premiers and held no party office. GKO's membership overlapped substantially with that of the Politburo and appears to have largely supplanted it as the apex of the decisionmaking process. For its part, the Central Committee secretariat dealt with most of the business channeled through the party apparatus. Much of this business was concerned with facilitating and enforcing high priority economic tasks, which involved local party officials in essentially managerial roles.[71] They thereby found themselves in the paradoxical position of enjoying extraordinary powers over local state personnel, but mostly in the furtherance of tasks determined by state rather than party bodies at higher echelons. Despite important structural and procedural changes, these basic features of the party–state relationship persisted after the war.

GKO was abolished on 4 September 1945. Meanwhile, in May 1944, the Bureau of the Council of People's Commissars, which had lapsed with the establishment of GKO after a very brief existence, was revived,[72] and on 30 July 1949 it was converted into a presidium of the Council of Ministers, the name suggesting a broader policymaking role.[73] A number of bureaus for specific areas of government set up in the period of *the* Bureau were now brought in under the presidium.[74] It seems likely that the presidium, whose existence was not made public at the time, included one or two additional members apart from the chairman and deputy chairmen of the Council. It transpired that a steering group––again, confusingly, termed the Bureau–– emerged, and may, indeed, have largely supplanted the full presidium.[75]

These years also saw an increasing identification of the Politburo with the Government leadership. Whereas in 1939 five of the Politburo's 11 full and candidate members had held office in the party Central Committee apparatus and five in the Government, by 1951 only three held Central Committee jobs and fully 10 held Government jobs (two out of the 12 held office in both). What, however, did membership of the Politburo mean in these years? From the memoirs of Khrushchev and others we know that it had ceased to operate as a regular decisionmaking body, and the essential political reality was now the changing pattern of relationships between Stalin as his "closest comrades in arms," a status that was signaled by inclusion in the (largely non–functional) Politburo.[76] It would seem that Stalin's role as head of the Soviet Government now meant more to him than his role as head of the party, and that he wanted most of the men closest to him to concern themselves primarily with the work of the state administration.

It is tempting to see the presidium of the Council of Ministers in Stalin's last years as an "inner cabinet," but this needs to be qualified. For one thing, there was, in effect, no "full cabinet" for it to be the "inner cabinet" of. If the Council of Ministers met at all it would have been very infrequently, and it was far too large to function as an executive body. Nor is it clear whether the presidium itself met regularly, although as noted its "Bureau" probably did.

While there are some respects in which the party can be said to have lost its primacy in Soviet political life in these years, we should again beware of simplistic generalizations. In the early postwar years great efforts were made to disengage local party organizations from day-to-day administration and management.[77] Nevertheless, they were still expected to constantly check the performance of Government-run (as well as formally voluntary) organizations and enterprises, and to correct them when they erred, as well as to transmit and enforce Moscow's priorities. To this end, the constitutional law of the time declared that the decisions of party organs possessed "the force of law."[78] Consequently, the central party apparatus, although separate from the Government, nevertheless made an important, if auxiliary, contribution to governing the country, and a crucial one in some areas (notably in the "ideological" area and in personnel administration).

There are two other ways in which wartime practices persisted into the "high Stalin" period of 1946–52. Only the most minimal gestures were made to reverse the atrophy of the formal organs of authority, in both party and state, which had been virtually complete during the war. Again, it was the party that received the lesser attention, for while the Supreme Soviet was at least brought together annually for a two to three day "budget" session, only two Central Committee plenums were held in this period, and the Nineteenth CPSU Congress was nine years overdue when it convened in 1952.

Meanwhile there was a marked stabilization of the Government's size and membership. Its headlong growth began to level off during the war, and between March 1946 and March 1953 its membership increased from 57 to 66, i.e. 2.5 percent per annum, compared with 20 percent per annum between 1936 and 1941. All but one of the eight deputy chairmen in 1946 were still in office at the time of Stalin's death,[79] and all six of the deputy chairmen added by 1953 had already been people's commissars at the end of the war. There was a considerably higher turnover among more junior Government members, although far less than in the prewar years. It is important to stress that, contrary to widespread suppositions, there was a remarkable stability in the core leadership of the Soviet Government in the late Stalin years.[80]

The Post–Stalin Governments

The basic structures of Soviet government, along with the rest of the mono–organizational system established under Stalin, survived the dictator's death for nearly four decades, but their operation was greatly affected by the shift from tyranny to oligarchy at the summit of power. After the Nineteenth CPSU Congress in October 1952, Stalin merged the Politburo into a much larger Central Committee presidium, in what was evidently intended, *inter alia*, to facilitate his disposing of several of his old "comrades in arms," who had now lost his favor. On his death on March 5, however, these old "comrades," who still retained most of the levers of power, managed to assert their collective authority and to impose a drastic narrowing and reshaping of the key executive bodies of the party and Government, sharing out the key positions among themselves. The Central Committee presidium was returned to approximately the size and membership of the old Politburo, and the Council of Ministers presidium was reduced from 14 to five members. Initially Malenkov was both "prime minister" (chairman of the Council of Ministers) and the most senior

Table 1.2
Membership of Key Executive Bodies
14 March 1953

Name	Politburo of CC	Secretariat	Pres C of M	Post(s) held
Malenkov	M		M	Ch CofM
Beria	M		M	1st DCh CofM; Min Internal Affairs
Molotov	M		M	1st DCh CofM; Min Foreign Affairs
Voroshilov	M			Ch Presidium Supreme Soviet
Khrushchev	M	M		Sec (later 1st) CC
Bulganin	M		M	1st DCh CofM; Min Armed Forces
Kaganovich	M		M	1st DCh CofM
Mikoyan	M			Min Trade
Saburov	M			Min Machine–building
Pervukhin	M			Min Electric Industry
Shvernik	C			Ch Trade Union Council
Ponomarenko	C			Min Culture
Mel'nikov	C			1st Sec CC Ukraine
Bagirov	C			1st Sec CC Azerbaidzhan
Suslov		M		Sec CC
Ignatiev		M		Sec CC
Pospelov		M		Sec CC
Shatalin		M		Sec CC

Note: M = Full member; C = Candidate member; Ch = Chairman; DCh = Deputy chairman Sec = Secretary; CofM = Council of Ministers; Min = Minister; CC = Central Committee.

member of the five–man Central Committee secretariat, but after a week he was constrained to give up the latter position, thus averting the first threat of a reassertion of one–man rule. A second such threat was defeated three months later, with the arrest (and later execution) of the police chief Beria.

Table 1.2 shows the distribution of formal roles within the oligarchy shortly after Stalin's death. It reveals a striking persistence of the pattern established in the late Stalin era, when most of the inner core of leaders had come to hold

Government rather than party jobs. Not surprisingly it was the prime minister, Malenkov, who figured initially as the oligarchy's *primus inter pares*. That was no doubt his expectation in opting for the key position in the Government rather than the party when confronted with the choice. Clearly, he underestimated the actual and latent powers inherent in the party apparatus, by virtue of its centrality in regime legitimation and in ideological and organizational authority. Nikita S. Khrushchev, the one Central Committee presidium member left in the secretariat after Malenkov's withdrawal, and therefore in effective control of it and of the whole party machine, now deployed impressive verve, shrewdness, and energy in reasserting the primacy of the party over the Government. In so doing, he assured his own primacy, as first secretary of the CPSU Central Committee, within the leadership. The crucial steps in Khrushchev's consolidation of power were the replacement of Malenkov as prime minister by Khrushchev's junior ally Bulganin in February 1955; Khrushchev's defeat in June 1957 of a Government-based majority in the Central Committee presidium that had sought to remove him, and were themselves removed (the "anti-party group" crisis); and his assumption nine months later of the prime minister's office in addition to his post of party first secretary.[81]

Khrushchev's victory of June 1957 was in one sense a victory of the Central Committee secretariat, where most of his key supporters worked, over the largely hostile Government presidium. This is reflected in the fact that by the end of the year the 15 members of the Central Committee presidium had come to include 10 members of the secretariat and only two members of the Government. Khrushchev, however, was not one to remain a mere spokesman for the party apparatus, as his prompt assumption of the post of prime minister and subsequent pruning and switching of personnel was to demonstrate. By 1960 the number of Central Committee presidium members holding office in the Council of Ministers was roughly in balance with those holding office in the party secretariat, and *neither* now formed a majority. As chairman of all three bodies, and the sole Central Committee presidium member with a place in the other two, Khrushchev had now given his personal authority a formidable structural basis, and had thus come to offer a *third* potential threat (after those earlier presented by Malenkov and Beria) to the developing oligarchical power structure. Of course, to become a despot in the Stalin mold Khrushchev would require such additional weapons as a mythologized "personality cult" and the power of life and death over his subordinates, and he showed little indication of seeking these. Nevertheless, between 1960 and 1964 he continued to impose a series of (largely unsuccessful) domestic and foreign policy moves, along with constant organizational and personnel changes, and ended by alarming and alienating all the major elites. In this context his leading colleagues and proteges could count on Central Committee support when they staged their "velvet" coup to remove him in October 1964. The bloodless and quasi-constitutional way in which this was effected, and the change in political culture which it reflects, is seen by some as his most impressive achievement.[82]

Let us now consider the major changes in the Soviet Government during the Khrushchev years. The drastic narrowing and consolidation of leadership bodies at the time of Stalin's death did not long outlive the immediate crisis of power. The full Council of Ministers, initially reduced from 66 to 29, grew to 55 by April 1954 and was up to 67 by May 1955.[83] This was not a simple restoration of the *status quo ante*, however, since there were several structural changes and a significant turnover of the Government leadership. Only 34 of the May 1955 Council of Ministers had been in Stalin's Government just over two years earlier.

Meanwhile, the constant expansion and growing complexity of the Soviet economy made it ever more difficult to run it effectively from a single center, and simply creating more and more specialized ministries was clearly no answer. One direction in which the post-Stalin leaders sought remedies was administrative decentralization. In industry this went through four stages, each more radical than the last.   In 1954–55, some 11,000 enterprises were transferred from Union to republican jurisdiction.[84] In May 1955, jurisdiction over a large number of decisions relating to planning and finance, previously vested in various central Government agencies, was devolved onto the republic governments.[85] In May 1956, enterprises administered by 12 central ministries were transferred to the full operative control of republic agencies.[86] And finally, in May 1957, most of the central industrial ministries were abolished and the focus for administering industry was shifted to roughly a hundred regional economic councils (*sovnarkhozy*).[87] Conflict over this radical measure proved a major factor in precipitating the attempt to overthrow Khrushchev in June 1957, but before amplifying this point we shall first need to note the changes in the structure and personnel of the Government since Stalin.

The re-expansion of the Council of Ministers in 1953–55 brought the restoration of several senior ministers to the status of deputy chairman of the Council of Ministers in order to coordinate this unwieldy body. At the time of Stalin's death, Beria, Molotov, Bulganin, and Voroshilov had been appointed *first* deputy premiers, while Mikoian remained a deputy premier. The official resolution stated that the chairman (Malenkov) and first deputy chairmen were to constitute the presidium of the Council of Ministers. In June 1953, Beria was arrested, reducing the presidium to four. Then, in December, Gosplan chief Maksim Z. Saburov and industrial ministers Mikhail G. Pervukhin, Ivan F. Tevosian, Viacheslav A. Malyshev, and Alexei N. Kosygin got their deputy

premierships back.[88] Further changes in early 1955[89] brought the number of
first deputy premiers to five,[90] and the deputy premiers to eight.[91] Meanwhile,
the presidium of the Council of Ministers was expanded to include the chairman,
first deputy chairmen, deputy chairmen, "and also individuals personally
appointed by the Council of Ministers of the USSR."[92] Given the size now
attained by the Central Committee presidium, it is not surprising to see evidence
that a system of specialized bureaus such as had operated under the Government
presidium in the late Stalin years had also been revived.[93] Furthermore, when
Bulganin replaced Malenkov as prime minister, a Commission on Current
Affairs (*Komissiia po tekuchim delam*), reminiscent of the various "vermicelli"
bodies over the decades, was established under the chairmanship of First Deputy
Premier Pervukhin, although it had an on–again, off–again existence in later
years.[94] To further complicate the picture, the State Economic Commission, an
offshoot of the State Planning Committee (Gosplan), was converted at the end
of 1956 into a kind of economic inner cabinet, which was chaired by Pervukhin
and contained several other members of the Government presidium. This was
an effort by Khrushchev's Government-based opponents to counter his
decentralizing measures with a radical recentralization. It proved very
short-lived, however, as Khrushchev soon regained the momentum and pushed
through his sovnarkhoz reform.[95]

According to an interview with Khrushchev in May 1957, the Government
presidium itself had established a practice of regular weekly meetings (as had
the Central Committee presidium),[96] and it remained the key organ for running
the state machine after Khrushchev took over the prime minister's office
personally. The Government presidium still consisted of the chairman, first
deputy chairmen, deputy chairmen, and "others personally appointed," and it
continued to operate by way both of collective "decisions" (*postanovleniia*) and
of "orders" (*rasporiazheniia*) issued by the chairman or one of his deputies.[97]

However, there was to be no quiet life under Khrushchev, for the Government
or for anyone else. The dysfunctions of his 1957 regionalization of industrial
administration soon made themselves felt, and recentralization measures, begun
modestly in 1958, led to the partial restoration, as "state committees," of most
of the abolished ministries. In March 1963, this process culminated in the
establishment of yet another economic inner cabinet, with the title, harking back
to the 1920s, of Supreme National Economic Council (VSNKh). It was
empowered to issue decisions and orders obligatory for both central economic
agencies and subordinate regional economic councils (*sovnarkhozy*).[98]

Considering the period 1953–64 as a whole, we observe a partial
reinstitutionalization of Soviet government, after three decades in which all
institutions had gradually dissolved in the acid of despotism. Not only did such

formal legitimating bodies as the Central Committee plenum and the Supreme Soviet resume regular meetings, but more vitally the three key executive bodies, the Central Committee presidium and secretariat and the Government presidium, previously convened at the whim of the despot, now met regularly and transacted the great business of government.   Formal structures and rules acquired greater force, and terror ceased to be a factor within the leadership and between it and wider circles of the elites and the masses.   But we have also noted two factors which worked against the reinstitutionalization process: Khrushchev's high-handed leadership style, and (largely due to this) the constant flux of Government and party structures, powers, and personnel.

The changes initiated by Khrushchev's successors, his erstwhile lieutenants, were designed to tackle these problems and to strengthen the oligarchy and promote stability.[99] The cornerstone here was a Central Committee endorsed decision that the post of party first secretary and the Council of Ministers' chairmanship should henceforth be kept in separate hands.   The power of each was further limited by keeping the numbers of Government and Central Committee officials in the party presidium roughly in balance.   A policy of "stability of cadres," that is, a reluctance to remove personnel from office, both reinforced elite support and reduced the opportunities for top leaders to acquire dominance through the exercise of patronage.   Most of Khrushchev's elaborate tinkerings with the structures of party and state were undone and jurisdictional demarcation simplified.   His arrangements for involving the party apparatus more closely in administering the economy were reversed.   More generally, rulers and ruled alike had had enough of mobilizational dynamism and were ready to settle for a blend of bureaucratic pragmatism and predictability.   Hence the concern to strengthen safeguards against the emergence of a new Khrushchev (or Stalin) by no means entailed a rejection of hierarchy, and the structural and procedural devices evolved over several decades now gradually congealed into fairly stable institutional shape.

The primacy of the Central Committee presidium over other executive bodies—-and the primacy of the first secretary within the presidium—-was acknowledged from the start of the post-Khrushchev era. It was reinforced by a 1966 CPSU Congress decision to restore the more authoritative, traditional titles of Political Bureau (Politburo) and general secretary. The chairman of the Council of Ministers (initially Kosygin) gained unequivocal acknowledgement as Number Two, while the positions of "second" Central Committee secretary and chairman of the Supreme Soviet presidium soon emerged as next in rank. The Council of Ministers presidium and the Central Committee secretariat each overlapped in membership with the Politburo and served it both as executants of second-order business and as channels to the Government and party machine, respectively. This "interlocking directorate" formed the central node of an increasingly intricate matrix of bureaucratic interest and policy communities engaged in a process of incremental, consultative, not to say ponderous, decisionmaking. These patterns were to become deeply entrenched in the two decades between Khrushchev's removal and Gorbachev's accession, and their impact on the structures and operation of government can be best summed up by the terms "conservatism" and "institutionalization."

The first step in the undoing of Khrushchev-era reforms was the recentralization of economic administration and the reassertion of the primacy of ministerial structures.[100] One consequence was the renewed growth of the Council of Ministers. By 1966 it was back to what it had been before Khrushchev's reforms, and in the next decade it grew by a further 17 ministries or state committees. By the time of Brezhnev's death it included 101 members, not counting the 15 republic premiers entitled to voting membership.

The new constitution adopted in 1977 at last gave formal recognition to the presidium of the Council of Ministers. Article 132 prescribed its composition as the chairman, first vice-chairmen and vice-chairmen, and its tasks as "the resolution of questions connected with providing leadership of the national economy, and of other questions"--hardly a restrictive definition. In 1981 this article was amended to allow "other members of the Government of the USSR" to be added to the presidium "by decision of the Council of Ministers of the USSR."[101]

A new Law on the Council of Ministers adopted in 1978 authorized the presidium to form permanent commissions and also "temporary commissions and other working agencies ... to prepare proposals connected with the development of branches of the national economy or spheres of administration, to work out draft decisions of the USSR government, to consider disagreements over draft decisions, and to implement particular instructions of the USSR Council of Ministers and its Presidium" (Article 30).[102] The presidium's Commission on Current Affairs, dropped by Khrushchev, was revived after his removal,[103] and about 1978 was transformed into a Commission on Operative Questions, whose task, as described by Prime Minister Kosygin, was "to consider and decide current questions of the economic system, and to exercise systematic control over the implementation of the State plan."[104] Other presidium standing commissions operating in the early 1980s included the Military Industrial Commission as well as those for the agroindustrial complex, environmental protection and the rational use of national resources, development of the West Siberian petroleum and gas complex, Comecon affairs, and foreign economic affairs.[105] They were chaired by one or other of the Council of Ministers deputy chairmen.[106]

The 1978 Law on the Council of Ministers also spelled out the "line" powers and responsibilities of the Government leadership. Thus the chairman "heads the Government and directs its activity ... coordinates the activity of the first vice-chairmen and vice-chairmen [and] in urgent cases, makes decisions on particular questions of state administration." For their part, "the first vice-chairmen and vice-chairmen, in accordance with the allocation of responsibilities, coordinate the activity of USSR ministries and state committees and other agencies under the jurisdiction of the USSR Council of Ministers, exercise control over the activity of these agencies and give them day-to-day instructions ... and give prior consideration to proposals and draft decisions and orders submitted to the USSR Council of Ministers" (Article 29).[107]

The ratio of first deputy chairmen to deputy chairmen, which had declined under Khrushchev, was now further reduced. From 1965 to 1973 there were only two first deputies, Kirill T. Mazurov (industry) and Dmitrii S. Polianskii (agriculture). With Polianskii's departure in 1973, Mazurov became the sole first deputy until he was joined by Nikolai A. Tikhonov in 1976. Mazurov retired in 1978, leaving Tikhonov alone in that post. Tikhonov became chairman of the Council of Ministers in 1980 and was replaced as the sole first deputy by Ivan V. Arkhipov. It was only after Brezhnev's death that this pattern showed signs of changing, with Arkhipov being joined as first deputy chairman by Gaidar A. Aliev in November 1982 and Foreign Affairs Minister Andrei A. Gromyko in March 1983. It seems clear that, instead of working with the chairman as a kind of inner-cabinet, such as existed in the 1940s and 1950s, the first deputies now served essentially as assistants to the prime minister, enabling him to devote more time to larger issues.

The number of deputy chairmen remained stable at 9 or 10 until Tikhonov replaced Kosygin as prime minister in 1980, when it was raised to 13. This increased the membership of the presidium to 15, plus perhaps two or three nominated members--still quite a comfortable number for an effective committee. Meetings of the full Council of Ministers were now regularly reported, albeit rather laconically, and the provision in the new Law (Article 28) that it meet at least once every three months was by and large observed. Most meetings were held within one working day, but occasionally carried over to a second. While their main function may have been to offer some credibility to constitutional forms, there was no attempt to represent them as taking concrete decisions or debating policy alternatives. They were occasions, it seems, for focusing attention on leadership priorities and problem areas and mobilizing effort to tackle them. They were occasionally addressed by General Secretary Brezhnev[108] and often attended by Central Committee secretaries Andrei P.

Kirilenko, Vladimir I. Dolgikh, or Mikhail S. Gorbachev.[109]   Annual plans and quarterly economic performance were the only topics mentioned in most reports.

There has been no space in this chapter to consider the background and career characteristics of Government members, but we should briefly note the main patterns in the two decades preceding *perestroika*.   "Stability of cadres" meant aging.   From 1965 to 1977, the average age of members of the Council of Ministers rose from 58 to 66.   Its subsequent rise was muted by an increasing death and retirement rate as well as by younger replacements brought in at Tikhonov's takeover of the chairmanship.   Ethnic Russians continued to predominate in both the presidium and the full Council, and those who were not Russians were mostly Ukrainians or Belorussians.   It was a man's world; after Elena A. Furtseva lost the Culture Ministry in 1974 there was not a single woman in the Council of Ministers.   Virtually all had a higher education, and they could be classified into "career specialists" (those who had worked all or most of their lives in a particular field) and "party generalists" (those who took Government posts after considerable experience in the party apparatus).   "Career specialists" began to take over industrial commissariats during the 1930s, an area they came to predominate by the 1950s, and the first two (Saburov and Pervukhin) were made deputy chairmen.   Khrushchev favored party generalists, but after his removal the career specialists came into their own.   Kosygin himself and most of the other presidium members had pursued technocratic careers, as had nearly two-thirds of the more junior Government members. Party generalists were to be found in such areas as security, control, media, and agriculture.[110]

Here we must return to the broader aspects of the party-state relationship. The balance struck at the time of Khrushchev's removal, and the related balance between the oligarchical structure of power and the primacy of the party general secretary, held on the whole throughout this period.   Despite the buttresses introduced to shore up the oligarchy, however, and despite the personal authority of Kosygin, bit by bit the balance moved in favor of the party and General Secretary Brezhnev.   This accelerated from the mid-1970s, and was reflected, *inter alia*, in the far stronger formula on the CPSU's "leading and directing" role in Article 6 of the 1977 Constitution, as compared with the laconic reference in the 1936 constitution; in stepped-up supervision of Government agencies by Central Committee departments; in the election of Brezhnev as chairman of the Supreme Soviet presidium (the nearest thing to formal head of state) and as chairman of the newly-formed State Defense Council (responsible to the Supreme Soviet presidium rather than the Council of Ministers); in a growing (if somewhat ridiculous) "cult of personality"; and in personnel changes, culminating in Kosygin's replacement in 1980 by

Brezhnev's crony Tikhonov. Nevertheless, no one imagined that the old and ailing General Secretary-"President" was set on establishing a personal dictatorship. The question is not whether the oligarchy was under threat, but how and to what extent its character had changed, specifically with respect to the party–Government relationship.

Unfortunately, there are no clear objective measures. For example, the incidence of joint Central Committee–Council of Ministers decrees or of Central Committee decisions bearing on Government operations can be no more than indicative.[111] A key factor is the nature and extent of Government representation in the Politburo, whose clear dominance in the "interlocking directorate" is generally agreed. A comparison of Table 1.3 with Table 1.2 above reveals some significant developments. As noted earlier, the predominance of Government officials over party officials in the Politburo at the end of the Stalin period was reversed following Khrushchev's victory over the "anti–party group"; but they were subsequently brought into a rough balance and this persisted in the early Brezhnev years. Toward the end of the Brezhnev period, however, the Politburo contained five Central Committee secretaries as full members and two more as candidate members, while the chairman of the Council of Ministers was the sole member of the Government presidium with a Politburo seat. On the other hand, there were now three other members of the Government who were not on its presidium, namely the ministers for foreign affairs and defense and the chairman of the KGB, but who *were* voting members of the Politburo.

To evaluate this it is worth recalling past practice in the representation of these three agencies in the top decisionmaking bodies. It is obvious that their political sensitivity would ensure that all substantive business in their areas would be dealt with directly by the Politburo. Indeed their status throughout the Soviet period appears to have resembled that of the "non–Council" agencies in the late tsarist period, referred to earlier, whose ministers normally dealt directly with the Sovereign, by–passing the Council of Ministers. Nevertheless in the late Stalin and early post–Stalin years, these agencies were either directly run or overlorded by Politburo members who were also deputy or first deputy chairmen of the Council of Ministers and therefore members of its presidium. Leadership changes which began with Beria's arrest in June 1953 and ran through Marshal Zhukov's ouster in October 1957 ushered in a new pattern where the heads of these bodies were members *neither* of the Central Committee presidium (Politburo from 1966) *nor* the Government presidium. This enhanced the collective role of Politburo members in the areas of defense, internal security, and foreign policy. This arrangement lasted for 16 years until in 1973 the heads of these bodies, Marshal Andrei A. Grechko, Iurii V. Andropov, and Andrei

Table 1.3
Membership of Key Executive Bodies
January 1982

Name	Politburo	Secretariat	Pres C of M	Post(s) held
Brezhnev	M	M		General Sec CC
				Ch Presidium Sup Soviet
				Ch State Defense Council
Andropov	M			Ch KGB
Grishin	M			1st Sec Moscow City Committee
Gromyko	M			Min Foreign Affairs
Kirilenko	M	M		Sec CC
Kunaev	M			1st Sec CC Kazakhstan
Pel'she	M			Ch Committee Party Control
Romanov	M			1st Sec Leningrad regional Committee
Suslov	M	M		Sec CC
Ustinov	M			Min Defense
Shcherbitsky	M			1st Sec CC Ukraine
Chernenko	M	M		Sec CC
Tikhonov	M		M	Ch CM
Gorbachev	M	M		Sec CC
Aliev	C			1st Sec CC Azerbaidzhan
Demichev	C			Min Culture
Ponomarev	C	M		Sec CC
Rashidov	C			1st Sec CC Uzbekistan
Solomentsev	C			Ch CM RSFSR
Kuznetsov	C			1st DCh Presidium Sup Soviet
Shevardnadze	C			1st Sec CC Georgia
Kiselev	C			1st Sec CC Belorussia
Dolgikh		M		Sec CC
Kapitonov		M		Sec CC
Zimianin		M		Sec CC
Rusakov		M		Sec CC
Arkhipov			M	1st DCh CM
Dymshits			M	DCh CM
Novikov			M	DCh CM
Smirnov			M	DCh CM
Baibakov			M	DCh CM
Nuriev			M	DCh CM
Martynov			M	DCh CM
Marchuk			M	DCh CM
Talyzin			M	DCh CM
Makeev			M	DCh CM
Kostandov			M	DCh CM
Antonov			M	DCh CM
Bodiul			M	DCh CM

Note: M = Full member, C = Candidate member, Sec = Secretary, Ch = Chairman, Min = Minister, DCh – Deputy chairman, CM = Council of Ministers, CC = Central Committee.

Gromyko, were simultaneously made full members of the Politburo, but without acquiring Government presidium status. This automatically diluted the influence of other Politburo members over policy in these areas. When in 1980 the presidium was reduced to only one member with a seat on the Politburo, that occupied by the new prime minister Tikhonov, a protege of General Secretary Brezhnev, the exclusion of the presidium of the Council of Ministers from even indirect say in the work of these agencies was virtually complete. When we further note that the Minister of Culture, Petr N. Demichev, was now also on the Politburo, albeit as a candidate (i.e. non–voting) member, the conclusion seems unavoidable that economic administration, which had always been the principle concern of the Government presidium, was now virtually the only field in which it could exercise any serious authority. Nothing happened between 1980 and the accession of Gorbachev to seriously change that situation.

On the Eve

We have now traced the development of the Council of Ministers and its place in the Soviet political system to the eve of Gorbachev's *perestroika*, which began to unravel the interwoven strands of that system and ended by severing them. As we have seen, most of those strands stretched back into the early years of Soviet rule, and some of them deep into Russia's history. Nevertheless it was arguably not until the 1960s that they settled into a stable relationship that then persisted for a mere quarter century.

It is tempting to suggest that if it was the Council of Ministers that governed, it was the Communist Party's Politburo that *ruled*. Our account, however, shows that things were not so simple. On the one hand, the Politburo was involved in the day-to-day running of Soviet society, and not just in major policy issues, while on the other hand the leading members of the Council of Ministers who formed its presidium overlapped with the Politburo, and along with its junior members figured as players in the political process out of which top–level decisions emerged. This said, it can certainly be argued that the Government and its agencies were engaged primarily in the more routine, "mechanistic," "rational–legal" aspects of governing, and the Politburo and party apparatus more with its *ad hoc*, "organic," "goal rational" aspects, so long as these contrasts are not absolutized.[112] This is all related to a point made early in this chapter, namely that the party executive embodies the theoretically unlimited prerogative that flows from the historical mission of "building communism."   This, as suggested, parallels the theoretically unlimited prerogative of the tsars, and like the latter is totally incompatible with any genuine system of constitutional and responsible government. It is a parallel, however, that needs to be carefully qualified, since the imperial regime did not seek to directly *run* everything that went on in society through its own bureaucracies, whereas the communist regime, unprecedently in human history, did seek exactly that. The size and complexity of government in Soviet society, and the interlocking and complementary roles of party and state executives and apparatuses that evolved to manage it, were an appropriate and indeed inevitable instrument of the very enterprise of mono–organizational socialism.

Now that enterprise is declared bankrupt and the "Soviet" system of government, starting with the "leading and directing" role of the Communist Party enshrined in Article 6 of the 1977 Constitution, has been scrapped. Nevertheless, as the political institutions of the 15 or so successor states and any coordinating political unit, such as the Commonwealth of Independent States, take shape, they will undoubtedly incorporate and adapt some of the structures, processes, and ways of thinking inherited from the old order, as the Bolsheviks did in their time. Moreover, elements of pre–1917 political thought and practice may now get a new lease on life. If Russia is finally to achieve a decisive breakthrough to a system of constitutional and responsible government, it is important that the right choices be made from both its pre–Soviet and Soviet legacy.

Notes

1. On imperial Russia's "prefectural governors," see John A. Armstrong, *The European Administrative Elite* (Princeton: Princeton University Press, 1973), 253ff; Daniel T. Orlovsky, *The Limits of Reform. The Ministry of Internal Affairs in Imperial Russia 1802–1881* (Cambridge Mass. and London: Harvard University Press, 1981), *passim*; P.A. Zaionchkovskii, *Pravitel'stvennyi apparat samoderzhavnoi Rossii v XIX v.* (Moscow: Mysl', 1978), chapter 3. More generally on the evolution of Russian governmental institutions before 1917, see N.P. Eroshkin, *Ocherki istorii gosudarstvennykh uchrezhdenii dorevoliutsionnoi Rossii* (Moscow: Uchpedgiz, 1960); S.V. Iushkov, *Istoriia gosudarstva i prava SSSR. Chast' pervaia* (Moscow: Gosiurizdat, 1950), and George L. Yaney, The *Systematization of Russian Government: Social Evolution in the Domestic Administration of Imperial Russia, 1711–1905* (Urbana: Ill.: University of Illinois Press, 1973). A valuable chronicle of the evolution of the central ministries from their pre–Petrine origins to the Stalin period is Boris Meissner, "Die Entwicklung der Ministerien in Russland", *Europa–Archiv*, February–April, 1948, pp. 1149–54, 1201–08 and 1253–62. On Speransky, see Marc Raeff, *Michael Speransky, Statesman of Imperial Russia, 1772–1839* (The Hague: Nijhoff, 1957).

2. Peter the Great's "Senate" also initially looked like serving as something approaching a "proto–cabinet" coordinating the work of the various agencies of government; but after a checkered career in the eighteenth century it evolved into a

large body lacking executive powers but exercising broad powers of judicial administration and administrative "control" (in the continental sense of the term).

3. Anatole Leroy-Beaulieu, *L'Empire des Tsars et les Russes, Tome II, Institutions* (Paris: 1882), p.88.

4. The best study of these developments is P.A. Zaionchkovskii, *Rossiiskoe samoderzhavie v rubezhe 1870–1880 godov* (Moscow, 1964).

5. On the formative stage of the new Council of Ministers created after the 1905 Revolution, see *Sovet Ministrov Rossiiskoi Imperii 1905–1906. Dokumenty i materialy*, ed. B.D. Gal'perin *et al.* (Leningrad: Nauka, 1990). This volume contains a valuable historical and analytical introduction. For further sources and a more extended outline of pre-revolutionary Government institutions, see my *Lenin's Government. Sovnarkom 1917–1922* (London/New York/Melbourne: Cambridge University Press, 1979), chapter 15.

6. The only monograph in a western language devoted entirely to the topic of this section is my *Lenin's Government: Sovnarkom 1917–1922.* Very valuable for this period is Walter Pietsch, *Revolution und Staat; Institutionen als Träger der Macht in Sowjetrussland 1917–1922* (Cologne: Verlag Wissenschaft und Politik, 1969). The one scholarly monograph devoted to the Soviet Council of Ministers for the entire period up to the 1970s is Ger P. van den Berg's invaluable *Organisation und Arbeitsweise der sowjetischen Regierung* (Baden–Baden: Nomos, 1984), which also examines the republic councils of ministers. Despite the restrictions imposed by official myths and censorship, several Soviet scholars, notably M.P. Iroshnikov and E.V. Genkina, provided much useful material for the study of the Soviet Government under Lenin. With the collapse of ideological censorship and the opening up of official archives we can now expect Russian scholars to lead the way in putting together a thorough picture of the operation of Soviet Government institutions from their origins.

7. On the origins of the name "Council of People's Commissars," see *Lenin's Government*, pp. 6–10.

8. See *ibid.*, chapter 2.

9. The next paragraphs closely follow the account given in my entry "Council of People's Commissars, 1917–1922", *Dictionary of the Russian Revolution*, ed. George Jackson and Robert Devlin (Westport, CT: Greenwood Press, 1989), pp. 168–71, which in turn summarizes the detailed analysis presented in *Lenin's Government*.

10. For details and sources relating to this revealing case where the Bolshevik leadership, encountering practical difficulties in the operation of their fledgling government, looked consciously to the structures and processes of prerevolutionary government for a solution, see *Lenin's Government*, pp. 36–38.

11. Van den Berg (*Organisation und Arbeitsweise*, p. 228) has calculated that the Little Sovnarkom averaged 18 meetings per month from April 1918 to January 1920, and 15 per month from then until August 1923.

12. There is a vast literature, but see especially George Leggett, *The Cheka: Lenin's Political Police* (Oxford: Oxford University Press, 1981).

13. See V.Z. Drobizhev, *Glavnyi shtab sotsialisticheskoi promyshlennosti (Ocherki istorii VSNKh, 1917-1932 gg.)* (Moscow, 1966), chapter 1; M.P. Iroshnikov, *Sozdanie sovetskogo tsentral'nogo gosudarstvennogo apparata* (Moscow, Leningrad: 1966), pp. 226-29, 244-46; M.P. Iroshnikov, *Predsedatel' Soveta Narodnykh Komissarov, V.I. Lenin (Ul'ianov)* (Leningrad, 1974), pp. 130-31.

14. For further details, see *Lenin's Government*, chapter 4.

15. See *ibid.*, pp. 169-70.

16. For details of the evolution of the Sovnarkom-CEC relationship, see *Lenin's Government*, chapter 12; Pietsch, *Revolution und Staat*, chapters 5 and 8; and van den Berg, *Organisation und Arbeitsweise*, chapters 1 and 3.

17. The following list of "the most important central commissions coming under Sovnarkom and STO" was attached to the official report on the work of the Government in the first half of 1923: Little Sovnarkom, Finance Committee, State Planning Commission, Chief Concessions Committee, Commission on domestic trade, Supreme Arbitration Commission, Commission on Industrial and Agricultural Immigration, Commission on Relieving Population Pressure (*razgruzka*) in Moscow, Special Temporary Science Committee, Commission on Recording and Sale of State Funds, Consultation on the Affairs of the Far East, Special Plenipotentiary Commission on Restoring and Developing the Grain Trade, and the Central Commission on Improving the Living Conditions of Scientists. See *Materialy o deiatel'nosti Soveta narodnykh komissarov, Soveta truda i oborony i tsentral'nykh pravitel'stvennykh uchrezhdenii: za pervoe polugodie ianvar'-iiun' 1923* (Moscow: Ekonomicheskaia zhizn', 1923), p. 245.

18. See *Lenin's Government*, pp. 176-89; Pietsch, *Revolution und Staat*, chapter 9; E.H. Carr, *The Bolshevik Revolution 1917-1923*, vol. 1 (London: Macmillan, 1950), chapters 8 and 9.

19. *Lenin's Government*, chapter 13.

20. *Ibid.*, chapter 14.

21. Cf. E.H. Carr, *Foundations of a Planned Economy 1926-1929*, vol. 2 (Harmondsworth: Penguin, 1967), p. 140. The fullest account and evaluation of Rykov's political career is Samuel A. Oppenheim's valuable Ph.D. dissertation, "Alexei Ivanovich Rykov (1881-1938): A Political Biography", Indiana University, 1972.

22. For Rykov's role in Lenin's Government, see my *Lenin's Government*, especially pp. 67, 88, 126, and chapter 13.

23. See Richard Pipes, *The Formation of the Soviet Union. Communism and Nationalism, 1917-1923* (Cambridge, MA: Harvard University Press, 1954), and E.H. Carr, *The Bolshevik Revolution*, vol. 1, part 3.

24. Carr, *The Bolshevik Revolution*, vol. 1, p. 409.

25. See *ibid.*, pp. 232-34.

26. See Carr, *The Bolshevik Revolution*, vol. 3, pp. 188-89, 218.

27. See *Lenin's Government*, chapter 8.

28. Carr, *The Bolshevik Revolution*, vol. 2, pp. 373-80.

29. See E.H. Carr, *Foundations of a Planned Economy, 1926–1929*, vol. 2 (Harmondsworth: Penguin, 1976), pp. 203–04.

30. *Lenin's Government*, pp. 65–66.

31. Van den Berg, *Organisation und Arbeitsweise*, p. 191.

32. N.P. Gorbunov *et al.*, *SSSR: God raboty pravitel'stva. Materialy k otchetu za 1925–26 biudzhetnyi god* (Moscow: Informatsionnoe Biuro SNK SSSR i STO, 1927), p. 38.

33. Its formal powers and responsibilities were listed rather laconically in an August 1923 "Regulation on the Council of Labor and Defense of the USSR." See *Sobranie uzakonenii RSFSR*, no. 95 (1923), item 946.

34. For example, in the course of September 1924 financial matters constituted 30 percent of STO's agenda items and 34 percent of the Sovnarkom's, industry 10 and 8 percent respectively, and military matters 5 percent of both. SNK dealt far more frequently with external trade questions and STO with internal trade, while SNK alone considered matters coming up at TsIK sessions. See "Obzor deiatel'nosti STO i SNK Soiuza SSR," *Vlast' sovetov*, no. 7 (October 1924), pp. 120, 123.

35. Cf. Van den Berg, *Organisation und Arbeitsweise*, p. 214.

36. See A. Malitskii, *Sovetskaia konstitutsiia*, 2nd ed. (Kharkov, 1925), p. 289; *Lenin's Government*, chapter 7 and p. 261, note 16.

37. See *Vlast' sovetov*, no. 8 (November 1924), p. 114.

38. Malitskii, *Sovetskaia konstitutsiia*, p. 289. In the two and a half years of its existence, the Legislative Proposals Commission considered about 400 of the 523 draft laws proposed by different Government agencies, sending about a quarter of them back and presenting the remainder to the Sovnarkom. See van den Berg, *Organisation und Arbeitsweise*, p. 229.

39. See Gorbunov, *God raboty pravitel'stva*, p. 39. A single Preparatory Commission had existed briefly in mid-1923 before dividing into the legislative proposals and administrative proposals commissions. For an analysis of the 1926 regulations governing its operation, see van den Berg, pp. 230.

40. See Derek Watson, "The Making of Molotov's Sovnarkom, 1928–1930," (Birmingham, UK: Soviet Industrialisation Project Series no. 25, CREES, University of Birmingham, 1984), p. 15.

41. See Carr, *Foundations of a Planned Economy*, vol. 2, p. 214.

42. For examples, see *Sovetskoe stroitel'stvo*, nos. 3–4 (1926), pp. 158–61.

43. Such appeals required the sanction of the Sovnarkom chairman, and in practice few went forward apart from cases of disagreement over social security entitlements. See E.E. Pontovich, "Konstitutsionnye vzaimootnosheniia pri razreshenii konfliktnykh voprosov," *Sovetskoe stroitel'stvo*, no. 6 (1929), p. 28.

44. Derek Watson gives an excellent account in "The Making of Molotov's Sovnarkom," pp. 17–37.

45. See R.W. Davies, *The Soviet Economy in Turmoil, 1929–1930* (Cambridge, MA: Harvard University Press, 1989), pp. 415–19.

46. See T.H. Rigby, *The Changing Soviet System. Monoorganizational Socialism from its Origins to Gorbachev's Perestroika* (Aldershot, UK, and Brookfield, VT: Edward Elgar, 1990).

47. *XIV S"ezd Vsesoiuznoi Kommunisticheskoi Partii (b), 2–19 dekabria 1925 g. Stenograficheskii otchet* (Moscow–Leningrad, 1926), p. 72.

48. V.M. Molotov, "Perevybory i perestroika sovetov," *V bor'be za sotsializm* (Moscow, 1935), p. 76.

49. The number of such joint decrees halved during Molotov's first year as chairman, and by 1935 it was down to one-fifth of the number in 1929. See van den Berg, *Organisation und Arbeitsweise*, p. 65. Concurrently, the essentially decorative role of TsIK was becoming more conspicuous; in 1931 it met for 16 days but by 1935 only for two. See *ibid.*, p. 39.

50. For counts of the number of such joint decrees see Watson, "The Making of Molotov's Sovnarkom," p. 2.

51. Van den Berg, *Organisation und Arbeitsweise*, p. 191.

52. G.V. Kuibysheva, O.A. Lezhava, N.N. Nelidov, and A.F. Charin, *Valerian Vladimirovich Kuibyshev. Biografiia* (Moscow, 1966), pp. 343–45. This arrangement seems to have originated under Rykov by at least 1927, but its operation between 1928 and 1930 was no doubt overshadowed by the struggles between "Rightists" and Stalinists. On the earlier period, see van den Berg, *Organisation und Arbeitsweise*, pp. 88, 220–21. A similar pattern at the republic level provides further indirect evidence, since changes in republic sovnarkom practices usually followed those at the center. In the Belorussian Sovnarkom the institution of "Consultative Meeting (*Soveshchanie*) of the Chairman of Sovnarkom" was established in December 1928 and was operating at least through the first half of the 1930s. It comprised the chairman and deputy chairmen, and agency heads took part as the agenda required. It met very frequently as a rule and covered the full range of Government business. The relation between this body, the full Sovnarkom, and the individual decisionmaking of chairman and deputy chairmen is described in terms very similar to those used by Kuibyshev's biographers with reference to the USSR Sovnarkom. See N.A. Slobodchikov, *Sovet narodnykh komissarov BSSR v 1920–1936 gg.* (Minsk, 1977), pp. 62–65.

53. Van den Berg, *Organisation und Arbeitsweise*, pp. 211–14.

54. *Sobranie zakonov*, part 1 (1931), pp. 4–48.

55. S.S. Studenikin, *Sovetskoe administrativnoe pravo* (Moscow, 1949), pp. 189–98.

56. *Resheniia partii i pravitel'stva po khoziaistvennym voprosam, 1917–1967gg. Tom 2, 1929–1940 gody* (Moscow, 1967), p. 639. Boards had to implement their people's commissar's decisions but were entitled to appeal them to the full Sovnarkom; I have not discovered any evidence on the exercise of this power. See also M. Gribanov, "K istorii razvitiia edinonachaliia i kollegial'nosti v narodnykh komissariatakh," *Sovetskoe gosudarstvo i pravo*, no. 3 (1940), pp. 61–67.

57. See V. Diablo in *Sovetskoe gosudarstvo*, no. 6 (1936), p. 58.

58. In 1931, the right of the permanent representatives of union republic governments to speak (but not vote) at sovnarkom meetings was reaffirmed.   See K.G. Fedorov, *Istoriia sovetskogo gosudarstva i prava* (Rostov, 1963), p. 178.

59. Further splits during these years: the Water Transport Commissariat separated out from the Transport Commissariat; an Armaments Industry Commissariat formed and later split into commissariats for aircraft industry, shipbuilding, munitions, and armaments; the Light Industry Commissariat split into commissariats for the light and textile industries; and the State Bank was given Sovnarkom representation separate from the Finance Commissariat.

60. Other peoples commissariats to divide in this 17–month period were Water Transport, Foodstuffs Industry, Lumber Industry, and Internal Affairs (NKVD), from which the State Security Commissariat was separated out in February 1941.

61. *Sobranie zakonov i rasporiazhenii Raboche–krestianskogo pravitel'stva SSSR,* no. 75 (1937), item 365; N. Kumykin, "Organy gosudarstvennogo upravleniia SSSR", *Sovetskogo stroitel'stvo,* no. 11 (1937), p. 42.

62. Van den Berg, *Organisation und Arbeitsweise,* pp. 240–41.

63. *Izvestiia,* 18 April 1940. The industry councils and their chairmen comprised: Metal and Chemical Industries (N.A. Bulganin), Machine–Building (V.A. Malyshev), Armaments Industry (N.A. Voznesenskii), Fuel and Electricity (M.G. Pervukhin), Consumer Goods (N.A. Kosygin) and Agriculture and Procurement (evidently no chairman was appointed and it is uncertain whether this council actually functioned).

64. See *Bol'shaia sovetskaia entsiklopediia,* 2nd ed., vol. 48, p. 399.   On this Bureau and its equivalents in the republics, see van den Berg, *Organisation und Arbeitsweise,* pp. 247–50.

65. Not even the *forms* of constitutional procedure were observed in Stalin's assumption of the Sovnarkom chairmanship.   The Supreme Soviet was not convened, nor was its presidium.   The latter's members were simply asked individually to signify their approval (*oprosnym poriadkom*).   See K.G. Fedorov, *Istoriia sovetskogo gosudarstva i prava* (Rostov, 1946) p. 133.

66. *KPSS o vooruzhennykh silakh Sovetskogo Soiuza. Dokumenty 1917–1968* (Moscow, 1969), p. 802; *Izvestiia,* 1 July 1941.

67. *Izvestiia,* 20 February 1942. In November 1944, Voroshilov was replaced by Bulganin. Voznesenskii, chairman of Gosplan from 1938, had been promoted to (the sole) first deputy chairman in March 1941 with overall responsibility for the economy. In October 1941, he was put in charge of evacuating a large part of the Government apparatus to Kuibyshev and other cities in the Volga–Urals area.

68. See See Sanford R. Lieberman, "Crisis Management in the USSR. The Wartime System of Administration and Control," in *The Impact of World War II on the Soviet Union,* ed. Susan J. Linz (Totowa, NJ: Rowman & Allanheld, 1985), pp. 59–76; A.B. Belikov, "Gosudarstvennyi Komitet Oborony i problemy sozdaniia slazhennoi voennoi ekonomiki," in *Sovetskii tyl v Velikoi Otechestvennoi Voine,* kniga pervaia, ed. P.N. Pospelov (Moscow: Mysl', 1974), pp. 70–79; Petr Studenikin and Ivan Taranenko, "Vvidu chrezvychainogo polozheniia," *Pravda,* 30 June 1986.   From

December 1942 GKO had an "Operative Bureau" that came to handle much of its second-order business (see Belikov, pp. 77).

69. G.I. Petrov, "Sovetskii gosudarstvennyi apparat v gody Velikoi otechestvennoi voiny," *Pravovedenie*, no. 3, (1975), pp. 16–27. See also Mark Harrison, *Soviet Planning in Peace and War* (Cambridge and New York: Cambridge University Press, 1985), pp. 93–97.

70. This historical precedent in imperial Russia was implicit rather than explicit in official accounts of this change, and another important motive for replacing the revolutionary-sounding title for the Soviet Government by a "normal" one was clearly to reassure international opinion. Cf. V.A. Vlasov, *Sovetskii gosudarstvennyi apparat* (Moscow, 1951), pp. 394–96.

71. See, e.g., P.S. Popkov, in *Partiinoe stroitel'stvo*, nos. 9–10 (1946), p. 19. For an example of the typical practice of a people's commissar wiring a regional party secretary to request his assistance in ensuring the carrying out of a GKO assignment by a locally-situated plant coming under his commissariat, see *Astrakhanskaia partiinaia organizatsiia v gody Velikoi otechestvennoi voiny* (Astrakhan, 1962), p. 62.

72. Vlasov, *Sovetskii gosudarstvennyi apparat*, p. 382.

73. Van den Berg, *Organisation und Arbeitsweise*, pp. 253–54.

74. Interview with Prof. Iu.M. Kozlov, Moscow State University, November 1973.

75. *Pravda*, 6 March 1953. An official biographical entry on Voroshilov states that he was "in 1946–53 a member of the Bureau (sic) of the Council of Ministers of the USSR. In 1947–51, Chairman of the Bureau for Culture of the Council of Ministers of the USSR." *Bol'shaia sovetskaia entsiklopediia. Ezhegodnik* (Moscow, 1966), p. 581. See also, van den Berg, *Organisation und Arbeitsweise*, 255ff, pp. 281–86.

76. See T.H. Rigby, "The Soviet Political Executive, 1917–1986," in *Political Leadership in the Soviet Union*, ed. Archie Brown (London: Macmillan, 1989), pp. 32–35.

77. For examples, see *Partiinoe stroitel'stvo*, no. 15, (1945), pp. 13–14; nos. 9–10 (1946), pp. 31–32; *Partiinaia zhizn'*, no. 23 (1947), p. 50; no. 2 (1948), p. 74; no. 3 (1948), pp. 31, 55; no. 4 (1948), p. 7; no. 5 (1948), pp. 12–13 (a report by Khrushchev); no. 7 (1948), pp. 9–10.

78. I.P. Trainin *et al.*, *Sovetskoe gosudarstvennoe pravo* (Moscow, 1948), p. 286.

79. The exception was Voznesenskii, who was shot in 1950.

80. As there was in the party leadership, with which it largely overlapped. See T.H. Rigby, *Political Elites in the USSR. Central Leaders and Local Cadres from Lenin to Gorbachev* (Aldershot, UK, and Brookfield, VT: Edward Elgar, 1990), chapter 6.

81. There is no space to deal closely here with the leadership politics and changes of the post-Stalin years, and these paragraphs draw on my earlier work, especially the following: "Khrushchev and the resuscitation of the Central Committee," in *Political Elites in the USSR*, chapter 7; "Towards a self-stabilizing oligarchy?" *ibid.*, chapter 9; "The Soviet Government since Khrushchev", *Politics*, vol. 12, no. 1 (1977), pp. 5–22; and "The Soviet Political Executive, 1917–1986," in Brown, *Political Leadership in the Soviet Union*, chapter 2.

82. I expand on this point in "Khrushchev and the rules of the game", chapter 2 in *Khrushchev and the Communist World*, ed. R.F. Miller and F. Feher (London and Sydney: Croom Helm, and Totowa, NJ: Barnes and Noble, 1964).

83. See *Pravda*, 16 March 1953; 10 February 1955; 1 March 1955; 7 April 1955; *Zasedaniia Verkhovnogo Soveta SSSR, 4-ogo sozyva, pervaia sessiia: Stenograficheskii otchet* (Moscow, 1954), pp. 555-58.

84. S.R. Vikharev and I.D. Vetrov, *Rasshirenie prav soiuznykh respublik* (Moscow: Gosiurizdat, 1963), p. 55.

85. See *Direktivy KPSS i Sovetskogo pravitel'stva po khoziaistvennym voprosam, 1953-1957*, vol. 4 (Moscow: Gospolitizdat, 1958), pp. 400-17.

86. *Spravochnik partiinogo rabotnika* (Moscow: Gospolitizdat, 1957), p. 178.

87. *Direktivy KPSS i Sovetskogo pravitel'stva po khoziaistvennym voprosam, 1953-1957*, vol. 4, pp. 732-38.   Under pressure, Khrushchev agreed to retain the defense industry ministries.

88. *Pravda*, 22 December 1953.

89. See *Pravda*, 10 February 1955 and 1 March 1955.

90. Molotov, Kaganovich, Mikoian, Saburov, and Pervukhin.

91. Malenkov, Tevosian, Malyshev, Kosygin, Zaveniagin, Kucherenko, Lobanov, and Khrunichev. V.V. Matskevich was added in April 1956--see *Pravda*, 10 April 1956.

92. *Sovetskoe administrativnoe pravo*, ed. Ia.N. Umanskii (Moscow, 1956), p. 49. Analogies from other periods and from republic governments suggest that the "personally appointed" presidium members probably numbered no more than two or three, and would have been chosen from such office holders as the Gosplan chairman, ministers of finance, agriculture and state control, and the trade union council chairman.

93. Thus a biographical note on D.V. Efremov states that in the period 1954-56 he was the deputy chairman of the Bureau on Chemistry and Electric Power under (*pri*) the Council of Ministers.   See *Ezhegodnik bol'shoi sovetskoi entsiklopedii: 1960* (Moscow, 1960), p. 597.

94. See N.N. Smeliakov, *S chego nachinaetsia rodina* (Moscow: Politizdat, 1975), pp. 176-77; van den Berg, *Organisation und Arbeitsweise*, pp. 286-89; Jerry F. Hough and Merle Fainsod, *How the Soviet Union is Governed* (Cambridge, MA, and London: Harvard University Press, 1979), p. 383; and V.I. Popova, "Razvitie sovetskogo zakonodatel'stva ob organakh gosudarstvennogo upravleniia", *Uchenye zapiski VNIISZ*, 1968, vol. 13, p. 53.

95. See Leonard Schapiro, *The Communist Party of the Soviet Union*, 2nd ed. (London: Methuen, 1974), 573 ff.

96. See N.S. Khrushchev, *Speeches and Interviews on World Problems: 1957* (Moscow: Foreign Languages Publishing House, 1958), pp. 53-54.

97. See Iu.M. Kozlov, *Organy gosudarstvennogo upravleniia* (Moscow: Gosiurizdat, 1960), p. 76, and N.A. Volkov, *Organy sovetskogo gosudarstvennogo upravleniia v sovremennyi period* (Kazan: Izdatel'stvo kazanskogo universiteta, 1962), pp. 85, 90.

98. See *Pravda*, 26 April 1963; Fedorov, *Istoriia sovetskogo gosudarstva i prava*, p. 314; V.I. Popova, "Sovet Ministrov RSFSR: vysshii ispolnitel'nyi, rasporiaditel'nyi organ gosudarstvennoi vlasti Rossiiskoi federatsii," *Uchenye zapiski VNIISZ*, 1964, vol. 3/20, p. 9. For background and further details, see van den Berg, *Organisation und Arbeitsweise*, pp. 295–300. Schapiro (*The Communist Party of the Soviet Union*, pp. 576–77), contrary to the view taken here, sees the establishment of VSNKh as a move by opponents of Khrushchev within the leadership. One consequence of VSNKh's establishment was the suspension of the Commission on Current Affairs.

99. For details, see "Toward a self–stabilizing oligarchy?" in Rigby, *Political Elites in the USSR*, chapter 9.

100. See Iu.M. Kozlov, *Sootnoshenie gosudarstvennogo i obshchestvennogo upravleniia v SSSR* (Moscow: 1966), pp. 26–35. A revised statute on ministries was not, however, promulgated until mid–1967. For text, see *Ekonomicheskaia gazeta*, no. 34 (August 1967), pp. 7–9.

101. *Pravda*, 25 June 1981. Such additional members may have been excluded for only a brief period, as sources in the early post–Khrushchev years indicate their presence (e.g. V.I. Vasilieva, *Sovetskoe stroitel'stvo* [Moscow: Vysshaia shkola, 1967], p. 109) and, at the Supreme Soviet session approving the amendment, the Supreme Soviet presidium secretary Georgadze said it was "based on the working practice" of the Council of Ministers.

102. *Izvestiia*, 6 July 1978.

103. Van den Berg, *Organisation und Arbeitsweise*, p. 304.

104. *Izvestiia*, 6 July 1978.

105. For others in earlier years, see van den Berg, *Organisation und Arbeitsweise*, p. 305.

106. For example, the Military Industrial Commission by L.V. Smirnov, the Agroindustrial Commission by Z.N. Nuriev, and the Environmental Protection Commission by I.T. Novikov.

107. On the role of deputy chairmen during this period, see van den Berg, *Organisation und Arbeitsweise*, pp. 343–76.

108. See, for example, *Pravda*, 2 June 1970 and 3 October 1974.

109. See, for example, *Pravda*, 16 July 1976, 19 April 1980, and 23 January 1982.

110. For further details see T.H. Rigby, "The Soviet Government since Khrushchev," *Politics*, vol. 12, no. 1 (1977), pp. 5–22, and *Der Ministerrat unter Kosygin*, Bericht No. 21/1977 (Cologne: Bundesinstitut für ostwissenschaftliche und internationale Studien, 1977). See also Jerry F. Hough, *Soviet Leadership in Transition* (Washington: Brookings Institution, 1980), and Seweryn Bialer, *Stalin's Successors. Leadership, Stability and Change in the Soviet Union* (Cambridge and New York: Cambridge University Press, 1980).

111. See van den Berg, *Organisation und Arbeitsweise*, pp. 113–24. Van den Berg's evidence (p.116) shows that joint Central Committee–Government decisions, which originated in the early 1930s, reached a maximum on the eve of the War,

dropped off sharply during the late Stalin years, stepped up after his death, and fluctuated at a moderate level through the 1960s and 1970s.

112. I develop these points in my chapters "A Conceptual Approach to Authority, Power and Policy in the USSR," in *Authority, Power and Policy in the USSR*, ed. T.H. Rigby, Archie Brown, and Peter Reddaway (London: Macmillan, 1980 and 1983), and "Introduction: Political Legitimacy, Weber, and Communist Mono-organisational Systems," in *Political Legitimation in Communist States*, ed. T.H. Rigby and Ferenc Feher (London: Macmillan, 1983).

2

PARTY-STATE RELATIONS

Cameron Ross

In recent years the Communist Party's fate has been developing in a truly tragic way. With the start of perestroika in society it gradually and then rapidly started lagging behind the changes taking place in the country. Having previously been the backbone of the state administration, the party was unable to find its place in the conditions of political pluralism and to overcome the conservative-bureaucratic nature of its structures.[1]

Introduction

Before Gorbachev unleashed his radical political reforms in the summer of 1988, there were two major bureaucracies in the Soviet Union, one for the Communist Party and one for the Soviet state. In each bureaucracy, centralism ruled. Decisions that in other societies might have been taken at lower levels were continually pushed upwards, to the all-union Politburo, Central Committee, and secretariat within the party and to the USSR Supreme Soviet and Council of Ministers within the state (see Table 2.1). This extraordinary concentration of power in central party and state institutions, and especially in their executive organs, was guaranteed by a tightly-regulated flow of information, by a prohibition against organized factions, and by the emasculation of legislative bodies. Neither delegates to party conferences nor deputies in the state's system of soviets were able to restrain the executive leadership of the party and state.

At the apex of this leadership was the general secretary of the party, who chaired meetings of the Politburo and embodied political authority for the average Soviet citizen. The state contributed two senior members of the leadership. The prime minister, formally the chairman of the USSR Council of Ministers, supervised over 100 ministries and state committees that comprised

Table 2.1
The Communist Party and the Soviet State
1986

PARTY		STATE	
Legislative	*Executive*	*Executive*	*Legislative*
Politburo*		Presidium of Council of Ministers	Presidium of Supreme Soviet
Central Committee	Secretariat	Council of Ministers	Supreme Soviet
Congress (Conference)	Departments	Ministries/ State Committees	Standing Commissions

* The Politburo exercised both legislative and executive functions.

the Soviet government. The chairman of the presidium of the USSR Supreme Soviet, often referred to as the president by the Western press, played a highly visible, if largely formal, role in the foreign affairs of the Soviet state.

The dominant position of the general secretary in the central leadership confirmed the traditional subordination of the Soviet state to the Communist Party. According to the 1977 Constitution, the party was the "leading and guiding force in society, the nucleus of the Soviet political system." The party was the chief policymaking body in the country, and armed with Marxist-Leninist ideology, it assumed responsibility for leading the country to communism. With the assistance of the secretariat and its twenty-odd departments, the Politburo formulated policy and then transferred it for adoption and implementation to the Supreme Soviet and the Council of Ministers of the USSR. The party apparatus then oversaw the faithful implementation of its

Table 2.2
The Central Committee Secretariat and Its Departments
1986

In the post-Stalin era, there were approximately a dozen secretaries who supervised, or managed directly, one or more of the following departments:

1) Administration of Affairs
2) Administrative Organs Department
3) Agriculture and Food Industry Department
4) Department for Cadres Abroad
5) Chemical Industry Department
6) Construction Department
7) Culture Department
8) Defense Industry Department
9) Economic Department
10) General Department
11) Heavy Industry and Power Engineering
12) International Department
13) Department for Liaison with Communist and Workers' Parties of Socialist Countries
14) Light Industry and Consumer Goods Department
15) Machine Building Department
16) Organizational Party Work Department
17) Propaganda Department
18) Science and Educational Institutions Department
19) Trade and Consumer Services Department
20) Transport and Communications Department
21) Main Directorate of the Army and Navy

Source: Alexander Rahr, "The Apparatus of the CPSU", *Radio Liberty Research Bulletin*, no. 15, April 15, 1987. pp. 1-8.

policy by the Government.   Such at least was the official theory of party-state relations.   As we shall see below, the division of political labor between partyand state was far less tidy.

An Overview of Party-State Relations

The Communist Party maintained its dominance over the state largely through its control over *nomenklatura*,[2] the country's patronage system.   Under the general supervision of the Politburo and the secretariat, and the immediate direction of a senior secretary, the Central Committee's Department of Organizational Party Work selected and placed personnel in all the top positions in Soviet society. Party organizations at lower administrative levels exercised similar patronage powers in their areas.

Besides hiring and firing state officials, the Communist Party placed leading state personnel in its own policymaking institutions and in turn appointed party officials to state institutions. Thus, all senior state officials held "dual membership" in party and state bureaucracies. The prime minister, the president, and other key figures of state, such as the ministers of defense and foreign affairs and the head of the KGB, were members of the Politburo, at least after the early 1970s. State functionaries accounted for 9 of the 18 members and candidate members of the Politburo in 1986 (see Table 2.3). Likewise, leading party officials, most notably the general secretary, held dual membership in party and state bodies. Both Stalin, from 1941 to 1953, and Khrushchev, from 1958 to 1964, served simultaneously as prime minister and general (or first) secretary of the party. The succeeding general secretaries—Brezhnev, Andropov, Chernenko, and Gorbachev—assumed the post of state president (chairman of the presidium of the Supreme Soviet), producing what Zhores Medvedev regarded as one of the many ironies of Soviet politics.

> The absurdity lay in the fact that the same person who, as general secretary, had to sign all proposals and drafts of legislation before they were put by the secretariat to the presidium [of the Supreme Soviet], then in his capacity as chairman of the presidium had to go to another building to sign the proposals again to make them laws or operative decrees.[3]

This interlocking membership of party and state bodies was evident in the composition of the party's Central Committee. In 1986, 124 members (22 percent) of the Central Committee were top officials from the USSR Council of Ministers. Among the full voting members of the Central Committee were all 13 members of the Council's inner cabinet, or presidium, 45 ministers and chairmen of state committees, and 22 first deputy or deputy heads of ministries or state committees. As Table 2.4 illustrates, the leaders of the powerful ministries responsible for industrial production and defense received full membership in the Central Committee. Candidate membership was reserved for ministers in important support sectors, such as education, health, justice, the chemical industry, and transport construction. The lowest status, membership in the party's Central Auditing Committee, was accorded to ministers in such fields as construction materials and medicine and microbiology. This hierarchy of representation in party bodies served as a reliable indicator of the political prominence of state institutions.[4]

Table 2.3
The Politburo
1986

Full Members

G. Aliev*	First Deputy Chairman of the USSR Council of Ministers
V. Chebrikov*	Chairman, USSR KGB
M. Gorbachev	General Secretary of CPSU
A. Gromyko*	Chairman, USSR Supreme Soviet Presidium
D. Kunaev	First Secretary, Communist Party of Kazakhstan
E. Ligachev	Secretary of CPSU
N. Ryzhkov*	Chairman, USSR Council of Ministers
V. Shcherbitskii	First Secretary, Communist Party of Ukraine
M. Solomentsev	Chairman, Party Control Committee of CPSU
E. Shevardnadze*	Minister of Foreign Affairs of USSR
V. Vorotnikov*	Chairman, RSFSR Council of Ministers
L. Zaikov	Secretary of CPSU

Candidate Members

P. Demichev*	Minister of Culture of USSR
V. Dolgikh	Secretary of CPSU
B. Yeltsin	First Secretary, Moscow City Party Committee
N. Sliun'kov	First Secretary, Communist Party of Belorussia
S. Sokolov*	Minister of Defense of USSR
Iu.Solov'ev	First Secretary, Leningrad Regional Party Committee
N. Talyzin*	First Deputy Chairman, USSR Council of Ministers and Chairman, USSR State Planning Committee (Gosplan)

* Denotes officials in state institutions.

There was also overlapping membership between party institutions and the Supreme Soviet, especially its presidium and standing commissions. Of the 38 members of the USSR Supreme Soviet presidium in 1986, 16 were full members of the Central Committee, six were candidate members, and a further eight were members of the Central Auditing Committee. Prominent among the members of the Supreme Soviet presidium, which enacted far more legislation than the full parliament, were ten high-ranking party functionaries, including seven members of the Politburo. Sitting on the presidium was the general secretary as well as the first secretaries of the Communist Party in the city of Moscow,

Table 2.4
Government Institutions and Their Representation
in the Central Committee
1986

Full Membership
Administrator of
  Affairs (SC)
Automative
Aviation
Civil Aviation
Coal Industry
Communications
Communications
  Equipment
Construction: Heavy
  Industry
Construction: Oil and
  Gas
Culture
Defense
Defense Industry
Electronics
Ferrous Metallurgy
Finance
Fish Industry
Foreign Affairs
Foreign Economic
  Relations (SC)
Foreign Trade
Gas Industry
General Mach. Building
Grain Products
Heavy and Transp.
  Machine Build.
Higher and Secondary
  Spec. Educ.
Install. and Spec.
  Constr.
Instr. Making and
  Contr. Systems

Internal Affairs
Land Reclamation and
  Water
Light Industry
Machine Building
Machine Tool and Tool
  Building
Maritime Fleet
Medium Machine
  Building
Non Ferrous Metallurgy
Petroleum Industry
Petroleum Refining and
  Petrochemical
Power and Electrification
Power Machine Build
Radio Industry
Railways
Security [KGB] (SC)
Shipbuilding
Television and Radio
Tractor and Ag. Mach.
  Build.
Trade

Candidate Membership
Chemical Industry
Chem. and Petro. Mach.
  Build.
Cinematography (SC)
Construction
Construction Far East
Const., Road, Mun.
  Mach. Build
Education

Electrical Equipment
  Industry
Geology
Health
Industrial Construction
Justice
Labor and Social
  Problems (SC)
Mach. Build. Animal
  Husbandry
Mach. Build. Light and
  Food
Mineral Fertilizer Prod.
Physical Culture and
  Sport (SC)
Prices (SC)
Publishing (SC)
Safe Working Practices
  (SC)
Standards (SC)
State Bank (SC)
Timber Pulp and Paper
Transport Construction

*Central Auditing
Committee*
Construction Materials
  Industry
Medical and
  Microbiology
State Commission
Forestry (SC)
Hydrometerology
Inventions and
  Discoveries (SC)
Vocat./Tech Education

All institutions are ministries except those followed by (SC), which are State Committees.
Source: For a list of the USSR Council of Ministers in 1986 see Herwig Kraus, "The Government of the USSR," *Radio Liberty Research Bulletin*, no. 24, 11 June 1986. For members of the Central Committee elected by the 27th Party Congress in March 1986, see the lists compiled by Sergei Belitsky, Valerii Konovalov and Herwig Kraus in *Radio Liberty Research Bulletin*, no. 15, 9 April 1986.

in the regions of Leningrad, Bashkiria, and Tatarstan, and in the republics of Ukraine, Kazakhstan, Uzbekistan, and Belorussia.

The British sociologist David Lane found that of the 1,140 members of the Supreme Soviet appointed to standing commissions in 1979, 72.4 percent were party members and 20 percent were party officials.[5] Not surprisingly, the party officials were the most likely to chair the commissions. In 1986, 18 of the chairmen of standing commissions were high-ranking party secretaries. Eight worked as republic secretaries and seven as first secretaries of regional-level party organizations. In addition, there were three Central Committee secretaries among standing committee chairmen. Georgii Razumovskii, the head of the Organizational Party Work Department, chaired the Legislative Proposals Committee in the Council of the Union, which played a key role in agenda setting for the parliament. Egor Ligachev, the unofficial second secretary of the party, headed the Foreign Affairs Commission in the Council of the Union, and Anatolii Dobrynin, the secretary in charge of foreign policy and head of the Central Committee's International Department, chaired the Foreign Affairs Commission in the Council of Nationalities. This biographical evidence indicates that officials with full-time responsibilities in the party apparatus played the dominant role in the operation of the state's legislative institutions.[6]

The party bureaucracy paralleled as well as overlapped state institutions, forming a kind of shadow government to the state. As Table 2.2 suggests, Central Committee departments, formed largely along economic branch lines, assumed responsibility for the supervision of ministries and state committees in their particular policy area. Depending on the sector of the economy and the politics and personalities of the day, this supervision ranged from a passive monitoring of the behavior of ministries to direct interference in their day-to-day operations.

The Communist Party also supervised the ministries from within through its primary party organizations (PPOs), which were the Communist cells located inside all major state and social organizations in the USSR. Within legislative bodies, from the USSR Supreme Soviet to local-level assemblies, PPOs functioned as party groups that rallied Communist deputies behind the policies of the party apparatus. In the post-Stalin era, there was much criticism of the ineffectual role of the PPOs as the eyes of the party apparatus within state institutions. During the last decade of Brezhnev's rule, the Central Committee adopted numerous resolutions that expanded the PPOs' formal authority within the ministries and directed the PPOs to intensify their oversight of ministerial behavior.[7] The PPOs failed, however, to satisfy the party bureaucracy's desire for tighter control over state institutions. As I have argued elsewhere, the fragmentation of the state administrative system into dozens of branch ministries and the lack of coordination among PPOs in different ministries enabled the state bureaucracy in many cases to circumvent party directives.   In the area of industrial development, for example, the ministries drove policy.   The interests and plans of the central ministries in Moscow determined to a large extent the economic development of cities and regions.[8]

The party leadership always insisted publicly that party bodies within and without the ministries should not engage in *podmena*,[9] the direct supplanting of state bodies.   Overall ideological and political leadership was the stated goal. According to the party rules:

> Party organizations must not act in place of government, trades union, co-operative or other public organizations of the working people; they must not allow either the merging of the functions of the Party and other organizations or undue parallelism in their work."[10]

Yet by holding party officials with unrestricted power responsible for the success or failure of the state bodies that they supervised, the system of party rule naturally bred *podmena*.   Georgii Razumovskii, former party secretary and head of the Organizational Party Work Department, graphically illustrated the negative aspects of *podmena* under Brezhnev.

> In previous years elements of excessive administrative and of a technocratic approach became deeply implanted in and made a strong impact on the work practice of party organs .... Party committees often assumed extrinsic functions and dealt directly with purely production matters. As a result, their attention to political questions relaxed and the main thing—vital work with people—was at times neglected. On the other hand, direct, and to put it frankly, not always competent interference in production by no means in all cases ensured its development and, frequently, impeded it.[11]

The theses of the 19th Party Conference were more blunt in their criticism of party-state relations in the Brezhnev period.

> Party organs increasingly began taking on the direct resolution of current tasks of economic and administrative management, supplanting the soviets and other state organs. This had an adverse effect on the exercise of the party's basic functions, led to the weakening of its political and ideological influence, and exacerbated many problems of social development.[12]

Instead of "leading and guiding," the party often appeared to be either trailing after or duplicating the work of the state.

There is evidence that Central Committee departments under Gorbachev lost their overall ideological and guiding role and became embroiled and even swamped by the ministries they were supposed to be controlling. The result was a departmentalism that stretched across the party-state divide. Because the party departments to a large degree took on the interests of the state bodies they were charged with managing, Gorbachev sought to abolish them at the end of the 1980s.

What were the appropriate boundaries between party and state bodies? What areas of work should the PPOs and the party apparatus have been engaged in? These questions were the subject of internal debates in the party throughout Soviet history. From the revolution of 1917 onwards, the party was suspicious of the state bureaucracy and its non-Bolshevik members. At first Lenin had to rely on bourgeois "experts" of the tsarist administration to run the new Soviet Government. In order to check on the work of these officials the party posted reliable functionaries, or "reds," in key staff positions in the bureaucracy. But as society became more technologically complex, the party had to rely on the "experts" for advice in policy making and implementation. Conflict soon arose between "reds" and "experts" as they fought over the slippery Weberian boundaries of politics and administration.

The Communist Party of the Soviet Union was clearly able to wield substantially more powers against institutions of state than parties in western multiparty "liberal democracies." This party domination of state and society in the USSR led a number of Western scholars, writing in the midst of the cold war, to advance the totalitarian model of Soviet politics.[13] According to this model, the party was said to maintain a totalistic control over a weak and passive state, dominating all aspects of policy making. The party was also thought to be monolithic, with no interest groups or factions operating within it.

In the late 1960s, Jerry Hough countered the totalitarian model with an "institutional pluralist" model, which posited a broker or umpire role for the party and stressed its ability to mediate conflicts between state institutions.[14] The pluralist model also refuted the idea of a monolithic party. It advanced instead an image of a fragmented CPSU, with loose groupings of members divided according to age, nationality, gender, and occupation. Policy was the result of bargaining and lobbying within the party and of conflict between party and state groups. For example, ministries involved in the military-industrial complex competed with those in agriculture or consumer goods production over the distribution of centrally allocated funds and resources.

Hough was certainly correct in alerting us to pluralist tendencies in Soviet society and to the sharp conflicts between state institutions over policy formulation. But he underestimated the ability of state institutions to exercise influence over policies at the output stage. I would argue that the party was largely dominant in the aggregation and articulation of interests, but that it was very weak in exercising control over the implementation of policies. Robert Putnam's statement about Western bureaucrats also holds true for those in the Soviet Union.

> Discretion, not merely for deciding individual cases, but for crafting the content of most legislation, has passed from the legislature [in the Soviet case, read "the party"] to the executive. Bureaucrats, monopolizing as they do much of the available information about the shortcomings of existing policies as well as much of the technical expertise necessary to design practical alternatives, have gained a predominant influence over the evolution of the agenda for decision. Elected officials [read "party apparatchiki" in the Soviet case] everywhere are outnumbered and outlasted by career civil servants. In a literal sense, the modern political system is essentially "bureaucratic"—characterized by "the rule of officials."[15]

My earlier work on Soviet local government noted the power of the ministries and their subordinate enterprises to ignore, block, or remold central party resolutions. From 1957 to the mid-1970s, for example, the Central Committee passed resolution after resolution demanding that the ministries relinquish their control over housing and transfer it to the soviets. But the ministries were so successful in thwarting party policies that they still controlled over 60 percent of all the housing stock in the mid-1980s.[16] During the Brezhnev period, as Gorbachev has noted, it was the state bureaucracy, and not the party or soviets, that ran the country.

> During the period of stagnation, the managerial apparatus, which had grown to almost 100 Union and 800 republic ministries and departments, to all intents and purposes began to dictate its will in the economy and in politics. It was departments and other managerial structures that had charge of the execution of adopted decisions, and through their action or inaction, they determined what would be or what would not be. The soviets and in many respects the party agencies as well proved unable to control the pressure of departmental interests.[17]

Relations between party and state institutions depended in part on the career patterns of officials within them. If officials regularly moved between party and state posts, a buildup of strong institutional loyalties would be less likely than if they followed narrow vertical careers within their respective bureaucracies. An examination of the biographies of leading party and state officials suggests that narrow vertical careers predominated.   The vast majority of the 195 members of the USSR Council of Ministers from 1984 to 1989 and the 100 top party officials in the secretariat from 1978 to 1989 spent the greater part of their careers in either the party or the state, and thus were likely to possess strong institutional bonds and loyalties.[18]

To emphasize this potential for policy conflict between party and state bodies is not to deny that officials of both bureaucracies had some interests in common. Undoubtedly, party and state officials who dealt with agriculture fought together for increased investment in this sector and against party and state officials who wanted more for heavy industry and the military. Elites in both the party and the state had a common interest in preserving their privileges and powers. They could act in concert to bloc reforms, whether undertaken by Khrushchev in the 1950s, Kosygin in the 1960s, or Gorbachev in the 1980s.

One may argue, along with the proponents of the state capitalist model, that party and state officials constituted a unified class. The bureaucracy in the Soviet Union did not *own* the means of production but *controlled* it and used it to its own advantage. In a real sense it extracted "surplus value" from the workers to uphold its privileged status.[19] Officials of both the party and state were therefore more likely to have stronger ties to their respective institutions than bureaucrats in the West. Not only did they receive higher wages, but more importantly their posts gave them access to special stores, to foreign travel, and to better housing, education, and health care. Dismissal from this elite meant an abrupt end to such privileges.

Cooperative behavior between elites and a common desire to preserve their privileges did not eliminate, however, the potential for significant conflict within and between party and state bureaucracies. Soviet history is replete with political competition on the personal, policy, institutional, and sectoral levels. An example is the conflict between the party's International Department (ID) and the Ministry of Foreign Affairs over the conduct of Soviet foreign policy, especially as it related to detente and the Third World. Jan Adams has written of the

> deeply embedded and seemingly inescapable conflict between these two major Soviet foreign policy institutions and their missions. On the one hand, the Ministry of Foreign Affairs seeks to cultivate formal state to state relationships; on the other the ID pursues the party's dream of building a communist world at the expense of capitalism.[20]

The party apparatus took a more aggressive "red," or ideological, stance in pursuing its policies in the Third World, even though this jeopardized the more pragmatic, and detente-oriented, policy of the Ministry of Foreign Affairs.

Party-State Relations under Gorbachev

At the beginning of his tenure, Gorbachev governed cautiously, content to put forward policies for limited decentralization of the economy while consolidating his power base in the Politburo and secretariat. Only after making significant personnel changes in the leading bodies of both the party and state—including a 40 percent turnover of full members of the Central Committee at the 27th Party Congress in March 1986—did a more politically secure Gorbachev begin to call for radical changes in the management of the economy. Gorbachev realized that curbing the power of the ministries was essential to revive an economy that had stagnated in the late Brezhnev years. He called on ministries to use "economic" measures to shape factory and enterprise behavior and to cease their rule by decree. The central ministries' "micromanagement" (*melochnaia opeka*) of their enterprises was also to be ended. Individuals, enterprises, and institutions were to be given incentives to provide more and better quality goods, and market forces were to replace centrally prescribed economic targets.

These economic initiatives required new relations between the party and the state. But the old problem of *podmena* stood in the way of radical economic reform. At the 27th Party Congress, Boris Yeltsin complained about the duplication of ministerial work by departments of the Central Committee.

> The party agencies ... have become so deeply immersed in economic affairs that they have sometimes begun to lose their positions of political leadership .... It's no accident that the structure of the Central Committee's departments have gradually become all but a copy of the Ministries. Many people in departments have simply forgotten what true Party work is. There is a complete duplication of the State Planning Committee and the Council of Ministers. We get bogged down in coordinating meetings which can last years for simple questions.[21]

Three years later, at a special conference of party and state officials, Gorbachev agreed that the party should abandon *podmena* and that the role of party and state officials should be more clearly differentiated.

> In essence what is involved here is the creation of a new mechanism of interaction between the party and the soviets, and political methods of party influence on their activity. What is involved, above all, is the elaboration of policy and its implementation through the Soviets ... party agencies can implement political decisions in bodies of people's rule only through

persuasion, recommendations and democratic agreements, through Communists working in the Soviets and their executive agencies.[22]

Economic reform, of course, demanded changes within the state as well as between party and state institutions. As part of a broad-based attack on command structures in the economy, Gorbachev began to streamline the ministries, reducing their number from over 100 to 70 by 1989. In the same period, the number of republic ministries fell from 800 to 600, and more than 1,000 ministerial departments were eliminated. By 1989 approximately one million officials of state bureaucracies had lost their jobs, and the central ministries had lost 23 percent of their staff.[23]

The state bureaucrats fought back, however. Jealous of their jobs, their privileges, and their power over the economy, state officials did everything they could to make the new laws on economic reform unworkable. Gorbachev was forced to admit that the economic reforms were meeting stiff resistance.

> In the third year of restructuring, we are still stuck with an unwieldy administrative apparatus, a considerable part of which is fighting tooth and nail to hold on to its positions without regard for the interests of society.[24]

By early 1988, Gorbachev realized that in order to implement his economic reforms he would also have to radically change the Soviet political system. He had attempted to instigate reforms within the party in January 1987, attacking both *nomenklatura* and "democratic centralism," the latter a euphemism for the dictatorship of the central party apparatus over lower party organs and the rank and file. Gorbachev had called for secret ballot elections for all leading party posts and a greater role in policy making for ordinary party members, but he was too weak in 1987 to press hard for these changes. In the spring of 1988, Gorbachev himself came under attack from an alliance of party and state conservatives, and there was an attempt by Egor Ligachev, the number two man in the party, to overthrow him.

This opposition forced Gorbachev onto the political offensive. At the 19th Party Conference in the summer of 1988, Gorbachev put forward new proposals to democratize the political system. These included the formation of a new state legislative body, the Congress of People's Deputies, a majority of whose members would be directly elected by the people. The Congress, in turn, would select from within itself a new Supreme Soviet, which would work as a standing parliament for up to eight months a year. There would be a new separation of executive and legislative bodies, with no members of the Government, except the Prime Minister and his deputies, permitted a place in the legislature. It was expected that a vigorous legislature would restrain and direct executive power over the economy and society, thereby diminishing the authority of party and ministerial apparatuses.

Gorbachev was not content, however, to create new state bodies. Radical changes were also made to the top party executive organizations, the CPSU Central Committee secretariat and its departments. These changes revealed for the first time that Gorbachev intended to move a number of the functions and powers of the party bureaucracy to the state. Gorbachev realized that he had enemies not only in the ministries but also among the party officials who had been charged with overseeing the reform of the state apparatus. Party and state bodies had been colluding, in his view, to block the reforms.

In 1988 Gorbachev attacked the party apparatus itself, most notably the secretariat, which Ligachev had been using as a base to rally the conservatives against the general secretary. At the July 1988 plenum of the Central Committee, Gorbachev noted that

> [t]he party apparatus must be completely freed from economic-administrative functions, concentrate its work on the key areas of domestic and foreign policy, and shift its center of gravity to political methods of leadership. This should be reflected both in the structure and the personnel makeup of the apparatus. It should be highly competent and significantly smaller than it is now.[25]

The plenum renounced "the fragmentation of the apparatus according to branches of management ...."[26]

At the next Central Committee plenum, in September 1988, Gorbachev made further changes to the Politburo that strengthened his position as general secretary and led a month later to his assumption of the post of chairman of the presidium of the Supreme Soviet. Gorbachev used the September plenum to launch a major assault on the CPSU secretariat and its apparatus. The number of departments in the party's shadow government was reduced from 20 to 9. The remaining departments were now supervised by six new Central Committee Commissions instead of the secretariat (see Table 2.5). The commissions, each with a membership of from 21 to 25 persons, were headed by senior members of the party who were to be kept in check by the wider and potentially more reformist membership drawn from the Central Committee.

Ligachev was demoted at this plenum from the number two position in the party and given the troublesome headship of the Agricultural Commission. His former institutional base, the secretariat, was no longer to play a major role in party life. Ligachev later noted that, following the September 1988 plenum, the secretariat "did not work for a long time. Then it met sporadically ...."[27]

In keeping with the demands of the 19th Party Conference, the branch economic departments of the Central Committee were subjected to the most

Table 2.5
The Central Party Apparatus
September 1988

Commissions of the Central Committee	Chairman	Members
1) Party Issues and Personnel Policy	G. Razumovskii	25
2) Ideology	V. Medvedev	25
3) Social and Economic Policy	N. Sliun'kov	21
4) Agrarian Policy	E. Ligachev	23
5) International Policy	A. Yakovlev	23
6) Legal Policy	V. Chebrikov	21

Departments of the Central Committee

1) Party Work and Cadres Policy	6) State and Law
2) Ideology	7) International
3) Socio-Economic	8) General Department
4) Agrarian	9) Administration of Affairs
5) Defense Industry	

Source: Adapted from Alexander Rahr, "Gorbachev Changes Party Structure," *Radio Liberty Research Bulletin*, 30 November 1988, pp. 1-4; Rahr, "Who is in Charge of the Party Apparatus?" *Report on the USSR*, 14 April 1989. pp. 19-23.

far-reaching restructuring. Seven departments were abolished outright: Chemical Industry, Construction, Heavy Industry and Power Engineering, Light Industry and Consumer Goods, Machine Building, Trade and Consumer Services, and Transport and Communications. A new Socio-Economic Department was created to deal with economic planning, but as CPSU Secretary Vadim Medvedev observed, much of the work of these former departments was "handed over to the Council of Ministers and to the Supreme Soviet and its commissions" (see Tables 2.2 and 2.5).[28] The central party apparatus also lost 30 percent of its staff, with many party personnel transferred to work in the government. The July 1988 Central Committee Plenum Resolution had stipulated that

> [i]t is necessary to use the reorganization of the Party apparatus and the release of some of its personnel to strengthen important sectors of the state, economic and social activity, as well as lower level Party units. In doing so, special attention should be devoted to strengthening the apparatus of the Soviets of People's Deputies and the People's Control agencies, taking into account their new role in the political system.[29]

Other important changes included the merger of the three Central Committee departments of Culture, Propaganda, and Science and Educational Institutions into a new Department of Ideology. The International Department absorbed the Cadres Abroad Department and the Department for Liaison with Socialist and Workers Parties. The latter had dealt with Soviet-East European relations, and its abolition signaled a more liberal attitude towards the reforms underway in that part of the world. Finally, a new State and Law Department was formed to oversee the work of the soviets and legal institutions. It took over the work of the abolished Administrative Organs Department, which had supervised the Armed Forces, the KGB, the courts, and law enforcement organs. Following these reforms, only one of the departments, Administration of Affairs, was still headed by an official appointed in the pre-Gorbachev period.

The period between the 19th Party Conference and the convening of the 28th Party Congress in the summer of 1990 witnessed further dramatic changes in party-state relations. The new legislative bodies, the Congress of People's Deputies and the Supreme Soviet, began to assume responsibilities for supervision of the ministries that had previously belonged to the party. No longer was the Supreme Soviet a passive, "rubber stamping" parliament. Although 87 percent of its deputies were party members, many Communist deputies took positions independent of those advanced by the party apparatus. In the summer of 1989, Prime Minister Ryzhkov was shocked to find that nine of his nominees for the USSR Council of Ministers had been rejected by the deputies. And for the first time a non-party minister was appointed to the Government. Ryzhkov gave this alarming account of how a "new triangle of relations" had been created between the Central Committee, the Supreme Soviet and the USSR Council of Ministers.

> In conditions of a permanently operating USSR Supreme Soviet and its constitutional powers, the functions that used to be performed by the plenary sessions [of the Central Committee] and the Politburo ... with respect to the elaboration of conceptions of the country's economic development, the formation of five-year and annual plans, the adoption of decisions involving state programs, etc., are becoming unclear. There can no longer be direct recommendations of economic construction, economic reform, scientific technical policy and many other questions solely in accordance with the party line, as in the past. Practice in recent months has shown that neither the USSR Supreme Soviet nor its commissions and committees will accept such recommendations. In short, a mighty real power has appeared—the Congress of People's Deputies and the Supreme Soviet.

Table 2.6
USSR Presidential Council
October 1990

Individual	Position
M. Gorbachev*	President of the USSR
C. Aitmatov	Novelist and Chairman, Board of Kirgiz Writers' Union
V. Bakatin*	Minister of Internal Affairs of USSR
V. Boldin	Head, General Department of CPSU
A. Kauls	Chairman, Agro-Industrial Enterprise, Latvia
V. Kriuchkov*	Chairman, USSR KGB
Iu. Masliukov*	First Deputy Chairman, USSR Council of Ministers and Chairman, USSR Planning Committee (Gosplan)
V. Medvedev	Former Politburo Member, 1988-90
Iu. Osip'ian	Vice President, USSR Academy of Sciences
E. Primakov	Chairman, Council of Union, USSR Supreme Soviet
V. Rasputin	Novelist and Secretary, Board of USSR and RSFSR Writers Union
N. Ryzhkov*	Chairman, USSR Council of Ministers
S. Shatalin	Economist/Academician and Secretary, Economics Department, USSR Academy of Sciences
E. Shevardnadze*	Minister of Foreign Affairs of USSR
A. Yakovlev	Chairman, Commission on International Policy, Central Committee of CPSU
V. Yarin	Worker and Cochairman, United Workers' Front of Russia
D. Yazov*	Minister of Defense of USSR

* Denotes officials in state executive institutions.

Source: Theodore Karasik, "The Defense Council & Soviet Presidency", *Perspective*, vol. 1, no. 2, 1990, p. 1.

He noted further that "a situation of uncertainty in relations among the CPSU Central Committee and the Council of Ministers has come about at the center."[30] According to a *Pravda* editorial of June 1989, "a considerable part of the party apparatus is in total disarray and is unable to find its bearings in the new situation."[31]

To still party conservatives as well as mounting ethnic and economic crises, Gorbachev sought to strengthen further his institutional base in the spring of 1990 with the creation of an executive presidency, which was placed at the pinnacle of the Soviet state. Elected by the Congress of People's Deputies to this new presidency, Gorbachev began to endow the office with powers that had previously been reserved for the Politburo and other executive institutions of the

Table 2.7
The Politburo
October 1990

Individual	Position
M. Gorbachev	General Secretary, USSR President
V. Ivashko	Deputy General Secretary, CPSU
M. Burakevicius	First Secretary, Communist Party of Lithuania
A. Dzasokhov	Secretary for Ideology, CPSU
I. Frolov	Editor in Chief, *Pravda*
S. Gumbaridze	First Secretary, Communist Party of Georgia
I. Karimov	First Secretary, Communist Party of Uzbekistan
P. Luchinsky	First Secretary, Communist Party of Moldavia
K. Makhkamov	First Secretary, Communist Party of Tajikistan
A. Masaliev	First Secretary, Communist Party of Kirgizia
V. Movsisyan	First Secretary, Communist Party of Armenia
A. Mutalibov	First Secretary, Communist Party of Azerbaijan
N. Nazarbaev	First Secretary, Communist Party of Kazakhstan
S. Niiazov	First Secretary, Communist Party of Turkmenistan
I. Polozkov	First Secretary, Communist Party of RSFSR
Iu. Prokof'ev	First Secretary, Moscow City Party Committee, and Secretary, CPSU Central Committee
A. Rubiks	First Secretary, Communist Party of Latvia
G. Semenova	Secretary for Women's Affairs, CPSU
O. Shenin	Secretary for Organizational Matters, CPSU
E. Sillari	First Secretary, Communist Party of Estonia
E. Sokolov	First Secretary, Communist Party of Belorussia
I. Stroev	Secretary for Agriculture, CPSU
G. Yanaev	Secretary for International Affairs, CPSU

Source: See "Politbiuro i sekretariat Tsentral'nogo komiteta KPSS," *Izvestiia TsK KPSS*, no. 8 (1990), pp. 8-61, which lists the membership of these leading party bodies, as elected at the 28th Party Congress in July 1990. This list was unchanged in October 1990.

party. Key state officials, such as the prime minister, the minister of foreign affairs, the minister of defense, and the head of the KGB, now held seats on the Politburo as well as on a new appendage to the presidency, the Presidential Council (see Table 2.6). It was clear that the center of political gravity was shifting away from the Politburo and toward the office of the president, which also contained a Federation Council, composed of top state officials from the republics.

Table 2.8
The CPSU Secretariat and Its Apparatus
October 1990

Senior Secretaries
M. Gorbachev	General Secretary
V. Ivashko	Deputy General Secretary
A. Dzasokhov	Secretary for Ideology
G. Semenova	Secretary for Women's Affairs
O. Shenin	Secretary for Organizational Matters
Iu. Stroev	Secretary for Agriculture
G. Yanaev	Secretary for International Affairs

Secretaries
O. Baklanov	Secretary for Defense Industry
V. Falin	Secretary for International Affairs
B. Gidaspov	First Secretary, Leningrad City and Regional Party Committees
A. Girenko	Secretary for Nationalities
V. Kuptsov	Secretary for Mass Organizations
Iu. Manaenkov	Secretary for RSFSR Communist Party

Central Committee Commissions with Chairmen
A. Dzasokhov	Ideology
V. Kuptsov	Socio-Political
V. Ivashko	Socio-Economic
E. Stroev	Agricultural Policy
A. Girenko	Nationalities Policy
G. Yanaev	International Policy
O. Shenin	Renewal of Primary Party Organizations
B. Gidaspov	Science, Education and Culture
O. Baklanov	Military Policy
Iu. Manaienkov	Youth Policy
G. Semenova	Women and Family Issues

Central Committee Departments
1) Ideology	8) Humanitarian
2) Ties with Socio-Political Orgs.	9) Information Center
3) Socio-Economic Policy	10) Legislative Initiatives and
4) Agricultural Policy	Questions of Law
5) Nationalities	11) General Department
6) International	12) Administration
7) Organizational	13) Press Center

Source: Alexander Rahr, "The CPSU after the Twenty-eighth Party Congress," *Report on the USSR*, no. 45, 9 November 1990, pp. 1-4.

At the 28th Party Congress, Gorbachev continued his policy of transferring power from the party to the state. After defeating a sizeable conservative opposition, the General Secretary dealt a new blow to the central party organs. The Politburo that emerged from the Congress was composed entirely of party functionaries, with no representatives from the state. Gorbachev alone held dual membership in the top state and party institutions. Although the secretariat was revived and strengthened with the appointment of 13 secretaries, 11 Central Committee Commissions, and 11 departments, its mandate was now limited to *intra-party* affairs and its staff reduced by 40 percent, to 850 persons (see Table 2.8).[32] The secretariat would oversee the work of local-level party bodies and would service the Politburo, but it now ruled only the party, not the country.[33] This decoupling of central party and state institutions was accompanied by the abolition of Article 6 of the Soviet constitution, which had granted to the Communist Party a monopoly of political power, and by the first attempts to remove primary party organizations from state institutions.

By August 1990, panic had set in among the conservatives in the party apparatus, as was revealed in a *Pravda* editorial on the party and soviets. The article began with the familiar Gorbachev line.

> Perestroika has put on the agenda the creation of a new democratic mechanism of interaction based on separating the functions of society's political vanguard, on the one hand, and power and administration, which are being transferred to the soviets, on the other. The party formulates policy and implements it via the soviets. And this applies not just to the CPSU Central Committee, the Supreme Soviet, and the USSR Council of Ministers, but also to the union republic communist party central committees, and krai, oblast, city and raion soviets.

But the editorial then went on to state that communist deputies were still subject to party discipline and had a dual responsibility to both party and state.

> They have a right to express their opinion on the problem being discussed, but when a decision has been made, they must carry it out. Their duty is to adopt the same stance as the Central Committee on questions arising from the party's political strategy and from the decisions of party organs at the corresponding level and to pursue and implement the party line in the soviet.[34]

Throughout 1990 and 1991, the Central Committee secretariat waged a battle to win back its "leading and guiding role in society."

To the chagrin of the party apparatus, the new legislative and executive bodies of state eclipsed the Politburo and secretariat. Under the new policy, the secretariat was only permitted to *recommend* policies, which then had to be

Table 2.9
Central Committee Members in State Institutions
1990

Central Committee Membership	412	
People's Deputies of USSR	103	(25%)
Members of USSR Supreme Soviet	27	(6.5%)
People's Deputies of Republics	46	(11.2%)
People's Deputies of Autonomous Republics	11	(2.7%)
Officials of USSR Supreme Soviet and of republic, autonomous republic, and regional-level soviets	8	(1.9%)
Officials of USSR Council of Ministers and of republic, autonomous republic, and regional-level executive committees	15	(3.6%)
Total	183	(44.4%)

Source: *Izvestiia TsK KPSS*, no. 8 (1990), p. 4., and author's calculations for members of Supreme Soviet from biographies of Central Committee members, published in numbers 10, 11 and 12 of *Izvestiia TsK KPSS*, 1990. The total figure of 183 includes doubling-counting of some Central Committee members who held more than one state post.

approved by the USSR Supreme Soviet. Henceforth, Gorbachev argued, the party would have to win seats in the country's parliaments. Persuasion and the ballot box were to replace coercion and rule by decree. Article 33 of the new party statutes, published in July 1990, stated that:

> The CPSU struggles for political leadership in society in free elections to the Soviets of People's Deputies and through other forms of expressing the will of Soviet citizens.[35]

In other words, the Communist Party of the Soviet Union was being transformed from a vanguard party to a Western-style parliamentary party.

As a parliamentary party, however, the Communists fared poorly in much of the country. On the surface, the party's presence in the soviets remained impressive even after competitive elections. As noted above, party members held approximately 87 percent of the seats in the Congress of People's Deputies and the USSR Supreme Soviet. Yet the party's authority within these bodies declined sharply because many Communists were no longer loyal to the party apparatus. While one quarter of the members of the Central Committee in 1990 were deputies to the Congress, only 27, or 6.5 percent, had seats in the Supreme Soviet (see Table 2.9). In the soviets of many republics, regions, and cities, including Moscow and Leningrad, the party apparatus found itself in the role of opposition.

By the autumn of 1990 it was clear that the central party apparatus would have a difficult fight to regain control over these bodies. Of particular concern was the role of party groups, now called "party factions," in the Supreme Soviet and local legislative bodies. In October 1990, the party established a Department on Legislative Initiatives and Questions of Law to strengthen the party's ties with the soviets. In a speech to the October Plenum of the Central Committee, party secretary O. Shenin delivered a devastating account of the poor level of party work in the soviets and the difficulties that the party faced in trying to form party factions and forge a unified policy.

> Communist deputies often lack openness and the ability to debate informally. Many of them, lacking experience in political speaking, get lost in the parliamentary polemics. The main thing is that we need a general line of behavior on fundamental questions. We must bear in mind that the idea of forming party groups or factions of Communists in the soviets is meeting with a cautious reception, particularly in the initial stages .... I refer above all to those who were elected on the bases of blocs and often scored points by criticizing the CPSU. There are party members who currently prefer not to advertise their party membership. Some still distrust the old style party groups. The creation of factions makes some Communists fear an increase in confrontation in the soviets. There are also those who are scared of being accused of conservatism.[36]

At the October 1990 Central Committee plenum, Deputy V.S. Lipitskii complained that the party was no longer the key decisionmaking body. The soviets, he argued, were now formulating policy.

We now have no real channels for influencing the choice made by our parliamentarians, since, because of the particular features of our historical situation, in many places, including the center, the soviets are not so much multi-party as non-party. Deputies there do not represent political parties but are elected to soviets thanks to their personal qualities and feel responsibility only to the voters. I think our party already effectively finds itself in the position of constructive opposition ....

Lipitskii's remarks at the plenum provoked this riposte from Gorbachev, who seemed to realize for the first time the absurdity of his position as both president and general secretary.

The most surprising thing is that it follows from this that the President as part of this power simultaneously heads the opposition to himself.[37]

Another participant at the plenum observed that the party had fallen behind the state in its ability to promote new policies.

... how can we explain the fact that we met to discuss the program for the transition to the market when the Russian Supreme Soviet had already approved the "500 days" program, and while the Union Supreme Soviet is near adopting an amended version of it ... the party is being transformed into an organization that catches up with Government decisions.[38]

As these comments suggest, Gorbachev's policy of transforming the vanguard party into a parliamentary party was not implemented without a fight. Many members of the secretariat and party apparatus, fortified by the country's political shift to the right in the autumn of 1990, allied themselves with conservatives in the state machinery. They launched a last-ditch attempt to reinstate the party's leading role in policy making and to assert its control over the new upstart legislative and executive bodies of the state.

In October 1990, new departments were set up in the Central Committee apparatus to deal with the soviets and the newly emerging, and now legally sanctioned, political parties and social movements (see Table 2.8). The new structure of the central party apparat was designed to win back for the party a stake in the political life of the country and to reverse its disastrous showing in the elections to the republic soviets in the spring of 1990. The Central Committee Commission on Socio-Political Work, headed by V. Kuptsov, and the Department for Ties with Socio-Political Organizations assumed the task of forging alliances with the new parties and social groups that were springing up daily throughout the Soviet Union. The newly-created Department for Legisla-

Table 2.10
The Communist Party and the Soviet State
January 1991

PARTY		STATE	
Legislative	*Executive*	*Executive*	*Legislative*
Politburo*		Presidency	Presidium of Supreme Soviet
Central Committee	Secretariat	Cabinet of Ministers	Supreme Soviet
Commissions		Ministries/ State Committees	Congress of People's Deputies
Congress (Conference)	Departments		

* The Politburo and Commissions exercised both legislative and executive functions.

tive Initiatives and Questions of Law played a major role in developing new ties between the party and the state. Another important addition to the apparatus was the Commission for the Renewal of Primary Party Organizations, which gave moral support to PPOs at a time when they were coming under increasing pressure to withdraw completely from state administrative bodies.[39]

During the winter of 1990-91 a fierce battle raged over the depoliticization of the state, that is, over whether primary party organizations should continue to function in non-party institutions. In his political report to the 28th Party Congress, Gorbachev had been unequivocal about the role of PPOs in economic enterprises.

> Primary Party Organizations do not consider it possible, and in fact no longer have the right, to exercise control over the management activity at enterprises and in organizations or over the work of the apparatus of ministries and departments and of Soviet and economic institutions .... The new role of Party organizations consists in collectively—at meetings, Congresses, conferences, and plenary sessions—working out positions on the most important questions

of the life of society, conveying these positions to the appropriate state and economic agencies, explaining these positions in public debates, and orienting Communists toward upholding them in practical deeds.[40]

Gorbachev's message was that the party must stand or fall on its policies and its support among the people and not as an administrative cog in the state machine. He did not, however, advocate the abolition of the PPOs.

At a Central Committee plenum on 8 October 1990, Vladimir Ivashko revealed that there were still more than 100,000 PPOs functioning in industrial, transport, communications, and construction enterprises and more than 40,000 in agriculture. The party continued to summon ministers before the secretariat to explain their actions. In the wake of the 28th Party Congress, for example, CPSU secretary Alexander Dzasokhov refered to the crucial role of the party in organizing agricultural work during the harvest period and in overcoming the crises in food provision for the cities. Dzasokhov realized that these were "purely economic problems," but they were studied, he explained, "exclusively through the prism of party work." He also explained that the party, in abandoning command and administrative functions in the economic arena, was not "divesting itself of responsibility for the formulation and implementation of an efficient socioeconomic policy corresponding to the working people's interest."[41]

For all the rhetoric of reform, then, the secretariat was still seeking to conduct business as usual. Only now there were new and powerful counterforces in the legislative and executive bodies of the state. No longer could the party simply issue orders to state officials. Decisions had to be debated and approved by the Congress and the Supreme Soviet. This did not, however, prevent the party from seeking to influence directly the executive institutions of state. For example, at its meeting of 27 March 1991, the party's Agrarian Commission requested that its decisions be given attention by the communist leaders of the USSR State Planning Committee, the USSR State Committee for Material and Technical Supply, and the USSR Ministry of Finance.[42]

Regarding party control of the state's military, security, and police institutions, Gorbachev was especially reluctant to decouple fully the party and state. At the 28th Congress he came out strongly against the depoliticization of these bodies.

> Another question is now being raised rather sharply: the question of depoliticizing bodies of state administration, the courts, the prosecutor's office, other law enforcement agencies and also the Army. Our position on this score is determined by the fact that the right of association is an inalienable political liberty. No one can prohibit Party members from setting up their own cells at enterprises, in institutions ....[43]

After the Congress had concluded, Gorbachev again took up this subject.

> We are against the de-Partyization of the Army and believe that the codification
> in the Statutes of the basic principles of Party work in the Army and Navy
> collectives is indispensable. In taking this position we proceed from the premise
> that from now on Party work in the Armed forces will be conducted only by
> primary party organizations and elected party agencies.[44]

The debate continued at the October 1990 plenum of the Central Committee,
which devoted considerable attention to the issue of depoliticizing state
institutions. In the words of Deputy General Secretary Ivashko,

> Discussion on the issue of depoliticizing work forces and on taking party
> committees out of enterprises have of late been initiated in every possible way.
> Unfortunately, in a number of places these discussions have turned into hasty
> actions which hinder the work of party committees. Supporters of the so-called
> depoliticization claim that recognition of the multiparty system allegedly
> demands that there are no parties at all at enterprises, for otherwise, it is said,
> they will stand in the administration's way to manage.[45]

At a session of the CPSU secretariat on 17 October 1990, the discussion focused
once again on the role of the party in law enforcement agencies. Participants in
the discussion included the reformist Minister of Internal Affairs, Vadim
Bakatin, as well as hardliners such as Boris Pugo, at the time chairman of the
party's disciplinary arm, the Central Control Committee. The subject of the
debate was emergent political forces in the Soviet Union that were not only
"outside the party's control" but openly hostile to the party's vanguard role in
state institutions.

> In certain places Communists working in law enforcement bodies are subjected
> to large scale moral and administrative pressure. An atmosphere of political
> uncertainty and lack of legal protection is evolving in their midst, and cases of
> people leaving the CPSU are becoming more frequent. A proportion of
> Communists who are highly skilled specialists are endeavoring to leave their
> jobs, which undermines the mechanism of state administration, the execution
> of the laws, the protection of law and order, and the anti-crime drive.[46]

The session reported numerous instances where republic and local authorities
had banned PPOs from their workplaces. In February 1990, for example, the
Supreme Soviet of Lithuania "prohibited the activity of PPOs in the organs of
internal affairs, state security, the customs service, justice, the procuracy, the

state arbitration service, state control and the people's courts." In March 1990, the presidium of the Estonian Supreme Soviet adopted a decree on the depoliticization of the law enforcement bodies. In July 1990, the Moscow city soviet recommended that officials of the law enforcement bodies in the city of Moscow refrain from joining political parties. The Moscow soviet also asked members of the Communist Party to consider whether their membership was commensurate with their state duties. Finally, in July 1990, a decree of the Supreme Soviet of Moldavia prohibited judges and other workers of state law enforcement bodies from belonging to political parties and sociopolitical movements.[47]

The attack on PPOs encouraged a massive exodus of members from the party's ranks. In 1989 alone 800,000 members left the Communist Party. It has been estimated that as many as four million left over the period from 1989 to 1991, reducing party membership from 19 million to 15 million.[48]

The Fall of Gorbachev, the Communist Party, and the Soviet State

In the autumn of 1990, Gorbachev came under intense criticism from conservative forces in the party and state. From their perspective, the only integrating institution in the country, the Communist Party, was in collapse. Law enforcement agencies were losing control of the streets. An alien market reform, based on Shatalin's 500 day plan, appeared imminent. And the center was losing the "war of laws" with the republics. Gorbachev's presidential decrees were continually ignored or classified as unconstitutional by the new republic supreme soviets, creating in effect 15 different and competing governments.

The country was gripped by a paralysis of power with neither the party nor the state in control. Deputy General Secretary Ivashko summed up the mood of the party in a statement made at the October 1990 Central Committee Plenum.

> The temperature of our long-sick and seriously ill society has reached the critical mark. The volume of production is being cut, there is a chain reaction under way in the disintegration of economic links, discipline is getting worse. Total shortage, speculation, the rise in prices, the stricken consumer market are poisoning the life of millions of Soviet people from day to day. The situation regarding providing Moscow and Leningrad with foodstuffs has become simply intolerable. The criminal world which is terrorizing the population is growing insolent. The hot beds of inter-ethnic strife and conflicts are not dying down. The polarization of political forces is continuing, anti-socialist trends are growing more active, attempts to drive the CPSU out into the backyard of

> social life are increasing ... the image of the enemy in the person of the CPSU
> is being instilled into the public consciousness.[49]

Nikolai Ryzhkov made this grim statement at a meeting of the Supreme Soviet
in November 1990.

> Control has been totally lost at all levels of the state structure. Authority has
> been paralyzed .... Universal destructiveness is basically becoming the norm.
> One can say with sufficient conviction and grounds that, throughout the greater
> part of the country's territory, a situation has been created in which no one is
> in charge, and this has led to a complete or partial deterioration of all systems
> of administration.[50]

In the midst of these economic and political crises, Gorbachev put forth yet
another round of radical proposals aimed at strengthening the state's executive
branch, most notably the presidency. In October 1990, he received additional
executive power to control the supply of foodstuffs to the cities. In November,
he announced that a USSR Cabinet of Ministers, directly subordinate to the
president, would replace the USSR Council of Ministers. The Presidential
Council was abolished and its powers transferred to a revamped Federation
Council, which was now to become the chief policymaking body in the country.
In addition, a Security Council and a Coordination Agency for the Supervision
of Law and Order were created, both answering directly to the president.
Gorbachev alone combined dual membership of these state bodies with
membership in the party Politburo and secretariat.[51]

But even the president's new executive powers could not hold the country back
from the brink of economic and political collapse. Gorbachev's inability to
implement his decrees gave renewed strength to the conservatives, and the
country now swung perceptibly to the Right. A number of personnel changes
made at the end of 1990 and the beginning of 1991 boded ill for the reform
movement. Boris Pugo, a hardline conservative and former head of the KGB in
Latvia, replaced the liberal Minister of Internal Affairs, Vadim Bakatin. On the
night of December 25, Prime Minister Ryzhkov suffered a heart attack,
removing him from political office. In January, Valentin Pavlov, the
conservative Minister of Finance, took over from Ryzhkov as the new chairman
of the Cabinet of Ministers. Less noticed at this time was the election of a gray
party bureaucrat, Gennadii Yanaev, to the post of vice president of the USSR.
Meanwhile, a number of radical reformers, the architects of perestroika, left the
Gorbachev camp in disgust at the President's support of the right. The most
prominent was the Foreign Minister Eduard Shevardnadze, who resigned his
office on 20 December 1990, warning of an impending dictatorship.

With a new, hardline leadership in place, there was a crackdown on the breakaway Baltic republics of Latvia and Estonia in late January 1991. Gorbachev seemed to have lost control over the army, KGB and police and was a hostage—how willing or unwilling history will tell—to the conservatives. There was also a clampdown on the press, which was part of a broader attempt by the party to roll back glasnost.

Gorbachev had played a very dangerous game. While remaining general secretary, he had precipitated the party's decline by abandoning Marxism-Leninism and supporting a market economy and a multi-party system. He had undermined the authority of the party and had tried to transfer power to the state. But he did not succeed in extracting the party from the state.   Most importantly, he was unable to transfer the party's tight control over the army, the KGB and the police to the new executive bodies in the presidency. It is indeed possible that he held on to the post of party general secretary in an attempt to maintain personal control over the security forces.

Amid this crisis of authority in Soviet politics, Prime Minister Pavlov staged an unsuccessful "constitutional coup" in June 1991. With the support of the armed forces, the KGB and the police, he asked the Supreme Soviet to grant "emergency powers" to the Cabinet of Ministers, which he directed. By strengthening cabinet government, Pavlov would have decisively weakened Gorbachev and the institution of the presidency.

Regrouping after the June setback, conservative officials in the party apparatus allied with Vice-President Yanaev, Prime Minister Pavlov, and the heads of the armed forces, KGB and police to remove Gorbachev physically from power on 19 August 1991.   Coming on the eve of a meeting between Gorbachev and republican leaders that would have shifted considerable political power from the center to the republics, the coup seemed to confirm Shevardnadze's prediction of a new dictatorship.   Gorbachev was replaced by the vice president, Gennadii Yanaev, an apparent puppet for the party and state officials who engineered the coup.   But through the indecision of the conspirators and the resistance of important sectors of the elite, the coup collapsed within three days, and with it more than 70 years of party-state relations. On August 29, the party was dissolved and its property handed over to state bodies at central and local levels. Party-state relations had come to abrupt end with the victory of the state over the party.

The failure of the August coup led inevitably to the collapse of the Soviet empire. The three Baltic republics quickly gained independence, and a number of other republics, including Ukraine, soon declared their intention to secede. The coup also redistributed power within the state.   As the directly elected president of the Russian Republic and the symbol of resistance to the coup,

Boris Yeltsin quickly emerged as the dominant political leader in the country. At the insistence of Yeltsin and other republican leaders, two new central executive institutions were created that eclipsed Gorbachev's presidency. They were the State Council, comprised of Gorbachev and the heads of the remaining republics, and the Committee for the Operational Administration of the Economy (later the Interrepublican Economic Committee), a successor to the Cabinet of Ministers, which had been discredited in the coup. These changes were accompanied by a major restructuring of central legislative institutions. The USSR Congress of People's Deputies reluctantly voted for its own dissolution, and a new and smaller Supreme Soviet was created, which functioned more as a coordinating council than a real parliament. Each republican parliament was to select its own delegation of deputies to the Supreme Soviet, with each delegation casting a single vote in the new assembly. These reforms confirmed the collapse of the center and the transfer of real power to the republics.

Perhaps even more dramatic than the collapse of the Soviet empire was the dissolution of the Communist Party, whose involvement in the August coup led to its proscription. The last formal bond between party and state was broken on 24 August 1991, when Gorbachev resigned his post as general secretary as well as his membership in the Communist Party. On 29 August 1991, the USSR Supreme Soviet adopted an historic resolution, "On Priority Measures for the Purpose of Preventing Attempts to Carry Out a Coup d'Etat," which stated that

> On the basis of available information about the participation of leading CPSU bodies in the preparation and conduct of the state coup of 18-21 August, 1991, the activities of the CPSU are to be suspended across the entire territory of the USSR.[52]

The all-union parliament also called upon banking institutions to "halt all operations involving CPSU funds." The offices of the Central Committee and secretariat were sealed and party property transferred to the jurisdiction of republican and local soviets.[53]   At the beginning of 1992, as the new Commonwealth of Independent States struggled to establish its viability as a political unit, the Communist Party showed few signs of life. But it was still not buried. New communist and socialist parties began to emerge from the remnants of the CPSU. Some, such as the Popular Democratic Party of Uzbekistan, continued the Communist legacy in all but name. Others, such as the Party of Communists, which was formed in Moscow shortly after the coup and supported by between one and a half and two million former Communist Party members, held aloft the Communist banner without apology.[54] It may be wise, therefore, to resist the temptation to write the obituary of the Communist movement. There may yet be a revival of Communist-style parties as forces of the Right regroup under the slogan, "The party is dead, long live the party!"

Notes

1. A. Ilin, "In Pravda's Editorial Office", *Pravda*, 30 September 1991, p. 1.

2. The classic work on *nomenklatura* is Bohdan Harasymiw, "Nomenklatura: The Soviet Communist Party's Leadership Recruitment System," *Canadian Journal of Political Science*, no. 3 (1969), pp. 493-512. See also Harasymiw's more extensive treatment of the subject, *Political Recruitment in the Soviet Union* (London: Macmillan, 1984). For a more recent discussion, see Ronald J. Hill and John Lowenhardt, "Nomenklatura and Perestroika," *Government and Opposition*, no. 2 (Spring 1991), pp. 229-244. Another informative work that treats party-state relations more generally and discusses nomenklatura is Rolf H.W. Theen, "Party and Bureaucracy," in *Public Policy and Administration in the Soviet Union*, ed. Gordon B. Smith (New York: Praeger, 1980), pp. 18-52.

3. Zhores Medvedev, *Gorbachev* (Oxford: Basil Blackwell, 1987), p. 178.

4. For an interesting discussion on the relationship between occupational status and membership in the Central Committee, see Robert V. Daniels, "Office Holding and Elite Status: The Central Committee of the CPSU," in *The Dynamics of Soviet Politics*, ed. Paul Cocks, Robert V. Daniels, and Nancy Whittier Heer (Cambridge, MA: Harvard University Press, 1976) pp. 77-95.

5. David Lane, *State and Politics in the USSR* (Oxford: Basil Blackwell, 1985), p. 189.

6. For more information about party membership in the standing commissions, see R.S. Siegler, *The Standing Commissions of the Supreme Soviet* (New York: Praeger, 1982).

7. See the following resolutions of the Central Committee of the CPSU, "O rabote partkoma Ministerstva miasnoi i molochnoi promyshlennosti SSSR [3 February 1970]," in *KPSS v rezoliutsiiakh i resheniiakh s"ezdov, konferentsii, i plenumov TsK*, X, 1969-1971 (Moscow: Politizdat, 1972) pp. 191-97 [hereafter, *KPSS v rezoliutsiiakh]*; "Ob osushchestvlenii partkomom Ministerstva sviazi SSSR kontrolia za rabotoi apparata po vypolneniu direktiv partii i pravitel'stva [19 November 1974]," in *KPSS v rezoliutsiiakh*, XI, 1972-5 (Moscow: Politizdat, 1978), pp. 463-5; "O sostoianii kontrolia i proverki ispolneniia v Ministerstve neftepererabatyvaiushcheii neftekhimicheskoi promyshlennosti SSSR [21 May 1980]," in *KPSS v rezoliutsiiakh*, XIII, 1978-80 (Moscow: Politizdat, 1981), pp.619-24; 16 February 1982, "O komissiiakh pervichnykh partiinykh organizatsii po osushchestvleniiu kontrolia deiatel'nosti administratsii i za rabotoi apparata [16 February 1982]," in *Partiinaia zhizn'*, no. 6 (1982), pp. 13-16.

8. C. Ross, *Local Government in the Soviet Union* (New York: St. Martin's Press, 1987).

9. The standard Soviet work on party-state relations in the pre-Gorbachev era is G.V. Barabashev and K.F. Sheremet, "KPSS i sovety," *Sovetskoe gosudarstvo i pravo*, no. 11 (1967), pp. 31-41. Ronald J. Hill provides an excellent discussion of such relations at the

local level in *Soviet Political Elites: The Case of Tiraspol* (London: St. Martin's Press, 1977); see also my chapter on party-state relations in C. Ross, *Local Government in the Soviet Union* (New York: St Martin's Press, 1987) pp. 17-61.

10. *Ustav Kommunisticheskoi Partii Sovetskovo Soiuza* (Moscow: 1980) p. 37 [Article 42c].

11. G. Razumovskii, "Bringing Party Work to the Level of the Tasks of Restructuring," in *Partinaia zhizn'*, no. 12 (June 1987), pp. 5-14, translated in *Foreign Broadcast Information Service*, Daily Report, Soviet Union [hereafter *FBIS*], annex, 3 August 1987, p. 6.

12. "CPSU Central Committee Theses for the 19th All-Union Party Conference," *FBIS*, 27 May 1988, reprinted in Baruch A. Hazan, *Gorbachev's Gamble. The 19th All-Union Party Conference* (Boulder, San Francisco and London: Westview Press, 1990), p. 84.

13. See C. Friedrich and Z. Brzezinski, *Totalitarian Dictatorship and Autocracy* (Cambridge, MA: Harvard University Press, 1956).

14. Jerry Hough, "The Soviet System: Petrification or Pluralism?" *Problems of Communism*, no. 2 (1972), pp. 25-45. See also J. Hough, *The Soviet Prefects* (Cambridge, MA: Harvard University Press, 1969), where Professor Hough argues that the party served as an essential coordinating apparatus for the economy.

15. Robert D. Putnam, "The Political Attitudes of Senior Civil Servants in Britain, Germany, and Italy," *The Mandarins of Western Europe: The Political Role of Top Civil Servants*, ed. Mattei Dogan (New York, London, Sydney, Toronto: John Wiley and Sons, 1975) p. 87.

16. C. Ross, *Local Government in the Soviet Union*, chapter 4.

17. "Gorbachev's Opening Speech to the 19th All-Union Party Conference, 28th June, 1988," in *FBIS*, no. 127, 1 July 1988, reprinted in B. Hazan, *Gorbachev's Gamble*, p. 122.

18. My biographical study in progress on top party and state officials shows that of the 98 members of the USSR Council of Ministers appointed in 1984, approximately 65 percent had careers entirely within the state, a further 15 percent had a mixed career with some experience of work in both the party apparatus and the state, and a third group, which made up 20 percent, had spent the majority of their time working for the party apparatus. Of the 70 members appointed to the USSR Council of Ministers in 1989, approximately 57 percent had spent the vast majority of their careers working for the state, 19 percent had a mixed career, and only 15 percent had been co-opted into the state from long careers in the party apparatus. Similar strong vertical careers were also to be found among party officials. In 1976, 75 percent, and in 1981, 70 percent, of secretaries had spent the majority of their working lives in the party apparatus. In 1989, 11 of 13 had strong vertical careers, or mixed career backgrounds; only 2 of 13 had spent a substantial period of time working outside the party apparatus.

19. See Tony Cliff, *State Capitalism in Russia* (London: Pluto Press, 1974), and Milovan Djilas, *The New Class* (London: George Allen and Unwin, 1966).

20. Jan S. Adams, "Incremental Activism in Soviet Third World Policy: The Role of the International Department of the CPSU Central Committee," *Slavic Review*, no. 4 (Winter 1989), pp. 615.

21. *Pravda*, 27 February 1986, pp. 2-3, translated in *Current Digest of the Soviet Press* [hereafter *CDSP*], no. 9 (1986), p. 5.

22. Report by M.S. Gorbachev, "Restructuring The Work Of The Party Is A Highly Important, Key Task Of The Day," *Pravda*, 19 July 1989, pp. 1-3, in *CDSP*, no. 29 (1989), p. 4.

23. "The State Statistics Committee Reports: Where Are The Managers And How Many Of The Are There?" *Izvestiia*, 7 March 1989, p. 1, in *CDSP*, no. 10 (1989), p. 8.

24. "Gorbachev's Opening Speech to 19th All-Union Party Conference," in Hazan, *Gorbachev's Gamble*, p. 136.

25. Report by M.S. Gorbachev, "On Practical Work To Implement the Decisions of the 19th All-Union Party Conference," *Pravda*, 30 July 1988, pp. 1-3, in *CDSP*, no. 30 (1988), p. 4.

26. "Resolution of the Plenary Session of the CPSU Central Committee, On Basic Guidelines for the Restructuring of the Party Apparatus," *Pravda*, 31 July 1988, p. 2, in *CDSP*, no. 30 (1988), p. 9.

27. "Report by Ye.K. Ligachev, Member of the Politburo and Secretary of the CPSU Central Committee," *Pravda*, 5 July 1990, p. 2, in *CDSP*, no. 29 (1990), pp. 10-11.

28. "Medvedev Answers Journalists Questions 30 September," *Tass*, 30 September 1988, in *FBIS*, 3 October 1988, p. 42.

29. "Resolution of the Plenary Session of the CPSU Central Committee, On Basic Guidelines for The Restructuring of the Party Apparatus," in *CDSP*, no. 30 (1988), p. 14.

30. "Speech by N.I. Ryzhkov at July 1989 CPSU Conference," *Pravda*, 21 July 1989, pp. 1-4, in *CDSP*, no. 30 (1989), p. 9.

31. "The Party and Restructuring: To Be Society's Political Vanguard," *Pravda*, 14 June 1989, p. 1, in *FBIS*, 20 June 1989, p. 63.

32. "Our Party Is Alive and Changing [interview with Valentin Kuptsov by Zdenek Porybny]," *Rude Pravo*, 17 October 1990, p. 7, in *FBIS*, 19 October 1990, p. 56.

33. For an excellent summary of the changes made to the party in 1990, see Dawn Mann, "Leading Bodies of CPSU Transformed," *Report on the USSR*, 20 July 1990, pp. 14-20.

34. "The Party and the Soviets," *Pravda,* 8 August 1989, p. 1, in *FBIS*, 18 August 1989, p. 62.

35. The statutes were published in *Pravda*, 18 July 1990, pp. 1-2. A translation may be found in *CDSP*, no. 38 (1990), p. 18.

36. "Speech by O.S. Shenin at 8 October session of CPSU Central Committee: Report on the CPSU Central Committee Commissions and Apparatus," *Pravda*, 10 October 1990, p. 2, in *FBIS*, 11 October 1990, p. 38.

37. "Speech by V.S. Lipitskii at 8 October session of CPSU Central Committee," *Pravda*, 10 October 1990, p. 4, in *FBIS*, 11 October 1990, p. 49.

38. "Speech by V.D. Kadochnikov at 8 October session of CPSU Central Committee," *Pravda*, 11 October 1990, pp. 3-4, in *FBIS*, 18 October 1990, p. 41.

39. For the first time, Central Committee commissions were formed on youth policy and on women and the family. The new secretary for women's affairs, Galina Semenova, was also a member of the Politburo. Presumably this was related to the party's attempts to increase its support among these previously neglected social groups. To draw up the party's economic policy a Socio-Economic Commission was created, headed by Deputy General Secretary V. Ivashko. There was also a subordinate Socio-Economic Policy Department. But unlike previous years these bodies now could only *recommend* policies to the Supreme Soviet. They were no longer, at least in theory, able to give direct commands to officials in state institutions.

40. M.S. Gorbachev, "The Political Report of the CPSU Central Committee to the 28th CPSU Congress and the Party's Tasks," *Pravda*, 3 July 1990, pp. 2-4, in *CDSP*, no. 27 (1990), p. 14.

41. A.S. Dzasokhov, "Sekretariat TsK posle s"ezda: pervye shagi," *Izvestiia TsK KPSS*, no. 9 (1990), p. 5.

42. "Session of Agrarian Commission, 27 March 1991," *Pravda*, 28 March 1991, p. 2, in *FBIS*, 4 April 1991, p. 34.

43. Gorbachev, "The Political Report of the CPSU Central Committee to the 28th CPSU Congress and the Party's Tasks," in *CDSP*, no. 27 (1990), p. 16.

44. "Chronicle Of The Congress, Day Eleven," *Pravda*, 13 July 1990, pp. 1-3, in *CDSP*, no. 35 (1990), p. 19.

45. "Report by V.A. Ivashko, Deputy General Secretary of the CPSU Central Committee, at the 8 October CPSU Central Committee Plenum in Moscow," *Pravda*, 9 October 1990, pp. 2-3, in *FBIS*, 9 October 1990, p. 48.

46. "Here is a report on a session of the CPSU Central Committee Secretariat," *TASS*, October 17, 1990, in *FBIS*, October 18, 1990, p. 28.

47. *Ibid.*

48. A. Ilin, "In Pravda's Editorial Office," *Pravda*, 30 September 1991, p. 1.

49. "Report by V.A. Ivashko, Deputy General Secretary of the CPSU Central Committee, at the 8 October CPSU Central Committee Plenum in Moscow," *Pravda*, 9 October 1990, pp. 2-3, in *FBIS*, 9 October 1990, pp. 41-2.

50. "Speech by N.I. Ryzhkov at USSR Supreme Soviet Session," *Moscow Domestic Service*, 0844 GMT, 17 November 1990, in *FBIS*, 19 November 1990, p. 29.

51. For further details about the Cabinet see, C. Ross, "The USSR Cabinet of Ministers", *Report on the USSR*, no. 26 (1991), pp. 1-14.

52. "USSR Supreme Soviet Resolution of 30 August, 1991, 'On Priority Measures for the Purpose of Preventing Attempts to Carry Out a Coup d'Etat'," *Moscow Tass International Service*, 1240 GMT, 1 September 1991, in *FBIS*, 3 September 1991, p. 21. According to Roy Medvedev, party factions in the USSR Supreme Soviet continued to function after this ban. *Moscow Radio Rossiia Network*, 1100 GMT, 21 October 1991, in *FBIS*, 22 October 1991, p. 30.

53. "Ob imushchestve Kommunisticheskoi partii Sovetskogo Soiuza," *Vedomosti S"ezda narodnykh deputatov SSSR i Verkhovnogo Soveta SSSR*, no. 35 (1991), item 1024.

54. Irina Lobanovskaia, "New, Entirely New Party of Communists", *Rossiiskaia gazeta*, 12 September 1991, p. 1, in *FBIS*, 13 September 1991, pp. 42-3.

3

EXECUTIVE-LEGISLATIVE RELATIONS

Eugene Huskey

On 25 May 1989, the first legislature worthy of the name met in the Kremlin. Few political events of this century aroused more interest and anticipation than the opening session of the Congress of People's Deputies of the USSR. The expectations for the new legislature were not to be realized, however. Within months of its formation, the Congress—and the smaller parliament, or Supreme Soviet, elected from within it—began voluntarily to transfer legislative authority to the executive. Following the abortive coup of August 1991, the Congress of People's Deputies effectively disbanded itself, leaving as its successors a restructured and emasculated parliament as well as a state council, which was a fused executive-legislative institution comprised of the heads of the republics. These institutions were in turn eliminated when the Soviet state collapsed in December 1991. Perhaps the final page in the history of the Soviet legislature was written on 17 March 1992 in a dimly lit state farm outside of Moscow, when a rump of the USSR Congress of People's Deputies met in a futile attempt to revive the institution, and with it the USSR.[1]

The impediments to the development of legislative power had been formidable in the final years of the Soviet era. Executive institutions gave up the prerogatives of rule only grudgingly. Legislators themselves remained ambivalent, and sometimes openly hostile, to the rise of powerful representative institutions in a period of mounting social and economic crisis. And the population, initially entranced by the novelty of open parliamentary debate, seemed to tire of the tortuous and arcane procedures of the legislature.[2] Both longstanding political tradition and the policy imperatives of the moment cried out for the firm hand of the executive.

Yet it would be inappropriate to conclude that this legislative experiment failed. As the pages below make clear, the last years of Soviet rule recast executive-legislative relations in the country. The idea and practice of executive accountability to popular representatives started to take root. The legislature began to displace the executive as the center of rule-making authority, and many of the laws enacted by the legislature remained in force in the successor states of the USSR. Further, the tradition of legitimate political opposition grew, if fitfully.   It is these elements of the Soviet legislative legacy on which parliaments in the successor states have begun to build.

Executive-Legislative Relations in Soviet History

The tension between legislative and executive power has been a staple of the liberal democratic order. To assure the accountability of the state to society, legislatures in the West have struggled over the centuries to influence and restrain the power of the executive.[3] For the Bolsheviks, however, this conflict between legislature and executive was not a universal principle of modern government but a vestige from the bourgeois order, a contradiction to be overcome in a socialist revolution.   Where capitalism subordinated the parliamentary "talking shop" to the class-aligned executive, socialism in Russia promised to combine legislative and executive functions in a new "working parliament," the soviets.[4]   Thus, Lenin's slogan "All Power to the Soviets," advanced in April 1917, was more than a tactical assault on the Provisional Government. It was also a summons to unite permanently the diverse functions of state into a single institution.

The Leninist vision of a "working parliament" did not accord, however, with the demands of revolutionary rule or with Bolshevik intolerance of opposition and open debate.   Once in power, the revolutionary leadership quickly abandoned attempts to govern through the unwieldy and unreliable soviets. Instead of channeling all power to the soviets it siphoned all power from the soviets and into a separate executive hierarchy (the Sovnarkom, later Council of Ministers) and the professional apparatus of the Communist Party.[5] By the mid-1930s, the soviets were functioning as a caricature of the lifeless legislatures attributed to capitalist societies by Lenin. Selected by a ruling bureaucratic class and not by the people, the soviets assembled only long enough each session to give unanimous approval to policies and laws advanced by party and Government. Thus, the Soviet political leadership overcame the tension between legislative and executive power not by fusing Government and parliament but by emasculating thoroughly the soviets as legislative institutions.

As the democratization campaign of Gorbachev breathed new life into the soviets at the end of the 1980s, it rekindled tensions between legislature and executive.   In so doing, it raised an array of elementary questions about the realignment of power and responsibility in the Soviet political system.   What was the division of labor between legislature and executive in a Soviet political order in transition?[6] How effective was the Soviet parliament in restraining the executive? What means did it use to achieve that end? How did the mounting crises of power and authority in the USSR shape the development of legislative-executive relations? To assess these and related questions, this chapter examines three traditional sources of legislative power as they developed in the last three years of Soviet parliamentary history. These legislative prerogatives were the confirmation of executive personnel, law-making, and the oversight of executive agencies.

Legislative Powers over Executive Appointments

In European parliamentary systems, the power of the legislature rests most directly on its ability to approve and remove a Government. The leading members of the Government come from parliament and rule at the pleasure of parliament. Subject continuously to immediate recall by the legislature, the executive must offer policies and personnel that can sustain a parliamentary majority and hence the support of society.

In its formal rules, the Soviet state system followed the parliamentary model. Yet the traditional patronage monopoly enjoyed by the Soviet Communist Party apparatus eliminated the accountability of Government to parliament, which is at the core of the liberal democratic order. Governments were made and unmade not in parliament but in the party. This patronage monopoly of the Communist Party ended, however, in the spring of 1989, when competitive elections in many districts returned legislators who refused to accede to party diktat. Characterized by open debate, weakened party discipline, and a politically diverse body of deputies, the new parliament[7] exercised its long-dormant prerogative of approving a Government. For the first time in Soviet history, the parliament vigorously challenged, and in some cases rejected, personnel nominated for the country's leading executive posts.

The new parliament had two sets of candidates for executive offices to consider when it assembled for its initial session in June 1989. The first group, nominated by the chair of the USSR Supreme Soviet, Mikhail Gorbachev, included the leading figures of state, the prime minister (Nikolai Ryzhkov), the head of the People's Control Commission (Gennadii Kolbin), chair of the USSR Supreme Court (Evgenii Smolentsev), procurator-general of the USSR (Alexander Sukharev), and the chief state arbiter (Yurii Matveev). In nominating the incumbent Ryzhkov to the post of prime minister, Gorbachev admitted that while he alone had the constitutional authority to propose the candidate for head of Government, "in view of the real position that the CPSU occupies in our society as the ruling party, consultations were held with the party Central Committee regarding the nomination."[8] Thus, while the party could no longer assure confirmation of its nominees,[9] it at least retained the power to veto candidates for high executive office.

Ryzhkov won confirmation handily from the 542 seat assembly (9 deputies voted against him and 31 abstained), but only after intense questioning from the floor.[10] More than 30 deputies directed questions at the prime minister or commented on his candidacy, which some regarded as sullied by "miscalculations" in economic policy. The parliament reserved its most serious criticism of the opening session, however, for the nominee to the People's Control Committee, Gennadii Kolbin. Having led the powerful, though troubled, Communist Party of Kazakhstan for the preceding three years, Kolbin seemed an unlikely candidate for the unglamorous post of chair of the People's Control Committee. When asked by the deputies whether he would be willing to assume the new post, Kolbin replied that the Communist Party had made its decision to nominate him for the position and he would therefore accept it. This explicit statement of fealty to party over parliament troubled many deputies, including the historian Roy Medvedev, who sought to scuttle Kolbin's candidacy by nominating Boris Yeltsin for the position. Even after Yeltsin turned down the nomination and threw his support behind Kolbin, almost 20 percent of the deputies refused to support Kolbin's candidacy.[11]

Once the prime minister and the heads of free-standing legal institutions had been approved, the parliament turned to the confirmation of the ministers and other executive personnel who would comprise the new Government. Nominated by the prime minister,[12] this second, and larger, group of candidates also stood for confirmation individually. Thus, instead of approving the Government as a team, the Soviet legislature scrutinized separately Government personnel and policy in each of the areas of ministerial competence. By examining candidates for high executive office individually, in the tradition of the United States Senate, the Soviet parliament was able to exercise a finer, more discriminating, and more pervasive influence on the formation of a Government.[13]

Discussions of the candidates for executive office began in legislative committees amid much confusion about appropriate procedures for examining the nominees. Where most candidates were examined by a single committee, others came before several committees, with one serving as the guiding committee for the nomination (*golovoi komitet*).[14] For example, the Minister of Health, Evgenii Chazov, appeared before committees on the family and ecology in addition to the Joint Committee on Public Health. Within the committees, deputies struggled to define their role in the confirmation of executive personnel.

The central issue was how much information to obtain before making a decision about a nominee. Where some deputies were satisfied with the brief official biographies distributed to the examining committees, many other deputies did not wish to recommend confirmation until the candidates had given detailed testimony before the committees about their political record and plans for their ministry.[15]

Judging by the published accounts of confirmation hearings, the more insistent deputies prevailed. The consideration of nominees in committee lasted three weeks, during which many committees subjected candidates to vigorous and lengthy questioning. Although the candidate for vice-chair of the Council of Ministers for Social Questions, Alexandra Biriukova, received the recommendation of the committee, the questioning of her was so hostile that Ryzhkov personally intervened at the hearing to demand greater respect for the aging former Politburo member. "After all, we're talking about a lady. Alexandra Pavlovna is here and every word leaves its mark. Let's be kinder to one another."[16]

Very few nominees escaped what Ryzhkov called the "purgatory" of the committees.[17] Of the senior ministerial appointments, only Eduard Shevardnadze (Foreign Affairs) and Valentin Pavlov (Finance), passed parliament with a unanimous or near unanimous recommendation of the deputies. The committee hearings were especially difficult for Lira Rozenova, nominated to chair the State Committee on Prices. Only one member of the examining committee voted to approve her candidacy.[18] In all, eight of the 72 nominees for ministerial posts failed to win committee recommendation.[19] Moreover, the Committee on Legislation and Legality refused to recommend the Leningrad procurator, Aleksei Vasiliev, for the post of first deputy procurator of the USSR, and Alexander Filatov, Sergei Gusev, and Robert Tikhomirnov as members of the USSR Supreme Court.[20] The most controversial appointments, therefore, were those to legal institutions, which had become a favorite target of popular and parliamentary criticism.

The committee decisions were not binding, however, on the prime minister or parliament. In submitting his final list of nominees to the full Supreme Soviet at the end of June 1989, Ryzhkov included several candidates rejected in committee as well as one new candidate advanced by the anti-reformist labor collective movement. He also excluded from the final list two nominees who had been approved in committee. These nominees were reform-oriented candidates for places on the military collegium of the USSR Supreme Court.[21]

The confirmation debates in the full Supreme Soviet illustrated the awkward coexistence of old and new politics in the USSR. In a dramatic departure from tradition, the head of the KGB, Vladimir Kriuchkov, came before the parliament to defend his candidacy and to respond to the many critical comments directed against the KGB. In his remarks, Kriuchkov offered an unprecedented statement on the functions and operation of his agency.[22] Likewise, the minister of defense, Dmitrii Yazov, appeared before the Supreme Soviet to answer pointed questions about the armed forces. In the interpellation of Yazov, the more insistent deputies behaved as Western parliamentarians. They sought to elicit new information about the activity of the ministry, to clarify the candidate's perception of the division of responsibility in military affairs between legislature and executive, and to receive assurances of his commitment to reform.[23]

Alongside these indications of a new parliamentary assertiveness were reminders of traditions of political deference and secrecy. The selection of ministers often followed what one observer called "Young Pioneer" logic. "Fellows, I know him. He's a good man!" (*Rebiata, ia ego znaiu - khoroshii muzhik!*).[24] At times one could hear cries from the floor: "Comrades, let's give Nikolai Ivanovich [Ryzhkov] a chance to form his own team!"[25] While Gorbachev generally refrained from using his post as head of state to support individual candidates, he threw aside protocol in the confirmation of the minister of defense. Gorbachev concluded the confirmation debate on Yazov with a vigorous speech in support of the defense minister. Although most of these debates reached a large and attentive national audience by television, on occasion coverage was suspended when the questioning of candidates raised volatile political issues. The most controversial appointments in this regard appear to have been nominees to the USSR Supreme Court and the USSR Procuracy.[26]

The consideration of Ryzhkov's nominees by the full Supreme Soviet resulted in a defeat for the prime minister in several portfolios. The parliament rejected nominees to head the Ministry of Rails, the Ministry of Timber Industry, and the Foreign Economic Commission, even though candidates for the latter two posts had received committee recommendations. If the parliament in fact contained an "aggressively obedient majority," its loyalties lay elsewhere than with the prime minister. It was evident from both the committee and parliamentary debates that the Supreme Soviet in most instances was using its confirmation prerogative to express its displeasure with Government policy in the minister's area of competence and not with the nominees themselves. A case in point was price policy. Echoing popular fear of rising prices, the parliament refused to approve the promotion of Lira Rozenova from deputy chair to chair of the State Committee on Prices. Yet the chair of the State Committee on Prices, Valentin Pavlov, won confirmation easily as the new minister of finance.

Conservative and reformist legislators appear to have united to defeat Ryzhkov's nominees for what might be termed thankless posts, where ministerial performance was both unpopular and unlikely to improve. With the Ministry of Rails threatened by strikes and pilloried in the press, the parliament refused to confirm a new railroad minister. One deputy admitted that the nominee "was not to blame and probably should be elected ... [but] we should make it understood that we are able to protect the people's interest from the department. I am going to vote against him."[27]   Similarly, candidates failed to receive confirmation to head departments responsible for environmental degradation, such as the water resources and timber industry ministries. The newly-created Environment Ministry was the target of such popular anger that Ryzhkov offered the post to four persons before he found someone—the only non-Communist in the Government—willing to be nominated for the position.

Once the Government was in place,[28] the confirmation power of parliament was used sparingly since there was neither a new parliamentary election nor a political crisis that might have required the formation of a new Government. During its subsequent sessions in 1989 and 1990 the Soviet parliament confirmed only a handful of nominees for vacant or newly-vacated ministerial positions before being asked at the beginning of 1991 to review candidates for a new institution, the Cabinet of Ministers, discussed below.   But while the confirmation prerogative was used only episodically, it established an important precedent of executive accountability to the legislature. Gorbachev reminded deputies in closing the initial session of the new Supreme Soviet that "for the first time in the entire post-Lenin period we have created a Government, each member of which must pass rigorous muster with the deputies ...."[29]

One must be cautious, however, in using the parliamentary confirmation of the Government in 1989 as evidence of a fundamental and permanent realignment of executive-legislative relations.   Executive power was broader than the Ryzhkov Government, and therefore in restraining Ryzhkov and the Government the parliament strengthened contending forces in the Soviet executive. Gorbachev and supporting elements in the party Central Committee apparatus may have encouraged a free vote, or even a no vote, on selected nominees for Government posts. Such a strategy would have enhanced Gorbachev's position by providing evidence that his campaign for democratization was taking root, by undermining the personal authority of his sometime rival Ryzhkov, and by refocusing elite and mass anger away from Gorbachev and the party and toward the Government and individual ministries. But whatever the role of Gorbachev in the formation and confirmation of the Ryzhkov Government, his relations with Ryzhkov were recast in early 1990 with the creation of the office of president of the USSR. This hastily-conceived institutional reform realigned executive power and weakened significantly parliament's ability to restrain and influence that power.[30] The rise of presidentialism dramatically reduced the role of the legislature in Soviet and post-Soviet politics.

At the end of 1989, amid building economic and ethnic crises, Gorbachev found himself without an effective institutional base from which to govern. He could no longer rely on the party as an instrument of rule. Its authority was collapsing, and the logic of his own campaign of democratization favored a shift of power from the party to the state. Yet his position as head of state (chair of the Supreme Soviet) enabled him to wield power only indirectly, through Government and parliament. There appeared to be only two avenues of escape. The first was to unseat Ryzhkov and rule as prime minister. Besides the political firestorm that a confrontation with Ryzhkov may have unleashed, this course would have exposed Gorbachev to direct parliamentary accountability and to the rigors of managing a national economy, a task for which he was ill prepared. The second, and more attractive, path for Gorbachev was to create a strong presidency for himself on the French model. The presidential option would give Gorbachev a base of power independent of Government and parliament. From this position well above the political fray, Gorbachev, like de Gaulle, could set the tone for the political debate and intervene at decisive moments to direct political developments.[31]

In grafting a strong presidency onto its traditional parliamentary system, the Soviet Union pushed executive-legislative relations even further in the direction of executive dominance. A hybrid presidential/parliamentary system, born in France of the frustrations with the overbearing parliaments of the Third and Fourth Republics, was now transplanted to a country with virtually no legislative tradition, much less legislative power.[32] This addition of the presidency to Government and parliament altered the politics of 1989 in two important respects. First, the Government gained an additional institutional master. The prime minister looked up to the president as well as down to the parliament. The parliament, therefore, was forced to share its oversight of Government with a president whose powers to dismiss and nominate ministers (the latter with the approval of parliament) made him a potent contender for the attention of the Government.[33] Furthermore, the president acquired new executive powers not enjoyed previously by the prime minister or the chair of the Supreme Soviet. Some enabled the president to restrict legislative action (e.g., the right to veto parliamentary legislation), while others enabled him to rule without reference to parliament (e.g., the right to issue binding decrees). Outlining the responsibilities of the presidency, Anatolii Lukianov, Gorbachev's protege and replacement as chair of the Supreme Soviet, explained that "the USSR Government, ministers, and state committees are guided in their activity not only by USSR laws [passed by parliament] but also by the decrees of the president."[34]

At the very moment when the Soviet parliament was beginning to assert its long dormant lawmaking power, the presidency appeared on the scene to challenge this traditional prerogative of the legislature.

Lawmaking in the Old and New Soviet Politics

The new politics in the USSR gave birth to a "war of laws." On one level, this war set legislation adopted by central Government and parliament against laws enacted by republican institutions. At stake was nothing less than the sovereignty of Soviet rule in the republics. But another war of laws was occuring at the center of the Soviet state. The combatants in this war were the laws of the parliament, the regulations of Government and its ministries, and, after March 1990, the decrees of the president. At stake here was the distribution of power within the executive and between the executive and the legislature.

Until 1989, the Soviet parliament had shown little signs of life as a lawmaking institution. Each year the Supreme Soviet adopted on average only 3-5 laws and 15-20 normative edicts.[35] The parliamentary laws that did appear were often ignored by the executives of the party and Government who were responsible for implementing policy.[36] But if the Soviet Union lacked a sizable and cohesive body of authoritative parliamentary laws, it was awash in a sea of normative acts issued by the Council of Ministers and its constituent ministries. Each year the Government issued more than a thousand decrees and the ministries tens of thousands of departmental instructions.[37] While most of these departmental instructions were internal directives designed to regulate the operation of a single bureaucracy, many ministries and state committees issued instructions that were binding on other central Government institutions and on the citizenry.[38] In 1987, approximately 10,000-15,000 all-union departmental instructions were binding beyond the issuing institution.[39] Alongside these governmental acts was a vast number of party directives and joint party-Government decrees that had the force of law even if they lacked its pedigree.[40]

Not only did Government and party decrees swamp parliamentary laws in number, they took precedent over them in shaping the behavior of the state and society. Although Government decrees were formally subordinate to the constitution and the laws of parliament, they outranked them in the daily administration of Soviet life. "One holds a bureaucrat accountable not for a 'violation' of the Constitution," one legal scholar remarked, "but for a violation of an instruction."[41] There was simply no enforcement mechanism in place to ensure that the hierarchical principle of legislation was respected in the Soviet Union.

The rulemaking power of the executive was one of the least visible but firmest pillars of traditional Soviet politics. It denied society the stability of laws found even in modern authoritarian states. Facing Government rules that were pervasive, obscure, and mercurial, Soviet officials sought refuge in networks of party patronage that could protect them from "state discipline," a term used to describe the respect due Government regulations. All Soviet citizens sought protection from the vagaries of Government rules by avoiding risks, by "overinsuring" themselves in the Soviet vernacular.

> Everyone, from ministers to primary school teachers, is waiting for instructions. Any act is preceded with the question: "Tell us first, is this all right?" For everything there is a need to secure preliminary consent and guaranteed success.[42]

Two institutional innovations at the end of the 1980s began to challenge this role of Government rules in the Soviet political system. The first was the invigoration of the Soviet parliament, the second the formation of a Constitutional Review Committee, one of whose tasks was the settlement of disputes in the war of laws. The new parliament formed in 1989 broke the virtual monopoly enjoyed by the Government and party in the purveying of legal norms. In its first year and a half, the new parliament adopted 69 laws,[43] an unprecedented level of legislative activity for a Soviet parliament. The new body of parliamentary laws was impressive both in its breadth and detail. By enacting laws that contained more specific provisions than was traditional in Soviet legislative practice, the new parliament sought to hinder attempts by the Government to fill the interstices of laws with regulations that violated legislative intent.

Even before parliamentary laws assumed a more prominent place in the Soviet normative order, Government rules themselves had come under attack. Following the Communist Party plenum of June 1987, commissions of the Supreme Soviet as well as internal working groups in Government ministries began to eliminate some substatutory legislation that had been overtaken by newer regulations or that stood in the path of reform legislation. A prominent legal official reported that by the summer of 1989 tens of thousands of Government decrees and departmental instructions had been annulled.[44]

At the end of the 1980s, the secrecy as well as the scale of Government rulemaking became a subject of reform. Traditionally, only the parliament's laws and a small portion of the decrees of the Council of Ministers were published. The vast body of Government instructions that gave direction to Soviet life was obscured from public view, distributed in effect as internal Government memoranda.[45] Unable to discover rules governing such basic questions as residence permits (*propiski*) and housing and labor rights, Soviet citizens operated in ignorance of the legal consequences of their actions. Lacking the direction of authoritative parliamentary laws and knowledge about most substatutory acts, Government officials regularly issued instructions that contravened other substatutory acts. The Soviet normative order, in short, was an impenetrable labyrinth that encouraged arbitrariness and not a rule of law.

In a decision that appeared at the time to have far-reaching implications for executive-legislative relations in the USSR, the Constitutional Review Committee ruled in November 1990 that the Soviet Government could no longer withhold publication of acts affecting the rights of citizens. Citing as authority Article 59 of the USSR Constitution as well as international treaties to which the Soviet Union was a signatory, the committee held that when citizens' rights were at issue publication must precede implementation. The committee gave the Government three months to publish these instructions. Instructions affecting citizens' rights that remained unpublished at the end of February 1991 were to lose legal force, though the Cabinet of Ministers ordered the publications of such acts only on 22 June 1991.[46]

The rulemaking prerogative of the executive came under attack, then, from two sides. The parliament sought to assert its claim to legislative sovereignty by adopting more detailed laws more frequently and by pruning from the normative pyramid large numbers of substatutory acts that are politically or legally compromised.[47] The Constitutional Review Committee, for its part, took a dramatic first step in asserting the primacy of constitutional principles enacted by the legislature over the detailed instructions issued by the Government. In this and other rulings that addressed disputes between legislature and executive, this proto-constitutional court used its authority to strengthen the parliament's role in the Soviet political system.[48]

A major question at the end of Soviet history was whether the executive would respect the laws of parliament and the rulings of the court. In the first years of Gorbachev's tenure, the Government and its ministries issued a wave of substatutory acts designed to block reform-oriented legislation enacted by the still party-controlled parliament. No sooner had the USSR Supreme Soviet adopted the Law on the State Enterprise than "ministries and departments so overloaded it with instructions that economic officials confirmed with one voice: the Law is not taking effect!"[49] After 1989 the resistance of some ministries to the laws of parliament lessened. For example, the mere threat of a ruling by the Constitutional Review Committee on the question of residence permits led the Council of Ministers to annul 30 decrees where the rules on *propiski* discriminated against the rights of certain categories of citizens.[50] But even officials as conservative as Anatolii Lukianov admitted that "new norms and principles meet with harsh resistance from old structures, which in essence are blocking laws."[51] When asked by the journal *Argumenty i fakty* in the fall of 1990 why the laws passed by parliament were not being enforced, Lukianov responded that the Soviet Union did not yet have "implementation discipline."[52]

Who was blocking the implementation of the laws? Most immediately, individual ministries who had traditionally pursued their own narrow branch or deparmental interests with scant regard for written norms from above. A basic ingredient of the old "command and administer" system, "departmentalism" (*vedomstvennost'*) remained largely unaltered in the Gorbachev era.   "Our ministries and ministers continue to feel themselves independent," complained a deputy at the end of 1990.[53] Another noted that

> the Supreme Soviet calmly looks on as the laws it has adopted go unfulfilled. The executors—ministries, departments, and officials—explain, in a mocking way, that your laws have no mechanism for implementing legal norms. Who should call to account those people who sabotage legislative acts adopted by the supreme body of power?[54]

Undoubtedly resistance to parliamentary legislation was at times encouraged, or at least acquiesced in, by the prime minister and other leading Government and party officials. But the continued existence of departmental fiefdoms devoted to economic and political autarky was as much a challenge to president or prime minister as to parliament.

It was in part to combat departmentalism that Gorbachev expanded the powers of the new presidency at the end of 1990.[55]   Where the original presidential mandate was to control the executive through the prime minister, subsequent changes granted the president more direct leadership of Government ministries. The Council of Ministers was transformed into a Cabinet of Ministers, signalling its direct subordination to the president and the loss of status and authority of its head, the prime minister. The creation of a vice-presidency weakened further the office of prime minister. Individual ministries with responsibilities in the areas of law enforcement, national defense, and foreign affairs were linked in a new Security Council, which answered directly to the president. In a move reminiscent of Lenin's formation of a workers' and peasants' inspectorate, Gorbachev sought to create a new state inspectorate to serve as the president's personal corps of observers of ministerial behavior.[56] Moreover, to direct that behavior into desired channels, Gorbachev issued numerous executive decrees in his almost two years as president.

These reforms did little to enhance implementation discipline but much to erode the power of parliament. In streamlining the executive, Gorbachev began to uncouple the Government from parliament, thereby shifting its formal as well as de facto accountability from the legislature to the supreme political leader. "If my perspectives begin to differ from those of the president," Prime Minister Pavlov noted in February 1991, "it would be better for me to resign immediately. Under presidential rule, disagreements between the prime minister and president are not acceptable."[57] (Pavlov had changed his mind by August of that year, when he chose to launch a coup against the president rather than resign.) According to revisions in the constitution adopted in 1990, the Supreme Soviet no longer confirmed (*utverzhdaet*) the members of the Government but merely gave its agreement (*daet svoe soglasie*) to nominees appointed by the president.[58]   Whereas previously the prime minister proposed ministerial candidates to parliament, beginning in late 1990 the president formally appointed (*naznachaet*) them by a decree. Although parliament had the option to overturn an appointment, there was a presumption of confirmation not present in 1989. In parliamentary debates in February 1991 on nominees to the Cabinet of Ministers, Prime Minister Pavlov asserted that deputies could no longer use the occasion of reviewing a candidate to raise issues of policy within the nominee's area of competence.[59] Parliament was increasingly forced into "take it or leave it" decisions on executive proposals, a traditional mark of executive dominance of the legislature.

Openly frustrated with what he perceived to be the lack of discipline and efficiency of the parliament, Gorbachev began to circumvent the legislative process altogether by issuing presidential decrees on pressing issues of public policy.[60] In September 1990, he succeeded in convincing the parliament to grant him extraordinary power for approximately 500 days to issue directives on economic policy that had the standing of law.[61] Although parliament retained the right to annul these decrees, it was reluctant to restrain presidential power in the midst of a deepening economic crisis. By acquiescing to the expansion of presidential power in 1990, an obedient and intimidated majority in parliament reduced significantly the ability of the legislature to hold the executive politically accountable. As Gorbachev turned to the Right in the last year of Soviet history, the parliament made only symbolic gestures to return the country to a more reform-oriented path.

Legislative Oversight of the Executive

A universal feature of modern government is the executive's superior access to information and expertise.   A monumental challenge for the Soviet parliament—and now for the parliaments in the successor states—was to develop from scratch access to information and expertise, both from the executive and from its own and independent sources. The policy of glasnost and the rise of a vigorous press gave the new parliament knowledge about executive behavior and social and economic conditions unrivalled since the early years of Soviet power. Parliamentary committees and commissions, for their part, were able to draw heavily on the expertise of specialists from universities and research institutes to educate deputies and to assist in legislative drafting. In addition, there were small but growing committee staffs,[62] though most parliamentary support personnel worked in the presidium, whose close political ties to the executive leadership made it as much an appendage of executive as legislative power.[63]

To oversee effectively the execution of the laws, a parliament must also have the means to extract information directly from Government agencies. While the interpellation of ministers making reports to parliament generated some information, it was the deputy's *zapros* that was designed to allow parliament to probe with depth and regularity into the bureaucracy.[64] An oral or written question posed by one or more deputies to an executive agency, a *zapros* had to be answered within a month by the official to whom it was directed. When a violation of the law was at issue, a response had to be made within three days.[65] From the middle of 1989 to the middle of 1990, deputies addressed 8200 *zaprosy* to the USSR Procuracy alone.[66] This avalanche of *zaprosy* directed to executive agencies was more than a request for information. It served to remind Government officials of the intensity of parliamentary concern about problems within their jurisdiction.[67]

Their heavy usage notwithstanding, the *zaprosy* were not always effective instruments of parliamentary oversight. Perceptions of their effectiveness varied according to the observer as well as the subject of the *zapros*. A.M. Yakovlev, a reformist legal scholar, insisted that deputies were granted ready access to information possessed by the executive.[68] Some deputies, however, were dissatisfied with responses to *zaprosy*, particularly on matters of foreign affairs, national security, and finance.[69] The Western analyst Michael Tsypkin reported that

> to counteract Ministry of Defense stonewalling, the more radical committee members [in the Committee for Defense and State Security] are coming to rely on individuals they euphemistically refer to as 'consultants'. These are in reality whistleblowers—defense industry specialists and military and KGB officers who, despite threats of retribution, are said to provide information that their agencies are trying to conceal.[70]

What was needed, one Soviet journalist argued, was a law on information that held accountable those in the executive who provided disinformation to parliament.[71]

The vigor of parliamentary oversight of the executive was limited on a very practical level by the deputies' continuing dependence on the state for the provision of scarce goods and services. As Peter Solomon illustrated in a study of the roots of localism in Soviet political culture, legal and political officials often abandoned professional and institutional loyalties to bind themselves to individuals or networks of officials who could supply the essentials of life, such as apartments, telephones, transportation, and education.[72] Soviet legislators were subject to many of the same pressures that this "goods dependency" created.[73] Indeed, the radical deputy Galina Starovoitova claimed that at the end of 1990 deputies succumbed to Gorbachev's pressure to shift power from parliament to presidency because they had been bought off by apartments and other goods provided by the executive.[74] In the ultimate demonstration of goods dependency, the members of the Congress of People's Deputies agreed in September 1991 to vote themselves out of existence provided they retained their pay and perquisites through the end of their term.   In a country without a market, where one made a life from politics and not for politics, the executive's virtual monopoly of economic resources encouraged deference in the attitudes and behavior of deputies.[75]

The Soviet executive also learned to court deputies by pursuing policies that benefitted certain electoral districts, a practice widespread in the United States and many other Western countries. In deliberations on the budget, for example, deputies tried to obtain from the ministries special projects for their constituencies. Ministerial officials, in turn, attempted to mobilize the support of potentially sympathetic deputies who could help them acquire resources above plan or budget.[76] This cooperation between "localist" and "departmentalist" interests, long a feature of behind-the-scenes bargaining in Soviet budgetary politics, was a revealing example of the adaptation of longstanding traditions to the reformed structures of Soviet politics. This adaptation was viewed with alarm by both Gorbachev and radical reformists, who shared a distaste for Madisonian principles that legitimated the open pursuit of partial interests.

Conclusion

At the end of the 1980s, the democratization campaign in the USSR set off a chain reaction in Soviet politics. Competitive elections brought the rise of a vigorous, if poorly organized, opposition in the USSR Supreme Soviet. The parliamentary opposition then transformed executive-legislative relations by challenging, for the first time in modern Soviet history, the personnel and policies advanced by the party and Government leadership. To be sure, these challenges usually failed. The Soviet Government, like governments in all parliamentary systems, relied on a majority in parliament to sustain most of its proposals. It also relied on a fifth column within the parliament, the presidium of the Supreme Soviet, headed by Anatolii Lukianov, to serve as a kind of institutional whip for the executive leadership. But some policies and personnel did not receive the support of parliament. Moreover, the mere use of parliamentary prerogatives so long ignored heightened the expectations in Government, in society, and in parliament itself that the executive would be, and should be, accountable to the legislature.[77]

The appearance in 1990 of a new executive institution, the presidency, dashed these expectations by reclaiming for the president much of the power that had flowed to the parliament from party and Government in 1989, most notably in the areas of lawmaking and Government oversight. In assuming the presidency, Gorbachev appeared to be less troubled by the realignment of executive-legislative relations than by the inability and/or unwillingness of the legislature to bring under control independent-minded ministries and republics.[78] Originally frustrated with the Communist Party as a vehicle of reform, Gorbachev abandoned the parliament as well in favor of the presidency, an instrument of rule that he believed would be at once more responsive and powerful.[79] But paradoxically it was the very efficiency of presidential rule in undermining the pillars of the old order—the Communist Party and Jacobin politics—that encouraged the coup against President Gorbachev in August 1991. The failure of that coup swept away the structures of central authority and opened a new era in executive-legislative relations, this time in the successor states of the USSR.

Notes

This is an updated and slightly revised version of "Legislative-Executive Relations in the New Soviet Political Order," *Perestroika-Era Politics: The New Soviet Legislature and Gorbachev's Political Reforms*, ed. Robert Huber and Donald Kelley (Armonk, NY: M.E. Sharpe, Inc., 1991), pp. 153-173.

1. *Novosti* (Russian Television Channel One), 17 March 1992, 18:05 GMT.

2. Polls indicated that popular support for representative institutions in Russia and the Soviet Union was limited. For example, a survey of 1600 Muscovites in late October 1991 found that only 28 percent supported the retention of an elected city council. "Moskovskie oprosy," *Rossiia*, 6-12 November 1991, p. 1.

3. The rise of modern, disciplined parties has of course moderated this tension in political systems that have strong parliamentary majorities.

4. V. Lenin, *The State and Revolution* (New York: International Publishers, 1932), pp. 35-44.

5. The most compelling account of this process remains L. Schapiro, *The Origins of the Communist Autocracy. Political Opposition in the Soviet State, First Phase, 1917-1922*, Second edition (Cambridge, MA: Harvard University Press, 1977).

6. Soviet scholars began in the mid-1980s to discuss the problem of the separation of powers in Soviet politics. See B. Lazarev, "'Razdelenie vlastei' i opyt sovetskogo gosudarstva," *Kommunist*, no. 16 (1988), and Iu. Tikhomirov, "Vlast' v obshchestve: edinstvo i razdelenie," *Sovetskoe gosudarstvo i pravo*, no. 2 (1990), pp. 35-43.

7. Unless otherwise specified, the term parliament will be used to refer to the USSR Supreme Soviet. The term legislature will be used more broadly, to embrace both the USSR Supreme Soviet and the USSR Congress of People's Deputies. The latter was an assembly of 2250 people's deputies that selected from among its members 542 persons to sit in the USSR Supreme Soviet, which was in effect the country's standing parliament. On the rise of Soviet legislative institutions at the end of the 1980s, see Michael E. Urban, *More Power to the Soviets. The Democratic Revolution in the USSR* (Aldershot, UK: Edward Elgar Publishing, 1990).

8. "The First Session of the USSR Supreme Soviet," *Izvestiia*, 9 June 1989, in *Current Digest of the Soviet Press* [hereafter *CDSP*], no. 31 (1989), p. 25.

9. Dawn Mann reported that nominees for Government posts in the summer of 1989 were still approved first in the Central Committee of the party. "Gorbachev's Personnel Policy: The USSR Council of Ministers," *Report on the USSR*, 17 November 1989, pp. 11-12.

10. "The First Session of the USSR Supreme Soviet," *Izvestiia*, 9 June 1989, in *CDSP*, no. 31 (1989), p. 25.

11. *Ibid.* The candidate for Procurator-General, A. Sukharev, proved to be almost as unpopular among the deputies as Kolbin. He was attacked from the Right for losing the war against crime and from the Left for failing to take more decisive measures to humanize Soviet justice. Sukharev's position was weakened further by a reputation for indecision within the Procuracy.

12. Formally, the Prime Minister presented only the leading members of Government to the parliament for confirmation. These included the deputy prime ministers, the Council of Ministers administrator of affairs (*upravliaiushchii delami*), the ministers of foreign affairs, defense, internal affairs, and finance, and the head of the KGB. The deputy prime ministers in turn proposed the remaining ministers and presented their resumes to the parliament. "N.I. Ryzhkov: Learning to Work Together," *Izvestiia*, 24 June 1989, p. 1, in *Foreign Broadcast Information Service* [hereafter *FBIS*], 26 June 1989, p. 45.

13. If the performance of the Government as a whole was regarded as unsatisfactory, the parliament could by a two-thirds majority express no confidence in the Government and "raise the question" about changing its composition. "Reglament S"ezda narodnykh deputatov SSSR i Verkhovnogo Soveta SSSR," *Vedomosti S"ezda narodnykh deputatov SSSR i Verkhovnogo Soveta SSSR* [hereafter *Vedomosti SSSR*], no. 29 (1989), item 565.

14. The distribution of committee responsibilities in the confirmation process was made by the presidium of the Supreme Soviet.

15. "A Good Beginning is Half the Job," *Izvestiia*, 20 June 1989, in *CDSP*, no. 34 (1989), pp. 17-18; A. Grobov *et al.*, "Examination for Minister," *Izvestiia*, 23 June 1989, in *CDSP*, no. 34 (1989), p. 19.

16. A. Luity *et al.*, "The Soviet Government is Being Formed," *Pravda*, 23 June 1989, in *CDSP*, no. 34 (1989), pp. 20-21.

17. "N.I. Ryzhkov's Report at the First Session of the USSR Supreme Soviet," *Pravda*, 28 June 1989, in *CDSP*, no. 35 (1989), pp. 13-14.

18. V. Dolganov *et al.*, "A Most Demanding Test," *Izvestiia*, 24 June 1989, in *CDSP*, no. 34 (1989), pp. 19-20.

19. Two of the nominees were withdrawn before being voted on by the committees.

20. A. Luity *et al.*, "The Soviet Government is Being Formed," *Pravda*, 23 June 1989, in *CDSP*, no. 34 (1989), pp. 20-21.

21. V. Dolganov *et al.*, "They will Stand Guard over the Law," *Izvestiia*, 7 July 1989, in *CDSP*, no. 36 (1989), pp. 11-12.

22. E. Gonzalez *et al.*, "The Formation of the Government nears Completion," *Izvestiia*, 14 July 1989, in *CDSP*, no. 36 (1989), p. 16; V. Dolganov and I. Korolkov, "The USSR State Security Committee in the Light of Glasnost," *Izvestiia*, 15 July 1989, in *CDSP*, no. 36 (1989), p. 17.

23. I. Korolkov *et al.*, "Ministers get the OKAY," *Izvestiia*, 3 July 1989, in *CDSP*, no. 35 (1989), p. 17.

24. P. Voshchanov, "Portfel' dlia ministra," *Komsomol'skaia pravda*, 22 July 1989, p. 3.

25. *Ibid.*

26. G. Alimov *et al.*, "Two Weeks of Debates are Behind Us," *Izvestiia*, 8 July 1989, in *CDSP*, no. 36 (1989), pp. 12-13.

27. V. Dolganov *et al.*, "The Situation in the Branch and the Minister's Program," *Izvestiia*, 6 July 1989, in *CDSP*, no. 36 (1989), p. 11. The same nominee was confirmed by parliament several weeks later. V. Dolganov and R. Lynyov, "The Session is Over, the Work Continues," *Izvestiia*, 5 August 1989, in *CDSP*, no. 38 (1989), p. 18.

28. On the composition of the new Government, see A. Rahr, "Ryzhkov's New Cabinet," *Report on the USSR*, 30 June 1989, pp. 13-16.

29. "Speech by M.S. Gorbachev on the Conclusion of the Work of the First Session of the USSR Supreme Soviet," *Pravda*, 5 August 1989, in *CDSP*, no. 38 (1989), p. 19.

30. On the formation of the presidency, see E. Teague, "Executive Presidency Approved," *Report on the USSR*, 9 March 1990, pp. 14-16; and E. Teague, "The Powers of the Soviet Presidency," *Report on the USSR*, 23 March 1990, pp. 4-7.

31. The leading figures of the political science and legal communities in the USSR rushed to justify the formation of a strong presidency. See, for example, F. Burlatskii, "Prezident i razdelenie vlasti," *Izvestiia*, 10 February 1990, p. 3, and a discussion with V. Kudriavtsev and others in "Dostatochno li vlasti v vlasti?" *Izvestiia*, 4 February 1990, p. 3.

32. On the functions and powers of the presidency, see "Ob uchrezhdenii posta Prezidenta SSSR i vnesenii izmenenii i dopolnenii v Konstitutsiiu (Osnovoi Zakon) SSSR," *Vedomosti SSSR*, no. 12 (1990), item 189.

33. The president was denied the power to dismiss members of the Supreme Court or the Constitutional Review Committee, reportedly a compromise forced on him by the legislature. E. Teague, "The Powers of the Soviet Presidency," *Report on the USSR*, 23 March 1990, pp. 6-7.

34. "On Making Changes in and Additions to the USSR Constitution (Basic Law) and Establishing the Post of President of the USSR," *Izvestiia*, 13 March 1990, in *CDSP*, no. 11 (1990), pp. 7-8. On the formation of the presidency, see B. Lazarev, "Prezident SSSR," *Sovetskoe gosudarstvo i pravo*, no. 7 (1990), pp. 3-14.

35. The following account of lawmaking in the Soviet Union draws heavily on E. Huskey, "Government Rulemaking as a Brake on Perestroika," *Law and Social Inquiry*, no. 3 (1990), pp. 419-432.

36. On the distinction between "declarative-propagangist" and "working" legislation, see A. Obolenskii, "Kakuiu politicheskuiu sistemu my unasledovali (anatomiia 'doaprel'skogo' politicheskogo rezhima)," *Sovetskoe gosudarstvo i pravo*, no. 10 (1990), pp. 69-71.

37. "O verkhovenstve zakona i stikhii podzakonnykh aktov," *Izvestiia*, 20 February 1989, p. 2.

38. These norms, variously labeled as generally obligatory (*obshcheobiazatel'nye*) or extradepartmental (*nadvedomstvennye*), emerged primarily from the most powerful governmental institutions, such as the Ministry of Finance, the Ministry of Internal Affairs, and the State Committee on Prices.

39. S. Polenina and N. Sil'chenko, *Nauchnye osnovy tipologii normativno-pravovykh aktov v SSSR* (Moscow, 1987), p. 93; "Opiat' ob instruktsiiakh," *Izvestiia*, 23 September 1987, p. 3.

40. On the role of party directives and joint party-Government decrees in the Soviet normative order, see S. Alekseev, *Pravo i perestroika: voprosy, razdum'ia, prognozy* (Moscow: Iuridicheskaia literatura, 1987), p. 51; and D. Barry, "The *Spravochnik Partiinogo Rabotnika* as a Source of Party Law," in *Ruling Communist Parties and Their Status under Law*, ed. D. Loeber (Dordrecht, Netherlands: Martinus Nijhoff Publishers, 1986), pp. 37-52. After the XIX Party Conference, the party and Government were to have halted the publication of joint decrees. But as V. Sazonov pointed out, because high-ranking officials of the Government represented a large share of the Central Committee, central party ties with the ministries continued to be very close, if at times troubled. "TsK KPSS i perestroika," *Argumenty i fakty*, no. 5 (1990), p. 6. In fact, there were instances of continued use of such party-Government decrees. See, for example, "O merakh po finansovomu ozdorovleniiu ekonomiki i ukrepleniiu denezhnogo obrashcheniia v strane 1989-1990 gg. i v trinadtsatoi piatiletke," of 15 March 1989. *Sobranie postanovlenii Pravitel'stva SSSR*, no. 22 (1989), item 69. E. Primakov reported that the Central Committee often complained that the Council of Ministers failed to implement party directive, while the Council of Ministers believed that the party issued unfulfillable orders. "O vlasti i privilegiiakh," *Argumenty i fakty*, no. 10 (1990), p. 2.

41. E. Lukianova, *Zakon kak istochnik sovetskogo gosudarstvennogo prava* (Moscow: Izdatel'stvo moskovskogo universiteta, 1988), p. 33.

42. N. Belyayeva, "Rule Out Loopholes in the Law," *Moscow News*, no. 21 (1989), p. 12.

43. This figure is based on a count of substantive laws (*zakony*) enacted by the USSR Supreme Soviet and published in *Vedomosti S"ezda narodnykh deputatov SSSR i Verkhovnogo Soveta SSSR* from June 1989 through December 1990.

44. "... s S. Emel'ianovym," *Sovetskaia iustitsiia*, no. 1 (1989), p. 6.

45. If only the entire ministerial "kitchen" was opened up, one reformist argued, there would be an end to the politics of stagnation.   V. Krichagin, "Vedomstvennaia glasnost'," *Argumenty i fakty*, no. 23 (1990), p. 3.

46. "O pravilakh, dopuskaiushchikh primenenie neopublikovannykh normativnykh aktov o pravakh, svobodakh i obiazannostiiakh grazhdan," *Vedomosti SSSR*, no. 50 (1990), item 1080; "O poriadke opublikovaniia postanovlenii Kabineta Ministrov SSSR i mezhdunarodnykh dogovorov," *Sobranie postanovlenii Pravitel'stva SSSR*, nos. 18-19 (1991), item 74.

47. In order to ensure the implementation of laws, some reformists wanted parliament to review in committee all ministerial instructions issued on the basis of laws.   M. Buzhkevich, "V dvukh ipostasiakh," *Pravda*, 29 June 1990, p. 3.

48. The head of the Constitutional Review Committee, Sergei Alekseev, recognized, however, that "a purely parliamentary solution historically has led to blind alleys."   In arguing for a strong and effective Government alongside a strong parliament, he referred to the lessons of France before the Fifth Republic.   "The Extraordinary Third Congress of USSR People's Deputies," *Izvestiia*, 13 March 1990, in *CDSP*, no. 11 (1990), pp. 2-3.

49. "Pravovoe gosudarstvo: kakim emu byt'?" *Pravda*, 2 August 1988, p. 2.

50. S. Alekseev, "Tret'ia vlast'," *Izvestiia*, 23 February 1991, p. 3.   This is an article of major significance for understanding the Constitutional Review Committee, written by its head.   See also D. Kerimov i A. Ekimov, "Konstitutsionnyi nadzor v SSSR," *Sovetskoe gosudarstvo i pravo*, no. 9 (1990), pp. 3-13.   On the question of *propiski* generally, see T. Merzliakova, "Izgoi po ... zakonu: sovmestima li sistema propiski s pravama cheloveka?" *Izvestiia*, 6 February 1991, p. 3.

51. "Vysokaia otvetstvennost' zakonodatel'noi vlasti (doklad Lukianova)," *Izvestiia*, 10 September 1990, p. 3.   See also A. Stepovoi, "Posle parlamentskikh kanikul," *Izvestiia*, 4 September 1990, p. 1.

52. "Nel'zia idti vpered, gliadia nazad," *Argumenty i fakty*, no. 39 (1990), p. 2.

53. Interview with V.A. Shapovalenko, USSR People's Deputy, Moscow Television Evening News (*Vremia*), 30 November, 1990, 18:10 GMT.

54. V. Dolganov and A. Stepovoi, "Time is Running Out," *Izvestiia*, 1 June 1990, in *CDSP*, no. 23 (1990), p. 10.

55. For an outline and justification of these changes, see "The President Proposes his Program," *Izvestiia*, 17 November 1990, in *CDSP*, no. 46 (1990), pp. 10-11; S. Chugayev, "The USSR President's Proposals are Supported," *Izvestiia*, 5 December 1990, in *CDSP*, no. 49 (1990), p. 13; and "Bring Life into the Constitution, and Bring the Constitution into Life," *Pravda*, 22 December 1990, in *CDSP*, no. 2 (1991), pp. 13-15.   On parliament's response to the proposed changes, see A. Stepovoi and S.

Chugayev, "Once Again about the Situation in the Country," *Izvestiia*, 23 November 1990, in *CDSP*, no. 47 (1990), p. 13.

56. In theory, "the functions of the Supreme State Inspectorate cannot and must not overlap either the functions of parliamentary control or the functions of prosecutor's supervision." "Bring Life into the Constitution, and Bring the Constitution into Life," p. 14. It is inconceivable, however, that there was not considerable overlap in practice.

57. M. Krushinskii, "Plan, rynok i ... kartoshka (Press-konferentsiia V.S. Pavlova)," *Izvestiia*, 23 February 1991, p. 1.

58. "Ob uchrezhdenii posta Prezidenta SSSR i vnesenii izmenenii i dopolnenii v Konstitutsiiu (Osnovnoi zakon) SSSR," *Vedomosti SSSR*, no. 12 (1990), item 189. The powers of the presidency were set out in Article 127 of the revised constitution.

59. A. Stepovoi i S. Chugaev, "Obsuzhdaetsia zakon o Kabinete ministrov," *Izvestiia*, 28 February 1991, p. 1.

60. Some deputies sought unsuccessfully to challenge the legal standing of presidential decrees. L. Aksenov *et al.*, "Otkrylas' sessiia Verkhovnogo Soveta SSSR," *Izvestiia*, 10 September 1990, p. 1.

61. D. Mann, "*Ukaz* and Effect: Gorbachev is Granted Additional Powers," *Report on the USSR*, 5 October 1990, pp. 1-4. Even before this formal shift of lawmaking authority in economic affairs, the Government appeared to be preparing drafts for presidential decrees on economic matters rather than submitting the legislation to parliament. "Vysokaia otvetstvennost' zakonodatel'noi vlasti (doklad Lukianova)," *Izvestiia*, 10 September 1990, p. 3.

62. Unlike American congressmen, members of European-style parliaments have modest personnel support, often only a single secretary. In the new Soviet parliament, individual deputies had no permanent staff but they did have the right to request that enterprises in their districts assist them with secretarial support. The response of enterprises to such requests varied widely, and therefore some deputies were much better supported than others. D. Mann, "Supreme Soviet Adopts Laws on the Status of People's Deputies," *Report on the USSR*, 28 September 1990, pp. 1-4. The use of enterprises as support bases began in the parliamentary elections of 1989, when candidates for the USSR Congress of People's Deputies were given the right to draw on factories and institutes for campaign assistance.

63. For the membership of the presidium, see *The Supreme Soviet: A Biographical Directory*, ed. Dawn Mann, Robert Monyak, and Elizabeth Teague (Munich and Washington, DC: Radio Free Europe/Radio Liberty and The Center for Strategic and International Studies, 1989), pp. 43-46. The secretariat of the presidium of the Supreme Soviet reportedly spent 6.5 million rubles on its staff in 1989, compared with 16.3 million rubles for the administrative staff of the USSR Council of Ministers. The central apparatus of the individual ministers and state committees reportedly cost the country 465 million rubles a year. The latter figure does not include the central staffs of the KGB or the Ministry of Internal Affairs, and presumably also the Ministry of Defense, all of whose budgets were secret. G. Alimov *et al.*, "The Difficult Path of Parliamentary Decisions," *Izvestiia*, 3 August 1989, in *CDSP*, no. 38 (1989), p. 17.

64. Oversight was also exercised by standing committees and by the select commissions created to investigate topical issues, such as the massacre in Tbilisi and the Gdlian-Ivanov affair. Most committees, however, appeared to be chaired by establishment politicians who did not encourage vigorous oversight of executive institutions.

65. "Reglament S"ezda narodnykh deputatov SSSR i Verkhovnogo Soveta SSSR," *Vedomosti SSSR*, no. 29 (1989), item 565; "O statuse narodnykh deputatov v SSSR," *Vedomosti SSSR*, no. 29 (1989), item 567. The latter law also granted deputies the right to conduct inspections of Government departments and to request immediate action by law enforcement organs if a violation of law was discovered. It should be noted that *zaprosy* had been in use for some years before the democratization campaigns of Gorbachev. See B. Khazyrev, "Deputatskii zapros: kak pomogaet on vypolniat' nakazy izbiratelei," *Izvestiia*, 21 January 1985, and D. Volgushev, "Deistvennost' zaprosa," *Izvestiia*, 25 March 1985.

66. "Gde nuzhno, vlast' upotrebit'," *Literaturnaia gazeta*, no. 25 (1990), p. 12.

67. In September 1990, for example, the head of the Social Democratic bloc in the Supreme Soviet, S. Belozertsev, directed a *zapros* to the Minister of Defense and the head of the KGB concerning the movement into the Moscow region of elite divisions of the armed forces. "Pervoi zakon chetvertoi sessii," *Izvestiia*, 25 September 1990, p. 2.

68. Interview with A.M. Yakovlev, 11 July 1990, Moscow.

69. Deputies also found it difficult to receive information about the perquisites of leaders. "E.A. Pamfilova, secretary of the USSR Congress of People's Deputies Commission on Reviewing Privileges Enjoyed by Certain Categories of Citizens, complained to the members of parliament that all the commission's inquiries to the Council of Ministers, particularly to first vice-chairmen L.A. Voronin and A.P. Biriukova, have been met with complete silence and a refusal to provide necessary information and documents." V. Dolganov and A. Stepovoi, "A Week for Reflection," *Izvestiia*, 12 September 1990, in *CDSP*, no. 37 (1990), p. 6.

70. M. Tsypkin, "The Committee for Defense and State Security of the USSR Supreme Soviet," *Report on the USSR*, 11 May 1990, pp. 10-11.

71. B. Sergeev, "Chelovek prokhodit kak khoziain," *Argumenty i fakty*, no. 37 (1990), p. 2. There was also concern among radical deputies that the parliament's right of oral *zapros* was limited illegally by the chair, A. Lukianov. In a heated debate in February 1991, a deputy directed a *zapros* to the Minister of Justice, asking him to comment on the legality of registering the Communist Party under the new law on public associations. Lukianov intervened to seek a vote on whether to accept the *zapros*, even though this privilege of deputies was not subject to a vote. In the event, the vote succeeded, by the slimmest of majorities, in preventing the request from being posed to the Minister. A. Stepovoi i S. Chugaev, "Sessiia obsuzhdaet plan raboty," *Izvestiia*, February 19, 1991, p. 1. As if the defeat of the vote were not enough, Vladimir Ivashko, the Deputy General Secretary of the Communist Party, attacked the "political" character of the deputy's *zapros* and warned that unless the deputy could prove all of his insults directed against the party, they [the party?] reserved the right to take "appropriate measures". *Ibid.*

72. P. Solomon, "Local Political Power and Soviet Criminal Justice, 1922-1941," *Soviet Studies*, no. 3 (1985), pp. 305-329.

73. The parliament was unable to oversee the Government, one deputy lamented, "because we're drowning in apartment problems and other such matters. Some bodies of power find it very advantageous to have USSR People's Deputies like that." V. Dolganov and A. Stepovoi, "Time is Running Out," *Izvestiia*, 1 June 1990, in *CDSP*, no. 23 (1990), p. 10.

74. "Power Structure Reform: Supreme Soviet Upstaged?" *Moscow News*, no. 50 (1990), p. 8.

75. Ministries were also able to coopt deputies by offering them personal "benefits". The Ministry of Foreign Affairs, for example, operated seminars for deputies to expose them to international law and diplomatic practice. Response to Reader's Question, *Argumenty i fakty*, no. 45 (1990), p. 8.

76. V. Dolganov and V. Romanyuk, "Everyone Needs Money - Where is it to Come From?" *Izvestiia*, 22 September 1989, in *CDSP*, no. 38 (1989), p. 22.

77. The expectations of fundamentally new legislative-executive relations were evident in Ryzhkov's comments in June 1989 following the first days of confirmation debates. "We must work together, constantly remembering the enormous tasks facing the country .... Those who come through this parliamentary procedure successfully cannot, of course, fail to have a sense of satisfaction in winning a vote of confidence from people's deputies. An important new quality will thereby appear in the position of the future Government members—reliance on the support of the people's representatives. And the formal act of appointment to a post thereby acquires fundamentally new importance as a democratic act that is part of the restructuring of our political system." "N.I. Ryzhkov: Learning to Work Together," *Izvestiia*, 24 June 1989, in *FBIS*, 26 June 1989, pp. 46-47. How different the politics of 1989 from the politics of 1990!

78. In a revealing speech to the cultural establishment at the end of November 1990, Gorbachev justified the subordination of the Council of Ministers to a strong presidency as essential to hold together the Union. "Speech by M.S. Gorbachev," *Pravda*, 1 December 1990, in *CDSP*, no. 48 (1990), pp. 1-5.

79. Like Gorbachev, many Western social scientists have reservations about the appropriateness of vigorous legislative institutions in countries in transition. According to Robert Packenham: "What little we do know suggests that strengthening legislatures in developing countries would, in most cases, probably impede the capacity for change which is often crucial for 'modernization' and economic development ...." "Legislatures and Political Development," *Legislatures*, ed. Philip Norton (Oxford: Oxford University Press, 1990), p. 82.

4

THE RISE OF PRESIDENTIAL POWER UNDER GORBACHEV

Brenda Horrigan
and
Theodore Karasik

The Early Reforms

Mikhail Gorbachev began to tinker with the organization of the Soviet political system soon after becoming general secretary in March 1985. Despite a long and successful career in the Communist Party, Gorbachev challenged the party's monopoly of power by investing new authority in the state's executive and legislative institutions and by seeking to maintain that authority through constitutional law and popular support. Through these reforms he intended to invigorate the nation, particularly its stagnating economy. He ended up transforming the state. A presidency replaced the Council of Ministers as the supreme executive institution; then, in the wake of the August coup, a state council in effect replaced the presidency. Finally, much to Gorbachev's dismay, the Commonwealth of Independent States replaced the Soviet Union itself at the end of 1991.

Gorbachev began his political reforms in earnest at the end of 1988 by revamping and empowering the legislative branch of the political system in a set of amendments to the existing constitution. Following these institutional changes, Soviet citizens in March 1989 elected a new representative body, the Congress of People's Deputies, from whose ranks a sitting legislature, the USSR Supreme Soviet, was selected to manage legislative affairs between congress meetings. These legislative bodies in turn began to support Gorbachev's attempts to recast the executive institutions of the Soviet state. In late 1989, members of the new Supreme Soviet drafted the Law on the USSR Council of Ministers. Many of these new Soviet legislators, who were part of the first popularly elected representative institution since revolutionary times, envisioned a Government responsible to the legislative branch.[1]

It soon became evident, however, at least to Gorbachev and his circle, that the Government could not be overseen effectively by two large and cumbersome legislative bodies.[2] And political oversight of the administrative machinery was especially important at this time, when the party apparatus was abandoning its traditional role of state overseer. As a means of filling this vacuum of authority and of enhancing his own personal power, Gorbachev decided to create a USSR presidency that could take charge of the unwieldy and often obstructionist Government.

Before October 1989, Gorbachev had been critical of the idea of a national presidency; he argued then that such a strong national leader would overwhelm the power of the local governing bodies, the soviets. Worse yet, Gorbachev feared a presidency would reestablish a "cult of personality" in Soviet politics.[3] Soon after voicing these concerns, however, Gorbachev apparently realized that broad reform of the Soviet political and economic systems could not be accomplished quickly and effectively through either the CPSU apparatus or the legislature. The former was filled with personnel hostile to fundamental change; the latter was inefficient as a policymaking and oversight body. In the first quarter of 1990, therefore, Gorbachev took his most dramatic step to that point in the reorganization of the Soviet political system by seeking legislative approval for the creation of a presidency, a move that promised to distance the CPSU even further from the leadership of the Soviet state.[4]

In February 1990, the USSR Supreme Soviet approved Gorbachev's proposal to establish an Office of the President. Within a matter of weeks, the USSR Congress of People's Deputies amended the Soviet constitution accordingly. What emerged at first was not an "executive" presidency but a unique, embryonic structure designed to place the focus of national leadership on a single individual. The Soviet president, according to the new Law on the Presidency, was to be chosen to a five-year term in a nationwide election with universal suffrage. However, in a concession to Gorbachev's fear of the divisiveness and uncertainty of an early presidential election campaign, the law allowed the Congress of People's Deputies to select the first president. The Congress chose Gorbachev, though by a margin (1329 out of a possible 2245 votes) that prevented the new president from claiming an overwhelming mandate.

The new law gave the Soviet president wide-ranging responsibilities, including the power to propose and veto legislation, to appoint Government officials, to act as the nation's top representative abroad, to sign international treaties, and to oversee the nation's defense. As president, Gorbachev could also call for national referendums on important issues, order a state of emergency or martial law in any region within the borders of the USSR, overrule Government decisions that he believed violated the USSR Constitution or endangered citizens' rights and freedoms, award military ranks and honorary titles, and restore citizenship to exiles or internal dissidents.[5]

The creation of the Office of the President was accompanied by the establishment of two advisory bodies: the Presidential Council and the Federation Council. The Presidential Council's day-to-day work, as described by Gorbachev and Presidential Council members, covered a vast range of policy concerns. The council itself, however, had no policymaking authority. Its job was to present to the president policy alternatives on social, economic, foreign, and defense problems facing the nation.[6] Each council member was to be aided by "special groups of experts and technical associates," and by staff advisers "whose task [would] be to prepare each day a very complete and objective picture of the state of society and the life of the country .... "[7]

The Presidential Council faced numerous obstacles from its inception and as a result never developed into an effective institution. In late 1990, Soviet legislators publicly complained that the Presidential Council's mission was still "unclear."[8] Apparent weaknesses in the council's operation encouraged Gorbachev to invite U.S. President George Bush's then chief of staff, John Sununu, to Moscow to advise him on organizing the presidential support staff. It seems, in retrospect, that the Presidential Council's internal political divisions contributed to its ineffectiveness. By attempting to include in the council representatives from many points on the Soviet political spectrum, from the conservative novelist Valentin Rasputin to the reformist international affairs expert, Alexander Nikolaevich Yakovlev, Gorbachev created a body unable to work as a team. Perhaps Gorbachev thought that they could work out their differences within the confines of a small but influential political body. The more cynical explanation is that Gorbachev intended the council to be merely a showpiece of functional representation of the country's diverse interests. In any event, that is what it became.

According to the Law on the Presidency, the second advisory body--the Federation Council—was to include all republic supreme soviet chairmen (unless membership was delegated by the republic chairmen to other local authorities). Leaders of the USSR's many autonomous regions could also attend Federation Council meetings.[9] The Federation Council's chief task was supervision of nationality and inter-republic issues, and its first major act was to develop a new union treaty, upon which future center-periphery relations would be based. In its initial stage of development (March-November 1990), the Federation Council faced problems similar to those of the Presidential Council. Federation Council meetings were infrequent and often proceeded without the participation of the Baltic republics, Georgia, Armenia, or Moldova, all of which sought independence from the Soviet Union.[10]

Along with these new advisory bodies, the Soviet president also began to build a personal staff. Among the first staff members recruited by Gorbachev were experts drawn from the CPSU apparatus, including several members of the Ideology Department.[11] Staff from this department and from two other critical Central Committee departments (the General Department and the State and Law Department) were given prominent positions within the new presidential Socioeconomic Department and the Defense and State Security Department.[12] That the Soviet president relied on personnel from the party apparatus, which he had criticized as resistant to reform, points to Gorbachev's need for managers who understood the mechanics of the Soviet system and could maneuver through the existing bureaucracy. Indeed, one may argue that in this transfer of personnel Gorbachev drained the central party apparatus of its most capable and progressive elements.

In the early autumn of 1990, barely six months into the experiment with a presidential system, Gorbachev returned to the USSR Supreme Soviet to request expanded powers for the presidency. His reasoning, as presented to the legislature, was the following.

> We describe the situation in the country as an emergency, as unstable. Features of an emergency abound .... The situation is full of danger and action is vital. The situation must be stabilized. Aren't we talking about power when we say all of this? The trouble today is that the system of executive power is not functioning.[13]

Gorbachev's immediate concern was the inability to get the central ministries and regional leaders to respond to presidential decrees. His decrees, directed at a plague of urgent problems, from armed conflict in Azerbaijan to fundamental reform in central economic planning, were going unnoticed, or at least unimplemented. On 24 September 1990, the USSR Supreme Soviet granted Gorbachev temporary powers (until 31 March 1992) to issue unrestricted decrees on the economy, law and order, and Government personnel. Gorbachev also won the important right to declare direct presidential rule in troubled regions and to abolish democratically elected bodies as he deemed necessary.[14]

Even these changes, however, failed to concentrate sufficient authority in the presidency, at least according to Gorbachev. Thus, in November 1990, the president unveiled a plan for reorganizing the entire Soviet political system. His surprise proposals included the creation of a stronger chief executive and an enhanced role for the 15 republics in national decisionmaking. The goal seemed to be a strong center and strong republics. Having opted in early 1990 for a French-style executive, with a president governing through a prime minister and council of ministers, Gorbachev now sought to establish presidential government based on the American model, which he hoped would arrest the country's deepening economic and social crises. In a speech appealing to the Supreme Soviet for acceptance of his plan, Gorbachev called upon the legislature to allow "without delay" the "radical reorganization of executive power and the center and to subordinate it ... directly to the president." [15] His plan envisioned a restructuring of the entire Government apparatus, including the replacement of the Council of Ministers by a Cabinet of Ministers and the establishment of the post of USSR Vice President.

Some critics claimed that these reforms were inappropriate prior to the signing of a new union treaty[16] that was designed to redefine political and legal relations between the center and the republics. But central leaders argued that negotiating a union treaty was a complex, long-term affair, and central institutions required immediate renovation. As the last chairman of the Council of Ministers, Nikolai Ryzhkov, put it:

> It is evident that the instability of the political situation in the country is having an increasingly adverse effect on the economy. The country is ceasing to take laws into account. Respect for the authorities and administrative bodies has been undermined--from the executive committee of the village soviet to the USSR Council of Ministers.[17]

Mikhail Gorbachev concurred and told his critics in his November 1990 State of the Union speech: "This government has to change decisively even before a Union treaty is adopted." He promised, though, that the treaty would be given "cardinal prominence" in the new government's work.[18]

The Council Becomes a Cabinet

The centerpiece of Gorbachev's November 1990 reorganization proposal was the creation of a Cabinet of Ministers. In effect, the separate institutions of the presidency and Government (Council of Ministers) were now integrated into a single state executive hierarchy. The Cabinet of Ministers, in operation from the beginning of 1991 but only established officially on 20 March 1991,[19] was to work immediately underneath the president. With this change, Gorbachev sought to tie the vast ministerial apparatus more closely to the president.

The top leadership body of the new Cabinet of Ministers was the presidium, which, according to the new law, included the prime minister, his deputies, and an administrator of affairs.[20] The list of the Cabinet's areas of responsibility, provided in the revised constitution, was a lengthy one and overlapped in large measure with the mandate of the former Council of Ministers. Among the responsibilities exclusive to the Cabinet were the development and execution of a Union budget, the administration of defense enterprises and space research, implementation of Soviet foreign policy, crime-fighting, and the maintenance of defense and state security. In cooperation with the republics, the Cabinet was also supposed to develop financial and credit policy, administer fuel and power supplies as well as the transport systems, and develop welfare and social programs. Finally, the Cabinet was to coordinate national policy on science and technology, patents, use of airspace, prices, the economy and market, housing, environmental protection, and military appointments.[21]

The law also allowed the Cabinet to issue decrees (*postanovleniia*) and resolutions (*rasporiazheniia*), but they were far narrower in scope than those of the old Council of Ministers.[22] According to the Cabinet's Legal Department chief, *postanovleniia* dealt with "questions of a normative character or those that have important state significance"; *rasporiazheniia* were instructions which were "nonprescriptive" and contended with day-to-day operations of industry or administration.[23]

The Law on the Cabinet required the entire Cabinet to meet at least quarterly.[24] In its first months of operation, however, the Cabinet met more frequently than required. Key Cabinet members also participated in meetings of other state bodies, including the Federation Council, in an attempt to guarantee that the Cabinet contributed to any discussion relating to central control of governmental organs.

These reforms of the Soviet political structure were designed to give Gorbachev greater formal control over the day-to-day activities of the state administrative apparatus. Whereas the old Council of Ministers had always been subordinate—at least in theory—to the national legislature, the new Cabinet reported directly to the president (though it was "accountable" to both the president and the USSR Supreme Soviet).[25] For Gorbachev, the most important difference between the old and new state systems lay in the chain of command. Put simply, the Government would now answer to the president first rather than to the legislature. While the tenure of the Council of Ministers had been tied to the election of a new Supreme Soviet, the Cabinet's term was linked directly to that of the USSR president. Upon election of a new USSR president, the

Cabinet was obliged by law to tender its resignation.[26] Furthermore, it was now the president who hired and fired the leading members of Government and the heads of ministries and state committees (though the Supreme Soviet did retain the right to confirm nominees). The Cabinet, with input from the ministers and other key officials, appointed and dismissed deputy ministers and deputy leaders of other bodies under its jurisdiction.[27]

Unlike the Council of Ministers, the Cabinet was only one of several executive structures within the reorganized Soviet state. Although an institution of limited authority vis-a-vis the CPSU in the pre-Gorbachev era, the Council of Ministers had been the sole focus of state executive and administrative activity. The new Cabinet, however, shared executive authority with the president's office, the USSR Federation Council, and other appendages of the presidency.[28] The Cabinet's central role, then, was as a link between the presidential offices and the ministerial and industrial infrastructure of the nation. Besides its own decisions, the Cabinet implemented the decrees of the president and the laws of the legislature.[29]

Even after the November 1990-March 1991 reorganization, the ministries and the state committees remained the basic units of government, responsible for carrying out the instructions issued by president and cabinet. As before the reforms, the major difference between a ministry and a state committee was the scope of the respective organ's policy responsibility.[30] A state committee was usually in charge of a policy area that cut across industrial branches--i.e., the State Committee for Science and Technology (GKNT) and the State Committee for Prices. A ministry, on the other hand, was typically in charge of a single line of industry; for example, there were ministries for the coal industry, the communications equipment industry, shipbuilding, and defense industry. Each national ministry was responsible for all policy in its particular branch. This distinction held true for a few non-industrial ministries as well, such as the ministries of foreign policy, defense, and finance. In some cases, though, the distinction between ministry and state committee could be obscure. For example, the KGB was a state committee--its full name was the Committee for State Security--while there was a *Ministry* of Justice.

There were two types of ministries in the Soviet Union: all-union and union-republic. The all-union ministry was a national-level, centralized organ that directly supervised policy in its sector throughout the country. Thus, all-union ministries in Moscow administered directly factories and enterprises in towns and cities throughout the Soviet Union. The union-republic ministries, for their part, supervised local enterprises indirectly, through associated republic-level ministries. For instance, the Ministry of Communications, a union-republic ministry, had an affiliated ministry of communications in each union republic.[31] The continuity in the system of ministries under Gorbachev, explored in detail in the following chapters, stood in sharp contrast to the fluidity of the leading executive institutions that stood above the ministries.

Among the many changes in these leading executive organs was the addition of the post of Vice-President of the USSR, again at Gorbachev's behest.[32] The Soviet vice-president was to stand in for the president when the latter could not fulfill his state duties. The first, and only, Soviet vice-president, senior CPSU official and former trade union leader Gennadii Yanaev, was nominated by Gorbachev and then confirmed by the Supreme Soviet on 27 December 1990.[33] Born in 1937, Yanaev, like Gorbachev, began his party career in the Komsomol and then rose through the ranks of other youth-oriented public organizations. Yanaev served briefly as chairman of the All-Union Central Council of Trade Unions and, in July 1990, became a CPSU Politburo member as well as the CPSU Secretary responsible for international affairs. Yanaev gave up his party posts upon assuming the vice-presidency.[34]

Gorbachev's selection of Yanaev as his vice president appeared a curious move, since Yanaev hardly fit the reformist mold. It is not clear to what extent Gorbachev, in making this appointment, was responding to pressure from a growing, dissatisfied conservative faction in the leadership. But Yanaev's politics were certainly in line with those of increasingly vocal Government conservatives, such as Defense Minister Dmitrii Yazov, KGB Chairman Vladimir Kriuchkov, and Minister of Internal Affairs Boris Pugo.

Another leading position in the newly reorganized Soviet state was that of prime minister. Although the chairman of the presidium of the USSR Council of Ministers had long carried the informal title of prime minister, it was only with the overhaul of executive institutions at the end of 1990 that the Soviet Union created the Office of Prime Minister, which was to sit atop the new Cabinet of Ministers.[35] In January 1991, the Soviet legislature approved the appointment of Gorbachev's nominee, Valentin Pavlov, to be the first USSR prime minister. A graduate of the Moscow Finance Institute, Pavlov had had a lengthy career in the central economic planning bureaucracy and, from 1989, had served as Minister of Finance under Nikolai Ryzhkov, the preceding "prime minister." Again, vocal conservative leaders in the party and Government apparently encouraged Gorbachev to choose Pavlov, an official who shared their desire to preserve strong central governmental institutions. The Soviet press described Pavlov at the time as a "bold" and complex man who attempted to prevent the introduction of market-oriented reforms, like production cooperatives, but who also condemned the USSR for being even more exploitative of workers than developed capitalist nations.[36]

Pavlov did act with great vigor in his first weeks as prime minister. The Cabinet, according to Pavlov, was "a 'survival Government'" and had to be willing and able to react quickly and decisively—terms seldom used to describe the old Council of Ministers.[37] To underscore the break between Council and Cabinet, one of Pavlov's first decisions was to move the Government offices from the Kremlin to the building of the former State Committee for Construction Affairs on Pushkin Street. "There was something symbolic about the leave-taking with the Oval Room in which Soviet Government sessions have been held for over 70 years," commented a TASS reporter covering the move.[38]

Pavlov moved swiftly and ominously to bolster his own position in the leadership by using the well-worn Soviet method of strengthening his institutional base.[39] In June 1991, Pavlov tried to win parliamentary approval for expanded powers for the prime minister, a move that ran directly counter to Gorbachev's campaign to strengthen the presidency. Specifically, the prime minister wanted the Cabinet to have the right to issue decrees on economic affairs without the prior approval of the president. This proposal came less than a week after Pavlov delivered a gloomy report on the state of the Soviet economy.[40] He linked his proposal for institutional reform, then, to his "anti-crisis" economic program and the need to smooth the USSR's transition to a market system. Attempting to justify his bid for greater power in front of the assembled legislators, he argued: "The president's working day is 14 hours long .... If we push all questions on to him, he simply will not be in any state to attend to them all ... there is a lot the president simply cannot do."[41] Vice President Yanaev quickly joined ranks with the prime minister, assuring the press that Pavlov's search for greater power was not politically motivated.[42]

In his bid for expanded power, Pavlov seemed intent on correcting what he saw as an institutional problem, the lack of real power in the post of prime minister, as well as a political problem, the imminent collapse of the Union and its central executive organs. Pavlov undoubtedly was frustrated by the unenviable position of the prime minister: he was responsible for the performance of the economy yet unable to make authoritative decisions on its activities. Press reports on Cabinet meetings—chaired by Gorbachev—barely mentioned the prime minister.[43] Like the US president, Gorbachev was seeking to fill the roles of head of state and head of government.

Gorbachev, of course, did not agree with Pavlov's assessment of the president's inability to attend to the economic affairs of the nation. With a speech made just days after Pavlov demanded broader lawmaking authority for the Cabinet of Ministers, Gorbachev won the legislature's support and denied Pavlov the expanded authority he sought. However, it would only be a matter of weeks before Pavlov, with the support of Yanaev and other Government conservatives, rebelled again, this time in a coup attempt.

A further appendage to the presidency added during the November 1990-March 1991 reforms was the USSR Security Council. The Security Council's concern was the day-to-day political and economic security of the country, which was interpreted to include such diverse areas as nationality issues, the pace and scope of economic reforms, environmental hazards, and "emergency situations."[44] The Council's first members, confirmed by the Supreme Soviet, included Prime Minister Valentin Pavlov, Vice-President Gennadii Yanaev, Foreign Minister Aleksandr Bessmertnykh, Defense Minister Dmitrii Yazov, KGB Chairman Vladimir Kriuchkov, and Minister of Internal Affairs Boris Pugo. Two leading pro-reform officials—Vadim Bakatin and Evgenii Primakov—were added as "special" members with full-time Security Council responsibilities. Bakatin focused on political affairs while Primakov had responsibility for economic issues.[45]

With the exception of Bakatin and Primakov, the council's members, who were nominated by President Gorbachev, did not inspire confidence even among moderate reformists. Indeed, Bakatin claimed that pro-reform analyses intended for the President ran into "a range of problems" created by "Council members who [were] ministers." Responsible for at least some of the obstruction was Prime Minister Pavlov, who reportedly withheld critical budget information from Bakatin and Primakov.[46] In retrospect it seems clear that the conservative members of the Security Council—most of whom were also members of the Defense Council that led the August coup attempt—actively worked against reform in 1991.[47]

The USSR Defense Council was a long-standing, if shadowy, fixture in the Soviet political system. In the early years of perestroika, it continued to supervise Soviet defense-related decisionmaking in the new governmental structure. In early 1991, however, Gorbachev transformed the Defense Council into a clearinghouse for defense information for other state institutions. This reform downgraded the Defense Council, since it no longer supervised all aspects of Soviet defense policymaking.

No official details of the Defense Council's membership during this period were published. It can be assumed, however, that it contained at least the president, the vice-president, the prime minister, as well as leaders of key security organizations, such as the MVD, the KGB and military. The Defense Council's relationship to such bodies as the Security Council and Cabinet of Ministers is also uncertain. In theory, the Defense Council should have fed information to the Security Council. Yet in practice the Defense Council seems to have bypassed the Security Council and reported directly to the president, perhaps because of the presence of Bakatin and Primakov on the Security Council.

Reforming Republican and Local Government

During 1990-91, the republics began to emulate the center by reorganizing their executive-administrative apparatuses. Soon after Gorbachev was named president, the republics started to draft legislation that created for the first time presidencies, and later prime ministerships, on their territories. The occupants of the new posts played an important role in the disintegration of the Soviet Union and the emergence of constituent states within the framework of the Commonwealth of Independent States.

Before the coup of August 1991, only two republics had held democratic elections for a Gorbachev-style executive president: Georgia's citizens elected Zviad Gamsakhurdia in April 1991 and citizens of the Russian Republic chose Boris Yeltsin in June 1991, both by overwhelming majorities.[48] Yeltsin's election was particularly significant because of the powers vested in the Russian presidency. During the March-April 1991 meeting of the Russian Congress of People's Deputies, pro-reform legislators amended the state structure of the Russian Federation with a Law on the Presidency. The Russian Supreme Soviet ratified the change in mid-April 1991, thereby strengthening the republic's executive organs vis-a-vis the party-dominated regional and city soviets.

Yeltsin's election was a dramatic development in Soviet politics. It established for the first time a leading state executive in the Russian Federation who was independent of USSR authority. The Russian Federation president possessed powers that made him an equal to Gorbachev within the republic. The new legislation, for example, gave the Russian president the ability to conduct his own international and interrepublic business through an RSFSR Security Council.[49] On paper at least, this meant that the Russian president could either support or veto USSR presidential decrees if the RSFSR's security interests were involved.

Other republics established powerful presidential posts as well, and in each republic new presidential support structures emerged, many of which mirrored those at the center. For example, Azerbaijan formed a National Security Council, headed by the chairman of the republic Council of Ministers. Its mission was "to elaborate recommendations for implementing policy in the field of defense, protect the state and territorial integrity of the republic, and deal with the aftermath of emergency situations."[50] In Kyrgyzstan, the reformist president, Askar Akaev, created a Presidential Council on 22 November 1990, shortly after his unexpected election to the post. The new Kyrgyz Presidential

Council had the authority "to work out measures for implementing the basic directions of the republic's domestic and foreign policy as well as ensuring its integrity and security."[51] President Nursultan Nazarbaev of Kazakhstan also set up a Presidential Council. The Kazakh Presidential Council consisted of 10 members, including the republic KGB and MVD chairmen.[52] In addition, Nazarbaev established a Supreme Economic Council to function under the president's office. Its stated task was to "create a legal foundation for new economic relations ... for the transfer to the market economy."[53]

Reflecting the trend towards "presidentialism," in mid-1991 some republics began to turn their councils of ministers into cabinets. As a corollary, these republics established republic prime ministerships. The Ukraine was a case in point. In April 1991, the Ukrainian Supreme Soviet created a republic Cabinet of Ministers[54] and named as prime minister the chairman of the Council of Ministers.[55] It also passed a law reorganizing the ministerial structure for the republic. Echoing the central leadership's efforts to streamline bureaucracy, the Ukrainian reform consolidated many ministries and even abolished a few.[56] While the Ukrainian reform reflected changes in the center, there were important differences. Some special ministries (such as the Ministry for Protecting the Population from the Consequences of the Accident at the Chernobyl' Atomic Energy Station) were created to handle issues unique to the republic. More importantly, only certain members of the Cabinet were responsible to the head of state. Others, such as the republic bank chief and republic KGB chairman, reported to the Ukrainian Supreme Soviet.[57]

The city and regional governments in the Soviet republics were not immune to the whirlwind of reform sweeping through the USSR during 1990-91. New local government structures began to emerge, distinguished by local tradition, population size, and relations with higher-level institutions. Moscow's city government was reorganized in June 1991, when its mayor, Gavriil Popov, established a new administrative structure that included a city duma and assembly as well as a department of the mayor and a government office. The latter body, headed by the mayor and a premier,[58] acted as a mini-cabinet of ministers that was responsible for the city's economic affairs.

In Belorussia, the basic units of local government were territorial soviets (councils) and smaller, self-governing committees located in housing complexes, residential communities, and villages.[59] Local soviets in Belorussia possessed considerable independence in areas once tightly controlled from the center, including foreign trade, industrial management, and economic development. Even before the collapse of the USSR at the end of 1991, legislation in Belorussia made almost no mention of the relationship between local soviets in the republic and central authorities in Moscow; discussion of chains of command was restricted to republic authorities.[60]

In February 1991, the president of Tajikistan signed a law on local government that was in many ways similar to Belorussia's. The principal unit of local government was also the soviet, though the Tajik law gave more prominence to the role of central government organs; multiple references were made to USSR law and the Soviet constitution as "guides" for the Tajik soviets.[61] This reliance on central models may have reflected the traditional deference of the Tajik elite toward the center as well as its suspicion of devolution within the republic amid a resurgent cultural Islam.[62]

Georgia broke with the other republics by establishing a system of local government based on prefectures. The prefect in Georgia was the highest official in each district and city and was accountable directly to the republic president, supreme court, and Government. The prefect was assisted by a deputy or deputies, whom he personally appointed. In some ways, the Georgian prefect resembled a "mini president" in that a cabinet aided him by acting as a "permanent consultative organ ... which develop[ed] proposals for performing tasks assigned to the prefect."[63] The prefect system was intended to control Georgia's "unruly" nationalities and clans. The prefect, for example, appointed the heads of locally-owned public enterprises and concluded contracts with local governments in other nations and Soviet republics. The prefect also managed the district and city budget and created funds needed for local government activities as well as for local disaster relief. In addition, he was the top local authority for "ensuring the constitutional rights" of the local citizens and investigating all reports of malfeasance.[64]

Relations between Center and Periphery

As a result of the 1990-91 reforms, the republics gained an increasingly stronger voice in central decisionmaking. The first step in this development came through the establishment of the Federation Council. Initially an advisory council, the Federation Council became a policymaking body attached to the Office of the USSR President in November 1990. In expanding the authority of the Federation Council, which contained the chairmen of the republic supreme soviets, Gorbachev argued that it needed more power in order to resolve increasingly complicated, and controversial, center-periphery issues.

Within the central Government, the new Cabinet of Ministers seemed to work more closely, and on a far more egalitarian basis, with republic officials than did the old Council of Ministers. Collaborative efforts may have been enhanced by the legally-mandated establishment of republic missions in Moscow that were "attached" to the Cabinet. The Law on the Cabinet of Ministers contained detailed provisions on how the republic government leaders should be included in Cabinet business. Heads of republic government organs, for instance, "participate[d] on a voting basis" in Cabinet meetings.[65] The Law gave republic governments

> ... the right to submit for consideration by the Cabinet of Ministers of the USSR proposals pertaining to questions of all-Union significance which are subject to compulsory examination in the Cabinet of Ministers of the USSR.[66]

While bound to consider republic proposals, the Cabinet had the final say on any decisions "of interrepublic significance"; on the other hand, it could elect to hand over to a republic any decision affecting only that republic. According to the new law, Union decisions affecting the rights of the republic were binding upon the republic governments, but could be adopted by the Cabinet of Ministers of the USSR only after consultation with them.[67]

Even before the August 1991 coup, some individual USSR ministries had taken steps to improve center-periphery cooperation in policy formation. Ministers of culture from the center and the union republics were the first to establish a sectoral council, called the Council of Ministers of Culture. According to an *Izvestiia* report on its second meeting, this new organ was intended "to unite representatives of different republics not within the structure of rigid 'vertical' subordination but on an equal footing."[68]

The USSR Ministry of Foreign Affairs and its union-republic affiliates gathered regularly to discuss policy-related issues at meetings of the new Council of Foreign Ministers of the USSR and Union Republics. This organization acted as

> ... a joint mechanism for republics' participation in the elaboration, implementation, and coordination of the Soviet Union's foreign policy, the specific discussion of international problems, and the finding of solutions to organization and other questions that arise.[69]

In November 1990, republic leaders had pushed for, and won, legislative approval for the creation of an Interrepublican Economic Committee, a body independent of the governmental apparatus that could play an important role in organizing the Federation Council's work. This new consultative body had oversight responsibility for center-republican economic relations.[70] It contained representatives nominated by the republics' supreme soviets; the chairmanship of the Committee rotated among the members.[71] Economic coordination among republics was clearly in evidence by the middle of 1991.

> Previously the [economic policy] document was the USSR Cabinet of Ministers program, but now it is the fruit of creative work by the Cabinet of Ministers and union republic governments .... the participants agreed that the economy can be extricated from crisis only given joint action by all republics; we cannot emerge from the crisis alone.[72]

Several republic officials expressed concern, however, that the Interrepublican Economic Committee was not functioning as originally envisioned.[73] Specific criticisms included its failure to establish a regular meeting schedule, a vital first step to effective operation.[74] Discussion of scrapping both the Federation Council and the Interrepublican Economic Committee began to appear in the Soviet press in June 1991. One proposal was to strengthen both institutions and add a Council of the Republics as one of the two parliamentary chambers in the Supreme Soviet.[75]

The Government, the Presidency, and the Coup

The August 1991 coup attempt against the Gorbachev presidency was launched on the eve of the signing of a new union treaty, a document that would have stripped considerable power from the Cabinet of Ministers and many other central institutions. Elements within the CPSU, the USSR Defense Council, the USSR Supreme Soviet, the KGB, the MVD, and the armed forces joined forces to oust Gorbachev. As noted earlier, despite his apparent support of Gorbachev's government reorganization, Prime Minister Pavlov clashed with the President over the scope of their respective areas of authority. Pavlov argued during the coup attempt that the USSR Cabinet of Ministers should "remain a governing body .... Either we fulfill instructions, or adopt decisions and implement them. Or else we will turn into an organ of recommendation."[76] The Cabinet's role in the conspiracy was revealed after the coup failed, when Yeltsin had Gorbachev publicly read the minutes from a Cabinet meeting that took place in the midst of the coup. The document revealed that a majority of the Cabinet had backed the coup attempt. Significantly, those who supported the president's ouster were figures who had a long history within the Government apparatus or the military-industrial complex.[77]

The post-coup Soviet Government underwent massive changes and lost most, if not all, of its authority by September 1991. Republican leaders insisted at once on the replacement of the Federation Council by a State Council, made up of Gorbachev and the leaders of the republic governments, each of whom had one vote. With the erosion of Gorbachev's authority as president in the wake of the coup, the State Council became in effect the supreme executive institution in the country.   One of its first acts was to grant independence to Estonia, Latvia, and Lithuania.[78]

Immediately following the coup, Yeltsin and the Russian Government launched a counterassault on the authority of the USSR Cabinet of Ministers' on Russian territory.   Yeltsin ordered the seizure by the Russian Federation of the USSR Ministry of Finance, Gosbank, and the USSR Bank for Foreign Economic Relations.   On August 24, the Russian Federation's Council of Ministers moved to take over operational control of the all-union economic ministries. Subsequently, Yeltsin—in defiance of existing constitutional norms—promoted several Russian Federation ministers to posts as all-union officials.[79] Among this group was Ivan Silaev, who left his post as Russian Federation prime minister to become the de facto prime minister of the USSR as head of the newly-formed Committee on the Operational Management of the Economy, the successor to the old Cabinet of Ministers.   Pavlov's two attempts to unseat Gorbachev had so tarnished the Cabinet of Ministers and the post of prime minister that neither survived into the autumn.

The remaining central Government institutions attempted to rebuff Yeltsin's actions but without success.[80]   In the twilight of the Soviet state, from August to December 1991, the ministries gradually slipped further from Gorbachev's reach.[81]   By November 1991, only a handful of central ministries was left, and with the collapse of the Union and the formation of a Commonwealth of Independent States in December 1991, the remaining central ministries passed to the Russian Federation and other republics.[82]   After three years of far-reaching political and administrative reorganization, the coup and Yeltsin's response to it left Gorbachev with neither party nor Government nor legislature through which to rule.

Notes

The authors would like to thank Justina Baskauskas, Derek Nowek, and Marie Steward for their research assistance.

1. V. Zvekov and L. Okunkov. "Pravitel'stvo i parlament: printsipy ikh vzaimodeistviia," *Pravitel'stvennii vestnik*, no. 22 (1989), p. 4.

2. Eduard Shevardnadze later called the restructuring of the state in the form of a parliamentary system a "crucial mistake" which led to the instability of the entire political system.   A. Rahr, "Shevardnadze on Leadership Mistake," *Radio Liberty Daily Report*, 2 May 1991.

3. "Vremia," Soviet television broadcast on Channel Two, 23 October 1989.

4. This continued a process begun in 1989 when the USSR Supreme Soviet was reformed and made a more powerful and independent institution in Soviet policymaking.

In July 1990, the CPSU Politburo was revamped at the 28th Party Congress. At this time all key government officials (except Gorbachev) left the Politburo, effectively separating party and state. On this point, see chapter 2 of this volume.

5. "Novye polnomochiia prezidenta," *Argumenty i fakty*, no. 39 (1990), pp. 1-2.

6. "Govoriat chleny prezidentskogo soveta," *Izvestiia*, 6 April 1990, p. 2.

7. "Po pyti reshitel'nykh preobrazovanii: vystyplenie M.S. Gorbacheva na prezidentskom sovete SSSR, 27 marta 1990 goda," *Pravda*, 28 March 1990, p. 1.

8. E. Iakovlev, "Farewell to the Presidential Council?" *Moscow News*, no. 49 (1990), p. 3.

9. "Uchrezhdenii posta prezidenta SSSR i vnesenii izmenenii i dopolnenii v konstitutsiiu (osnovnoi zakon) SSSR," *Krasnaia zvezda*, 16 March 1990, pp. 2-3.

10. A presidential Committee on Coordinating Law Enforcement Bodies' Activities as well as three other departments--the secretariat, the Protocol Department, and the Press Department--were also established in this period. Each of these carried out typical bureaucratic functions found in other governmental systems.

11. John Lloyd and Quentin Peel, "Counsellor for a New Way of Life," *Financial Times*, 2 April 1991, p. 36.

12. "Vsesoiuznyi seminar," *Krasnaia zvezda*, 15 May 1991, p. 1.

13. D. Mann, "Gorbachev: Ukaz and Effect," *Report on the USSR*, 25 September 1990, p. 1.

14. "O dopolnitel'nykh merakh po stabilizatsii ekonomicheskoi i obshchestvenno-politicheskoi zhizni strany," *Vedomosti S"ezda narodnykh deputatov SSSR i Verkhovnogo Soveta SSSR*, no. 40 (1990), item 802. With these powers, Gorbachev could have abolished local elected bodies like the republic supreme soviets. Some legislators objected to Gorbachev's quest for more power. They argued that the power of the Supreme Soviet "would be reduced to zero". Others maintained that the passage of this law allowed for the "law and order" powers needed to keep the country from breaking apart. "Gorbachev Seeks Sweeping Powers to Save His Reforms," *Los Angeles Times*, 22 September 1990, p. 1.

15. See, for example, the letter signed by 23 liberal figures including Oleg Bogomolov, Iurii Afanasev, and Tatiana Zaslavskaia in "Strana ustala zhdat'," *Moskovskie novosti*, 18 November 1990, pp. 1, 4.

16. See, for example, Fedor Burlatskii, "Na perelome: zametki deputata," *Literaturnaia gazeta*, 21 November 1990, pp.1-2.

17. N.I. Ryzhkov, "Speech at USSR Supreme Soviet session in the Kremlin on 11 September--Recorded," in *Foreign Broadcast Information Service* (Soviet Union: Daily Report) [hereafter *FBIS*], 12 September 1990, pp. 40-45 [FBIS-SOV-90-177].

18. These phrases appear in a recording of Gorbachev's speech. See Mikhail Gorbachev, "Speech at the USSR Supreme Soviet session in Moscow on 16 November - Recorded." *Moscow Domestic Service* in Russian, 0942 GMT, 16 November 1990, in *FBIS*, 19 November 1990, pp. 15-26 [FBIS-SOV-90-223].

19. M. Gorbachev, "Zakon Soiuza Sovetskikh Sotsialisticheskikh Respublik: O Kabinete ministrov SSSR," *Izvestiia*, 28 March 1991, p. 2. The law on the Cabinet, as its preamble noted, "determines the competence of the Cabinet of Ministers of the USSR,

the procedure of its activity, and its relations with other official bodies." *Ibid.* See also, V. Isachenkov, Radio broadcast, Moscow TASS in English, 1423 GMT, 20 March 1991, in *FBIS*, 21 March 1991, pp. 21-22 [FBIS-SOV-91-055].

20. "19 March Session Discusses Cabinet Powers," Moscow Central Television Second Program Network in Russian at 1852 GMT on 19 March 1991, in *FBIS*, 20 March 1991, p. 13 [FBIS-SOV-91-054].

21. *Ibid.*

22. *Ibid.*

23. Decrees had to be signed by the prime minister *and* the administrator of the Cabinet; resolutions were signed by the prime minister *or* a first deputy prime minister. Both decrees and resolutions were binding for all central government institutions; those which addressed organs under joint jurisdiction of the Union and a republic government had to be ratified by the republic government. V. Lvov and V. Iurteev, "Radius polnomochii," *Pravitel'stvennii vestnik*, no. 14 (1991), p. 5. Cabinet decrees and resolutions could only be reversed by the joint action of the USSR Supreme Soviet and the USSR President. (M. Gorbachev, "Zakon Soiuza Sovetskikh Sotsialisticheskikh Respublik: O Kabinete ministrov SSSR," pp. 3-4.)

24. "19 March Session Discusses Cabinet Powers," p. 13.

25. M. Gorbachev, "Zakon Soiuza Sovetskikh Sotsialisticheskikh Respublik: O Kabinete ministrov SSSR," pp. 3-4.

26. *Ibid.*

27. *Ibid.*

28. V. Lvov and V. Iurteev, "Radius polnomochii," *Pravitelstvennii vestnik*, no. 14 (1991), p. 5.

29. M. Gorbachev, "Zakon Soiuza Sovetskikh Sotsialisticheskikh Respublik: O Kabinete ministrov SSSR," pp. 3-4.

30. J.F. Hough and M. Fainsod, *How the Soviet Union is Governed* (Cambridge, MA: Harvard University Press, 1979).

31. The two types of ministerial organization were maintained in the 1991 government reorganization. The distinction between all-union and union-republic ministries became very important as republics within the USSR sought to make more policy decisions independently of Moscow. "Pravitel'stvo strany: ego funktsii, polnomochiia, otvetstvennost'," *Pravitel'stvennii vestnik*, no. 18 (1989), pp. 2-3.

32. TASS, 16 November 1990.

33. On 5 September 1991, in the wake of the August 1991 coup attempt, an extraordinary Congress of People's Deputies approved the abolition of the post of USSR Vice President and the establishment of new succession procedures aimed at ruling out a repetition of August's coup. See TASS, 5 September 1991.

34. Theodore Karasik, *The CPSU Central Committee: Members, Commissions, and Departments* (Sherman Oaks, CA, 1991).

35. In case of the prime minister's absence, a first deputy assumed the duties of the prime minister.

36. V. Golovachev, "Simply a Change of Government?" *Trud*, 15 January 1991, p.1, in *FBIS*, 23 January 1991 [FBIS-SOV-91-015].

37. V. Pavlov, "Otoiti ot kraia propasti--dosporit' mozhno potom," *Ogonek*, no. 17 (1991), pp. 4-5.

38. B. Grishchenko and B. Shestakov, "Light at the End of the Tunnel? From a USSR Cabinet of Ministers Session," *Sovetskaia Rossiia*, 5 May 1991, p. 1, in *FBIS*, 6 May 1991, pp. 13-14 [FBIS-SOV-91-087].

39. Pavlov actively supported a consultative "think-tank" outside the governmental apparatus, apparently to develop and give legitimacy to his own, more cautious economic program. The Experimental Creative Center Corporation, headed by one of the authors of Pavlov's "anti-crisis program" for the Soviet economy, grew influential through its ties with the Prime Minister. In May 1991, it reportedly had "a turnover of 100 million rubles" and received preferential treatment through an decree of the USSR Cabinet of Ministers. TASS, 7 May 1991; see also, Victor Yasmann, "Elite Think-Tank Prepares Post-Perestroika Strategy," *Report on the USSR*, 13 May 1991.

40. V. Pavlov, "At the USSR Supreme Soviet," Moscow Central Television Second Program Network in Russian, 2039 GMT, 11 June 1991, in *FBIS*, 12 June 1991 [FBIS-SOV-91-113].

41. *The Washington Post*, 19 June 1991, quoted in D. Mann, "An Abortive Constitutional Coup D'Etat?" *Report on the USSR*, 26 June 1991.

42. TASS Report, 18 June 1991, quoted in *ibid.*

43. See, for example, "V Kabinete Ministrov," *Pravda*, 5 March 1991, pp. 1-2.

44. "Ob izmeneniiakh i dopolneniiakh konstitutsii (osnovnogo zakona) v sviazi s sovershenstovaniem sistemy gosudarstvennogo upravleniia," *Pravda*, 27 December 1990, p. 2. Interestingly, an MVD official stated that the USSR Security Council should have its own police forces in the republics--specifically in "hot spots." See "Iskliuchit' vnezapnost'," *Sovetskaia Rossiia*, 2 December 1990, p. 1.

45. A. Stepovoi and S. Shugaev, "Formiruetsia Sovet bezopasnosti SSSR," *Izvestiia*, 8 March 1991, p. 2. Security Council members Pavlov, Yanaev, and Kriuchkov were arrested for their involvement in the August 1991 coup attempt. Pugo committed suicide and Bessmertnykh was forced to resign because he did not speak out against the coup. After the coup, Gorbachev, as leader of the new USSR State Council, dissolved the KGB and appointed Bakatin to head a new Interrepublican Security Service; Primakov was appointed to head the new Central Intelligence Service. Bakatin assumed responsibility for all security focusing on "political" affairs while Primakov controlled the former KGB's spy network and its work in acquiring advanced economic and technological data. TASS, 6 November 1991. With the formation of the Commonwealth of Independent States in December 1991, the Russian Federation absorbed the entire central security network into its administrative apparatus.

46. Igor Mendelentsev, Moscow Russian Television Network, 1545 GMT, 10 June 1991, in *FBIS*, 11 June 1991, pp. 66-76 [FBIS-SOV-91-112].

47. It is important to recognize that the USSR Security Council did not instigate the coup. The Defense Council, along with the Cabinet of Ministers, led the coup.

48. Other republics held the following direct presidential elections: Azerbaijan (8 September 1991); Kyrgyzstan (12 October 1991); Armenia (16 October 1991); Tajikistan (25 November 1991); Ukraine (1 December 1991); Kazakhstan (1 December 1991);

Moldavia (8 December 1991); Uzbekistan (29 December 1991). See T. Karasik, *USSR: Facts and Figures Annual* (Gulf Breeze, FL: Academic International Press, 1992).

49. "RSFSR Law on the RSFSR President," *Sovetskaia Rossia*, 30 April 1991, p. 1, in *FBIS*, 1 May 1991, pp. 57-58 [FBIS-SOV-91-084].

50. Moscow All-Union Radio Maiak Network, 1530 GMT, 14 May 1991, in *FBIS*, 15 May 1991, p. 90 [FBIS-SOV-91-094].

51. A. Akaev, "On the Statute Concerning the Kirghiz SSR Presidential Council," *Sovetskaia Kirgizia*, 28 November 1990, p. 2, in *Joint Publications Research Service* (USSR: Political Affairs) [hereafter *JPRS*], 23 January 1991, pp. 78-80 [JPRS-UPA-91-003].

52. A. Rahr, "Presidential Councils in the Republics," *Radio Liberty Daily Report*, 1 August 1990.

53. N. Nazarbaev, "Decree of the Kazakh President on the Formation of the Supreme Economic Council of the Kazakh SSR," *Kazakhstanskaia pravda*, 22 November 1990, p. 1, in *FBIS*, 23 January 1991, p. 88 [FBIS-SOV-91-015-S].

54. L. Kravchuk, "Law of the Ukrainian SSR on the Formation of a Ukrainian SSR Cabinet of Ministers." *Pravda Ukrainy*, 23 April 1991, p. 1, in *JPRS*, 16 May 1991, pp. 50-51 [JPRS-UPA-91-027].

55. *Ibid.*

56. The only state committee outside the republic Council of Minister's control was the republic Committee for State Security (KGB).

57. "Ukraine Cabinet of Ministers Structure Approved." Moscow All-Union Radio First Program Network in Russian, 1600 GMT, 13 May 1991, in *FBIS*, 14 May 1991, p. 61 [FBIS-SOV-91-093].

58. D. Mann, "Executive Structure of Moscow Revamped," *Radio Liberty Daily Report*, 25 June 1991.

59. N. Dementei, "On Local Self-Government and Local Economy in the Belorussian SSSR." *Sovetskaia Belorussiia*, 15 March 1991, pp. 2-4, in *JPRS*, 6 May 1991, pp. 23-42 [JPRS-UPA-91-025]. The purpose and tasks of the self-governing committees were set by the Belorussian constitution. The new Belorussian law on local government included guidelines for the establishment and work of presidiums—the executive bodies of local soviets—and the duties and jurisdiction of a soviet chairman's executive-managerial committee.

60. *Ibid.*

61. K. Makhkamov, "Law of Tadzhik Soviet Socialist Republic 'On Local Self-Government and Local Economy in Tadzhik SSR'," *Kommunist Tadzhikistana*, 9-10 April 1991, pp. 2-3, in *JPRS* (Soviet Union: Economic Affairs), 20 May 1991, pp. 10-39 [JPRS-UEA-91-025].

62. TASS, 27 October 1991.

63. Z. Gamsakhurdia, "Law of the Republic of Georgia: 'On Prefectures'," *Svobodnaia Gruziia*, 27 April 1991, pp. 2-3, in *FBIS*, 4 June 1991, pp. 37-40 [FBIS-USR-91-002].

64. *Ibid.*

65. "V Kabinete ministrov," *Pravda*, 5 March 1991, pp. 1-2.

66. *Ibid.*
67. *Ibid.*
68. V. Ardaiaev, "'Sovmin kultury' v Alma-Ate," *Izvestiia*, 10 June 1991, p. 1.
69. "Ofitsial'noe soobshchenie," *Pravda*, 16 February 1991, p. 6.
70. TASS, 17 November 1990; Agence France Press, 7 January 1991. See also Gorbachev's discussion of establishing such a body in "Osnovnye napravleniia po stabilizatsii narodnogo khoziaistva i perekhodu k rynochnoi ekonomike," *Pravda*, 18 October 1990, pp. 1-4.
71. *Radio Liberty Daily Report*, 31 October 1990; TASS, 4 January 1991.
72. D. Valovoi, "Programma sovmestnykh deistvii," *Pravda*, 16 May 1991, pp. 1-2.
73. "Interv'iu M.S. Gorbacheva dlia sovetskogo i frantsuzskogo televideniia," *Pravda*, 22 November 1990, p. 1.
74. TASS, 7 June 1991.
75. TASS, 10 June 1991.
76. "If We Backtrack One Iota We Will Sacrifice Our Jobs and Our Lives. We Will Not Get a Second Chance," *Rossiiskaia gazeta*, 24 August 1991, p. 2, in *FBIS*, 29 August 1991, pp. 46-48 [FBIS-SOV-91-168].
77. "Speech by USSR President Mikhail Gorbachev to the RSFSR Supreme Soviet in Moscow," Moscow Russian Television Network, 1308 GMT, 23 August 1991, in *FBIS*, 26 August 1991, p. 64. One of the coup leaders, Aleksandr Tiziakov, participated in the Cabinet meeting. He was most likely sent as a representative of the coup leader's Emergency Committee as well as to confirm that the state of emergency sought to preserve and strengthen the Cabinet of Ministers.
78. TASS, 5 September 1991.
79. Yeltsin made the following appointments: Andrei Zverev, chairman of the USSR Gosbank; Igor' Lazarev, USSR Minister of Finance; Aleksandr Khlystov, USSR Minister of Trade; Evgenii Saburov, USSR Minister of Economy and Forecasting; Valerii Mangazaev, USSR Minister for Foreign Economic Relations; Valerii Telegin, Chairman of USSR Vneshekonombank; Mikhail Kuriachev, head of USSR Chamber of Commerce and Industry; and Alla Zakharova, Administrator of Affairs of the USSR Cabinet of Ministers. TASS, 26 August 1991.
80. Gorbachev's associate, Arkadii Volskii, announced a decision to cancel the Russian Federation's actions. He claimed that the Soviet ministries' first deputy chairmen would do the jobs of their "disgraced bosses." TASS, 28 August 1991.
81. TASS, 29 August 1991. The USSR Supreme Soviet vote was 279-37 with 38 abstentions.
82. See, for example, reports on the central Government's demise in TASS, 1 November 1991. Ministries dealing with foreign affairs, defense, transportation, energy, and communications were the only ones in existence at the end of November 1991.

THE STATE AND THE ECONOMY

5

THE MINISTRY OF FINANCE

Peter B. Maggs

History has recorded the exact circumstances of the founding of the People's Commissariat of Finance (which became the USSR Ministry of Finance).

> It became necessary to organize a Commissariat of Finance. Comrade Menzhinsky was made Commissar of Finance. His appointment came late at night. Menzhinsky was at the time extraordinarily fatigued by work. So as to immediately put the Government's order into effect, he with one of his comrades carried in a large divan, placed it against a wall right there in the Management Office and wrote in big letters on a piece of writing paper, "Commissariat of Finance." After posting this sign above the divan, he lay down on the divan and immediately fell asleep. His peaceful snoring carried throughout the Management Office of the Council of People's Commissars.[1]

Despite this beginning, the job of minister of finance has not been a restful one. Since 1917 there have been repeated financial crises, culminating in the financial collapse of 1991. Two people's commissars of finance were convicted in the Moscow Purge Trials.[2] Valentin Pavlov, minister of finance and later prime minister under Gorbachev, was jailed on treason charges after the failure of the August 1991 coup.

History

The new Soviet regime drew on centuries of Russian experience in public finance. The Russian empire transformed its financial institutions into a Ministry of Finance in 1802; the ministry published an elegant jubilee history celebrating its centennial in 1902.[3] When the Bolsheviks took power in 1917, they were able to draw both on the experience of the Russian Government[4] and on their own experience in managing party finances. The Imperial Ministry of Finance was headed by a minister, to whom were subordinate: (1) the Department of the State Treasury, responsible for accounting for state receipts and expenditures; (2) the Department of Tax Revenues; (3) the Head Office for Non-Tax Revenues and the Government Sale of Beverages (the state alcohol monopoly); (4) the Department of Customs Revenues; (5) the Department of Railway Affairs (which set railway tariffs); (6) the Special Chancery for Credit (which dealt with credit institutions, foreign loans, Treasury debt, currency, and the mint); and (7) the Minister's Special Chancellery. There were also a number of other organizations subordinated to the minister, including the state savings banks. Local authorities had no role in the operation of the ministry.[5]

This structure was replaced by (or, rather, renamed as) the Russian Republic People's Commissariat of Finance in 1917. With the creation of the Soviet Union in the early 1920s, a USSR People's Commissariat of Finance was established, along with commissariats of finance in each republic and local finance departments in local governments.[6] The republic commissariats and the local finance departments were in theory subordinate both to the republic and local governments respectively and to the Union People's Commissariat of Finance. Continuity in the Stalin and post-Stalin periods was provided by Minister of Finance A.G. Zverev, who served from 1938 to 1959.[7] In 1946, the Union and republic people's commissariats of finance, like the other people's commissariats were renamed "ministries." This change of name did not involve any change of function.

The Ministry of Finance in 1987 was remarkably similar in structure and duties to the Imperial Ministry of Finance of early 1917, with one important exception. This exception was the dual subordination of the republic ministries of finance and the local finance offices. In Imperial Russia, lower level agencies of the Ministry of Finance reported only to Moscow; they were in no way subordinate to local governments. Until the late 1980s, the subordination to republic and local governments existed much more on paper than in fact. Policy differences between Moscow and the republic and local governments were minimized by the strong hand of the Communist Party, which ensured a uniform policy throughout the country, and the iron fist of the KGB, which detected and neutralized individuals who might struggle for local governmental autonomy. In 1990 and 1991, however, as will be discussed below, the dual subordination of the republic financial agencies played a crucial role in the unraveling of the Union of Soviet Socialist Republics.

The main function of the Ministry of Finance was, as its name implies, to finance government operations. It used three means of financing: (1) robbery, confiscation, and requisition; (2) printing or creating money, and (3) taxation. In the first months of Bolshevik power, forcible taking of resources was the primary means of supporting government operations. Printing money was important until the inflation bubble burst, but taxation was slow to develop. By the late 1930s, there was nothing left to confiscate. The memory of the disastrous inflation of the 1920s discouraged financing government operations by printing money. Taxation came to be the primary method of providing money to pay bureaucrats and soldiers.

Financing by robbery was the initial basis of both Bolshevik Party and Soviet Government finance. In 1907, armed robbers, acting on behalf of the Bolsheviks, probably under Stalin's orders, stole 500,000 rubles from the State Bank in Tiflis, the Georgian capital.[8] In the early days of Bolshevik power, Lenin ordered the creation of the first Soviet treasury confiscation—the forcible seizure of 10,000,000 rubles from the State Bank.[9]

> In those days our "staff" carried out the most varied tasks for Vladimir Ilich. For instance, once Vladimir Ilich handed me a decree over his own signature ... with an order to the State Bank, outside all rules and formalities and as an exception to those rules, to hand over to the Secretary of the Council of People's Commissars 10,000,000 rubles to the disposition of the Government. V.V. Obolensky-Osinsky was named Government Commissar. Giving me this decree in the presence of Comrade Osinsky, Vladimir Ilich said, "If you don't get the money, don't come back." ... After receiving the assignment from Lenin, Comrade Osinsky and I drove together to the State Bank .... Relying on lower level staff and couriers, who were on our side, and also threatening that the Red Guard already had surrounded the bank, we succeeded in getting into the cash office of the bank, despite all sorts of excuses that were made up by the higher officers of the State Bank, such as false alarms, etc., and we made the cashier give out the amount required. We conducted the receipt of the money at a counting table under the cocked guns of the soldiers of the military guard of the bank. There was a difficulty with bags for money. We had not brought anything with us. One of the couriers finally lent a pair of some sort of large old bags. We filled them to the top with money, put them over our backs and carried them to our vehicle.
>
> We went to Smolny smiling. At Smolny, we personally carried the bags into Lenin's office. Vladimir Ilich was out. While waiting for him, I sat on the bags holding a revolver: "on guard." I ceremoniously turned the bags over to Vladimir Ilich. He accepted them with an expression as if it were perfectly natural, but in fact he was very pleased. He had a wardrobe chest brought into a nearby room to hold the first Soviet treasury, surrounded this chest with a

semicircle of chairs and posted a sentry. A special decree of the Council of People's Commissars established the procedure for safekeeping and use of this money.

Within a very short period, the Bolsheviks had control of the banks and thus of the existing money supply. At this point there was no more money to confiscate. They next turned to printing money. The printing plants inherited from the prerevolutionary Ministry of Finance worked overtime, producing billions of increasingly worthless rubles. This policy was self-defeating, since it led, by the early 1920s, to the total collapse of Soviet currency. However, the Government, in times of crisis, returned to the policy of financing by creating money, during the Second World War and most recently during 1991. The Soviet Union never had an independent currency emission body, like the Federal Reserve Bank in the United States or the Bundesbank in Germany. As a result, when the Government decided to issue money, it met with no resistance from the Ministry of Finance or the State Bank.

Financing by taxation began early in the Soviet period and continued throughout its history. During 1990 and 1991, at both the USSR and republic levels there was an attempt to reform the tax system, to create a system suited to a market economy. When Soviet enterprises all belonged to the state and were closely monitored by ministries and the party, there was little problem in getting payment of taxes and profits due from the enterprises. As state planning weakened, enterprises became more interested in making money (and in paying it out to their managers and employees) than in filling plans. Individuals began to get sources of income not subject to tax withholding. In response, legislation created new tax enforcement mechanisms in the USSR and republic ministries of finance. A 1990 law established a Main Tax Inspectorate of the USSR Ministry of Finance, with auditing and collection powers similar to those of the United States Internal Revenue Service.[10] The legislature ordered the ministry to become more active in closing tax loopholes. Legislation in 1990 ordered it to issue new accounting regulations to prevent state enterprises from using cooperatives to evade financial rules.[11] The republics initiated similar revenue collection services and issued similar rules.[12] Creating a modern tax enforcement system is no simple task, and the changes failed to keep up with the changes in the economy.

In 1990 and 1991 the USSR Ministry of Finance faced a problem much more serious that modernizing its tax enforcement system. Under its charter, the Ministry of Finance was responsible for ensuring the receipt of the income anticipated by the Union budget.[13] However, the republics' revolt against Union authority in 1990 and 1991 made it impossible for the ministry to carry out this function.   Previously, the republics had collected tax money from state enterprises under their jurisdiction and had transferred the money to the Union Ministry of Finance.   By 1990, not only were enterprises resisting tax collection, the republics themselves were systematically withholding contributions from the USSR Ministry. Under the system of strong central party rule, the republic ministries of finance, although theoretically subordinate both to the republic governments and the Union Ministry of Finance, in fact collected taxes for the center and remitted money to the center substantially as ordered by the Union Ministry of Finance.   By 1990-91, the Union ministry had become unable to obtain payments due from the republics.[14] Union officials must have seriously regretted the decision taken in the 1920s to abandon the Russian empire's policy of subordinating all tax collection bodies directly to the central Ministry of Finance.

Russian Republic Takeover

In the summer of 1990, the Russian Republic unsuccessfully attempted to seize the assets and operations of the USSR State Bank on Russian Republic territory.[15]   The Union authorities resisted Russian Republic financial moves through August 1991. During a financial scandal in early 1991, involving a huge rubles-for-dollars deal negotiated by officials of the Russian Republic Government, the Union Ministry of Finance offered an expert opinion that the deal was illegal.[16] An unconfirmed Soviet press story indicated that the whole deal was part of a KGB sting operation undertaken by the Union authorities to discredit the Russian Republic.[17]

In the aftermath of the failed August 1991 coup, the Russian Republic claimed authority over the USSR Ministry of Finance and the other USSR financial organs. A Radio Russia broadcast reported that

> Russian President Boris Yeltsin has issued an instruction according to which all financial and foreign currency operations and operations involving precious metals and stones may be carried out by the Ministry of Finance, State Bank and Bank for Foreign Economic Activity of the USSR exclusively with the agreement of the RSFSR Ministry of Finance and its central bank and the Foreign Trade Bank. All the material and technical assets of the USSR Ministry of Finance, State Bank and Bank for Foreign Economic Activity are transferred to the jurisdiction of these Russian departments. According to the instruction, proposals for the procedure for the relations between the budget of Russia and the budgets of the union and the other republics are to be submitted to the Russian President within a month.[18]

However, in one of the many twists in the war of laws, the Russian authorities redelegated some of the powers back to the Union level.[19] In fact the Union Ministry continued functioning until mid-November 1991, when the Russian Republic issued a decree completing its takeover.

> The non-fulfillment by USSR bodies of obligations which are directly envisaged by the treaty on an economic community is hampering the implementation of the provisions of the treaty, destabilizing the economic situation, reinforcing inflationary processes and exacerbating the financial crisis in the RSFSR, and in the USSR as a whole. In the interests of financial provision for the reforms in the RSFSR and also with the aim of protecting the RSFSR's economic sovereignty, and establishing the necessary control over circulation and emission of money, the government of the RSFSR resolves:
>
> 1. That the central apparatus of the Ministry of Finance of the RSFSR be included in the structure of the RSFSR Ministry of Economy and Finance, and that the necessary organizational changes be made. That the structures, subdivisions and organizations of the former USSR Ministry of Finance, including the Precious Metals and Precious Stones Administration, the subdivisions of the State Valuables Depository [USSR Gokhran] and administrations of the State Assay Office of the USSR Ministry of Finance, located on the territory of the RSFSR, should be subordinated to the RSFSR Ministry of Economy and Finance.
>
> 2. Enterprises and institutions of the State Production Association for the Production of State Banknotes of the USSR [Goznak] located on the territory of the RSFSR are to be transferred to the jurisdiction of the RSFSR Ministry of Economy and Finance. The RSFSR Ministry of Economy and Finance is to ensure the fulfillment of contracts and other obligations of Goznak towards sovereign states—former union republics.
>
> 3. From 20th November 1991 the financing of ministries and departments of the USSR is to be ended, apart from those to which part of the functions of state administration have been transferred in accordance with RSFSR legislation. Ministries and departments of the RSFSR are to take measures to recruit qualified officials of the former central departments of the USSR to work in RSFSR institutions.
>
> 4. That the RSFSR Ministry of Economy and Finance, jointly with the RSFSR central bank, should by 10th December 1991 prepare and put forward a system of measures to protect the interests of the RSFSR in its relations with the former union republics intending to introduce their own currencies.
>
> 5. That the RSFSR Ministry of Economy and Finance be empowered to conduct talks with the leadership of the sovereign states—the former union republics—on matters to do with the apportionment of the diamond and hard currency reserves, and the further utilization of them.[20]

The Future

Although it is unclear how financial powers will be allocated between the republics in the new Commonwealth of Independent States, the functions of the former USSR Ministry of Finance should survive the reallocation of power over finances to the republics. Nearly all of these functions are essential to the operation of a modern society. Regardless of the fate of the Commonwealth and its constituent republics, the functions will have to be performed. Many of the them had already migrated to the republic ministries of finance before the Russian Republic takeover of the Union ministry. Others may migrate eventually from the republic ministries to other organizations at the republic or local level or even to non-governmental organizations.

In its last days, the Union Ministry of Finance still had, on paper, a wide variety of legal powers. It was not easy to determine exactly what these formal legal powers were or to what extent the formal powers were available in practice. The charter of the Ministry was two decades old. After it was adopted, numerous legislative acts gave additional functions to the Ministry but did not revise the charter to reflect these powers. This process accelerated during the period of rapid change in 1990-91. During the same period, as finances became a major battlefield in a "war of laws" between the Union and the republics, republic legislation often denied to the Union Ministry of Finance powers granted to it by USSR legislation. The 1971 charter summed up the tasks of the ministry as follows: "The USSR Ministry of Finance prepares the draft of the USSR State Budget and bears responsibility for the fulfillment of the USSR State Budget, both for receipts and for expenditures .... "

Examples of shifting of power during 1990-91 are numerous. Until 1990, the USSR Ministry of Finance played an important role in approving foreign investments. However, the Russian Republic Law on Foreign Investments required foreign investors to obtain the approval of the republic's ministry of finance.[21] Likewise, the Kazakh Law on Foreign Investment listed the republic's ministry of finance as one of the agencies that would grant approval to foreign investments.[22] In the domestic economy, the Russian Republic Law on Privatization of State and Municipal Enterprises provided for the creation of investment funds (like mutual funds) and required these funds to make quarterly, semiannual, and annual reports in forms specified by the republic's ministry of finance.[23] The Statute on the Russian Fund of Federal Property provided that expenditures by the fund and its local departments should be made on the basis of financial norms approved by the republics's ministry of finance.[24] The republic's ministry of finance also acted as the registry for joint stock companies[25] and maintained a register of enterprises registered by local authorities.[26] These registers are important, because the ministry had to have information on all companies and enterprises for tax enforcement purposes.[27] Finally, the republic's ministry of finance was responsible for securities regulation.[28] This gradual transfer of powers should ease the shock of the completion of the Russian takeover of the Union ministry.

The broad legislative power of the USSR Ministry of Finance was long important at both the Union and the republic levels. The ministry's charter authorized the minister to issue orders, instructions, and directives obligatory for all organizations and enterprises. Because almost every action of every organization has a financial aspect, these general legislative powers made the Ministry of Finance a government within a government. It exercised the power to set standards and rules for accounting and bookkeeping, for all organizations, institutions, and enterprises, governmental and non-governmental. It also had the related power to issue regulations providing for the detailed application of the general principles of tax legislation. Both these functions are necessary in any modern economy. In the United States, for instance, the Treasury Department issues tax regulations, while a variety of institutions, the General Accounting Office, the Securities and Exchange Commission, and a private accounting organization, issue accounting standards. Under United States law all such regulations issued by governmental bodies must be published and may be attacked in court by dissatisfied affected parties. The power of the Ministry of Finance differed in that it was more centralized, in that its regulations were published haphazardly or not at all, and in that no effective legal channels existed for challenge. Often the USSR Ministry of Finance exercised its rulemaking power jointly with other state agencies. A good example is the 1990 Basic Provisions on the Composition of Expenditures Included in the Cost of Production, which was adopted jointly by the USSR State Planning Committee, the USSR Ministry of Finance, the USSR State Committee on Prices, and the USSR State Committee on Statistics.[29]

The rulemaking power of the USSR Ministry of Finance also devolved to the republics during 1990 and 1991. However, this change alone will make little difference. Even after the disappearance of the Union Ministry of Finance, many of its regulations will have to stay in force because the republics will take years to develop a comparable body of rules. The real legal question is whether the system can be reformed to meet the standards necessary for a law-governed market economy, namely that all accounting and tax regulations be published and be subject to judicial review for legality. The real practical question is how this mass of regulations, which enshrine the precepts of the command-administrative economy, can be rewritten to provide working rules for a market economy.

The Ministry of Finance had a major role in the development and implementation of the Union budget. It was supposed to prepare the first draft of the budget and present it to the USSR Government. Even after the power shifts resulting from the failure of the August 1991 coup, the Union Ministry of Finance retained its function of preparing a draft budget. However, a new institution created in the aftermath of the coup, the Committee for the Operational Administration of the Economy, assumed the leading role in the formation of the budget, as indicated by its rejection of the ministry's draft budget.[30] The ministry also had the power to inspect the fulfillment of the budget by all Government agencies and the fulfillment by state banks of the plan of capital investments, involving both investments with state funds and investments with enterprise funds. Clearly, if at some point Government functions are revived at the center of the new Commonwealth, some finance agency will be needed to audit and inspect to be sure that budget funds are spent for the purposes designated. Whatever the ultimate division of labor between Commonwealth and republican institutions, the ministries of finance are likely to lose much of their role in auditing enterprise investment with the decline of centralized investment planning and the growth of commercial banking and joint stock companies. Commercial banks will naturally engage in their own verification operations to ensure that loans are spent for the purposes for which they are borrowed. Joint stock company legislation provides for stockholder election of audit commissions.[31]

The USSR ministry's charter also provided that the ministry would participate in the operations of the USSR State Committee on Prices. Here two changes took place in the transition from the Soviet Union to a Commonwealth of Independent States. First, price-setting functions devolved to the republics, so that prices are set by the republic ministries of finance together with the republic committees on prices. Second, with the move toward a market economy, a variety of commodities are being freed by law, or in spite of the law, from price controls, so that the price-setting function is "withering away."

The USSR ministry also participated in the setting of salaries for employees of government departments and of state enterprises. Even with the shrinking size of the Union Government in the last months of Soviet rule, the ministry still had many employees and still needed an organization to coordinate their salaries. However, as the Government moves from direct to indirect wage controls of enterprise employee wages in the republics, so the wage-setting will "wither away" at the enterprise level and lessen, or eliminate, the need for salary setting by the republic ministries of finance.

The charter also provided that the USSR ministry was to work with the State Planning Committee and the State Bank in making and fulfilling plans for foreign currency, precious metals, and precious stones. The "foreign currency plan" was essentially a plan for taxing those organizations that earned foreign currency, by paying them far below the market value of the currency in rubles and for subsidizing certain organizations that spend foreign currency, and by selling them foreign currency for far below its market value in rubles. As mentioned above, the republics moved to take over control of their own natural resources and foreign currency. To the extent that they also move toward elimination of subsidies and creation of a market economy, and toward the creation of convertible currencies, the "foreign currency plan" will wither away.

The charter provided for the Ministry of Finance to exercise general supervision of state insurance. *Gosstrakh*, the state monopoly insurance agency, was subordinate to the ministry. Now, increasingly, private companies are starting to compete, and the fate of *Gosstrakh* is unclear.[32] However, unlike some areas, where they may be unfettered competition in the future, it seems likely that there will always be a need for fairly strict regulation of insurance companies. Thus, even if insurance is privatized, it is likely that the republic ministries of finance will continue to regulate the insurance industry.

The USSR ministry was also responsible for arrangement with other agencies for the handling of the payment of pensions. In the past, the discredited "official" trade union system played an important role in pension payments. It is likely that in the future the republics will dispense pensions directly, bypassing the "official" trade unions.

The "500 day plan" almost adopted in the fall of 1990 called for the passage of legislation to create a "USSR Reserve System," "an independent nongovernmental organization" modeled after the United States and German systems. It also envisioned a board consisting of the heads of the central banks of the republics, which was designed to limit the power of the political leadership to create money.[33] However, the December 1990 law on the State Bank [*Gosbank*] created instead a state organization, controlled by the Union authorities and charged with the task of "conduct of a uniform government policy."[34] Transition provisions emphasized the subservience of the financial agencies to Government policy by ordering the uncompensated transfer of a portion of the Ministry of Finance's gold reserves to the State Bank.[35] Thus, while the Ministry of Finance was responsible for the physical manufacture of paper money, coins, and government bonds, it did not have the authority to regulate the money supply. As long as the ruble survives as a currency, the plants that belonged to the USSR Ministry of Finance will print it. If the ruble is replaced by republic currencies, the same plants may print them too. The newly freed Baltic countries have had difficulty mastering the technical task of printing counterfeiting-resistant currency, despite the fact that they are superior in technology to most of the Soviet Union.

Gorbachev continued the tradition of regulating the money supply by political decision. Soon after taking power, Gorbachev began an anti-alcohol campaign. Whatever the success of the campaign in reducing drunkenness, it was a budgetary disaster, as alcohol tax revenues fell precipitously. Gorbachev retreated from the campaign, and alcohol tax revenues rose by 1989. But at this point, the republics started withholding budgetary contributions, with the result that the USSR Government relied more and more on creation of money to finance its operations and to finance transfer payments to the poorer republics and pensioners. Gorbachev's Government met its obligations by ordering the Ministry of Finance to create money. In addition to printing currency, the ministry created money by obtaining huge loans from the State Bank in paper transactions.[36] Government officials responsible for economic reform threw the blame upon Gorbachev, saying that lower level officials were powerless to control the Ministry of Finance and the State Bank.[37] The republics have been equally undisciplined. They too have been ordering their ministries of finance to "find" the money for various projects.[38] The result by 1991 was runaway inflation.[39] The Union and republic governments continued price controls on the sale of goods in state stores despite the inflation, partly for ideological reasons, partly from well-justified fear of popular reaction to major price increases. The result was the virtually total disappearance of goods from the state retail store network. (The goods moved to areas outside the price control system: the black market, the farmers' market, and barter.) Whether it was intended or not, the bare store shelves convinced the Soviet public and foreign public that communism had failed.

The September 1991 draft treaty on an economic union envisioned the creation of a true reserve system that would control the money supply of a new economic union independent of the wishes of the political leadership of the Union.[40] If adopted, this reserve system would have been independent of the USSR and republic ministries of finance. Such a reserve system would, in theory, have created a unified and strong currency for the Union. However, in December 1991, the republics decided to abandon the Union and form a Commonwealth with indeterminate powers and purpose. Within this new Commonwealth, many republics are threatening to issue their own currency. Efforts are still underway by some republics, notably Russia, to find a compromise that would tie the value of republic currencies firmly to the ruble. And while no one has suggested allowing the leadership of the Russian Republic to continue to control the supply of rubles by political decision, that is in fact what is happening. In this sense, then, the collapse of the Union may prove to have been a setback in negotiating an end to the irresponsible printing of money. The ministries of finance of the now independent republics are showing no more signs of self-restraint in monetary emission than the USSR Ministry of Finance.

Whatever monetary systems emerge in the Commonwealth, taxes will have to be collected, money will have to be printed, and businesses will be subject to financial regulation. The question is at what administrative level those functions are performed. Perhaps the most important measure of the independence of the constituent states of the Commonwealth will be their ability to prevent these financial functions from being recentralized in Commonwealth institutions or in the institutions of other, more powerful, republics.

Notes

1. V.D. Bonch-Bruevich, *Vospominanie o Lenine*, 2nd ed. (Moscow: Nauka, 1969), p. 133.

2. G.Ia. Sokolnikov, People's Commissar of Finance in the 1920s, confessed that his "public utterances of 1925 and 1926 already contained all the principal elements of a program of capitalist restoration." *Report of Court Proceedings in the Case of the Anti-Soviet Trotskyite Centre Heard Before the Military Collegium of the Supreme Court of the USSR, Moscow, January 23-30, 1937* (Moscow: People's Commissariat of Justice of the USSR, 1937), p. 551. G.F. Grinko, People's Commissar of Finance in the 1930s, confessed to using the commissariat to further plans for "wrecking." *Sudebnyi otchet po delu antisovetskogo "Pravo-trotskistkogo bloka" rassmatrennomu Voennoi Kollegiei Verkhovnogo Suda Soiuza SSR, 2-13 marta 1938 g.* (Moscow: Iuridicheskoe izdatel'stvo NKIu SSSR, 1938), pp. 51-60.

3. *Ministerstvo finansov 1802-1902* (St. Petersburg: Ekspeditsiia zagotovleniia gosudarstvennykh bumag, 1902).

4. See *Ministerstvo finansov 1904-1913* (n.p., n.d.) and S.S. Katzenellenbaum, *Russian Currency and Banking 1914-1924* (London: P.S. King & Son, 1925).

5. I. Reingold, "Finance Administration in the USSR," in Sokolnikov *et al.*, *Soviet Policy in Public Finance 1917-1928* (Stanford: Stanford University Press, 1931), p. 442-43.

6. For the history of Soviet finance in the 1920s and 1930s, see: Arthur Z. Arnold, *Banks, Credit, and Money in Soviet Russia* (New York: Columbia University Press, 1937); and Gregory Y. Sokolnikov *et al.*, *Soviet Policy in Public Finance 1917-1928* (Stanford: Stanford University Press, 1931).

7. A.G. Zverev, *Zapiski ministra* (Moscow: Politizdat, 1973).

8. Isaac Deutscher, *Stalin: A Political Biography*, 2nd ed. (New York: Oxford University Press, 1967), pp. 87-88; Robert C. Tucker, *Stalin as Revolutionary 1897-1929*, (New York: W.W. Norton, 1973), pp. 102-103.

9. N.P. Gorbunov, "Kak sozdavalsia v oktiabr'skie dni rabochii apparat Soveta narodnykh komissarov," in *Vospominaniia o Vladimire Il'iche Lenine*, vol. 3 (Moscow: Politizdat, 1969), pp. 58-59.

10. "O pravakh, obiazannostiiakh i otvetstvennosti gosudarstvennykh nalogovykh inspektsii," *Vedomosti s"ezda narodnykh deputatov SSSR i Verkhovnogo Soveta SSSR*, no. 22 (1990), item 394.

11. "O vzaimootnosheniiakh gosudarstvennykh predpriiatii s sozdannymi pri nikh kooperativami," *Sobranie postanovlenii pravitel'stva SSSR*, no. 30 (1990), item 146.

12. "RSFSR State Tax Service Act 1991," SovData DiaLine, SovLegisLine, 21 March 1991 in LEXIS, EUROPE library, SOVLEG file.

13. "Polozhenie o Ministerstve finansov SSSR," *Sobranie postanovlenii Pravitel'stva SSSR*, no. 4 (1971), item 28; as amended, *Sobranie postanovlenii Pravitel'stva SSSR*, no. 2 (1981), item 3. See also "O perestroike finansovogo mekhanizma i povyshenii roli Ministerstva finansov SSSR v novykh usloviiakh khoziaistvovaniia," *Sobranie postanovlenii Pravitel'stva SSSR*, no. 36 (1987), item 119.

14. "USSR Finance Minister Optimistic About Solving Economic Crisis," Soviet television, 20 July 1991, BBC Summary of World Broadcasts, July 22, 1991, LEXIS, EUROPE library, BBCSWB file. It is the duty of finance ministers to be optimistic, even when there is nothing to be optimistic about.

15. "O gosudarstvennom banke RSFSR i bankakh na territorii respubliki," *Vedomosti s"ezda narodnykh deputatov RSFSR i Verkhovnogo Soveta RSFSR*, no. 11 (1990), item 146; "Russian Republic-USSR Dispute Over Banks Highlights Importance of Bank Law Reform," *Soviet Business Law Report*, no. 5 (September 1989), in LEXIS, EUROPE Library, SBLAW File.

16. "Deal to Sell Rubles for Dollars Invalid, Experts State," TASS, 25 January 1991, Lexis, EUROPE library, TASS file.

17. "On Launching 'Case', Take Time Off," *Megapolis Express*, no. 39 (1991), p. 22, translated in *Soviet Press Digest*, LEXIS, EUROPE library, SPD file.

18. "Jurisdiction Over Financial Operations," Russia's Radio, 28 August 1991, BBC Summary of World Broadcasts, 6 September 1991, LEXIS, EUROPE library, BBCSWB file.

19. "Jurisdiction Over Financial Operations," TASS, 29 August 1991, BBC Summary of World Broadcasts, 6 September 1991, LEXIS, EUROPE library, BBCSWB file.

20. "Resolution on Financial Provision for Reforms," TASS, 17 November 1991, translated in BBC Summary of World Broadcasts, 19 November 1991, in LEXIS; NEXIS library; CURRNT file.

21. "Ob inostrannykh investitsiiakh v RSFSR," *Sovetskaia Rossiia*, 25 July 1991, pp. 1, 4.

22. "Text of Kazakh Law on Foreign Investment," *Soviet Business Law Report*, no. 1 (May 1991), in LEXIS, EUROPE library, SBLAW file.

23. "O privatizatsii gosudarstvennykh i munitsipal'nykh predpriiatii v RSFSR," *Rossiiskaia gazeta*, 19 July 1991, pp. 15-16.

24. "Polozhenie o Rossiiskom fonde federal'nogo imushchestva," *Ekonomika i zhizn'*, no. 31 (1991), p. 16.

25. "[RSFSR] Polozhenie ob aktsionernykh obshchestvakh," *Biznes i banki*, no. 2 (1991), p. 4, ch. III.

26. "O predpriiatiiakh i predprinimatel'skoi deiatel'nosti," *Vedomosti s "ezda narodnykh deputatov RSFSR i Verkhovnogo Soveta RSFSR*, no. 30 (1990), item 418.

27. Registration at the Union level has a long history.   See N.D. Ignatov, "O gosudarstvennoi registratsii predpriiatii," *Finansy SSSR*, no. 5 (1991), p. 28; *Ukazatel' deistvuiushchikh v Imperii aktsionernykh predpriiatii: sostavlen po dannym, izvlechennym iz materiala Otdela torgovli, Osobennoi kantseliarii po kreditnoi chasti Departamenta zheleznodorozhnykh del Ministerstva finansov*, ed. V. A. Dmitriev-Mamonov with G. Andreev *et al.* (St. Petersburg: A.I. Dmitriev-Mamonov, 1903).

28. "Ob utverzhdenii polozheniia ob aktsionernykh obshchestvakh," *Biznes i banki*, no. 2 (1991), p. 4, Art. 5.

29. "Osnovnye polozheniia po sostavu zatrat, vkliuchaemykh v sebestoimost' produktsii (rabot, uslug) na predpriiatiiakh SSSR," *Biulleten' normativnykh aktov ministerstv i vedomstv SSSR*, no. 5 (1991), p. 3.

30. Vladimir Isachenkov, "Economic Management Committee Discusses Budget Crisis," TASS World Service in English, 13 September 1991, reported in BBC Summary of World Broadcasts, 17 September 1991, LEXIS, EUROPE library, BBCSWB file.

31. For example, "[RSFSR] Polozhenie ob aktsionernykh obshchestvakh," *Biznes i banki*, no. 2 (1991), p. 4, ch. 19.

32. V.V. Shakhov, "Gosstrakh na puti obnovleniia," *Finansy SSSR*, no. 2 (1991), p. 3.

33. "Proekt Zakona SSSR 'O Rezervnoi sisteme SSSR'," in *Perekhod k rynku: Chast' 2—Proekty zakonodatel'nykh aktov* (Moscow: Arkhangel'skoe, 1990).

34. "O gosudarstvennom banke SSSR," *Vedomosti s "ezda narodykh deputatov SSSR i Verkhovnogo Soveta SSSR*, no. 52 (1990), item 1154.

35. "O vvedenii v deistvie Zakona SSSR 'O gosudarstvennom banke SSSR' i Zakona SSSR 'O bankakh i bankovskoi deiatel'nosti'," *Vedomosti s "ezda narodykh deputatov SSSR i Verkhovnogo Soveta SSSR*, no. 52 (1990), item 1156.

36. See, for instance, Ivan Ivanov and Vladimir Isachenkov, "USSR Parliament Endorsed Gosbank Credit to Finance Ministry," TASS, 27 May 1991, in LEXIS, EUROPE library, TASS file.

37. Andrei Orlov, "Academician Abalkin: Lessons for the Future," TASS, 24 January 1991, in LEXIS, EUROPE library, TASS file.

38. For example, "RSFSR Government Resolution on Ways to Improve Grain Storage," *TASS World Service in Russian*, 9 September 1991, BBC Summary of World Broadcasts, 11 September 1991, LEXIS, EUROPE Library, BBCSWB file.

39. Ivan Ivanov and Vladimir Isachenkov, "USSR Parliament Warns of Threat of Budgetary Collapse," TASS, 4 April 1991, LEXIS, EUROPE library, TASS file.

40. I. Demchenko, "Economic Union Without Political Conditions—This is How G. Yavlinsky's Group sees It," *Izvestiia*, 11 September 1971, BBC Summary of World Broadcasts, 12 September 1991, LEXIS, EUROPE library, BBCSWB file.

6

THE INDUSTRIAL MINISTRIES

Stephen Fortescue

Just as the Soviet Union had a very special economic structure, so it had a very special administrative structure. The economy was for a long time almost totally nationalized and tightly controlled from the center. This chapter describes the state apparatus that was developed to run the industrial sector of the economy. It was organized on a highly specialized branch, or industry-by-industry, basis. The branches were organized into vertical hierarchies, with a powerful chain of command from top to bottom. We will examine here that chain of command, working downward from the branch-specialized units of the top Government administrative body, the Council of Ministers (renamed the Cabinet of Ministers in the waning months of the Soviet Union). Most attention will be devoted to the industrial ministries, which served as the "transmission belts" between the top-level bodies and enterprises. The treatment will be limited to civilian industry.

History and Antecedents

It might appear simple to declare that the origins of the Soviet bureaucracy lie in the pre-revolutionary tsarist bureaucracy. The oppressively bureaucratic traditions of tsarism could be used to explain, and to imply the inevitability of, an oppressive bureaucracy under the communists. Once Lenin realized that a change of political leadership in Russia had not brought about the end of bureaucratism, he laid the blame on the "tsarist hangovers" in his state apparatus (although he far from absolved from blame the new "Soviet" bureaucrats). The "tsarist hangover" thesis remained the standard Soviet explanation of bureaucratism until very recently.

The extent to which there was continuity between the tsarist and Soviet bureaucracies in general, and the effect of such continuity on the political culture of the Soviet Union, fall outside the concerns of this chapter. However, some attention needs to be paid more narrowly to possible continuities in the state management of industry. Tsarist industry was, relative to other industrializing countries of the time, highly state-directed. In the defense industry sector there was a high degree of state ownership and close control over production by central government agencies. In the civilian sector the situation was rather different. There the state, while highly interventionist, relied on private ownership of industry, exercising its influence through tariff regimes, provision and guarantees of credit, and guarantees of markets and prices through government contracts. The approach was reflected in the Government's bureaucratic structure, with an independent Ministry of Trade and Industry established only in 1905 on the basis of departments transferred from the Ministry of Finance and other agencies.[1]

Most historians have focused on non-governmental structures of pre-revolutionary industrial management. They draw attention to the highly concentrated structure of Russian private sector industry and the increasing dominance of oligopolistic trusts formed in response to the economic downturn of the early twentieth century and the special needs of the First World War.[2] It is claimed that these large-scale enterprises and associations, rather than the tsarist state apparatus, were the most direct precursors of the highly interventionist Soviet ministries. Indeed, in the first months after the revolution, Lenin described the pre-revolutionary industrial structures as representing an advanced form of capitalism, which could be used by the new regime.

The Bolsheviks' central industrial management body, the All-Russian Council of the National Economy (*VSNKh*), took over the pre-revolutionary state and particularly private industry structures and transformed them into its own branch-based units. Set up on 2 December 1917,[3] *VSNKh* directly supervised nationalized enterprises. Non-nationalized enterprises, usually of a smaller-scale, were supervised by regional management bodies, the *sovnarkhozy*, which reported to *VSNKh* on their industrial management activities.

Branch specialization was immediately evident in *VSNKh*'s structural units. As nationalization spread, particularly as the Civil War got underway, the branch units of *VSNKh* became more numerous and more formalized. The first of these branch units, known as *glavki*, short for *glavnye upravleniia* (chief administrations), was formed in mid-1918. By September 1918 there were eighteen *glavki*; fifty-two existed by the end of 1920. During the Civil War the *glavki* were exercising as much day-to-day control over the production and particularly supply and distribution activities of enterprises as was possible in the chaos of the time.

From this early period two important tensions in Soviet economic management were evident. First, there was the struggle for control over economic resources between the center and periphery. *VSNKh* and its *glavki* struggled, with increasing success, to gain control of even those medium and small-scale enterprises that had originally been under regional control. The central political authorities well understood the political and strategic importance of central economic control and supported *VSNKh*.[4] Secondly, from these earliest stages the center faced the problem of control of its own operational industrial management bodies, at this stage the *glavki*, later the ministries. These organizations have always had the tendency to look after their own narrow interests at the expense of the state interest. As the extent of state ownership and the complexity of the economy increased, this problem, summed up in the word *vedomstvennost'* (usually translated as "sectionalism" or "departmentalism"), became ever more serious.

The end of the Civil War and introduction of the New Economic Policy brought major economic changes. However these changes had far less relevance for large-scale industry than for other sectors of the economy. There was some delegation of *VSNKh* control to regional authorities and a sharp reduction in the number of *glavki*, to 17. However, as an organizational chart of *VSNKh* at this time shows, the remaining *glavki* were highly specialized and had many even more specialized sections under them.[5] New organizations called trusts were set up at the production level. These were amalgamations of enterprises that were supposed to operate on a profit-and-loss basis. In 1921, 421 trusts were formed covering about 90 percent of state enterprises. The trusts in turn "voluntarily" formed "syndicates," which had responsibility for providing the trusts with supplies, something which they did on a commercial basis. This reduced to a limited extent central operational control over enterprises, but *VSNKh*, through its *glavki*, still approved production plans, provided capital, and appointed managers.[6]

Whether NEP was a brief interlude in a continuous process of centralization of economic management or a distinct stage of economic development that preceded a qualitatively new Stalinist system is an historical argument that cannot concern us here. What can be stated confidently is that Stalinist industrialization brought with it the "classical" model of the command economy, which in turn brought the "classical" model of industrial management, a model which changed remarkably little in the next six decades. By the time industrialization got underway, all threats to central state power over industry had been dealt with, whether the Workers' Opposition and its concept of workers' control of industry, the Right Opposition with its gradualist and decentralized approach to industrial development, or the "bourgeois specialists," who were removed in "*spets*-baiting" trials and the *vydvizhenie* movement.[7] The Stalinist system adopted the same basic industrial structure as had been evident since the revolution, branch-based, line-dominated vertical hierarchies. But new, more specialized, arrangements were required because the tempos of industrialization set by Stalin demanded even tighter central control.[8] In 1932, *VSNKh* was abolished and a number of people's commissariats were established in its place. People's commissariat was the name that had been given to ministries at the time of the revolution, but up to 1932 there had been no commissariats in the industrial sector. Now commissariats for heavy industry, light industry and the timber industry were set up, with the first (*Narkomtiazhprom*) being the most important for our purposes. During the 1930s, the number of independent commissariats increased, as new industrial commissariats split off from *Narkomtiazhprom*. In 1946, the commissariats were renamed ministries, but the same process of multiplication and occasional contraction continued.[9]

It presumably was after the abolition of *VSNKh* that branch-specialized units began to be set up within the top-level state executive body, the Council of People's Commissars, renamed the Council of Ministers in 1946. To help overcome burgeoning "departmentalism," these branch-specialized supervisory units were placed above the commissariats/ministries. Parallel to these branch departments of the central apparatus of the Council of Ministers[10] were added the branch departments of the Communist Party's Central Committee apparatus.[11] The curtain finally fell on the latter in 1991.[12] The former seemed to have a chance of maintaining a rump existence even as the Soviet Union was collapsing. The Interrepublican Economic Committee was retained in the fall of 1991 as a successor of sorts to the Council of Ministers. It had an apparatus of no more than 1500 staff, of whom 500 were to be in the Department of Economics and Finance, presumably all that was left of Gosplan and the Ministry of Finance. The rest of the staff was to be divided up between approximately 15 to 20 departments, a number of which presumably were to be branch departments.[13] However, the final collapse of the Soviet Union in December 1991 seems to have brought an end to the Interrepublican Economic Committee, though something akin to it may yet emerge to coordinate economic activity in the Commonwealth of Independent States.

Historically, the only major development affecting the ministries after industrialization was Khrushchev's *sovnarkhoz* reorganization of 1957. Partly out of a genuine desire to improve industrial management and partly out of a desire to give himself, with a power base in the party apparatus, an advantage over his political rivals with their power bases in the state apparatus, Khrushchev abolished the civilian industrial ministries and introduced a regional system of industrial management. The experiment was not a success, and even before

Khrushchev's removal from power the old centralized branch structure reasserted itself in the form of an increasing number of state committees.[14]

Once Khrushchev was out of the way, the new leadership reestablished the ministerial system in its familiar form, including the familiar expansion and contraction in the number of ministries. Many commentators consider that the industrial ministry system reached its apogee under Brezhnev. The breakdown of central political will aggravated the old problem of "departmentalism." The industrial ministries and the whole "sectional society" that they represented played an increasingly obstructive role in policy making and implementation, contributing to the economic paralysis of the period. While the period was not devoid of attempts at reform, they were depressingly ineffective in conception and implementation. As one would expect, after Gorbachev came to power the pace of change rapidly increased. Whether the changes introduced were more radical or effective than their numerous predecessors is a controversial issue to which we will return.

Functions of the Ministries

Ministries do not stand at the top of the economic decision-making hierarchy. Since we are dealing with a centrally planned economy, higher organs than the ministries set policy and the broad parameters of its implementation. These bodies for most of the USSR's history were, at the top, the Politburo and Council of Ministers, then Gosplan and lesser functional agencies such as the Ministry of Finance, *Gossnab* (State Supply Committee), *Gostsen* (State Prices Committee), and the State Committee for Science and Technology. In addition, there were the already mentioned higher-level line agencies within the Council of Ministers apparatus.

It is in the nature of a complex society, however, that the center could not run everything--Gosplan could not plan everything, *Gossnab* could not allocate everything, *Gostsen* could not set every price--and therefore many operational functions were delegated to the ministries, with the "departmentalism" consequences noted earlier. Given the close historical links between the centrally planned economy and the ministries, it is not surprising that their functions were essentially those of operational administrative units of the command economy.[15] The most important ministry functions are briefly described below.

Plan formulation

The basis of the command economy is the plan. Given that no one has yet managed to invent a computer that can plan everything, central planning inevitably involves an intermediary between central political and planning agencies and producers. At the plan formulation stage the central planners' most important requirement is accurate information on the production capacities and input requirements of producers. For the most important enterprises and product lines the ministries provided the information required for the central agencies to enter single-line items into the plan; for other items the ministries aggregated at the branch level. In theory the process should have been a purely technical one, with all participants sharing the same interest in maximizing national output. In practice, of course, narrow interests could not be ignored. It was a controversial issue in Soviet commentary as to whether ministries were, or should have been, representatives of the state interest or whether the only realistic expectation was that they would represent their own narrow "departmental" interests.[16] The reality would appear to be the latter, meaning that to a very considerable extent the ministries' shared their enterprises' interest in setting plan targets at the lowest possible level and inputs at the highest possible level.

Plan fulfillment

Plan fulfillment was undoubtedly the most important function of the ministries. Ensuring the fulfillment of branch output plans often required considerable shifting around of output targets for different enterprises, including giving emergency orders to some to cover production shortfalls in others. This subsidization of poorly performing enterprises by good performers, something which was also achieved by the application of differential branch-level taxation rates, was seen as having a negative incentive effect in enterprises. Moreover, ministries themselves had little incentive to improve the performance of weak enterprises.

The stress above all else on plan fulfillment as the measure of ministries' performance had various other baleful consequences for overall economic performance. One of the best known is the practice of "micro-management" (*melochnaia opeka*). In its narrowest sense "micro-management" referred to excessive demands from ministries for reports on enterprise performance. This might mean no more than having to send into ministry headquarters hundreds of statistical reports that were simply filed away at no more cost than time and paper. More importantly, however, it likely meant very regular reporting on fulfillment of key plan indicators, something which made it extremely difficult for enterprises to take a long-term approach to innovation and renovation.

Particularly if an enterprise was having difficulty with plan fulfillment we meet the broader meaning of "micro-management," the excessive interference of ministry officials in the day-to-day activities of enterprises. Such interference was not always unwelcome, particularly when it entailed helping with the provision of inputs, but it could also mean administrative, party, and even judicial pressure on managers as well as the imposition of inappropriate operating methods. The phenomenon was considered to lead to sub-optimal decisionmaking by remote bureaucrats and the reduction of the initiative and flexibility of enterprise managers. The imperative of plan fulfillment affected virtually every aspect of the ministries' activities.

Capital investment

Capital investment was planned in the same way as production, meaning that ministries both bid for capital investment funds and distributed them among enterprises.[17] Investment projects worth more than a set amount, usually no more than a few million rubles, had to be approved centrally; smaller projects could be funded independently by the ministries from their own funds. The ministries overbid for capital investment inputs as they did for all inputs. Indeed, "investment hunger" was a typical phenomenon of the planned economy. Ministries (and enterprises) were subject to constant demands to increase output. They attempted to control this by underestimating capacity. But to the extent that they received increased targets each year (the infamous "ratchet principle") they tried to expand production capacity through new capital investment, usually in the form of the physical expansion of production facilities. This was the essence of the so-called "extensive" approach to growth, in which increases in output were achieved through increased inputs rather than the more efficient use of existing inputs. That was the standard approach of the command economy to expansion, and one which suited the capital investment policies of the ministries very well. In this their interests and those of their subordinate enterprises seemed to coincide pretty well.

Material-technical supplies

"Material-technical supplies" (MTS) was the rather pompous Soviet phrase for that most difficult of problems for Soviet managers, obtaining scarce inputs. As has been demonstrated all too conclusively, the command economy was synonymous with the deficit economy. The ministries contributed to creating the deficit and, at the same time, struggled to overcome it. Through their responsibility for plan fulfillment, ministries had to ensure that deliveries were made according to *Gossnab*'s centrally-set targets. They also had to ensure that their own enterprises got the inputs necessary for their production activity, both by getting inputs through *Gossnab* and allocating within the branch those inputs which were not provided through the central plan.

MTS was one of the ministries' biggest headaches. The ministries attempted to overcome the headache by engaging in overbidding for inputs, hoarding the inputs they did obtain, and laying a very considerable stress on "autarchism," i.e. ensuring that as many of the inputs as possible were produced within the branch itself. These tactics led to very low levels of specialization within the economy, despite the existence of highly specialized branch ministries. An example was the strange phenomenon of timber production. More than 70 ministries and agencies produced timber products, and the Ministry of Forestry accounted for only 37 percent of total timber output. At the level of the enterprise the situation was no less extraordinary. For example, an electronics factory made its own chisels at a cost 22 times higher than in a specialized factory.[18]   As well as being a headache, MTS was also one of the ministries' most effective weapons over their enterprises. The threat of witholding supplies was usually enough to bring the most recalcitrant enterprise to heel.

Budget formation

An important proportion of the Soviet budget was formed at ministry level, with a significant share of enterprise "profits" paid into central ministry accounts. (Profits is put in quotes because to an important degree the level of profits was determined by the ministries through their setting or negotiation of input and output quotas and prices.) Besides research and development, the money in these accounts was then used to finance capital investment, both in productive plant and non-productive "social" assets, such as sanitoria and health clinics, including of course those for ministry officials. The process was very widely used for the cross-subsidization of weaker, or more favored, plants, as described above.

Ministries also assumed an increasing role in credit provision. Credit became more important as economic reform supposedly gave primacy to "economic" methods over administrative methods. In response, a number of branch-specialized banks were established that provided credit for the enterprises in those branches. There was evidence that the banks were controlled by the ministries and that they manipulated the availability of credit and interest rates to continue the cross-subsidization already referred to as well as to maintain control over subordinate enterprises.

Personnel

The industrial ministries always had the right to appoint and dismiss senior enterprise management. Before Gorbachev, they appointed directors and their deputies. Beginning in the late 1980s, under new contract forms of employment, the ministry appointed only the director, who then had the right to appoint his own managerial team (although ministry officials stated that they still took a keen interest in the members of that team). But to make up for what might have been a small loss in formal personnel power, the ministries were the big winners from the collapse of the Communist Party *nomenklatura* system. We do not know precisely what the division of personnel powers was between the ministries and local Communist Party authorities. It was usually assumed by Western commentators that the party apparatus' power over personnel appointments was unquestioned. The predominance of managerial appointments from within the region in which the enterprise was situated (although not, it needs to be said, across branch boundaries) might be seen to support this assumption. However, the local party role was removed in the last months of Soviet rule, which increased considerably the ministries' powers and responsibilities in this area. Patronage as a source of power over enterprises obviously could not be overestimated at the end of the Soviet era.

Science and technology

One of the most heavily-stressed functions of the ministries in the official literature was the maintenance of an "integrated science and technology policy for the branch."[19] This entailed the granting of considerable powers to bodies within the ministries, such as the Scientific-Technical Council, the Technical Administration, and "head" institutes. Usually the ministries had control over the funding of research and development within their branch. For many years that funding came through the Integrated Fund for the Development of Science and Technology. Although Gorbachev's economic reform should have given research institutes greater financial independence, the ministries still in fact controlled much of the funding through the *goszakaz* (state order) system, which made the institutes heavily dependent on work ordered by the ministry.

As one would expect from organizations with strong autarchic tendencies, the ministries, and their leading research institutes in particular, were not enthusiastic about research and development work done outside their branches. Neither were they generous in making their own research available to others. But an even more important and baleful attitudinal disposition was their general distaste for research, development, and innovation no matter what its origin, for the usual reason that it disrupted the fulfillment of short-term production plans. The ministries certainly shared this distaste with their enterprises, and it does not seem to have particularly antagonized even their institutes.

Staff and structure

Until the end of the 1980s, although the number of industrial ministries fluctuated considerably, they were plentiful and highly specialized. But Gorbachev carried out a determined program of abolition and amalgamation, reducing dramatically the number of ministries.[20] From more than two dozen under Brezhnev, the number of industrial ministries declined by about half at the beginning of the 1990s. Another general feature of the organizational structure of industry was the tendency to have producers and users in different ministries. This was particularly evident in machine-tool and equipment building. An enterprise that made even highly specialized machine tools and equipment for specific end uses had usually been subordinate to one ministry while the enterprise using the product was subordinate to another. Thus, in the heyday of the specialized equipment sector under Brezhnev we had ministries such as the Ministry for Animal Industry Machine Building making equipment for the enterprises of the Ministry of Food Processing. In the Western context such specialization does not necessarily seem unusual or undesirable. However in the Soviet context, with its strong tendencies towards "departmentalism," the consequences were often negative.

In terms of internal structure, Soviet organizational theorists usually described the ministries as "line-functional," that is, sometimes the hierarchical chain of command passed through line units directly responsible for production management, sometimes through functional or staff units responsible for specialized management functions. While it is true that functional units such as the Technical Administration and the Supply Administration did in some areas have direct operational powers over production activities, in general those powers were completely overshadowed by the powers of line units. It would certainly not be inaccurate to describe the internal structures of the ministries as line-dominated.

The ministry was headed by a minister. Traditionally he was formally appointed by the Supreme Soviet, although clearly the real appointment was made within top-level party bodies. Under Gorbachev's reorganization of 1990, ministers were appointed by the president and ratified by the Supreme Soviet. Because ministries operated according to the dominant Soviet administrative principle of one-man management (*edinonachalie*), the minister bore full individual responsibility for the running of the ministry. As we will see in a moment, although there were collegial organs in the ministries, only the minister, or someone to whom he delegated power, had the right to issue obligatory orders. The minister had a number of deputies, including between one and three first deputies. There were usually about ten ordinary deputies, some of whom held other lower-level positions simultaneously.[21] The deputies had their own specific responsibilities, usually a combination of line and functional areas.

The top collective decision-making body of the ministry was the board (*kollegiia*). Its membership usually consisted of the minister, who chaired the body, his deputies, and the heads of the most important constituent units of the ministry apparatus. Occasionally, important outsiders, such as research scientists and heads of major enterprises, were also included. The collegium considered all major decisions facing the ministry in its regular meetings, and despite the fact that it was only a consultative body making recommendations to the minister, Soviet accounts suggest that it was important and influential.

Because the ministries were line dominated, the chain of command ran from the minister, usually through a deputy minister, to the production enterprises. In the middle of this chain was what many would see as the core of the traditional command-administrative ministry, the notorious "middle link." Particularly in recent times, the middle link went through a bewildering series of reorganizations, including its de facto abolition.[22] However the essence of the middle link was always summed up in the word *glavk*, no matter what the current name or status of the middle-link unit. To repeat, *glavk* is an abbreviation of *glavnoe upravlenie* (chief administration) and referred to the administrative unit of the central ministerial apparatus that was most directly responsible for giving operational orders to production enterprises. Each *glavk* supervised the enterprises in its own specialized sub-branch. For example, the Tractor Spare Parts *glavk* of the Ministry of Tractors and Agricultural Machinery contained 22 factories and associations, such as the Kharkov Tractor Spare Parts Association and the Odessa Piston Ring Factory.[23]

The rest of the apparatus consisted of the functional units. These included the usual "nuts and bolts" units such as the chancellery and registry as well as more important policy and operational units such as the technical, capital construction, supply, and personnel administrations. These had important powers in their own specific fields of competence, although the line-dominant nature of the ministries meant that their decisions were usually put into effect only by means of an order of a line manager.[24]

Before the savage staff cuts of the last years of the Soviet era, an industrial ministry appeared typically to have about 1000 persons working in its central apparatus. These personnel were broken down fairly evenly between functional and line units. Managerial personnel in both functional and line units overwhelmingly had production enterprise backgrounds. Particularly those in the all-important line *glavki* were quite likely to have begun their careers at the work bench, gained an engineering degree at night school, and then moved into production management in an enterprise before moving to the ministry apparatus. Personnel in the functional units were likely to have had considerable experience in their own specializations, but again usually with an enterprise background. In terms of staff and structure the ministries were about what one would expect of the enginerooms of the command economy. They were large and highly specialized bureaucracies, staffed by personnel with very narrow engineering-production backgrounds. The stress was on line units able and willing to exercise close day-to-day operational control over production enterprises, with functional units of considerable capacity providing backup in more specialized fields.

Reforms and Reorganizations

We have described the history, functions, and structures of the industrial ministries in terms of their close fit with the development and operation of the command economy. This might suggest that the ministries could claim some of the praise for what successes the command economy might have had, but that they also had to accept a good share of the blame for the failures of that form of economic management. Certainly the ministries always attracted very harsh criticism from both ends of the political spectrum. Conservative supporters of central planning blamed them for distorting and corrupting a system that would otherwise have worked very much better; marketizing reformers saw the ministries as bureaucratic monsters that had to be destroyed along with the command economy that spawned them.

The rhetoric of economic reform in recent decades has usually been that of the market variety. That was certainly the case after Gorbachev came to power in 1985. It is therefore understandable that the ministries had a particularly torrid time over the last half-decade. It was also in the nature of the Soviet system that even under glasnost there was a tendency for all sides of a debate to adopt what seemed to be the dominant language at the moment. This meant that everyone, even ministers, tended to talk of radically changing, even abolishing, the ministries, making it sometimes very difficult to sort out what the genuine positions and intentions of various people were and even the significance of measures taken.[25]

One of the most important pieces of economic legislation as far as the ministries were concerned was the 1990 Law on the Enterprise. It granted enterprises considerably increased formal independence in day-to-day management. Those provisions appeared to be severely compromised, however, by other provisions of the legislation that retained significant powers, particularly in the areas of planning and taxation, for the "organs of state management," which included the ministries.

Even more important as a basis of continued ministry power was the emphasis in new legislation on the rights in economic management of the "owner" (*sobstvennik*). The "owner" of the great bulk of Soviet industry was the state, even at the system's collapse in December 1991. This was true even in those enterprises that had been transferred to the joint-stock form of collective ownership, since the majority of shares was usually retained by the state. The owner had the right to dispose of its property and therefore effectively determine which basic form of management would be adopted. It had the right to appoint and dismiss leading personnel and to determine the basic development and investment strategies of the enterprise. In the case of most industrial enterprises, the owner, i.e. the state, exercised these rights through its agents, the ministries.

In other areas, however, there is evidence that the powers and capacities of the ministries declined in the last years of Soviet rule. This can be seen when one looks at staff and structural changes. The ministries were subjected to a savage round of staff cuts in 1987, apparently losing as much as 50 percent of their establishments, and further cuts followed. There was also a series of abolitions and amalgamations that reduced the number of ministries. Although there is some evidence that many of the cuts were fudged in one way or another, there seems to be little doubt that the staff capacities of the ministries were seriously affected. Certainly the combination of persistently harsh criticism in the press, legislative changes, and job insecurity led to a crisis of morale among ministry officials, leading to what one minister described in disgust as a "no-work mood".[26] This crisis no doubt contributed to the support for the August 1991 coup within broad segments of the Government apparatus.

The staff cuts were accompanied by major ongoing structural reorganizations. Here the evidence of ministry resistance to and frustration of change is strong. In particular, a determined effort by higher authorities to force the ministries to abolish the middle link was met by a farcical series of "nameplate" changes. Organizations with a variety of market-sounding names such as "concerns," "consortiums," and "associations" took the place of the old *glavki* and other middle-link units. Occasionally they even replaced the ministries themselves. A recent example of the latter was the State Joint-Stock Association "*Stankoinstrument*" replacing the Ministry of Machine-Tool Industry and Instruments (*Minstankoinstrument*).[27] In supervising its 511 enterprises and organizations, this association employed 348 persons in the summer of 1991, where the ministry only a few years earlier had employed 1450 persons.[28]

At the end of the Soviet era, references became increasingly common to so-called "holding companies" (*kholdingi*), part of the process of the privatization of Soviet industry. There were referred to in the USSR legislation on privatization as potential "founders" of joint-stock companies and the holders of the state's shares in those companies (Article 7.5 of the Law on the Basic Foundations of the Destatization and Privatization of Enterprises of 1 July 1991). That they were intended to replace the branch ministries was confirmed by the transformation of the Ministry of Automobile and Agricultural Machine Building (*Minavtosel'khozmash*) into the joint-stock company *Avtosel'khozmash-Kholding*.[29] These new structures were joint-stock companies in which shares were held by the state and by the enterprises in the relevant branch; they in turn held shares on behalf of the state majority or controlling shareholdings in those enterprises. Those who were more optimistic about the USSR's movement toward a market economy saw holding companies as temporary bodies that would gradually divest themselves of their shareholdings into private hands and eventually disappear.[30] The pessimists said that they were simply designed to ensure the continuation in one form or another of the old branch ministries, and in particular to avoid the threat of their abolition as outdated "organs of state management." Thus, when the abolition of virtually all USSR administrative bodies did come in November 1991, the branch ministries in the civilian sector had already managed to tranform themselves into new "commercial" structures. It remains to be seen how these new "commercial" structures will be transferred to republic authority after December 1991, and the extent to which the republics' ministries themselves use holding companies as a vehicle for institutional reform.

While the old structures were still there under one name or another at the end of 1991, there was evidence that the old functions were breaking down even before the collapse of the Soviet Union. Commentators spoke of a decline in "micro-management," and even more striking was the serious breakdown in contract discipline between Soviet enterprises. Given that contract discipline was a modern form of the old plan fulfillment requirement, it could be said that the ministries were failing in what was always their most important function.

The ministries were also under serious threat from two other sources in 1991. The first was the privatization process, of which joint-stock structures were a part. The stated long-term intention of privatization is to remove the state from the ownership of economic assets, leaving the ministries with no basis for operational control. While there is good evidence that privatization was used in some cases to maintain centralized branch control, a truly privatized economy is incompatible with the traditional branch ministries. Ministries have acted as owners toward enterprises, and as privatization deepens ownership will pass from state to private institutions.

The final blow to the central ministries was, of course, the decentralization of economic powers to republican and regional authorities at the end of 1991. But even before the attempted coup of August 1991, demands for control over local economic resources had been key to center-periphery relations. It was one area where the central political authorities showed some willingness to negotiate and the republics to take action regardless of the center's attitudes. In February 1991, for example, the Russian Government issued a decree giving all-union enterprises the opportunity to transfer to republican subordination.

After the coup, the Russian Federation and other republics simply appropriated all enterprises on their territories to their own jurisdictions, something in which the center had to concur. The ministries appeared to be the most direct and immediate losers of such transfers, since most republican leaders claimed to be extremely antipathetic toward them. But even here we see signs of the ministries' extraordinary ability to survive. In the summer of 1991, President Nursultan Nazarbaev of Kazakhstan signed an agreement with a number of USSR ministries granting them the right to manage enterprises on Kazakh territory.[31] There was also a fascinating clause in the RSFSR Law on Privatization which, in describing Russian territorial privatization agencies, stated that "representatives of all-union bodies which manage property owned by the RSFSR are involved in the operation of territorial agencies."[32] It appeared that the republics were unable or unwilling to proceed immediately themselves to the radical marketization of the economy and therefore needed some sort of "command" structures, since they had not had such structures of their own in the heavy industry sphere. They were therefore forced to turn to the only existing "command" structures, the central branch ministries.

As we now know, this was destined to be a short-term arrangement. Under the new Commonwealth of Independent States, the central ministries passed into history. Yet it may be too early to write off industrial ministries entirely. As long as elements of the command economy remain in the republics, there will be a need for administrative units to manage enterprises. Whether industrial ministries gain a new lease on life in the republics depends on the success of the "destatization" (*razgosudarstvlenie*) of the republican economies launched at the beginning of the 1990s.

Notes

1. N.P. Eroshkin, *Istoriia gosudarstvennykh uchrezhdenii dorevoliutsionnoi Rossii* (Moscow: Vysshaia shkola, 1983), p.281.

2. On the wartime war-industries committees, see L. Seigelbaum, *The Politics of Industrial Mobilization in Russia, 1914-17. A Study of the War-Industries Committees* (London and Basingstoke: Macmillan, 1983).

3. For English-language accounts of the immediate post-October and Civil War periods, see E.H. Carr, *The Bolshevik Revolution 1917-1923*, vol. 2 (London: Macmillan, 1952), chapters 16 and 17; E. Zaleski, *Planning for Economic Growth in the Soviet Union, 1918-1932* (Chapel Hill: University of North Carolina Press, 1971), esp. pp. 24-29; S. Malle, *The Economic Organization of War Communism, 1918-21* (Cambridge: Cambridge University Press, 1985), especially chapter 5. The standard Soviet accounts are A.V. Venediktov, *Organizatsiia gosudarstvennoi promyshlennosti v SSSR*, 2 vols. (Leningrad: Gosudarstvennyi universitet im. A.A. Zhdanova, 1957-61); E.G. Gimpel'son, *Velikii Oktiabr' i stanovlenie sovetskoi sistemy upravleniia narodnym khoziaistvom (noiabr' 1917-1920gg)* (Moscow: Nauka, 1977); M.P. Iroshnikov, *Sozdanie sovetskogo tsentral'nogo gosudarstvennogo apparata. Sovet narodnykh komissarov i narodnye komissariaty (oktiabr' 1917g - ianvar' 1918g)* (Leningrad: Nauka, 1966); Iu.K. Avdakov, *Organizatsionno-khoziaistvennaia deiatel'nost' VSNKh v pervye gody sovetskoi vlasti (1917-21 gg.)* (Moscow: Izdatel'stvo moskovskogo universiteta, 1971).

4. For a brief list of relevant decrees and decisions, see R. Sakwa, *Soviet Communists in Power. A Study of Moscow during the Civil War, 1918-21* (New York: St Martin's, 1988), p. 50. For an attempt to put the industrial management aspect of central control over the periphery in broader context, see S. Fortescue, "The Regional Party Apparatus in the 'Sectional Society'," *Studies in Comparative Communism*, no.1 (1988), pp. 11-23.

5. For a chart showing the structure of *VSNKh* in 1921-22, see Zaleski, *Planning for Economic Growth*, p. 26.

6. For details on NEP, see Zaleski, *Planning for Economic Growth*; Carr, *The Bolshevik Revolution*, vol. 2, chapter 19; E.H. Carr and R.W. Davies, *Foundations of a Planned Economy, 1926-1929* (London and Basingstoke: Macmillan, 1969), chapters 12-14.

7. '*Spets*-baiting' referred to the persecution of 'bourgeois specialists'; the *vydvizhenie* movement involved pushing huge numbers of workers and peasants through higher education into technical and industrial management positions. See K.E. Bailes, *Technology and Society under Lenin and Stalin. Origins of the Soviet Technical Intelligentsia, 1917-1941* (Princeton: Princeton University Press, 1978).

8. On Stalin's industrialization, see Carr and Davies, *Foundations of a Planned Economy*, vol. 1, especially chapter 12; E. Zaleski, *Stalinist Planning for Economic Growth, 1933-1952* (London and Basingstoke: Macmillan, 1980), part 1; H. Kuromiya, *Stalin's Industrial Revolution* (Cambridge: Cambridge University Press, 1988).

9. For as clear a description as possible, see, in Russian, T.P. Korzhikhina, *Istoriia gosudarstvennykh uchrezhdenii SSSR* (Moscow: Vysshaia shkola, 1986); in English, Zaleski, *Stalinist Planning for Economic Growth*, chapter 2; J. Crowfoot and M. Harrison, "The USSR Council of Ministers under Late Stalinism, 1945-54: Its Production Branch Composition and the Requirements of National Economy and Policy," *Soviet Studies*, no. 1 (1980), pp. 39-58, plus unpublished appendices.

10. For a detailed description of their structures and functions over recent decades, see S. Freidzon, *Top-Level Administration of the Soviet Economy. A Partial View*, Rand Paper P-7178 (Santa Monica, CA), January 1986.

11. J.F. Hough and M. Fainsod, *How the Soviet Union is Governed* (Cambridge, MA: Harvard University Press, 1979), pp. 409-48.

12. On the fate of the branch departments of the Communist Party under Gorbachev, see chapter 2 in this volume, by Cameron Ross.

13. G. Alimov, "Chto zhe budet, esli ustanet ne karaul, a narod?" *Izvestiia*, 5 November 1991, p. 1.

14. Korzhikhina, *Istoriia gosudarstvennykh uchrezhdenii*, pp.286-90.

15. For a formal listing of functions in the ministries' general statute, see *Sobranie postanovlenii pravitel'stva SSSR*, no. 17 (1967), item 116. For recent general accounts of the ministries' activities in English, see A.C. Gorlin, "The Power of the Soviet Industrial Ministries in the 1980s," *Soviet Studies*, no. 3 (1985), pp. 353-70; D.A. Dyker, "The Power of the Industrial Ministries," in *Elites and Political Power in the USSR*, ed. David Lane (Aldershot, UK: Edward Elgar, 1988), chapter 8.

16. For some discussion of this issue, see S. Fortescue, "Soviet Bureaucracy and Civil Society," in *The Transition from Socialism. State and Civil Society in Gorbachev's USSR*, ed. C. Kukathas, D.W. Lovell, and W. Maley (Melbourne: Longman Cheshire, 1991), chapter 8.

17. For a detailed account of investment processes, see D.A. Dyker, *The Process of Investment in the Soviet Union* (Cambridge: Cambridge University Press, 1983), especially chapter 2.

18. Dyker, *The Process of Investment in the Soviet Union*, pp. 38-46.

19. For details, see S. Fortescue, *Science Policy in the Soviet Union* (London: Routledge, 1990), chapter 4.

20. For a list of ministries and state committees at the end of the Soviet era, see "O perechne ministerstv i drugikh tsentral'nykh organov gosudarstvennogo upravleniia," *Izvestiia*, 9 April 1991, p. 2.

21. For a recent list of ministers and their deputies, see *Sovet Ministrov SSSR. Spravochnik serii "Kto est' kto"* (Moscow: Vneshtorgizdat, 1990).

22. For the reorganizations of the 1970s, see L. Holmes, *The Policy Process in Communist States. Politics and Industrial Administration* (London: Sage, 1981); W.J. Conyngham, *The Modernization of Soviet Industrial Management. Socio-economic Development and the Search for Viability* (Cambridge: Cambridge University Press, 1982), especially chapter 6.

23. V.N. Goncharov, I.R. Budyko and V.D. Evstigneev, *Finansirovanie rabot po razvitiiu nauki i tekhniki* (Moscow: Finansy i statistika, 1987), pp. 18, 32, 76.

24. For a reasonably detailed account of the work of the Technical Administration, see Fortescue, *Science Policy in the Soviet Union*, pp. 65-72.

25. For an attempt to do so, see Fortescue, "Soviet Bureaucracy and Civil Society," in *The Transition from Socialism*. For a more detailed account of changes up to late 1990, see S. Fortescue, "The Restructuring of Soviet Industrial Ministries since 1985,"

in *Market Socialism or the Restoration of Capitalism?* ed. A. Aslund (Cambridge: Cambridge University Press, 1991).

26. R. Lynev, "Kto sleduiushchii?" *Izvestiia*, 1 October 1990, p. 2.

27. For an interview with the old minister/new board chairman, see *Pravda*, 4 April 1991, p. 2.

28. V. Romaniuk, "Ministr stanovitsia prezidentom," *Izvestiia*, 1 July 1991, p. 2.

29. *Izvestiia*, 14 September 1991, p. 2.

30. For an example of such an argument, see V. Tarasov, "Arenda, kollektivnaia sobstvennost', narodnoe predpriiatie ... ," *Ekonomika i zhizn'*, no. 9 (1991), p. 5.

31. *Pravda*, 5 July 1991, p. 2; "Otzhivshee—v pereplavku! " *Pravitel'stvennyi vestnik*, no. 29 (1991), p. 10.

32. See Article 4.1, "O privatizatsii gosudarstvennykh i munitsipal'nykh predpriatiiakh v RSFSR," *Rossiiskaia gazeta*, 19 July 1991, p. 2.

7

THE AGRICULTURAL MINISTRIES

Barbara Ann Chotiner

Agriculture was perhaps the most intractable and important area of policy in the Soviet era. In 1989, James H. Noren noted that "[a]lmost half the population's consumption comes directly from agriculture or indirectly through the food processing industry and part of light industry."[1] Long-time students of rural affairs, Roy and Betty Laird, characterized the "agricultur[al sector as] the largest single segment of the Soviet economy."[2]

A vital area of politics as well as policy, agriculture helped to make and unmake Soviet political leaders. For example, difficulties in providing dependable supplies of a wide assortment of comestibles at reasonable prices, especially through the state stores, contributed to the turn toward the right in central governmental policy in early 1991. Participants in the August 1991 coup almost certainly believed that the increasing scarcity of affordable food would encourage Soviet citizens to accept a curtailment of newly-gained freedoms in exchange for a more reliable administration of the economy. After the failure of the coup, one of the first acts of the new State Council was to tie the ten participating republics into a joint scheme to channel interrepublican food flows and to deal with commodity imports (including assistance).[3] The link between the provision of food and political stability remained painfully apparent in the winter of 1991–92, as the new governments of the Commonwealth of Independent States sought to manage unwieldy economies and societies.

Although this chapter focuses on Soviet Government institutions in the agricultural sector, it should be noted at the outset that until the repeal of Article 6 of the Soviet Constitution in 1990, the central leadership of the Communist Party made agricultural policy. And the party's responsibilities were not limited to policy initiation. Lower-level CPSU organs monitored compliance with party policy in agriculture, rendered assistance in meeting its goals, and resolved disputes when existing party and/or state decrees and laws were in conflict or did not cover a particular situation. Local party committees also helped to lay the groundwork for new official enactments. Thus, Soviet Government agencies were by no means the only authoritative institutional actors in agricultural affairs. In agriculture more than in perhaps any other sector, the party substituted itself for the Government in the administration of the economy.[4]

Government Agricultural Agencies Before Gorbachev

People's commissariats (as ministries were called before 1946) of agriculture and of food were represented in the first Government, or Council of People's Commissars, formed after the Bolshevik Revolution. Vladimir P. Miliutin, a member of the Communist Party Central Committee, served as the first agricultural commissar, while the revolutionary Ivan A. Teodorovich was named first commissar of food. When the Bolsheviks briefly entered into a Government coalition, the former position was given to their partners, the Socialist Revolutionaries.[5]

Even after the collectivization of agriculture and the Great Purges in the 1930s, an era that brought major discontinuities in the rural economy and society, a Commissariat of Agriculture continued to function. With the exception of an eight-month period of consolidation with the Ministry of State Procurements in the immediate aftermath of Stalin's death, a farming department existed within the central Government until several months after Gorbachev's election to the CPSU general secretaryship. In addition, ministries or commissariats of state procurement or grain products, charged with obtaining required deliveries of agricultural products from farms, existed for all but eight months in the period from January 1938 until 1985. These major agricultural bureaucracies often functioned alongside even more specialized agencies of Government. At various times in Soviet history, separate institutions existed to administer state farms, livestock-raising, cotton, fruits and vegetables, meat and milk products, land improvement, and water usage.[6]

The personnel and bureaucracies of these specialized commissariats, ministries, or state committees were commonly spun off larger Government departments, such as the Ministry of Agriculture. The creation of separate, stand-alone ministries or state committees from parts of larger agriculturally-related Government bureaucracies was designed to enhance oversight of poorly-managed sectors, to achieve different types of economic efficiency, and to coordinate programs that cut across several traditional economic branches. At times, of course, more purely political goals were served by the creation of additional agricultural agencies or the disestablishment of old ones, with top leaders using administrative reorganization to reward their supporters and punish their detractors.[7]

A major institutional reform of agricultural management came at the end of the Brezhnev era, when the leadership introduced the Food Program. Its stated purpose was to coordinate more closely the farming sector with its suppliers and consumers in order to expand the amount and kinds of food available to the Soviet population. Approved by the May 1982 Plenum of the CPSU Central Committee, this initiative fused collective and state farms (*kolkhozy* and *sovkhozy*) as well as organizations supporting production, processing, and trade in food into unified intra-branch agencies, known as district (*raion*), regional (*oblast'*), and territorial (*krai*) agroindustrial associations. At the republican and all-union levels existing ministries and state committees in farming and related branches, such as the light and food industries and agricultural machine-building, were linked in new agricultural commissions under the presidia of the councils of ministers.[8] These commissions permitted concentration and linkage of activities while preserving the identity of the specialized departments. The idea was to improve coordination among the agricultural organs and between these organs and institutions managing other branches of the economy.

The Creation of the *Gosagroprom* USSR

Less than nine months after Gorbachev's selection as general secretary of the Communist Party, a major reorganization of the Government's agricultural agencies was launched. On 27 November 1985, a new superministry, the State Agroindustrial Committee (*Gosagroprom*) USSR, replaced five existing ministries—Agriculture, Fruit and Vegetable Economy, Agricultural Construction, the Meat and Milk Industry, and the Food Industry—as well as the State Committee for Productive-Technical Supply of Agriculture. Segments of the ministries of procurements, light industry, and melioration and water economy were also shifted to *Gosagroprom*. In a related reform, the USSR Ministry of Procurement became the Ministry of Grain Products USSR.[9]

The formation of *Gosagroprom* represented in some respects a traditional attempt to improve economic performance through organizational change, though the hypercentralization of *Gosagroprom* was clearly at one end of the continuum of agency proliferation and consolidation that characterized the history of Soviet Government.[10] This reorganization was an even more radical effort to unify farming and related non-farming branches than had been attempted under Khrushchev, who had viewed institutional restructuring as a panacea for many economic ills. Certainly *Gosagroprom* had the formal powers to make and impose binding rules in the supplying of the agricultural sector, the production of food and raw materials, and the preparation of comestibles for consumers. *Gosagroprom* directed funds and state plan requirements to the remaining ministries and state committee concerned with land and water usage, food, and the provision of goods and services to farmers.   Furthermore, ministries manufacturing for agriculture were required "[to] closely coordinate their work with *Gosagroprom* USSR."[11]   Among members of the board of *Gosagroprom* were representatives of all such related departments.

Structurally, *Gosagroprom* USSR was a union-republic organ, in which rule-making and administrative powers were shared between the central agency and similar bodies at the republican level.   Therefore, the organizational network of *Gosagroprom* USSR included, as subordinate entities, republican, *krai*, and *oblast'* agroindustrial committees, and *raion* agroindustrial associations.   At least formally, *Gosagroprom* directives were binding on all other government bodies.[12]   Thus, officials of *Gosagroprom* possessed legal authority both horizontally and vertically to regulate development of farming and related production.

The formal positions and personal backgrounds of the highest executives in *Gosagroprom* enhanced the institution's powers of regulation, policy-making, and oversight.   Its chairman, Vsevolod S. Murakhovskii, a Central Committee member since 1981, had served as superior and then subordinate to Gorbachev in the Komsomol and the Communist Party bureaucracies.   Murakhovskii's job at *Gosagroprom* carried with it the rank of first deputy chairman of the USSR Council of Ministers, which confirmed his supervision of the entire "agroindustrial complex."   Murakhovskii outranked almost all other members of the Council of Ministers and therefore possessed the formal status to make his views prevail in disagreements with ministers or state committee chairmen in organizations whose activities affected farming or food.   There were two first deputy chairmen of *Gosagroprom*, Evgenii I. Sizenko and Alexander I. Ievlev, each of whom held the rank of minister of the Soviet Union, a title that enabled them to deal with the heads of other ministries and state committees from a position of strength.   A member of the Central Committee since 1981, Sizenko had an advanced economics degree and had worked previously as the first secretary of an oblast party committee (*obkom*) and as the USSR Minister of Meat and Milk Industry.   For his part, Ievlev had been an *obkom* first secretary and deputy USSR minister of agriculture.   The backgrounds of even the deputy chairmen of *Gosagroprom* USSR suggest that they were powerful actors in Soviet politics who enjoyed impressive contacts and authority within the party and state bureaucracies.   These officials included two more Central Committee members, who were former *obkom* first secretaries, as well as the president of the All-Union Agricultural Academy.[13]

With such personnel and organizational strengths, *Gosagroprom* USSR was able to move horizontally beyond traditional agricultural management to activities that were outside the competence of its ministerial predecessors. Vertically within its own bureaucracy, *Gosagroprom* USSR engaged in micro-management of its subordinate institutions. In so doing, *Gosagroprom* undercut some of the first steps toward economic reform by making economic decisions that were supposed to have been left to local personnel, on such questions as leaseholds and product assortment. Subdivisions of *Gosagroprom* dealt with questions of pricing, wages, and even bookkeeping. Along with the USSR State Planning Committee (Gosplan), *Gosagroprom* issued instructions on the appropriate methods for calculating state crop-purchasing parameters. As leasing became the preferred method for relating peasants' work to farm administration, *Gosagroprom* not only indicated national norms for the lease contract but also suggested how much rent leaseholders should pay for assets. As always, of course, *Gosagroprom* remained subject to Communist Party guidance. When Boris Yeltsin, at the time the first secretary of the Moscow city party organization, tried to improve the food supply for his constituents, he enlisted the help of the Central Committee secretary for agriculture. The secretary in turn issued a directive to *Gosagroprom*, whose head, Murakhovskii, reported that his organization and others were providing additional comestibles to the national capital.[14]

The more traditional concerns of agricultural administration also occupied subdivisions of *Gosagroprom*. Its All-Union Scientific Research Institute for the Processing of Fruits and Vegetables developed some novel methods and equipment, while employees of the central and republican agroindustrial committees cooperated with scientists of the All-Union Agricultural Academy to devise measures for soil improvement. Reviewing the activities of the Georgian and Kirov *oblast'* agroindustrial committees, the board (*kollegiia*) of *Gosagroprom* USSR ordered improvements in the farm balance sheets and apparently even authorized agencies in those regions to change output profiles and production arrangements of *kolkhozy*.[15]

Pursuant to a joint party-Government decree, the "agroindustrial complex" as well as the industrial sector began to be managed contractually in 1988 rather than solely by directives.[16] The state order (*goszakaz*) became the new vehicle for managing production and related services. The state order system, which replaced planning directives with near-monopoly purchase orders, was designed to introduce some formal elements of a market while ensuring that output would be responsive to Government and party goals. According to scholar Vladimir

A. Tikhonov, this system authorized "state planning, procurement [and] supply" bodies to contract on a "wholesale" basis "for the delivery of an exactly stipulated product, in a fixed period, in exactly fixed conditions."[17] Vasilii Uzun of the All-Union Scientific Research Institute of the Economics of Agriculture contended that

> by decisions of Gosplan USSR and Gosagroprom USSR from 1988, the state order was equated with state purchases. In this way [the state order] ... preserved the system of planning .... The state order ... was established for all kinds of production, for which earlier tasks were managed according to state purchases and procurements.[18]

These orders, which were transmitted to the *raion* agroindustrial associations in the cases of food and raw materials, could even be used to arrange for road construction! In 1988, state orders of *Gosagroprom* USSR were configured according to 242 criteria. *Gosagroprom* in turn continued to receive plan directives from the USSR State Planning Commission, though there were fewer categories of requirements that year—171 as opposed to 296 the year before. Thus, *Gosagroprom* USSR constrained autonomous economic activity of productive units like farms[19] and was itself constrained by traditional mechanisms of control.

Decentralization of Agricultural Administration

In November 1988, a Politburo commission chaired by Nikolai Ryzhkov proposed a reorganization of central economic institutions. The commission, which included no members from the agricultural sector, envisioned devolution of some responsibilities discharged by *Gosagroprom* USSR to union-republican agencies. Furthermore, it favored the creation of a new central Government institution to resolve "all-union, large-scale tasks of the development of ... agriculture and the processing of agricultural products ...." These changes seemed to be expected to establish "prerequisites for administration by primarily economic methods."[20]

The March 1989 Central Committee plenum appeared to push devolution of agricultural management further by mandating leasing by farmers and agricultural organizations. At this plenum, Gorbachev advocated the dissolution of *Gosagroprom* USSR and its replacement by a State Commission for Food and Purchasing within the Council of Ministers USSR. Gorbachev related his recommendations to ongoing efforts to enlarge the prerogatives of the union-republican governments in domestic affairs and to make republican socio-economic activities "self-administ[ered] and self-financing." He stated that

> in principle, the matter is about broadening of the rights of the union republics
> in the solution of all problems of the agroindustrial complex and strengthening
> ... their responsibility for the food supply of the population of their own
> regions.[21]

One unintended result of this initiative, economist Karen M. Brooks suggests, may have been the subsequent difficulties in supplying agricultural commodities to the consumer.[22] Although Gorbachev's organizational reform retained *gosagropromy* at the republic level, it limited their authority to control the behavior of agricultural producers.[23]

Following the Central Committee's endorsement of Gorbachev's proposals, the USSR Council of Ministers and the presidium of the USSR Supreme Soviet enacted these suggestions into law in April 1989. A new State Commission for Food and Purchasing was established to discharge technical and "staff" functions, with the agency's main "line" responsibility being the amassing and operation of the all-union food fund. Other commission tasks included coordination and regulation within the agroindustrial sector, between it and other components of the economy, and among "regions." The commission retained some planning responsibilities as well. Nonetheless, while the jurisdiction of the new state commission may have appeared wide, in many cases it shared its rights and responsibilities with other central and republican organs. In important instances, the State Commission for Food and Purchasing was not legally delegated to be the primary actor in policy implementation. Furthermore, the State Commission for Food and Purchasing was shorn of a significant portion of the operating agencies that had reported to *Gosagroprom*.[24] Hence, the successor to *Gosagroprom* USSR had limited ability to make policy or to assure its implementation. Given the limits of its powers and jurisdiction, the commission often had to negotiate with other bureaucratic entities from a position of weakness. As a consequence, the new agency could not function as the lynchpin or the major instrument of party and Government direction of farming and related sectors.

An examination of some organizational resources of the State Commission for Food and Purchasing and of its republican affiliates highlights the weakness of the institution. A number of departments of the State Commission for Food and Purchasing were removed from direct involvement in production. These included subdivisions for "economic analysis and interbranch proportions, improvement of the economic mechanism and price regulation, scientific-technical progress, ... [and] investment and social development" as well as two offices dealing with "long-term development" issues.[25] The relatively small size of the all-union food fund, whose creation and distribution was one of the national agency's major operational tasks, illustrated the commission's limited capacity to ensure adequate supplies. The commission's deputy chairman, B.I. Poshkus, noted in 1991 that the "fund comprise[d] only 13 percent of commodity output" in the Soviet Union.[26]

The State Commission for Food and Purchasing did not set state orders for agricultural commodities to be included in the national food fund; instead, it was the USSR State Planning Commission and the councils of ministers of the union republics that made these decisions.[27] Hence, the State Commission had no direct leverage over production decisions that would later affect the viability of comestible and raw material supplies for the country as a whole. Moreover, additional responsibilities devolved to the republican governments because agroindustrial committees continued to exist at this level. These republic *gosagropromy* now wielded jurisdiction over farms as well as service and food-processing enterprises. Thus, with the scrapping of *Gosagroprom* USSR, its subordinate organizations at lower levels enjoyed broader jurisdiction in agricultural affairs than the new agricultural management body sitting atop the system in Moscow. Discussing the jurisdiction of *Gosagroprom* of the Ukrainian SSR, its chairman, N. Sidorenko, noted that

> in its system are upwards of 23,000 farms, associations, establishments, and organizations in which work around 40 percent of the workers and service personnel of the republic .... [They] produced upwards of a third of the gross output of the entire national economy of the Ukraine.[28]

Given such administrative control, the authority for determining supply performance criteria, and the size of the all-union food fund, it is not surprising that 12 issues of that republic's agroindustrial magazine contained no mention of the USSR State Commission for Food and Purchasing![29] It would appear that the activities of this organ of the USSR Council of Ministers were peripheral to management of one of the country's major agricultural regions.

The political resources of major officials of the State Commission for Food and Purchasing were also limited. They certainly appear less impressive than those of the leaders of *Gosagroprom* USSR. The first chairman of the new State Commission for Food and Purchasing, Vladilen V. Nikitin, had previously served as Minister of Agriculture of the Russian Republic and as first deputy chairman of *Gosagroprom* RSFSR. In terms of political authority, Nikitin seemed to be outranked by his old superior at *Gosagroprom* RSFSR, Lev B. Yermin, who had been a full member of the party Central Committee since 1970 (another bit of evidence that the republic *gosagropromy* overshadowed the primary institution for agricultural affairs in the center). Likewise, negotiations with Gosplan USSR were probably not helped by the fact that its deputy chairman for agricultural matters had the same party rank as Nikitin himself. Following criticism of his work by Communist Party officials, Nikitin was replaced by his first deputy, Viacheslav I. Chernoivanov.[30]

In comparison with the leaders of *Gosagroprom* USSR, Nikitin and Chernoivanov appeared to lack informal, as well as formal, resources to coordinate the management of agricultural production and nourishment of the populace. Not only did Murakhovskii and several of his assistants possess higher party standing than Nikitin, chairman of the State Commission for Food and Purchasing, but Murakhovskii also had longstanding personal ties to the head of the party and state hierarchies, Mikhail S. Gorbachev. This higher status in what, until 1990, was the primary political institution in the Soviet Union undoubtedly allowed officials of *Gosagroprom* USSR to bring additional pressure to bear in negotiations with lower-ranking officials and producers. Shared experiences as CPSU apparatchiks might also have aided the *Gosagroprom* chairman and some of his deputies in securing cooperation from local party bureaucrats who directly oversaw performance by farmers and agriculturally related enterprises. One may speculate that Nikitin's previous subordination to the chief of the Russian Agroindustrial Committee and his parity in party rank with the Gosplan deputy chairman for food and farming questions had a purpose, namely to reinforce the restricted role of the State Committee on Food and Purchasing. With limited authority, this new state commission was probably less likely to substitute administrative decisions for economic ones or to try to control production processes in collective and state farms, processing plants, and service enterprises.

Despite its limited powers and leverage, the State Commission for Food and Purchasing undertook a broad range of tasks. Various organizations turned to the commission to solve problems or to blame it for difficulties in farming and in the supply of agricultural goods. In one area for which the state commission clearly had responsibility, pricing, a number of USSR Council of Ministers decrees specified ends toward which this authority should be used. For example, the commission—by itself or with other agencies—was empowered to authorize more than one price for commodities like grain, millet, and oil-seeds. Along with union-republican governments and other official entities, the State Committee for Food and Purchasing was ordered to employ price manipulation "to ensure control over the observance of parity of the economic interrelations of agriculture with other branches of the national economy."[31] The commission did establish a price list for food by commodity.[32]

The commission also offered technical input into the policy process. The USSR Supreme Soviet Committee on Agrarian Questions and Food requested that the commission help to draft legislation on the "Fundamentals of Veterinary Affairs in the USSR." In addition, the supreme soviet committee indicated that the Commission for Food and Purchasing, union republican councils of ministers, and a public construction organization should collaborate in drawing up a land improvement scheme. And one or more representatives of the State Commission participated in official discussions about ameliorating the consequences of the Chernobyl' nuclear accident.[33]

In fostering economic change, the Commission for Food and Purchasing seemed to have varied opportunities for input. Its deputy chairman sat on the State Commission for Economic Reform of the USSR Council of Ministers, a commission formed in July 1989. The Soviet Government enjoined the central comestibles authority to join with other official bodies

> to work out a program of actions for the stimulation of competition in the production and processing of agricultural output and for the restriction of monopoly manifestations in the actions of large-scale producers in the market of agricultural output.[34]

With the USSR Ministry of Finances and the Agroindustrial Bank, the Commission for Food and Purchasing also endorsed a sample leasing agreement.[35] As a result, these organizations may have helped to influence the form that tenancy relationships assumed across the country.

The State Commission for Food and Purchasing was, understandably, the target of criticism. Complaints focused upon shortfalls of food and tobacco for shoppers as well as supplies for producers. Such objections originated from a variety of sources. The Agricultural Department of the CC CPSU blamed problems with grain products and cigarettes on poor administration by officials of the USSR Commission for Food and Purchasing. The USSR Supreme Soviet Committee on Agrarian Questions and Food investigated difficulties in obtaining "veterinary preparations, disinfection means, and polythene articles."[36] After reviewing the availability of sausage, the USSR People's Control Committee ordered the State Commission for Food and Purchasing to foster joint ventures to manufacture "flavoring[s and] food colorings!" The state commission was also encouraged to find "economic" means to induce production of more diverse sausages.[37]

An analyst may question the degree to which the commission--with its contingent authority, large number of "staff" functions, and direct jurisdiction over a very limited proportion of the Soviet food supply--could have been expected to prevent or remedy shortages. Even Soviet critics recognized the agency's weaknesses. For instance, the agricultural department of the party Central Committee faulted union-republican leaders for failure to provide required quantities of "meat and meat products to the all-union fund."[38] For its part, the Supreme Soviet Committee on Agrarian Policy and Food conducted an investigation of grain imports. Its findings indicated that

> the role of the State Commission of the Council of Ministers USSR for Food and Purchasing is undervalued; in practice it does not have control of the means ... allotted for the import of grain.[39]

In fulfilling its functions, then, the State Commission for Food and Purchasing was hampered by the additional political and administrative powers acquired by the republic *gosagropromy* after 1989, by its restricted role as an actor in central politics, and by its lack of organizational autonomy.

Final Attempts to Improve Soviet Agricultural Administration

In 1990, critics of agricultural management expressed concerns about reduced coordination and focus within the community of agricultural producers. Members of the Congress of People's Deputies "insisted on a meeting with the Government ... to receive a competent answer from competent people" about supply problems experienced by farms and related enterprises. Gorbachev presided over the session, which was convened at Communist Party headquarters![40] One functionary lamented the fact that no particular state agency seemed responsible for accounting practices related to contracts and leases in the "agroindustrial complex," yet utilization of these arrangements was supposed to constitute a major reform! The chief of a department of the State Planning Commission observed that with the abolition of *Gosagroprom* USSR, "decentralization of administration" was linked to decisions being made "unsatisfactorily both in the center and in the localities."[41] At the beginning of 1991, even an editorial in the journal of the State Commission for Food and Purchasing reminded readers of its organizational predecessor's

> rights of leadership of the branches of the APK [agroindustrial complex] and the entire plenitude of responsibility for the production of agricultural output, its procurement and processing, for the provision of the population with food.[42]

This criticism seems to have led to the creation in March 1991 of a new Ministry of Agriculture and Food, headed by Viacheslav Chernoivanov. Speaking to farmers and perhaps others in related occupations, President Gorbachev described the new cabinet department as having been "created at your request." Alongside the new ministry, a new State Committee for Purchases of Food Resources also functioned in the months before the August coup.[43] Thus, in the last months of Soviet politics, analogues were established to Government agricultural organs that had functioned for decades before 1985. In organizational terms, the Gorbachev reforms in agriculture had come full circle, though a full restoration of the agricultural and state procurement institutions did not occur. The new ministry and state committee functioned under novel constitutional conditions, with a strong presidency and a new Cabinet of Ministers, and in an environment of growing republican autonomy.

Following the failure of the August 1991 coup, central institutions increasingly lost relevance and authority as the republics asserted independence, as Russia laid claim to Union agencies, and as the USSR itself gave way to a new political organization, the Commonwealth of Independent States. In the transitional months of late 1991, these trends could be observed in the administration of the farming and food sector. In September 1991, the State Council announced that the republics would determine agricultural policy but that the Committee for the Operative Administration of the Economy of the USSR would administer programs already approved by the republics. However, an *Izvestiia* report in October of "an agreement of the sovereign states on the food supply for 1992" made no mention of any role for central Government organizations. The story did note that republican "heads of governments" would negotiate about the method of payment for imports of agricultural products. This second accord was concluded as discussions on the inter-republican economic union were being brought to close.[44]

In the wake of the establishment of the Commonwealth of Independent States in December 1991, the central institutions of agricultural policymaking and implementation were formally abolished. But the need remained for institutions to carry out at least some of the functions exercised by traditional Soviet institutions of agricultural administration. Over the short term, the founding documents of the Commonwealth of Independent States may have envisioned coordination of agricultural policy through regular meetings of the heads of state and heads of Government (and their staffs). The question for the long term is to what extent decisions in agriculture will be made by Government institutions—whether at central, republic, or local levels—or by the market.

Notes

The author wishes to thank Ann B. Chotiner for helpful comments.

1. James H. Noren, "The Soviet Economic Crisis: Another Perspective," *Soviet Economy*, no. 1 (January-March 1989), p. 51.

2. Roy D. and Betty A. Laird, "*Glasnost'*, *Perestroika*, and Gorbachev's Policies: The Built in Contradictions of Soviet Socialism," *Studies in Comparative Communism*, no. 2 (Summer 1990), p. 115.

3. Francis X. Clines, "10 Soviet Republics Agree to Coordinate Food Supply," *The New York Times*, 17 September 1991, p. A5. See also "Zaiavlenie Gosudarstvennogo soveta SSSR o normalizatsii prodovol'stvennogo obespecheniia i agrarnoi politike v 1991-1992 godakh," *Izvestiia*, 17 September 1991, p. 1.

4. See [Nikita S. Khrushchev], *Khrushchev Remembers*, trans. Strobe Talbott (New York: Little Brown and Company, 1970); Gregory Bienstock, Solomon M. Schwartz, and Aaron Yugow, *Management in Russian Industry and Agriculture* (London: Oxford University Press, 1944); Merle Fainsod, *Smolensk under Soviet Rule* (New York: Alfred A. Knopf, 1958); Cynthia S. Kaplan, *The Party and Agricultural Crisis Management in the USSR* (Ithaca, NY: Cornell University Press, 1987); Barbara Ann Chotiner, *Khrushchev's Party Reform: Coalition-Building and Institutional Innovation* (Westport, CT: Greenwood Press, 1984); Zhores A. Medvedev, *Gorbachev* (New York: W.W. Norton and Company, 1986); Robert F. Miller, *One Hundred Thousand Tractors: The MTS and the Development of Controls in Soviet Agriculture* (Cambridge: Harvard University Press, 1970); Leonid I. Brezhnev, *Virgin Lands: Two Years in Kazakhstan, 1954-1955* (Oxford: Pergamon Press, 1979); Barbara Ann Chotiner, "Soviet Local Party Organs and the RAPOs," in *The Soviet Union: Party and Society*, ed. Peter J. Potichnyi (Cambridge: Cambridge University Press, 1988); *idem*, "Organizational Change, Local Party Committees and Farms: Soviet Local Party Committees and Farms after the Inception of Raion Agro-industrial Associations," *Studies in Comparative Communism*, no. 1 (Spring 1988), pp. 45-60; Robert Conquest, *Power and Policy in the USSR: The Struggle for Stalin's Succession, 1945-1960* (New York: Macmillan and Company, 1961); Carl A. Linden, *Khrushchev and the Soviet Leadership*, updated ed. (Baltimore, MD: The Johns Hopkins University Press, 1990); Michel Tatu, *Power in the Kremlin: From Khrushchev to Kosygin*, trans. Helen Katel (New York: The Viking Press, 1969); Fedor Timofeevich Morgun, *Khleb i liudi*, 2nd enlarged ed. (Moscow: Izdatel'stvo politicheskoi literatury, 1975).

5. T.H. Rigby, *Lenin's Government: Sovnarkom, 1917-1922* (Cambridge: Cambridge University Press, 1979), pp. 2-3, 27, 130, 147, 241.

6. *Vedomosti Verkhovnogo soveta SSSR*, no. 1 (1938) - no. 48 (1985).

7. Changing the number and type of agricultural organs in the USSR Council of Ministers altered bargaining channels for middle and lower-level administrators and changed the scope and type of oversight exercised by bureaucratic superiors. Barbara Ann Chotiner, "Structural Change and Personnel Circulation in the Bureaucracy of the U.S.S.R. Council of Ministers, 1938-1969," (Seminar paper, Columbia University, 1971), pp. 21-30; Alec Nove, *The Soviet Economy: An Introduction*, paperback ed. (New York: Frederick A. Praeger, 1965), pp. 64-65; John Crowfoot and Mark Harrison, "The USSR Council of Ministers Under Late Stalinism, 1945-54: Its Production Branch Composition and the Requirements of National Economy and Policy," *Soviet Studies*, no. 1 (1990), pp. 39-45.

8. "Postanovlenie plenuma Tsentral'nogo komiteta KPSS 24 maia 1982 g. 'O proekte Prodovol'stvennoi programmy SSSR na period do 1990 goda'," in *Resheniia partii i pravitel'stva po khoziaistvennym voprosam*, vol. XIV, ed. K. M. Bogoliubov and M. S. Smirtiukov (Moscow: Izdatel'stvo politicheskoi literatury, 1983), pp. 399-400; "Prodovol'stvennaia programma SSSR na period do 1990 goda odobrena 24 maia 1982 g. plenumom Tsentral'nogo komiteta KPSS (izlozhenie)," *ibid.*, pp. 401, 403-404, 407-408, 410-413; "Postanovlenie TsK KPSS i Soveta Ministrov SSSR 24 maia 1982 g. 'Ob uluchshenii upravleniia sel'skim khoziaistvom i drugimi otrasliami agropromyshlennogo kompleksa'," *ibid.*, pp. 440-443.

9. "Ob izmeneniiakh v sisteme organov upravleniia agropromyshlennym kompleksom," *Vedomosti Verkhovnogo soveta SSSR*, no. 48 (1985), item 938; "O dal'neishem sovershenstvovanii upravleniia agropromyshlennym kompleksom (izlozhenie)," *Resheniia partii i pravitel'stva po khoziaistvennym voprosam*, vol. 16, part 1 (Moscow: Izdatel'stvo politicheskoi literatury, 1988), p. 233. The statute on the Council of Ministers had already been changed to accommodate entities like *Gosagroprom*, which combined features of ministries and traditional state committees. "O dopolnenii zakona SSSR 'O Sovete Ministrov SSSR'," *Vedomosti Verkhovnogo soveta SSSR*, no. 44 (1985), item 838; A.P. Alekhin, "O razrabotke teoreticheskikh problem sovershenstvovaniia gosudarstvennogo upravleniia ekonomikoi v svete reshenii XXVII s"ezda KPSS," in *Problemy sovershenstvovaniia gosudarstvennogo upravleniia*, ed. M.I. Piskotin, B.M. Lazarev, and N.G. Starovoitov (Moscow: Institut gosudarstva i prava AN SSSR, 1987), p. 39. Generally, ministries exercised operative direction over productive units like farms or factories; state committees usually provided coordinative guidance and supporting services for producers.

10. See comments by Alekhin, *ibid.*, p. 37; Don Van Atta, "'Full-Scale, Like Collectivization, but without Collectivization's Excesses': The Campaign to Introduce the Family and Lease Contract in Soviet Agriculture," in *Perestroika in the Countryside: Agricultural Reform in the Gorbachev Era*, ed. William Moskoff (Armonk, NY: M.E. Sharpe, Inc., 1990), p. 90; Kenneth Gray, "Soviet Utilization of Food: Focus on Meat and Dairy Processing," in *Soviet Agriculture: Comparative Perspectives* (Ames, IA: Iowa State University Press, 1990), p. 108; *idem.*, "Introduction," in *ibid.*, p. 10.

11. "O dal'neishem sovershenstvovanii upravleniia agropromyshelennym kompleksom," pp. 232-235.

12. *Ibid.*

13. "O naznachenii tov. Murakhovskego V.S. predsedatelem Gosudarstvennogo agropromyshlennogo komiteta SSSR," *Vedomosti Verkhovnogo soveta SSSR*, no. 48 (1985), item 939; "O naznachenii pervogo zamestitelia predsedatelia Gosudarstvennogo agropromyshlennogo komiteta SSSR tov. Sizenko E.I. ministrom SSSR," *ibid.*, no. 49 (1985), item 962; "O naznachenii pervogo zamestitelia predsedatelia Gosudarstvennogo agropromyshlennogo komiteta SSSR tov. Ievleva A.I. ministrom SSSR," *ibid.*, no. 51 (1985), item 989; "Sostav Tsentral'nogo komiteta Kommunisticheskoi partii Sovetskogo soiuza, Izbrannogo XXVII s"ezdom KPSS: chleny TsK KPSS," *Izvestiia TsK KPSS*, no. 2 (February 1989) pp. 49, 68, 86, 98; "Ob itogakh Vsesoiuznoi nauchno-prakticheskoi konferentsii po sovershenstvovaniiu nauchnogo obespecheniia agropromyshlennogo

kompleksa strany: zapiska agrarnogo otdela KPSS," *ibid.*, p. 153; "Kandidaty v chleny Tsentral'nogo komiteta KPSS," *ibid.*, no. 6 (June 1989), p. 32; Medvedev, *Gorbachev*, pp. 46-47.

14. "Nam otvechaiut," *APK*, no. 5 (1989), p. 80; I. Balgazin, "Sovershenstvovanie arendnykh otnoshenii," *ibid.*, no. 6 (1989), p. 32; "Problemy razvitiia ekonomicheski slabykh kolkhozov i sovkhozov," *ibid.*, no. 6 (1989), p. 127; "Nam otvechaiut," *ibid.*, no. 8 (1989), p. 9; Van Atta, "Full-Scale, Like Collectivization," p. 96; Z. Beridze and M. Kozlov, "Arendnie otnosheniia v sisteme APK," *APK*, no. 6 (1989), p. 19; "Kak reshalsia v Moskve prodovol'stvennyi vopros," *Izvestiia TsK KPSS*, no. 12 (1990), p. 125.

15. I. Kalin, "Agropromyshlennomy kompleksu--nadezhnuiu nauchnuiu osnovu," *Planovoe khoziaistvo*, no. 5 (May 1988), p. 30; A. I. Tiutiunnikov, "Intensivnoe sel'skoe khoziaistvo: problema effektivnosti," in *Sel'sko-khoziaistvennaia praktika: protivorechiia perestroiki*, ed. M.M. Badina *et al.* (Moscow: VO "Agropromizdat," 1989), p. 302; "O rabote Gosagroproma Gruzinskoi SSR i agropromyshlennogo komiteta Kirovskoi oblasti po likvidatsii ubytochnosti predpriiatii i organizatsii," *APK*, no. 3 (1989), pp. 124, 126.

16. N. Borochenko, "Reservy popolneniia prodovol'stvennykh resursov," *Planovoe khoziaistvo*, no. 2 (February 1988), p. 84; A. Kirin, "Tsenoobrazovanie v APK," *APK*, no. 4 (1989), p. 68; V.Ia. Uzun, *Realizatsiia ekonomicheskoi reformy v APK*, Novoe v zhizni, nauke, tekhnika, Seriia ekonomika, no. 6 (Moscow: Izdatel'stvo "Znanie," 1989), p. 39.

17. "Kakaia khoziaistvennaia sistema nam nuzhna," in *Sel'sko-khoziaistvennaia praktika*, p. 177.

18. Uzun, *Realizatsiia ekonomicheskoi reforma v APK*, p. 39.

19. N. Aver'ianov, "Planirovanie, sistema planovnykh pokazatelei i normativov v APK," *APK*, no. 1 (1989), p. 94; G. Atrakhimovich, "Sovershenstvovanie planirovaniia v usloviiakh raboty na polnom khozraschete i samofinasirovanii," *ibid.*, pp. 54-55; Uzun, *Realizatsiia ekonomicheskoi reforma v APK*, pp. 5-6; Tikhonov, "Kakaia khoziaistvennaia sistema nam nuzhna," p. 168; R. Tonkonog, "Sovremennaia agrarnaia politika", *Sovety narodnykh deputatov*, no. 5 (1989), p. 31.

20. "Doklad komissii Politbiuro TsK KPSS po perestroike organizatsionnykh struktur tsentral'nykh ekonomicheskikh organov, ministerstv i vedomstv SSSR," *Izvestiia TsK KPSS*, no. 1 (1989), pp. 69, 70, 73; Politbiuro TsK KPSS, "O rabote Komissii Politbiuro TsK KPSS po perestroike organizatsionnykh struktur tsentral'nykh ekonomicheskikh organov, ministertv i vedomstv SSSR," *ibid.*, pp. 68-69.

21. M.S. Gorbachev, "Ob agrarnoi politike KPSS v sovremennykh usloviiakh," *Materiały plenuma Tsentral'nogo komiteta KPSS, 15-16 marta 1989 goda* (Moscow: Izdatel'stvo politcheskoi literatury, 1989), pp. 62, 63; "Ob agrarnoi politike KPSS v sovremennykh usloviiakh: postanovlenie plenuma Tsentral'nogo komiteta KPSS 16 marta 1989 goda," *ibid.*, pp. 87-89.

22. Karen M. Brooks, "Soviet Agriculture's Halting Reform," *Problems of Communism*, no. 2 (March-April 1990), p. 31.

23. Gorbachev, "Ob agrarnoi politike KPSS v sovremennykh usloviiakh," p. 63.

24. "Ob agrarnoi politike KPSS v sovremennykh usloviiakh: postanovlenie ... ," pp. 86, 91, 94; "Ob izmeneniiakh v sisteme organov upravleniia agropromyshlennym kompleksom strany," *Vedomosti Verkhovnogo soveta SSSR*, no. 15 (1989), item 107; "Ob uluchshenii prodovol'stvennogo obespecheniia naseleniia strany na osnove korennogo povysheniia effektivnosti i dal'neishego razvitiia agropromyshlennogo proizvodstva," *Sobranie postanovlenii Pravitel'stva SSSR*, no. 19-20 (1989), item 60; "O korennoi perestroike ekonomicheskikh otnoshenii i upravleniia v agropromyshlennom komplekse strany," *ibid.*, item 61.

25. A. Gonchar, I. Gumeniuk, and I. Kurochka, "Sistema vedeniia khoziaistva i planomernoe razvitie sel'skokhoziaistvennogo proizvodstva v strukture APK," *APK*, no. 5 (1990).

26. Sovershenstvovanie upravleniia APK v novykh usloviiakh khoziaistvovaniia," *APK*, no. 2 (1991), p. 43.

27. "O korennoi perestroike ekonomicheskikh otnoshenii i upravleniia v agropromyshlennom komplekse strany," item 61.

28. P. Buchel, "Odnimi zakonami syt ne budesh'," *Ekonomika i zhizn'*, no. 9 (1991), p. 10.

29. *Agroprom Ukrainy*, no. 12 (1989), nos. 2-12 (1990).

30. "Kandidaty v chleny Tsentral'nogo komiteta KPSS," *Izvestiia TsK KPSS*, no. 6 (1989), pp. 39, 40; "Sostav Tsentral'nogo komiteta izbrannogo XXVII s"ezdom KPSS: chleny TsK KPSS," p. 65; P. Paskar', "Agrarnaia politika i zadachi agropromyshlennogo proizvodstva," *Planovoe khoziaistvo*, no. 5 (May 1989), p. 3; Sekretariat TsK KPSS, "Ob usilenii politicheskoi napriazhennosti v sviazi s ukhudsheniem obespecheniia naseleniia prodovol'stvennymi i drugimi tovarami," *Izvestiia TsK KPSS*, no. 10 (October 1990), pp. 14, n. 18; "Sokrashchenie," *ibid.*, no. 12 (December 1989), p. 26; Sekretariat TsK KPSS, "O rabote partiinykh organizatsii Rostovskoi oblasti po sodeistvuiu v formirovanii mnogokladnoi agrarnoi ekonomiki s uchetom politicheskikh ustanovok XXVIII s"ezda KPSS," *ibid.*, no. 4 (April 1991), p. 19.

31. "O korennoi perestroike ekonomicheskikh otnoshenii i upravleniia v agropromyshlennom komplekse strany," item 61; "O stimulirovanii prodazhi gosudarstvu v 1989-1990 godakh vysokokachestvennogo zerna pshenitsy, bobovykh i semyan maslichnykh kul'tur putem oplaty valiutoi, vysvobozhdaemoi v sviazi s sokrashcheniem zakupok zerna i prodovol'stviia za rubezhom," *Sobranie postanovlenii Pravitel'stva SSSR*, no. 29 (1989), item 123; "O merakh stimulirovaniiu v 1990 godu gosudarstvennykh zakupok zerna," *ibid.*, no. 13 (1990), item 74; "O vvedenii novykh gosudarstvennykh zakupochnykh tsen na sel'skokhoziaistvennykh produktsii u," *ibid.*, no. 20 (1990), item 103.

32. "Forma 3," *Agropromyshlennyi kompleks Rossii*, no. 1 (January 1990), pp. 13-14.

33. S. Smolianskii, "V interesakh razvitiia sel'skogo khoziaistva," *APK*, no. 3 (1991), pp. 104, 106; "V Gosplane SSSR," *Planovoe khoziastvo*," no. 6 (June 1990), p. 125.

34. "O Gosudarstvennoi komissii Soveta Ministrov SSSR po ekonomikoi reforme," *Sobranie postanovlenie Pravitel'stva SSSR*, no. 28 (1989); item 108; "O merakh po demonopolizatsii narodnogo khoziaistva," *ibid.*, no. 24 (1990), item 114.

35. I. Kostik, "Vnutrikhoziaistvennaia arenda: pravovye aspekty," *APK*, no. 2 (1991), p. 29.

36. [Otdel agrarnoi politiki TsK KPSS], "Ob usilenii vnimaniia partiinykh organizatsii voprosam stabilizatsii i uluchsheniia prodovol'stvennogo polozheniia strany v usloviiakh perekhoda k rynochnoi ekonomike," *Izvestiia TsK KPSS*, no. 2 (February 1991), pp. 15, 18; Smolianskii, "V interesakh razvitiia sel'skogo khoziaistva," p. 105.

37. "O neudovletvoritel'nom sostoianii proizvodstva i kachestve vyrabatyvaemykh kolbasnykh izdelii," p. 103.

38. [Otdel agrarnoi politiki TsK KPSS], "Ob usilenii vnimaniia partiinykh organizatsii voprosam stabilizatsii i uluchsheniia prodovol'stvennogo polozheniia," pp. 15-16.

39. S. Smolianskii, "O gosudarstvennoi politike zakupok zerna za rubezhom," *APK*, no. 2 (1991), p. 119.

40. B. Prokopchuk, "Nabolelo!," *Agropromyshlennyi kompleks Rossii*, no. 7 (1990), p. 2.

41. I. Ernazarov, "Sel'skokhoziaistvennye predpriiatiia v novykh usloviiakh khoziaistvovaniia", *APK*, no. 1 (1991), p. 80; G. Elistratov, "Rynok prodovol'stviia – kakim emu byt'," *Planovoe khoziaistvo*, no. 11 (1990), p. 33.

42. "Po puti stabilizatsii," *APK*, no. 1 (1991), p. 3.

43. Its chairman, Mikhail Timoshishin, was accused of having acquiesced to this effort to seize power. "O chlenakh Kabineta Ministrov SSSR," *Vedomosti S"ezda narodnykh deputatov i Verkhovnogo soveta SSSR*, no. 10 (1991), item 255; "Za novye formy khoziaistvovaniia na sele, za prioritet agropromyshlennogo kompleksa: vstrecha M.S. Gorbacheva s rukovoditeliami kolkhozov, sovkhozov, agropromyshlennykh predpriiatii, pereshedshikh na novye formy khoziaistvovaniia," *Sel'skaia zhizn'*, 30 March 1991, p. 1; Kabinet Ministrov SSSR, "O merakh po obespecheniiu soglasovannykh deistvii soiuznykh i respublikanskikh organov v formirovanii gosudarstvennykh resursov zerna iz urozhaia 1991 goda," *Sel'skaia zhizn'*, 16 July 1991, pp. 1-2; "Gorbachev's Speech to Russians: 'A Major Regrouping of Political Forces'," *New York Times*, 24 August 1991, p. 6.

44. "Zaiavlenie Gosudarstvennogo soveta SSSR o normalizatsii," p. 1; A. Stepovoi, "Vzory vsekh opiat' prikovany k kremliu: rukovoditeli desiati respublik vyskazalis' za podpisanie Ekonomicheskogo dogovora k 15 oktiabria," *Izvestiia*, 12 October 1991, p.1.

THE STATE AND
SECURITY

8

THE MINISTRY OF DEFENSE

Ellen Jones and James Brusstar

On 8 December 1991, leaders of the three Slavic republics signed an agreement in the Belarus capital of Minsk establishing a Commonwealth of Independent States and declaring "that the USSR as a subject of international law and a geopolitical entity has ceased to exist."[1] On 21 December, the three Slavic states were joined by Kazakhstan, Armenia, Azerbaijan, Moldova, and the four Central Asian republics, whose leaders agreed to name Defense Minister Evgenii Shaposhnikov as Commonwealth Commander.[2] The decree naming Shaposhnikov to his new post heralded the demise of the USSR Ministry of Defense.[3]

The Ministry of Defense, to be sure, lived on under a different name: the Commonwealth Command. Former Deputy Defense Minister and Commander in Chief of the Navy Vladimir N. Chernavin became known simply as the Commander of the Navy.[4] General Staff officers still made their way each morning to General Staff headquarters at the end of the old Arbat market place in downtown Moscow. The Defense Ministry's numerous components still functioned much as they had in the past.

Despite these continuities, the legal demise of the old USSR Defense Ministry–an event made necessary by the collapse of the old USSR itself–is an appropriate marker to the end of an era. As the old Defense Ministry leadership struggles to find a place for the old Armed Forces in the new political environment, now is a fitting time to assess an organization that finds itself without a mission and without a country.

The Defense Ministry's Place in the Soviet Federal Structure

The USSR Defense Ministry was part of a huge bureaucracy and cannot be understood without a knowledge of how that bureaucracy functioned within the

181

larger Soviet policymaking system. Soviet policies were made and implemented through a dual party-Government structure. The Communist Party leadership formulated policy and oversaw its execution. The real policymakers in the country worked in the party Central Committee building. The role of the Government--of which the Defense Ministry was a part--was to elaborate party policy through laws and administrative acts, and to implement it.

The Soviet Government exercised authority through an administrative system that was composed of three distinct types of organizations. Some agencies were based on fulfilling a specific administrative function; USSR Gosplan, which oversaw the economic planning process, is an example of such an agency. Other agencies, known as "sectoral" agencies, provided specialized products or services throughout the country as a whole. Examples included the Ministry of Defense and the Ministry of Chemical Industry. The third type of organization managed a wide variety of functional and sectoral agencies within a specific geographical area; the Ukrainian Council of Ministers is an example of this kind of organization. The functional and sectoral agencies and the territorial governments were connected through an intricate web of relationships.

The Soviet system has often been characterized as highly centralized, and this characterization is largely correct. The degree of centralization, however, varied widely, with some activities literally run out of the Kremlin and others delegated to local authorities in the hinterlands. This variation was reflected in the three basic types of Soviet ministries. Most highly centralized were the all-union ministries in Moscow, which managed their assigned sector through field offices subordinate solely to the Moscow headquarters. Union-republic ministries represented an intermediate level of centralization; most of their agencies were administered through republic bureaucracies and answered to republic agencies, which were "dual subordinate" to the republic government and the parent ministry in Moscow. The most decentralized functions (like social welfare) were run through republic ministries, with no parent ministry at the national level.

The Defense Ministry's legal status varied over time. The 1936 Stalin constitution included a provision allowing each of the Soviet Union's 15 republics to raise and maintain its own military forces. On 1 February 1944, in connection with a law authorizing republics to set up their own military formations, the ministry (then the People's Commissariat of Defense) was reorganized into a union-republic ministry. As national formations were phased out in the post-war period, the ministry began functioning in a more centralized manner.[5] However, the Defense Ministry remained a union-republic ministry. In 1977, a new constitution was adopted that eliminated the provision empowering republics to maintain their own armed forces. Accordingly, in July

1978, when a new law on the Council of Ministers was adopted, the Defense Ministry was listed among the all-union ministries.[6]

The 1978 shift in legal status was official acknowledgement of existing practices, since the Ministry of Defense had already long been operating as a highly centralized agency.   There had been no republic defense ministries. Republic and regional governments had virtually no role in making defense policy, and they had only a limited impact on how certain aspects of that policy, such as manpower procurement, were carried out.

Structure of the Ministry of Defense in the Soviet Era

The Soviet leadership also faced the problem of how to group related missions under the various ministries. For instance, major categories of products, such as machinery, could be grouped together into one huge ministry or multiple ministries could be set up to handle machine building, each with responsibility for one specialized subset of products (e.g., automobiles). The possibilities are endless, to which Soviet experiments with different arrangements attests.

The Soviets faced similar choices in the way they organized defense.   All services could be grouped together in one ministry or individual services could be handled by separate ministries. Centralizing the control and management of all services in one ministry had the advantage of facilitating uniform manpower and training programs. On the other hand, dividing out certain components with specialized missions and unique needs, such as the Navy, offered its own advantages, such as less bureaucratic interference and outside constraints on force building.

The Soviets experimented with a long series of organizational arrangements. The People's Commissariat for Military Affairs, organized in late 1917, combined all services under one organizational umbrella.[7] By early 1918, however, the Navy was split off into an independent commissariat.[8] In 1923, the two functions were brought together again into an all-union Commissariat for Military and Naval Affairs.[9] In 1934, this organization was restructured into a Commissariat of Defense.[10]   The Navy once again gained its own administration with the establishment of the Commissariat of the Navy in 1937.[11] This division of authority lasted until after World War II. In 1946, the two organizations were combined into a unified Commissariat for Armed Forces (later renamed the Ministry of the Armed Forces.)[12] The Navy once again enjoyed a brief period of organizational autonomy with the formation of two separate ministries--the Ministry of War and the Ministry of the Navy--in the early 1950s.[13] In March 1953, the two ministries were once again merged into

Table 8.1
Structure of the Armed Forces

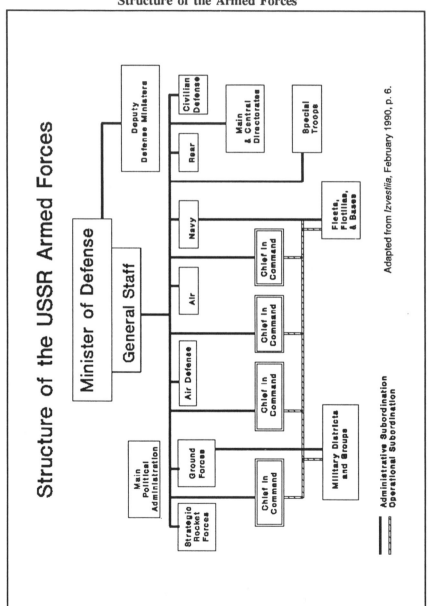

Adapted from *Izvestiia*, February 1990, p. 6.

a unified Defense Ministry, which survived until December 1991 and the collapse of the Soviet Union.

Management of the Armed Forces in the Soviet Era

Every state that has a large military faces choices about how to administer and manage it.   Two basic questions to be resolved are how to set up the headquarters elements and how to handle troop units, both operationally and administratively.   In dealing with the former issue, the Soviets favored a General Staff type structure, opting for weak service commands and a strong centralized staff.

At the pinnacle of the military hierarchy was the Defense Minister, who served as an executive agent for military policies approved by the Politburo and the Defense Council (a state body specializing in national security issues, but operating more as a sub-committee of the Politburo).[14]   Like all Soviet ministries, the Defense Minister had an advisory committee--the Ministry of Defense board (*kollegiia*).[15]   Patterned roughly after the tsarist Military Council, which was formed in 1832, the board brought together the deputy ministers of defense and the Chief of the Main Political Administration (who headed the military's hierarchy of political and party bodies).[16]

The General Staff was the real focus of bureaucratic power in the Defense Ministry.[17]   It served as an extended headquarters staff for the Defense Minister, coordinating the activities of the main and central MOD headquarters directorates (such as the Main Cadres Directorate and the Main Directorate for Military Educational Services), as well as the General Staff's own directorates and departments.[18]   The General Staff also served as a policy and program focal point for the various MOD agencies and the service commands.

From 1959 to late 1991, the USSR Armed Forces consisted of five services: the Strategic Rocket Forces, the Ground Forces, Air Defense Forces (PVO), Air Forces, and Navy.[19]   In November 1991, the SRF, the missile early warning system, the space monitoring and ABM defense systems, and the directorate of the chief of space systems were merged to form a Strategic Deterrence Force.[20] The services were responsible for the development of tactics and aspects of training and logistical support of their service-related units throughout the Soviet Armed Forces.   The service headquarters of the Strategic Rocket Forces (and later Strategic Deterrence Force), the Navy, and the Air Forces also had operational responsbilities.

The vast majority of Defense Ministry personnel, of course, were assigned to troop units and administrative elements throughout the country.   These "field offices" were roughly analogous to the factories and stores run by the economic ministries. Like the economic ministries, the Defense Ministry had several organizational options. Some industrial ministries in the USSR organized their far-flung factories into production associations run directly from Moscow. Other ministries, such as the Ministry of Internal Affairs (MVD), sub-divided their field offices by territory, running them through analogous ministries at republic level. The MVD's territorial administration mirrored republic and regional boundary lines and was knit into the federal system, with regional MVD offices being dual subordinate to both the regional government and the MVD office at the next highest level.

Like the MVD, the Defense Ministry was sub-divided for administrative purposes into territorial headquarters--military districts, fleets and (for units outside the USSR) groups of forces.[21] Unlike the MVD, the MOD's territorial units (the military districts) were not subordinate to republic or local governments.[22] In some cases, the boundaries of the military districts coincided with those of federal administrative-territorial units (as was the case, for instance, with the Belorussian Military District); in other cases, a single military district encompassed several republics.

In adopting this form of territorial arrangement, early Soviet leaders were drawing on the tsarist past.[23] Until 1862, there were essentially no local military administrative entities. Several of the War Ministry's departments had regional representatives, and the individual field units were forced to negotiate with each of them to satisfy needs for food, clothing, and weapons. The system was decentralized in 1862, when military district administrations were set up to handle troop supply and administration. The powers of the district commander were roughly analogous to those of the war minister. Like the war minister, the district commander had a staff and was assisted by a military district council analogous to the War Ministry's Military Council. The tsarist military districts were abolished in January 1918, but resurrected several months later. The military district structure was retained throughout the Soviet period.

The Soviet military district was a microcosm of the Defense Ministry itself.[24] The military district commander was subordinate to the Defense Ministry in Moscow through the Ground Forces Commander in Chief.[25] Each military district contained troop units, schools, and administrative entities (personnel directorate, billeting directorate) subordinate to the district commander but having a "special subordination" relationship with the analogous component at Defense Ministry headquarters in Moscow.[26] The military district commander administered the components of the district through the military district staff--a district level analog to the General Staff.[27] Like the General Staff, it was subdivided into directorates and departments. The military discrict commander also had an advisory board (another holdover from the tsarist era)--the military district Military Council.

For force operations, the Defense Ministry employed a second system of headquarters that was subordinate to the General Staff. Three service headquarters--the Strategic Rocket Forces, the Air Force, and the Navy-- exercised operational control over the strategic nuclear forces in their services. A separate set of headquarters, called High Commands of Forces, exercised operational control over the USSR's sizable general purpose forces and non-strategic nuclear weapons.[28] Fronts (the equivalent of an Army Group in Western terminology) and army headquarters (whose units were administratively assigned to military district and groups of forces) were subordinate to the high commands of forces for operational purposes.

Another key element in the Ministry of Defense's territorial network-- occupying an intermediary position between the military district and the civilian territorial system (the network of republic, regional and city governments)--was the military commissariat system.[29] This system was based on the civilian territorial structure, with commissariats at republic, region (*oblast'*), city, and district (*raion*) level. The commissariats were part of the Defense Ministry, while operating with the rights of a department of the corresponding local government. Their work was directed by the General Staff's Organization-Mobilization Directorate and the relevant military district commander.

Military commissariats were combined draft boards and recruitment centers that were responsible for manpower procurement, mobilization, and civilian military training. They also administered service pensions and allowances. The Ministry of Defense was thus dependent on the military commissariat system to implement the semi-annual draft. Beginning in the late 1980s, when republic and regional governments were taken over by politicians intent on autonomy and later independence from Moscow, their control of the local manpower procurement system resulted in widespread disruption of the draft.

Civil-Military Relations in the Soviet Era

All states face the potential threat of military intervention in politics. Military leaders command most of the coercive capability in a given state, and this raises the possibility that they may use (or threaten to use) that capability to usurp civilian power. To counter this threat, many Western democracies have devised systems that ensure that the military remains apolitical, with the officer corps legally excluded from an active political role. The Soviets faced a similar problem, but the mechanisms they developed to safeguard the political leadership from military pressure were very different.

One part of the Soviet strategy to ensure political control of the military involved giving civilians the predominant role in all aspects of decisionmaking. This domination by civilian politicians was carried out not through legislative oversight (since there were no independent legislatures), but through the Communist Party leadership's preeminent role in military policy. The top decisionmaking body within the party hierarchy, the Politburo, set overall policy in virtually all areas, including defense.[30] The Politburo generally met about once a week, as did the Central Committee secretariat--another party decisionmaking body that focused on overseeing appointments and controlling policy implementation.[31] The highest government body that specialized in national security issues was the USSR Defense Council.[32]

Members of these committees--a handful of the USSR's top policymakers-- played a key role in formulating defense policy. Unlike democratic systems, where elected representatives reflect public interests, the Soviet system employed both policymaking and advisory committees to represent organizational interests. Committees like the Politburo, secretariat, and Defense Council represented one of several mechanisms to ensure that relevant organizational interests were represented in the decisionmaking process. For instance, Politburo membership generally included the heads of key organizations--party chiefs from key republics, the heads of important ministries, and Central Committee secretaries charged with priority missions.[33]

Military leaders, however, played a distinctly secondary role. Except for brief periods, the Defense Ministry was not represented on the Politburo until 1973, when Defense Minister Andrei Grechko became a member.[34] Grechko was succeeded in 1976 by Dmitrii Ustinov, a full member of the Politburo. Ustinov, however, was not a career military officer but a defense industrialist.[35] In December 1984, he was succeeded by Sergei Sokolov, a professional military officer who was given candidate Politburo status in 1985. Sokolov was removed in May 1987 in the wake of the Rust incident, during which a German citizen piloting a Cessna aircraft penetrated Soviet airspace and landed on Red Square.[36] Sokolov was succeeded by Dmitrii Yazov, another military professional who became a candidate member of the Politburo the following month.[37] Yazov's career came to an abrupt end when he participated in the abortive August 1991 coup. He is at this writing in prison awaiting trial for treason.

Defense Ministry interests were also represented through the membership and participation of top Ministry of Defense officials in the USSR Defense Council. Chaired by the party general secretary, this top national security policy board generally included the defense minister and the chief of the General Staff. Like the Politburo, however, the Defense Council was dominated by civilians--party functionaries and heads of key civilian Government agencies.

The primary role of Defense Ministry officials in the decisionmaking process was that of providing expert advice. Military officers drafted recommendations, devised alternatives, and assembled supporting data. They did not make decisions. Civilian politicians, not military professionals, dominated the Kremlin's corridors of power. Defense Ministry officials played only a supportive role, even in decisions directly affecting the Armed Forces. Their power depended on their ability to convince the political leadership that their position on individual issues was the right one. As noted above, the one exception to this generalization, Dmitrii Ustinov, was not a military professional but a civilian defense industrialist by background and thinking.

Another mechanism for civilian political control over the military was the Communist Party's control of key appointments. Each party committee had its own *nomenklatura*, a list of positions over which that committee exercised authority to approve or disapprove personnel appointments. Nominees for high-level military posts, for instance, were apparently reviewed at Politburo or Central Committee secretariat level. The party's power to hire and fire was crucial in ensuring military responsiveness to civilian authority.

Leaving nothing to chance, Soviet politicians supplemented these mechanisms with yet another--a network of Communist Party organizations. Every Government bureaucracy had its own primary party organizations. In the military, this network of party bodies was only one of a series of redundant civilian control mechanisms built into the military structure. The rationale for this difference in military and civilian supervisory mechanisms must be sought in the early Soviet period.

When the Bolsheviks seized power in 1917, they faced the immediate problem of ensuring that the army functioned as a loyal instrument of civilian authority. In the early Bolshevik period, this was a daunting task. Many of the former tsarist military officers were actively hostile to the new regime, yet the Bolsheviks were forced to rely on them in great numbers during the Civil War.[38] To counter potential sabotage by these men, the fledgling regime created a system of military commissars, whose main role was to serve as a political watchdog over the former tsarist officers. At all operational levels, orders by the military commander were not binding unless they were also signed by the commissar. The Bolsheviks also moved rapidly to replace these professionally qualified, but politically suspect, officers with "Red" commanders. The proportion of ex-tsarist military officials, who accounted for 75 percent of military commanders in 1918, dropped to about two thirds by the close of the Civil War and to less than 11 percent by 1929.[39]

At the same time, the proportion of officers with desirable political credentials (in particular, Communist Party membership) grew rapidly. By 1930, over half of the military's command personnel (compared to just 13 percent of white-collar professionals in the civilian workplace) were members or candidate members of the party.[40] In the 1970s and 1980s, party membership among Soviet officers probably ranged from 75 to 80 percent, compared to less than a third for most civilian professionals.[41] For most officers, then, a military career meant party membership. Limiting the officer corps largely to party members provided a way of filtering out political dissidents and ensuring that the military remained subservient to its political bosses. Ironically, the officer corps was "depoliticized," not because they were prohibited from actively participating in political parties, but because the vast majority of officers belonged to the only political party that existed.

Responsibility for administering the armed forces' party organizations and its Komsomol bodies (the party's "farm league" for teenagers and young adults) fell to the Main Political Administration (MPA)—an agency that was in theory part of the Communist Party hierarchy but in practice operated as an arm of the Ministry of Defense. The MPA started out as a political watchdog. By the mid-1930s, however, this role had largely atrophied, in part because the officer corps was dominated by loyal party members and in part due to the existence of another control mechanism within the military—the network of "special departments" subordinate to the KGB. The role of these bodies was to gather personal information on servicemen through a network of informers in order to identify and dismiss political dissidents.[42] These strategies were fairly effective, at least until the waning days of the Soviet period, in ensuring that the military remained an apolitical instrument of the party leadership. The military, despite its near monopoly of coercive power, remained largely outside of politics and played only a secondary role in political decisions that shaped the Armed Forces future.[43]

Because the politicians who dominated decisionmaking placed a high priority on military power, the military as an institution prospered, at least from the Brezhnev period on. Military programs were accorded high priority, even in the late Brezhnev period when a slowing economy made it ever more difficult to insulate defense projects from the restraints that bedeviled most civilian programs. Military officers, although excluded from a political role, were a pampered and respected group within Soviet society.

The Defense Ministry and the Gorbachev Reforms

In a very real sense, the end of the Soviet Union began with the political reforms introduced by Gorbachev in the late 1980s. Gorbachev's innovation was to introduce political pluralism, through greater tolerance of alternative political viewpoints in the press and by breathing life into the moribund Soviet legislatures, which had existed theretofore merely as rubber-stamps for Communist Party decisions. These developments resulted in the slow death of the Communist Party, which was unable to compete in competitive elections. The relaxation of centralized political authority also undermined the political links tying republics to Moscow.

The consequences for the Defense Ministry were profound.[44] The military's role in Soviet society changed from that of a privileged body to an institution under siege. Once the favorite son of the command economy, it faced increasingly persistent calls for deep budget cuts. Once the object of media adulation, it found itself a target of growing resentment and criticism. Soviet officers, once respected and rewarded, were faced with an uncertain future of force cuts, declining living standards, and (in some regions) a hostile and dangerous citizenry.

Gorbachev's political reforms also led to significant changes in how national security policy was made. The military policy process became far more decentralized, involving a host of new institutions and players. Legislators at both national and provincial levels began playing an increasing role in military decisions. Military officials once accustomed to working with a small circle of Communist Party apparatchiks with a strong commitment to military power were forced to defend their programs before a more diverse and less accommodating array of decisionmakers. Moreover, the formerly quiescent Soviet public, once a non-player in security politics, began acquiring increasing clout. Regional and local interests that the Defense Ministry could previously ignore with impunity began interfering with a vengeance in Defense Ministry business.

Increasingly strident republic demands for autonomy began threatening the very basis of the centrally controlled Armed Forces. By the late 1980s, control of military policy emerged as a key issue in the struggle between Moscow and her ever more restive republics, including the Russian republic. Many republics began demanding a major role in shaping military programs; others simply declared unilaterally that Moscow's military service requirements had no validity on republic territory. By 1990, provincial authorities in the Baltic and Caucasus republics and the Western Ukraine were successfully encouraging draft resistance.

These developments resulted in the gradual breakdown of many of the previous constraints on the military's political activity. As the Soviet domestic situation rapidly spun out of control in 1990 and the first half of 1991, Gorbachev was forced to rely increasingly on the support of the military and other security bodies. As Soviet politics became more polarized, the system of redundant political control mechanisms, designed to ensure that the Defense Ministry served as a reliable instrument of Communist Party politics, began to break down. Some officers began to take sides in political conflicts, emerging as active participants in policy debates ranging from issues directly affecting the armed forces to domestic matters.

The officer corps' new political activism took many forms. With no prohibitions on political activity, military personnel began running for legislative office and playing a vocal role in legislative politics. Officers also began running for executive offices. The prominence of military candidates in the June 1991 Russian presidential election was an example.[45] Yeltsin chose popular Afghan war veteran Colonel Alexander Rutskoi as his vice-presidential running mate. Yeltsin's most serious rival, former Council of Ministers Chairman Nikolai Ryzhkov, chose another prominent Afghanistan veteran, Colonel General Boris Gromov. Another military officer—Colonel General Albert Makashov, Commander of the Volga-Urals Military District—ran for president, campaigning in military uniform.[46] Both the Yeltsin-Rutskoi and the Ryzhkov-Gromov teams attempted to cultivate the military during the campaign, with promises of more resources for social programs and benefits and more respectful treatment in the media. These efforts to curry military favor reflected an attempt both to gain military votes and placate an institution that controlled the nation's most powerful coercive forces.

Military personnel also emerged during this period as an influential political force outside the realm of formal institutions. Top-ranking Defense Ministry leaders lent their authority to highly publicized attempts to mobilize public opinion and pressure the leadership on domestic issues. For example, in December 1990, Chief of the General Staff Mikhail Moiseev (along with Deputy Defense Minister Valentin I. Varennikov and Commander in Chief of the Navy Chernavin) signed a public letter urging Gorbachev to use his presidential powers to restore stability and halt republic separatism.[47]

Uniformed personnel also became involved in local and regional politics, particularly in regions where separatist sentiment was strong and servicemen had come under attack by local civilians. In such cases, the military took a strong anti-independence stance. For example, servicemen in the Baltic met in Riga on 21 December 1990 to demand that the Soviet legislature introduce presidential rule in the Baltic region.[48]

As military personnel became more enmeshed in politics, strong divisions within the officer corps surfaced. Top Defense Ministry leaders took fairly traditionalist approaches. They believed that the changes of the late 1980s had weakened Soviet national security, pointing to the loss of Soviet dominance over East Europe and the resulting withdrawal of forces, the reunification of Europe, and what they saw as one-sided concessions in the Conventional Forces in

Europe (CFE) process.[49] Senior military leaders were also profoundly troubled by the chaotic situation on the home front. They saw the potential breakup of the Union as threatening the security of the country and the integrity of the armed forces.

Below the level of the top leadership, however, deep political divisions emerged. Some officers joined more extreme conservative coalitions, like Soiuz--a traditionalist faction of the USSR legislature that advocated preserving the union and blocking ethnic separatism. Military officers such as Colonel Viktor Alksnis, an ethnic Latvian favoring policies that would reinstate order and crush republic separatism, emerged as prominent spokesmen of such groups.[50] Officers also assumed high profiles in conservative groups at republic level. Other members of the officer corps joined groups espousing radical reform or allied themselves with reform-minded republic leaders like Russian chief Boris Yeltsin.

The emergence of these political divisions within the officer corps undermined its cohesiveness and helped ensure the failure of the August 1991 coup. While some top Defense Ministry officials supported Defense Minister Yazov and the other coup conspirators, many officers hesitated and a few actively joined Yeltsin's effort to reverse the coup. The military's failure to support the conspiracy contributed to its collapse, Yazov's arrest, and his replacement by Marshal Shaposhnikov.

The Defense Ministry in the Post-Soviet Era

Although the Defense Ministry emerged surprisingly unscathed by the coup, the subsequent demise of the old center and the old framework for tying together the republics effectively set the military adrift. After the coup, the Soviet high command still clung to the hope that the Soviet Armed Forces could be preserved.[51] These hopes were shattered by Ukraine. Unwilling to participate in a military alliance that would jeopardize her chances to be part of a larger all-European security system, Kiev repeatedly and firmly rejected the Defense Ministry plans to preserve a single military.

Yeltsin's decision in early December 1991 to abandon Gorbachev and his attempt to revive the Union forced military leaders to make a choice. They could either continue to support Gorbachev or shift allegiance to Yeltsin and his plan to keep the former republics linked through a commonwealth arrangement. Shaposhnikov chose the latter course and on 21 December was named interim Commander in Chief of the newly formed Commonwealth. It became clear almost immediately, however, that Shaposhnikov's hopes for the Commonwealth were unrealistic. The Commonwealth was never conceived as a successor state to the Soviet Union. It is not a government and has no permanent governing bodies with authority over member states. Commonwealth member states may decline to participate in any Commonwealth discussion and to sign Commonwealth agreements.[52]

The main role of the Commonwealth is to facilitate a negotiated divorce between the former republics by providing a forum for dividing the assets and responsibilities of the defunct union. So far it has made little progress in this regard. Contention between the successor states represents a continuing obstacle to smooth relations. Conflict between the two largest Commonwealth states, Russia and Ukraine, over economic, military, and territorial issues (such as the Crimea) emerged immediately. The dispute between Azerbaijan and Armenia over Nagorno-Karabakh, which in late January 1992 deteriorated into war between the two states, further strained the Commonwealth.

Nor did creation of the Commonwealth solve the problem of what to do with the centralized Soviet Armed Forces. Shaposhnikov clearly hoped that the 11 member states of the new Commonwealth could be persuaded to participate in a defense coalition, with much of the old Soviet Armed Forces retained under allied command. It also became clear that he, like many others in the officer corps, viewed the Commonwealth as the nucleus of a new center.

However, Ukraine consistently frustrated the high command's hopes. While Ukraine signed a series of superficial agreements acceding in principle to the need for allied Commonwealth control of strategic forces, Kiev refused any involvement in a Commonwealth defense arrangement involving either a single armed forces or allied Commonwealth control of national forces.[53] Underlining its determination to disengage from its former partners, Ukraine began in early January 1992 to move ahead unilaterally to nationalize former union troops on its soil, including assets--such as the Black Sea Fleet--that both Shaposhnikov and Russia claimed as Commonwealth forces. Ukrainian Defense Minister Morozov ordered a cessation of direct communication between troop units located in Ukraine and the General Staff in Moscow.[54] Kiev also announced that military personnel in "non-strategic" units on Ukrainian territory would be obliged to sign a new oath of allegiance to Ukraine.

Both the high command and Russian officials denounced Ukraine's actions. Shaposhnikov accused Ukraine of violating the Commonwealth accords. Russian legislators published an open letter to their Ukrainian counterparts requesting that Kiev revoke its demands on Black Sea officers to take the Ukrainian oath of allegiance.[55] Ukraine, of course, turned a deaf ear to these complaints and continued to make good on its commitment to nationalize forces on Ukrainian soil. Russia, meanwhile, moved to exert her jurisdiction over forces deployed outside the Commonwealth.[56] At this writing, there is as yet no agreement among Ukraine, the Commonwealth high command, Russia, and other Commonwealth states on the division of military assets.

Moreover, the thorny issue of civilian political control of the military still remains to be worked out. At this writing, Commonwealth states have not yet reached agreement on command arrangements. Although Shaposhnikov was appointed Commander of the Joint Commonwealth forces by the Commonwealth Council of Heads of States, he has thus far not been legally subordinated to the Council itself.[57] Russian President Yeltsin clearly wields the greatest de facto influence over Shaposhnikov, as a result of his budgetary authority and the fact that he heads the largest country in the Commonwealth. However, Shaposhnikov is not legally subordinate to Yeltsin either. A series of proposals that would have clarified the command arrangements and subordinated the military directly to civilian Commonwealth bodies was repeatedly rejected by Commonwealth leaders, apparently because states like Ukraine saw this as an effort to recreate the old center.[58] As a result, the military—except those servicemen in Ukraine who have sworn an oath of allegiance to Ukrainian political authorities—is not legally accountable to any civilian leadership.

These developments have been profoundly disturbing to the officer corps, which is only with great reluctance becoming reconciled to the breakup of the military.[59] Many officers, particularly at the senior levels, lament the demise of the old Union and the loss of control over most forces in Ukraine. A poll taken at a meeting of officers in Moscow on 17 January revealed that 71 percent of the assembly participants favored restoration of the old USSR. Seventy-nine percent felt that the military should have the deciding say in determining the future of the armed forces; only 19 percent felt that the army must await decisions by politicians on the army's future.[60]

The final chapter still remains to be written. Russia's preference is a truncated defense alliance with Belarus, Kazakhstan, and the Central Asian states. Only if other states begin to take the same path as Ukraine is Russia likely to abandon the Commonwealth and adopt a "Russia alone" defense strategy. Russian participation in a Commonwealth defense coalition does not preclude, however, creation of both a Russian Defense Ministry and a Russian Armed Forces, which were authorized by Yeltsin in the spring of 1992.[61] If Russia does elect to participate in a more limited general purpose force coalition with some of the other states, she would provide some troops and financial resources to a central allied command, while retaining a larger number of forces subordinate exclusively to Russia.

On 14 February 1992, Russia and seven other states (Belarus, Kazakhstan, Armenia, and the Central Asian states) took the first step in the direction of a truncated defense alliance (without Ukraine). The eight states signed a transitional agreement setting up joint Commonwealth General Purpose Forces, which will apparently consist of some common forces plus some national forces operationally subordinate to the Commonwealth command.[62] Whether this agreement in principle will be carried out in practice remains to be seen. In any event, elements of the old USSR Ministry of Defense and General Staff will likely be incorporated into the Russian Armed Forces. If the Commonwealth strategic arrangements hold, other MOD elements associated with strategic forces will probably be retained as part of a Commonwealth strategic command. If Russia and the other seven states follow through on their commitment to create joint Commonwealth General Purpose Forces, other elements of the old Defense Ministry will form the basis of a Commonwealth general purpose command. The shape of the future Russian Defense Ministry and the Commonwealth high command (assuming that some joint command arrangements are retained) will, of course, depend on the viability of Commonwealth political links, as well as decisions in Moscow on the level of Russia's participation in allied defense structures.

Like the Bolsheviks who seized control from the tsarist government, the Russian reformers who supplanted the Soviet system—clearly anxious to distance themselves from their predecessors—will stress the differences that divide the emerging Russian democracy from the despised totalitarian past. Indeed, the new arrangements for defense decisionmaking in Russia (assuming Russia avoids an authoritarian reaction) will surely include elements—such as mechanisms for legislative control, judicial review, and separation of powers—that were foreign to the Soviet system, at least as Gorbachev inherited it in 1985.

However, these differences should not obscure important continuities between the Soviet and post-Soviet political systems. Many of the same organizational principles that characterized the Soviet-era Defense Ministry will likely be preserved in the new command and administrative arrangements. The temporary charter of Russia's new Ministry of Security provides an example of such continuity. It includes a section setting up a ministry board (*kollegiia*). The wording of this provision is almost identical to analogous sections in the charters of Soviet-era ministries.[63] Just as the Bolsheviks adapted tsarist collegial arrangements as a way of providing a check on the minister's authority, Russian reformers are modifying the Soviet-era ministerial board for the same purpose. Old administrative habits, it seems, die hard.

Notes

The views expressed in this chapter reflect the personal opinions of the authors and do not represent the views of the Defense Department or the U.S. Government.

1. "Full Text of Agreement Establishing a Commonwealth of Independent States," Moscow TASS International Service, 9 December 91.

2. "Protocol of the Conference of Heads of Independent States," *Krasnaia zvezda*, 24 December 1991, p. 2.

3. On the last day of 1991, the Defense Ministry's newspaper (*Krasnaia zvezda*) described itself in its masthead as "the daily newspaper of the Defense Ministry." On 1 January 1992, the newspaper declared itself "the daily newspaper of the Armed Forces."

4. *Krasnaia zvezda*, 16 January 1992, p. 2. Chernavin was also referred to in the media as "Commander in Chief of the former USSR Navy." See *Sovetskaia Rossiia*, 9 January 1992, p. 1.

5. "Ministerstvo oborony SSSR," *Sovetskaia voennaia entsiklopediia*, vol. 5, pp. 294-296 [hereafter *SVE*].

6. "O sovete ministrov SSSR," *Vedomosti Verkhovnogo Soveta SSSR*, no. 28 (1978), p. 436.

7. "Ministerstvo oborony SSSR," *Voennyi entsiklopedicheskii slovar'* (Moscow: Voenizdat, 1986), p. 445 [hereafter *VES*]. See also, "Ministerstvo oborony SSSR," *SVE*, vol. 5 (Moscow: Voenizdat, 1978), pp. 294-296.

8. "Narodnyi komissariat po voennym delam," *VES*, p. 474; and "Narodnyi komissariat po morskim delam," *ibid.*

9. "Narodnyi komissariat po voennym i morskim delam," *VES*, p. 474; and "Narodnyi komissariat po voennym i morskim delam SSSR," *SVE*, vol. 5, p. 508.

10. "Narodnyi komissariat oborony," *VES*, p. 474; and "Narodnyi komissariat oborony SSSR," *SVE*, vol. 5, p. 508.

11. "Narodnyi komissariat voenno-morskogo flota," *VES*, p. 474; and "Narodnyi komissariat voenno-morskogo flota SSR," *SVE*, vol. 5, p. 508. See also "Polozhenie o narodnom komissariate oborony soiuza SSR," in *Zakonodatel'stvo ob oborone SSSR* (Moscow: Voenizdat, 1939), pp. 10-12; and "Ob obrazovanii narodnogo komissariate voenno-morskogo flota SSSR," *ibid.*, p. 13.

12. "Narodnyi komissariat vooruzhennykh sil," *VES*, p. 474.

13. "Voennoe ministerstvo SSSR," *VES*, p. 140; and "Voenno-morskoe Ministervsto SSSR," *VES*, p. 141.

14. *Sovetskoe administrativnoe pravo*, ed. Iu.M. Kozlov (Moscow: Iuridicheskaia literatura, 1971), *passim*; and *Administrativnoe pravo*, ed. A.Ie. Lunev (Moscow: Iuridicheskaia literatura, 1967), p. 458.

15. "Kollegiia ministerstvo oborony SSSR," *VES*, p. 340; and "Kollegiia ministerstva oborony SSSR," *SVE*, vol. 4, pp. 235-36.

16. A.V. Fedorov, *Russkaia armiia v 50-70 godakh XIX veka. Ocherki* (Leningrad: Izdatel'stvo leningradskogo universiteta, 1959), pp. 123-36.

17. "General'nyi shtab," *VES*, pp. 185-186; and V.G. Kulikov, "General'nyi shtab," *SVE*, vol. 2, pp. 510-513. On the tsarist General Staff, see A. Kavtaradze, "From the History of the Russian General Staff," *Voenno-istoricheskii zhurnal*, no. 3 (1976), pp. 103-109.

18. "Glavnye i tsentral'nye upravleniia," *VES*, p. 195; "Glavnye i tsentral'nye upravleniia," *SVE*, vol. 2, p. 565;

19. *Voennoe zakonodatel'stvo i pravovoe vospitaniia voinov*, ed. A.G. Gornii *et al.* (Moscow: Voenizdat, 1983), pp. 29-33; "Vid vooruzhennykh sil," *VES*, p. 129; and "Vooruzhennye sily SSSR," *VES*, pp. 158-160.

20. Air and sea-based strategic nuclear forces were made operationally subordinate to the commander of the Strategic Deterrence Forces. Interview with Iu. Maksimov, "Military Reform in Action," *Krasnaia zvezda*, 7 December 1991, p. 3.

21. M.I. Eropkin and A.P. Kliushnichenko, *Sovetskoe administrativnoe pravo* (Moscow: Iuridicheskaia literatura, 1979), pp. 234-35; and Iu.M. Kozlov, *Upravlenie v oblasti administrativno-politicheskoi deiatel'nosti* (Moscow: Iuridicheskaia literatura, 1979), p. 42.

22. *Administrativnoe pravo*, ed. Iu.M. Kozlov (Moscow: Iuridicheskaia literatura, 1968), pp. 512-13.

23. Forrest A. Miller, *Dmitrii Miliutin and the Reform Era in Russia* (Nashville, TN: Vanderbilt University Press, 1968), pp. 26-53.

24. "Voennyi okrug," *VES*, p. 146; A. Babakov, "The Soviet Military Districts: Toward a History of Their Development," *Voenno-istoricheskii zhurnal*, no. 9 (1982), pp. 62-67.

25. *Voennoe pravo*, ed. A.G. Gornii (Moscow: Voenizdat, 1984), p. 46.

26. *Voennaia administratsiia. Uchebnik*, ed. P.I. Romanov (Moscow: Glavnoe politicheskoe upravlenie), pp. 85-86.

27. N.T. Konashenko, "Voennyi okrug," *SVE*, vol. 2, pp. 270-271.

28. Soviet officials long maintained that the high commands of forces were a wartime phenomenon and did not exist in peacetime. The existence of this command arrangement was publicized during the Gorbachev era. This discussion is drawn largely from the chart found in V. Litovkin, "Secrets without Secrets," *Izvestiia*, 21 February 1990, p. 6.

29. "Voennyi komissariat," *VES*, p. 146; and P.I. Romanov, "Voennyi komissariat," *SVE*, vol. 2, pp. 269-270.

30. A.A. Epishev, *KPSS i voennoe stroitel'stvo* (Moscow: Voenizdat, 1974); and *Partiino-politicheskaia rabota v sovetskikh vooruzhenikh silakh*, ed. M.G. Sobolev (Moscow: Voenizdat, 1974), p. 103.

31. *Ustav kommunisticheskoi partii Sovetskogo Soiuza* (Moscow: Politizdat, 1977), Article 38, p. 65.

32. "Sovet oborony SSSR," *VES*, p. 684. See also, S.S. Maksimov, *Osnovy sovetskogo voennogo zakonodatel'stva* (Moscow: Voenizdat, 1978), pp. 50-51; and P.I. Romanov and V.G. Beliavskii, *Konstitutsiia SSSR i zashchita otechestva* (Moscow: Voenizdat, 1979), pp. 51-52.

33. For instance, of the 23 full and candidate members of the Politburo in June 1980, eight were party functionaries in various republic and regional party organizations (the areas represented were Moscow city, Kazakhstan, Leningrad oblast, Georgia, Ukraine, Azerbaijan, Belorussia, and Uzbekistan). Six members had full time posts in the national level party apparatus. Eight were top officials in various government departments, such

as the Foreign Ministry, KGB, and Defense Ministry. *Knizhka partiinogo aktivista* (Moscow: Politizdat, 1980), pp. 7-20.

34. "Grechko, Andrei Antonovich," *VES*, p. 213.

35. "Ustinov, Dmitrii Fedorovich," *VES*, p. 769.

36. *Pravda*, 31 May 1987.

37. Moscow Domestic Service, 1430 GMT, 26 June 1987.

38. "Voennyi komissar," *VES*, p. 145; V.G. Kolychev, "Voennyi komissar," *SVE*, vol. 2, pp. 268-9; A. Chiliants, "V.I. Lenin and the Creation of the Political Organs and Party Political Apparatus in the Soviet Armed Forces," *Voenno-istoricheskii zhurnal*, no. 2 (1983), pp. 12-17.

39. P. Spirin, "V.I. Lenin and the Creation of Soviet Command Cadres," *Voenno-istoricheskii zhurnal*, no. 4 (1965), pp. 3-16.

40. D.A. Voropaev and A.M. Evlev, *Bor'ba KPSS za sozdanie voennykh kadrov* (Moscow: Voenizdat, 1960), pp. 145-46; *X let krasnoi armii. Albom diagram* (Moscow: Izdatel'stvo "Voennyi Vestnik", 1928), p. 35; and *Narodnoe khoziaistvo SSSR. Statisticheskii spravochnik, 1932* (Leningrad and Moscow: Gosudarstvennoe sotsial'no-ekonomicheskoe izdatel'stvo, 1932), pp. 494-95.

41. Estimates of party membership in the officer corps are from V. Khrobostrov, "Political Organs and Party and Komsomol Organizations in the Soviet Armed Forces," *Kommunist vooruzhennykh sil*, no. 4 (1974), pp. 69-76; and V. Izmalov, "The 26th CPSU Congress on Strengthening the Nation's Defense Might," *Kommunist vooruzhennykh sil*, no. 8 (1981), pp. 77-84. The civilian comparison was calculated from "KPSS v tsifrakh," *Partiinaia zhizn'*, no. 21 (1977), pp. 20-43; and *Narodnoe khoziaistvo SSSR v 1977 g* (Moscow: Statistika, 1978), p. 48.

42. "Osobye otdely," *SVE*, vol. 6, pp. 142-43.

43. Timothy J. Colton, *Commissars, Commanders, and Civilian Authority: The Structure of Soviet Military Politics* (Cambridge, MA: Harvard University Press, 1979), *passim*.

44. For a discussion of the impact of developments during this period, see Ellen Jones, "Social Change and Civil-Military Relations," in *Soldiers and the Soviet State: Civil-Military Relations from Brezhnev to Gorbachev*, ed. Timothy J. Colton and Thane Gustafson (Princeton, NJ: Princeton University Press, 1990), pp. 239-84.

45. E. Ivanov, "Who Will Be President?" *Pravda*, 20 May 1991, p. 2.

46. "Albert Makashov: By Birth I am One of My People," *Pravda*, 29 May 1991, p. 2.

47. "With Hope and Belief: Appeal to Comrade M.S. Gorbachev," *Sovetskaia Rossiia*, 22 December 1990, p. 1.

48. Moscow Television Service, 2057 GMT, 24 December 1990.

49. For a description of changes in the strategic balance, see Ye. G. Korotchenko, "The Contemporary Military-Political Situation and Problems of Military Art," *Voennaia mysl'*, no. 8 (1991), pp. 19-24.

50. See, for instance, "Things Are Heating Up All the Time," *Sovetskaia Rossiia*, 20 June 1991, p. 2; and Interview with Viktor Alksnis, "Gorbachev's Concept Have Led Us into Anarchy and Chaos," *Der Morgan*, 6 May 1991, p. 4. Alksnis' call for a state of

emergency in the spring of 1991 is presented in "The Army Will Play First Fiddle," *Komsomolskaia pravda*, 14 March 1991, p. 3. See also, *Moscow News*, no. 6, 10-17 February 1991, p. 7.

51. See, for instance, the 5 November press conference by Defense Minister Shaposhnikov, "USSR State Council Says 'Yes' to Unified Armed Forces," *Krasnaia zvezda*, 7 November 1991, p. 1; and "Armed Forces Must be Unified. USSR Defense Minister's News Conference," *Krasnaia zvezda*, 7 September 91, p. 1.

52. "Temporary Agreement on the Council of Heads of State and the Council of Heads of Government of the Commonwealth of Independent States," *Rossiiskaia gazeta*, 1 January 1992, p. 2.

53. The agreements on strategic forces signed to date have papered over contentious issues, such as the successor states' operational control of nuclear weapons, relocation of nuclear weapons located on their territory, and how START reductions will be implemented. Copies of the relevant Commonwealth agreements are found in "Agreement on Joint Measures in Relation to Nuclear Weapons," *Krasnaia zvezda*, 24 December 1991, p. 3; "Agreement Between Commonwealth Nuclear States on Strategic Forces (30 December 1991)," *Rossiiskaia gazeta*, 1 January 1992, p. 2; "Agreement of CIS Member States on the Military Oath in Strategic Forces," *Rossiiskaia gazeta*, 18 January 1992, p. 2; and "Agreement Between CIS Members States on the Status of Strategic Forces," *Rossiiskaia gazeta*, 19 February 1992, p. 2. The Commonwealth's inability to reach a stable agreement on key issues, such as the relocation of nuclear weapons, was reflected by Kiev's 12 March announcement that Ukraine was halting the transfer of tactical nuclear weapons to Russia. See *Izvestiia*, 12 March 1992, p.1.

54. Interview with General Piankov, "Major Maneuvers in a Mine Filed," *Trud*, 9 January 1992, p. 4. See also V. Pasyakin, "The Divison of the Navy Means Its Destruction," *Krasnaia zvezda*, 10 January 1992, p. 1; *Izvestiia*, 4 January 1992, p. 1, and 7 January 1992, p. 1.

55. The text of the appeal is available in *Rossiiskaia gazeta*, 1 February 1992, p. 1.

56. "Decree of the Russian President on Transferring the Northwest Group of Forces and the Baltic Fleet to the Jurisdiction of the Russian Federation," *Rossiiskaia gazeta*, 1 February 1992, p. 2.

57. Shaposhnikov was named Commander of the Armed Forces at the 21 December Commonwealth summit in Alma-Ata. At the 14 February 1992 Commonwealth summit in Mensk, nine of the eleven Commonwealth states (all but Moldova and Turkmenistan) signed an agreement changing Shaposhnikov's title to Commander in Chief of the Allied Armed Forces of the Commonwealth. See "Protocol of the Meeting of Heads of Independent States," *Krasnaia zvezda*, 24 December 1991, p. 2; and *Rossiiskaia gazeta*, 19 February 1992, p. 2.

58. L. Ivashov, "Armed Forces Await Political Decisions," *Krasnaia zvezda*, 5 February 1992, p. 1; and Moscow Interfax, 1526 GMT, 14 February 1992.

59. Results of a poll taken in early February in all branches of the armed forces indicate that 80 percent favor a unified military doctrine. G. Andreev, "80 Percent Favor Unified Military Doctrine," *Krasnaia zvezda*, 14 February 1992, p. 1.

60. Aleksandr Putko, "Sentiments in the Army Worry the Military Itself," *Nezavisimaia gazeta*, 5 February 1992, p. 2. A subsequent analysis of the poll results challenged Putko's conclusion about the military's propensity to intervene in politics. However, the data presented in this article, which breaks down the results from several key questions by service tenure, strongly supports the conclusions from the original article. For instance, 55 percent of the officers under ten years of service and 57 percent of those with 10 to 15 years of service support the idea of restoring the former USSR, compared with 71 percent of the officers with 20 to 25 years service and 78 percent with over 25 years service. Over 80 percent of those with over 20 years of service felt that the military should have the deciding say in questions pertaining the future of the armed forces, and 70-77 percent of the younger officers subscribed to that opinion. In sum, although the more detailed breakdown reveals some age differences, junior officers are only slightly less supportive of reviving the USSR and of an active military role in determining the army's fate. See Elena Koneva, "Real Support for Army Reform," *Nezavisimaia gazeta*, 20 February 1992, p. 2.

61. At the end of 1991, Russia had a State Defense Committee, consisting of several dozen staffers. See "O preobrazovanii Gosudarstvennyi komitet RSFSR po oborone i bezopasnosti v Gosudarstvennyi komitet po delam oborony i Komitet gosudarstvennoi besopasnosti RSFSR," *Vedomosti S"ezda narodnykh deputatov RSFSR i Verkhovnogo Soveta RSFSR*, no. 19 (1991), item 632. For the formation of a Russian Ministry of Defense and Armed Forces, see Serge Schmemann, "Yeltsin Acts to Create a Separate Army for Russia," *The New York Times*, 8 May 1992, p. A4.

62. "Agreement Between the Republic of Armenia, the Republic of Belarus, the Republic of Kazakhstan, the Republic of Kyrgyzstan, the Russian Federation, Republic of Tadzhikistan, Turkmenistan, and the Republic of Uzbekistan on General Purpose Forces for the Transitional Period. 14 February 1992," *Rossiiskaia gazeta*, 21 February 1992, p. 3.

63. "Temporary Charter of the Ministry of Security of the Russian Federation," *Rossiiskaia gazeta*, 30 January 1992, p. 3. Article 8 covers provisions setting up the ministry collegium. Provisions governing the activities of Soviet-era collegia are found in "General Charter of USSR Ministries. 10 July 1967," *Svod zakonov SSSR* (Moscow: Prezidium Verkhovnogo Soveta SSR, 1980), pp. 193-204. The relevant articles are 15 and 18.

9

THE MINISTRY OF INTERNAL AFFAIRS

Louise Shelley

The Ministry of Internal Affairs (MVD) was responsible for the maintenance of order in the Soviet Union. Its mandate, grounded in the ideology of Marxism-Leninism, was to control crime, isolate political opposition (including localist and nationalist movements), and combat economic activity outside the state sector. Like other ministries, the MVD was highly centralized. Its massive apparatus, which extended into every corner of the USSR, contained several functional branches: the police, the internal security troops (*vnutrennye voiska*, or *VV*), ground units, the fire service, and the prison and labor camp systems.

Until the Gorbachev era, the MVD remained an extremely powerful, and seemingly unshakeable, institution of state control despite occasional changes in its name and in the scope of its activities. But the restructuring of the economy and society and the rise of nationalism in the republics gradually undermined the institutional integrity of the ministry. In the late 1980s, numerous republics seeking greater autonomy from the center established independent republic ministries of internal affairs, which served as a prelude to the acquisition of full sovereignty. The central authorities in Moscow, in turn, made increasing use of the internal security troops and other combat forces under the USSR Ministry of Internal Affairs to fight the disintegration of the Soviet Union. In advance of the breakup of the USSR in December, 1991, USSR MVD personnel operated on the frontlines in numerous republics in an attempt to halt separatist movements and violent inter-ethnic conflict. When the final collapse of the Soviet Union occurred, one of the first measures of the new Commonwealth of Independent States was to remove the troops of the former USSR MVD from warring regions in the Caucasus. The pages that follow set these developments in the context of the ministry's historical development, its functions, and its critical role in the final period of the Soviet state.

The Development of the Internal Affairs Ministry

The original institution in charge of internal affairs, the NKVD (People's Commissariat of Internal Affairs), was established in October 1917. Initially, the NKVD had primarily police functions; responsibility for prisons and corrections fell to other institutions. The NKVD was not, however, a traditional police force. The early administrators of the NKVD as well as many of its personnel were distinguished by their ideological commitment rather than their professional competence. Individuals who had made their name in fighting political opponents and armed criminals in the first stages of the post-revolutionary period were often promoted to leadership positions. It was not until the Stalin years that a professional and entrenched bureaucracy governed the ministry.

The intense centralization of the Soviet state, apparent in the immediate post-revolutionary period, resulted in the establishment of a central *militsiia* (ordinary police) administration in Moscow as part of the NKVD. A complex chain of command descended from the national headquarters in Moscow to the republic level and then down to the regional and local levels, where precincts of small size were created to facilitate policing. The 36 people who first ran the central office in Moscow, with its responsibilities for criminal investigation, information and, supplies[1], would have had difficulty imagining the size and complexity of the internal affairs apparatus that would soon exist. Once the Soviet leaders abandoned the idea of a popular police, responsive and accountable to the local community, they wasted little time in establishing a complex bureaucratic structure to police the immense territory of the Soviet state. By 1920, five specialized police forces, divided by territory or function, existed within the NKVD. They were the urban and district police, the criminal investigative unit, and the river, industrial, and railway police.[2]

Because the growth of the Treasury could not keep pace with the expansion of the state bureaucracy, even the most essential operations of the Soviet state, the army and the secret police (Cheka, later GPU and OGPU), were strapped for funding. The regular police, an organization of much lower priority, received even less support from the central budget. Thus, while the *militsiia* received some funding from the NKVD in Moscow, it had to rely on local budgets[3] for much of its support. In an attempt to streamline operations in 1925, the NKVD consolidated in one act the diverse responsibilities assigned to the police.[4]

The structural changes in the NKVD in the early years of Stalin were dizzying in their complexity and in the extent to which they augmented the authority and independence of the commissariat. When Stalin assumed power in the late 1920s, two distinct organizations performed the police function. Ordinary criminal offenses were under the jurisdiction of the NKVD while political crime was the responsibility of the OGPU (Unified State Political Administration). By 1932, the Soviet leadership had placed the NKVD under the OGPU, consolidating the two police functions for the first time.[5] Only two years later, the OGPU was absorbed into an expanded NKVD, where all police functions were now concentrated.[6] Writing in 1968, Robert Conquest noted that "[i]n the NKVD the Soviet police forces reached their full development and the USSR finally evolved the widespread system of police controls which is substantially that of today."[7]

The USSR NKVD acquired such extensive authority that there were no effective local controls over its activities throughout the Stalinist period. Its head reported directly to the Communist Party leader, Stalin, who closely supervised its activities. While the NKVD, unlike its tsarist counterpart, was organized formally along federal lines, and was therefore subject to some direction by governmental authorities at the republican and local levels, by the 1930s the central organization in Moscow exercised direct control over all NKVD activities in the different republics. As the Smolensk archives reveal, local party officials were forbidden to interfere in NKVD work and could not summon its employees to do their bidding.[8] Further insulating the NKVD from local party influence was the commissariat's control over its own appointments. While the region (oblast') and district (raion) NKVD offices were part of the nomenklatura (the party-controlled patronage system), it was the NKVD itself that suggested the appointment or dismissal of its personnel. The party only confirmed the internal NKVD decisions. All this was possible because the NKVD answered to no governmental agency or party structure. With such unbridled authority, the NKVD was able to conduct the purges of the 1930s as almost a free-standing bureaucracy of repression.

Throughout the 1930s there was organizational continuity in the law enforcement apparatus: all police power was consolidated in the NKVD.[9] But no such continuity was observed in the leadership of the police. Between 1934 and 1938 there were three leaders of the NKVD. The first two, Genrikh Yagoda and Nikolai Yezhov, suffered the same fate as the numerous victims of the purges they had overseen. Only Lavrenti Beria, who assumed power in 1938, was able to remain in office for a lengthy tenure. He was finally removed in 1953 in the wake of Stalin's death.

In 1941, the NKVD was split into two commissariats. The one under Beria retained the title NKVD while the new commissariat, the NKGB (People's Commissariat for State Security), under the direction of Beria's crony, Vsevolod N. Merkulov, specialized in the narrow functions of the political police. This division lasted only six months, with the two commissariats reuniting at the outbreak of war.   These two commissariats were revived under the same leadership in 1943, a division that lasted through the war.[10]

Following the war, in 1946, the NKVD and NKGB were renamed the MVD and MGB (ministries of interior and state security).[11] The wartime division of labor between the two organizations continued until 1950, when a significant shift occurred in their responsibilities. The MVD, which had previously controlled most law enforcement activities, lost several of its most important components. The *militsiia*, the border troops (the armed police that guarded the entire Soviet border), and probably the special purpose troops were transferred to the MGB.[12]

Beria used Stalin's death in 1953 to launch yet another reorganization of the police apparatus. It was now the turn for the MGB to be absorbed by Beria's institution, the MVD.[13] Beria's maneuver, designed to strengthen his position in the succession struggle, did not have its intended effect.   He was soon checked by the leaders of party and Government, who feared the concentration of power in the hands of the police chief. Arrested in June 1953, Beria was tried in December of that year along with several of his associates from the security apparatus.   They were executed following their trial.[14] It should be noted that the execution of Beria and his henchmen was not an anomaly. Trials and executions of other police leaders continued for three more years, and the same pattern was repeated more recently.   Brezhnev's police leaders either committed suicide or were prosecuted following his death. In other centralized societies key police personnel have managed to survive different regimes.[15] In the USSR, the Ministry of Internal Affairs was too central an institution to permit career continuity under different party secretaries. Its leaders were devoured as the party secretaries they served were discredited.

The first decade after Stalin's death brought frequent reshuffling of the police structure, as Stalin's successors sought to ensure that the MVD leadership never again achieved the power it enjoyed during the purges. The major consequence of the trials and the executions of the immediate post-Stalin years was the permanent division of the police apparatus between its ordinary and political functions. In 1954, the political police, now known as the KGB (Committee for State Security), was established with jurisdiction over the security police and border guards. The regular police remained under the MVD, whose new leadership recruitment policy favored personnel who were trained in party work and did not have law enforcement experience in the Stalinist police apparatus. While this policy facilitated the dismantling of the machinery of terror, it ushered in a long period of party justice.[16] The appointment of party personnel without specialized training encouraged party pressure on law enforcement. The extent of this party intervention in legal affairs, and of corruption more broadly defined, was only revealed after Brezhnev's death.

In 1956, as part of an attempt to combat the Stalinist legacy in law and to weaken the institutions of the central Government, the Khrushchev leadership decentralized power in the MVD.[17] At this time, regional-level MVD organs were reorganized and made accountable to the corresponding units of government, the soviet executive committees. *Militia* departments in cities and districts were in turn made accountable to the soviet executive committees on those levels.[18] Then, in 1960, the USSR Ministry of Internal Affairs became a hollow shell after its functions were transferred to the ministries of internal affairs of the union republics.[19] In 1961, Vadim S. Tikunov, a former deputy KGB chairman under Alexander Shelepin, was appointed to head this emasculated ministry in Moscow. The appointment of Tikunov, an individual with close personal ties to Shelepin, a newly appointed secretary of the party Central Committee, enhanced the political standing of the beleaguered MVD. Tikunov's standing as the first lawyer to serve as head of the MVD contributed to the professionalism of the ministry.[20] Although Tikunov survived the temporary name change of his ministry in 1962 from the MVD (the dreaded name of the Stalinist period) to the Ministry for Defense of Public Order (MOOP)[21], he was ousted by Brezhnev in 1966 and spent the rest of his career in diplomatic exile as ambassador to Romania and then to several countries in Africa.[22]

Brezhnev undid Khrushchev's structural changes in the police apparatus, reviving a strong central ministerial apparatus and reinstating the onerous name of the Stalin police authority, the MVD, in 1968.[23] In the early 1970s, the Brezhnev stamp was impressed more deeply on the police apparatus with personnel changes and with the issuance of new legislation on the MVD, on the internal affairs departments of the executive committees, and on the police itself, measures that augmented the authority of the ministry.[24] Among other things, the regular police acquired additional administrative and data collection responsibilities and a greater role in conducting criminal investigations.

A primary source of recruitment for MVD officials in the Brezhnev era remained party *apparatchiki* without experience in law enforcement. Leaders of the MVD were frequently party officials who used service in the ministry as a stepping stone to higher party positions. As one western student of the law enforcement apparatus explained, MVD officials in this period had often served

> in the Party apparatus (as heads of Administrative Organs departments, Party secretaries or in the Komsomol) or in some cases in the procuracy, prior to going to the MVD. Not infrequently, MVD cadres later moved back into these positions. Of 28 MVD officials serving in leading posts at the republic or

national level during the seventies, only six could be classified as "career" MVD personnel. This trend reflects the Brezhnev regime's deliberate policy of bringing in Party *apparatchiki* to serve in the MVD, a policy that was begun in the late 1960's in an effort to strengthen the Party's supervision over the MVD.[25]

During the Brezhnev period there were very close links between the MVD and the general secretary of the Communist Party. As one Soviet official noted:

> Nepotism, string-pulling and servility, which increasingly ousted party principledness, entered our life .... Thus the number of untouchables protected by highly-placed patrons increased.[26]

Among the most prominent of these untouchables was Nikolai Shchelokov, a Brezhnev protege and head of the MVD for most of the Brezhnev period. Perhaps the classic example of patronage was the promotion in 1979 of Yurii Churbanov, Brezhnev's son-in-law, to the post of first deputy minister of the MVD ahead of colleagues with more seniority.

The close association of the MVD chiefs with the party general secretary innoculated the ministry against careful scrutiny of the rising corruption in the law enforcement apparatus.[27] However, as Brezhnev's authority waned in the early 1980s, the KGB under Yurii Andropov began an investigation of corruption in the MVD. These investigations increased not only Andropov's personal power but the influence of the KGB relative to that of the regular police.[28] Here Andropov—like Beria before him—used his skills as the ultimate police chief to advance his political career.

After assuming the post of party general secretary, Andropov moved rapidly to strengthen law and order. Only a month after he became the party leader, *Pravda* reported that a Politburo meeting had discussed complaints from the public about widespread corruption and growing crime. Laying the groundwork for a major change in the MVD, the article noted that "[t]he procurator's office and the MVD have been notified of the necessity of taking steps to improve law and order."[29] The following day, Moscow Radio announced that Shchelokov had been deprived of his post as USSR Minister of Internal Affairs.[30]

Speculation as to Shchelokov's successor was short-lived. Less than a week after his removal, Vitalii Fedorchuk, Andropov's successor as head of the KGB merely six months before, assumed the post of Minister of Internal Affairs.[31] Fedorchuk had served in the state security organs since 1939,[32] and had gained a reputation for toughness while in his prior post as chief of the Ukrainian security apparatus. The transfer of a KGB man to the MVD was a familiar strategy to control and at the same time revive the beleaguered ordinary police.

In his new role as MVD chief, Fedorchuk quickly initiated major changes. In January 1983, at a conference of senior MVD personnel, he spoke of a need "to eliminate shortcomings in the performance of internal affairs organs."[33] To do that, he investigated and dismissed large numbers of personnel at all levels of the MVD hierarchy throughout the USSR. MVD sources indicate that 161,000 MVD personnel were fired in 1983.[34]

The disgrace of Fedorchuk's predecessor, Shchelokov, was made more complete at a Central Committee meeting in June 1983. The former MVD minister was dismissed from his seat on the Central Committee "for allowing mistakes in his work."[35] Long-term associates of Shchelokov suffered as well. In the spring and summer of 1983, two of the eight deputy ministers at the MVD were forced into early retirement at age 61. Their replacements came from the KGB, another example of personnel from the reliable security organs being used to revamp the MVD. In addition, approximately one-half of the republic MVD ministers were purged in an effort to root out corruption and strengthen law enforcement in the periphery.[36] Many of the newly appointed MVD ministers were Slavs, unlike the ousted ministers, who were often members of titular nationalities. The Russification of the MVD leadership followed the national trend toward increased Great Russian presence in political posts under Andropov.

The appointment of Slavs to leadership positions in the non-Slavic republics reduced the influence of local party and government officials over the MVD apparatus. The flipside of these appointments was that they exacerbated the problems of national identity that surfaced with greater frequency and intensity under Gorbachev. Members of the diverse ethnic groups in the Soviet Union increasingly sought to determine their own affairs without direction from Moscow.

Following Andropov's death in 1984, a reversal in policy toward law enforcement might have been expected with the accession of Konstantin Chernenko, a Brezhnev supporter, to the post of party general secretary. Contrary to expectations, however, Fedorchuk continued his decisive restructuring of the MVD. While Shchelokov might have anticipated better treatment as a result of his former close association with the Brezhnev mafia, no reprieve for him was forthcoming.[37] A November 1984 decree stripped Shchelokov of his military title "for abuse of his official position for motives of personal gain."[38] A month later Shchelokov committed suicide.[39] His deputy, Yurii Churbanov, Brezhnev's son-in-law, was arrested and tried. Churbanov is now serving a 14-year labor camp sentence. Such measures anticipated the major changes to the MVD that would occur under perestroika, changes that will be discussed in greater depth below.

The Structure of the MVD

At the end of the Gorbachev era, three million employees of the Ministry of Internal Affairs performed law enforcement, corrections, and public safety functions in the USSR. The diverse and often conflicting responsibilities of MVD personnel made it difficult to reform this major organization. Whereas the police and correctional authorities were under instructions to humanize their activities at the end of the 1980s, the increasing ethnic conflict caused ever more frequent deployment of the para-military internal security troops of the MVD in nationalist conflicts. At the end of the Soviet period, there was a marked division of responsibility between the central and peripheral offices of the internal affairs ministry. While the local MVD devoted itself to the control of crime, the central MVD concerned itself with "internal and state security tasks."[40]

The USSR MVD offices in Moscow contained the main directorates of its operational branches: the criminal investigative division (*ugolovnyi rozysk*), the BKHSS (the division that combatted the theft of socialist property), the social order branch, GAI (State Automobile Inspectorate), the internal passport division as well as OVIR (which issued passports for travel abroad), the departmental guard, the extra-departmental guard, corrective labor, and the fire service.[41] Only the first five of these were considered parts of the *militsiia*. The center set policy, monitored enforcement, and maintained statistics in these operational areas. Furthermore, the national headquarters had responsibility for finances, medical programs, education and last, but certainly not least, political work. It also oversaw the selection of cadres for this highly centralized system. Before the autonomy drive of various republics, all major appointments went through Moscow. To ensure the smooth operation of this process, the second in command (the deputy MVD chief in each republic) was a Russian whose primary function was cadre selection.

These diverse responsibilities of the MVD were supervised by a board (*kollegiia*), which was headed by the Minister of Internal Affairs and included the deputy ministers, the heads of directorates, and other ministerial management personnel. The composition of the board, which met once or twice monthly, was approved by the Council of Ministers upon nomination by the Minister of Internal Affairs.[42] The board considered the plans and normative acts that were to be implemented by the Ministry. In its deliberations, the board relied heavily on the Communist Party apparatus for guidance.

The USSR MVD provided centralized leadership and immediate direction for all subordinate organizations. The MVD had numerous schools and institutes in different republics to train its entry level personnel, and it operated advanced training institutes and programs at both the republic and national level. The MVD headquarters staff also developed the work plans that guided the *militsiia* and other subordinate organizations,[43] much as any other ministry in the centrally-planned Soviet state. These central staff personnel oversaw the implementation of the numerous directives and instructions of the ministry.[44]

Beneath its central headquarters in Moscow, the MVD was divided into republic, region, city, and district offices, known as administrations (*upravleniia*), which reported to the party organizations and soviet executive comittees at their administrative levels as well as to the next-higher level office of the MVD. All republics in the USSR, with the exception of the RSFSR (Russian Republic), had longstanding ministries of internal affairs. In 1989, in an effort to appease Russian nationalists, a republic-level MVD was established in the RSFSR. It was this newly-established body that inherited many of the resources of the former Soviet MVD at the collapse of the USSR.[45]

The responsibilities of the republic ministries were in many respects analogous to the USSR ministry, except that the former's jurisdiction was confined to their republic.[46] Each republic ministry had a *militsiia* service with the following divisions: criminal investigation (*ugolovnyi rozysk*), BKHSS, administrative service (patrol-post work, passport, licensing)[47], and GAI (automobile inspectorate). These branches also existed at all administrative levels within the republic. At each administrative level, the *militsiia* was accountable to the internal affairs administration (*upravlenie vnutrennykh del*, or *UVD*) of the local soviet executive committee. Thus, the local *militsiia*, like most institutions of the Soviet state, was subject to dual subordination (*dvoinoe podchinenie*), answering vertically to higher-level offices of the MVD and laterally to the local government (and, as noted above, to the local apparatus of the Communist Party).

Attached to the *militsiia* at the regional level were specialized units such as the guard services. Of the approximately 200,000 men employed in these services, nearly 80,000 worked in the departmental guard (*vedomstvennaia okhrana*),[48] which operated under the *militsiia* statute and was subordinate to the USSR MVD.[49] In existence for over six decades, the departmental guard was assigned to institutions, territories, and economic enterprises, such as the USSR State Bank, air terminals, and reservoirs.[50] In Moscow, for example, special guards belonging to the MVD were employed by the metro, the Exhibition of Economic Achievement (*VDNKh*), the Lenin Library, and the Ostankino radio and television tower.[51]

A more sophisticated extra-departmental guard (*vnevedomstvennaia okhrana*) operated in both civilian and militarized units of the MVD. Organized in 1952 as part of the *militsiia*'s external (*naruzhnaia*) administrative division, it was transferred later in the decade to the public order division of the *militsiia*.[52] The civilian part of this force resembled in function U.S. private guard services. Working under contract, this agency maintained discipline at enterprises, construction sites, and organizations such as clinics, hospitals, pioneer camps, children's nurseries in cities, work settlements, and regional centers.[53] Under perestroika it provided guards to more than 1,000 church buildings.[54] Extra-departmental guards also supervised the transport of goods, especially *spetsproduktsiia* (special products), which had to be protected from public scrutiny.

The MVD fire guards existed under a separate MVD administration. With a central administrative staff in Moscow, the fire guards existed at the republic, regional, and district levels to enforce fire safety laws and fight fires. Another important branch of the MVD was the Corrective Labor Administration (*ispravitel'no-trudovoe upravlenie*, or *ITU*). The MVD employees who worked in this branch trained at many of the same institutes as those employed in the police. Their responsibility was to run the corrective labor camps and prisons that before perestroika housed approximately 1.75 million inmates. Employees in this branch of the MVD worked solely in the prison system and were not interchangeable with police personnel.

The MVD's internal security troops assumed an active, and controversial, role during perestroika. As ethnic tensions rose, the internal security troops were called on increasingly to quell unrest in the republics. In response to these new demands, in 1990 approximately six divisions, or 65,000 men, were added to this MVD division, which already numbered 300,000 men.[55] Many of these forces were sent to the frontlines, where they suppressed separatist movements in the republics or attempted to curb ethnic conflict in the Nagorno-Karabakh region of the Caucasus or the Fergana valley of Central Asia.[56] In these situations, they were fulfilling the role envisioned for them at the time of their establishment in the early post-revolutionary period. Separate from military units and reporting directly to the head of the MVD, they were always on call to control strikes, ethnic conflict, and even outbreaks at sport events. Unlike police personnel, internal security troops were conscripts rather than long-term employees of the MVD.[57]

Seeing that the conscripts of the internal security troops were unable to control ethnic conflict and unrest during perestroika, the leadership of the MVD created a new elite branch of the ministry, known as the Special Purpose Security Detachments, or *OMON*. The MVD began training personnel for *OMON* in 1987, although its black-bereted troops were first deployed only in the summer of 1988, against demonstrators in Moscow. Established as a special unit, *OMON* was incorporated in 1988 into the MVD Internal Security Troops[58]. Numbering approximately 25,000 to 35,000 men,[59] it employed much more violent techniques in the republics than in the Soviet capital. The most notorious role of the *OMON* was in the Baltics in the final period before independence. *OMON* troops shot unarmed civilians during the January 1991 crackdown throughout the Baltic region[60] and they stormed the Latvian Interior Ministry in an effort to reverse the autonomy drive of that ministry.[61] In May 1991, *OMON* troops attacked custom posts on the Latvian-Lithuanian and Latvian-Belorussian borders.[62] *OMON* units were also sent to Moldavia by the central government without requesting first the permission of local authorities.[63] In the attacks in the Baltics, the USSR Minister of Internal Affairs disclaimed responsibility for the actions of *OMON*, even though these troops were directly under his command. This denial of responsibility was not accepted, however, by the Procurator General of the USSR, Nikolai Trubin, who investigated charges of *OMON* abuse in Latvia.[64] Although the last *OMON* units departed the Baltics after independence, Baltic republics are still trying to extradite members of the *OMON* now living in Russia.

Control and Coordination

The MVD responded both to the commands of the Government and the Communist Party[65]. But in law enforcement, as in some other policy areas, the party and not the Government (the Council of Ministers) assumed direct responsibility for the supervision of the ministry. The division of the party apparatus charged with oversight of the MVD, as well as other legal institutions, was the Department of Administrative Organs (*otdel administrativnykh organov*), renamed the State and Law Department (*pravovo-gosudarstvennyi otdel*) in the late 1980s. The State and Law Department operated within the Central Committee apparatus in Moscow as well as in republic and regional party committees. Below that level party officials responsible for supervising law enforcement activities were attached to other, more broad-based departments of the party apparatus.

Party guidance of state legal institutions assumed several forms. As one distinguished foreign commentator on Soviet law has written:

> There are several basic means by which the CPSU (Communist Party of the Soviet Union) controls the activities of state agencies. First, the CPSU monopolizes the power to appoint persons to all key positions within the state agencies .... Second, various party organizations closely monitor and control the daily activities of state agencies. They [also] form the policy at the respective level of the hierarchy together with the state agencies.[66]

In the MVD, as in most other legal institutions, party supervision included the issuance of written instructions that set out goals to be achieved by the ministry; attendance and participation of party officials at ministry meetings; the evaluation of the *militsiia*'s performance in maintaining order and fulfilling party directives; and examination by party officials of citizen complaints and press criticism of improprieties within the MVD.[67] Furthermore, prior to the collapse of Communist Party authority at the beginning of the 1990s, at each administrative level representatives of the MVD, together with officials from the courts, the Procuracy, and the Ministry of Justice, met regularly with party representatives to discuss legal policy. These diverse forms of external supervision, especially intrusive in the case of the MVD, gave the party the potential to finely tune the behavior of the ministry.

Control of the MVD was ensured from within as well as from above. To maintain party control in such a massive bureaucracy, the party relied on its members and organizers inside the ministry. Because career advancement was limited without party membership, "[m]ore than 500,000 Communists work within the USSR MVD system, [and] there are 10,000 primary party organizations and 17,000 political workers."[68] While many line personnel were not party members, half of all officers belonged to the party,[69] and at the upper echelons of the officer corps, party membership was nearly universal because of the *nomenklatura* system.

Political organs reintroduced into the MVD under Andropov in the early 1980s were a major means of reasserting party control at a time of rising corruption in the ranks.[70] These organs were intended to provide greater direction than the political education departments, which had previously conducted the ideological indoctrination of MVD personnel. Reporting directly to the party Central Committee and acting only on its instructions, the political organs were designed to combat the "incidence of collusion between Party and MVD officials at the local level."[71]

In the final years of the Soviet Union, the party tried to rely on the political organs and party groups within the MVD to restore discipline in the ministry.[72] Evidence of the intensive effort to shore up party control was the establishment of "an additional ... 1,632 party groups ... and 646 party organizers" within the Ukrainian MVD apparatus.[73] Supervising political education and aiding cadre selection, they were a significant force in communicating party policy in a time of political flux.

At the very end of the 1980s, democratic reformers sought to eliminate these political organs as well as the party cells, which were important symbols of party power. One of the major strike demands of Siberian miners, for example, was the depoliticization of state bodies such as the police, which meant the removal of the party cells, known as primary party organizations, which functioned inside institutions of state. Even officials in the MVD itself seemed to view with increasing ambivalence the party presence in the ministry. After the elimination of the constitutionally guaranteed party monopoly of power in 1990, the deputy chief of the ministry's Political Administration explained, "MVD employees will soon belong to different political organizations, not just the Communist Party."[74]

In July 1991, Russian Federation President Boris Yeltsin banned all primary party organizations in state institutions, thereby accelerating the atrophy of the Communist Party. The leadership of the MVD, rudderless without direction from the party, joined forces with other conservative elements in the August coup to seek a restoration of party hegemony over state institutions. The coup failed, however, and the party was soon banned from political life. But even though there is no longer direct party influence in the MVD, the party legacy lives on in the supervisory personnel selected and trained in the years of Communist Party domination.

The Challenges of Perestroika

The Soviet state ultimately could not survive the challenges of perestroika. Its collapse was due in part to the inability of the MVD, one of the most formidable elements of the state social control apparatus, to stem separatism and national conflicts, the increase in black markets and organized crime, and the mounting regular crime that threatened to destroy the country's social fabric. In the twilight of Soviet rule, various structural changes were made in the police, new branches were added, and municipal policing was developed to supplement the centralized state apparatus. But all of this proved incapable of reversing the larger forces for disunion in the Soviet state.

The last years of the USSR MVD were marked by an almost frantic search for enhanced powers that would prevent the dissolution of the Soviet Union. Throughout the late 1980s and into 1991, there was a constant conflict between the mandated openness of *glasnost'* and the attempts by the MVD and other organizations of state to restrain the fundamental changes occurring in the USSR, changes which included an increase in free enterprise, a decentralization of power to the ever more assertive republics, and a diminished fear of the state by the Soviet populace. Among the measures designed to regain control of society for the state was the establishment in 1988 of a sixth directorate of the MVD to fight organized crime. However, its 1200 employees were unable to control the organized crime that had grown dramatically following the anti-alcohol campaign launched in May 1985. Corruption in government was so severe that in one area a MVD unit threatened to strike to protest inappropriate pressure from local politicians. Leading police officials also attempted to create a national organization, a Soviet-style FBI, that would be immune to local patronage and pressure. The state budget crisis, however, prevented the establishment of such a body.[75]

Another major structural response to the conditions created by perestroika was the establishment in May 1989 of an MVD directorate of preventive services—the Workers' Detachments to Support the Militia—to supervise citizen and volunteer militia groups. First established in the industrial city of Gorkii (now Nizhnii Novgorod) to supplement the understaffed police and to replace police personnel sent to areas of unrest, such as Nagorno-Karabakh,[76] the workers' detachments subsequently spread to Uzbekistan, Kazakhstan, Ukraine, Moldavia and 15 regions in the RSFSR. Their rapid expansion was reportedly encouraged by the Central Committee Department of State and Law.[77] The worker detachments consisted of factory workers released on a temporary basis from their enterprises for *militsiia* service. Paid substantially better than *militsiia* employees, these individuals started patrols after only rudimentary training in the legal norms they were to enforce. Their mandate was large and there were no restrictions on their right to enter "residential quarters in pursuit of an escaped lawbreaker."[78] Many reformers feared that they were a force for order alone rather than for the establishment of a law-based state.[79]

The formation and the deployment of the *OMON* in 1988 was another major initiative of the MVD. As previously noted, the use of *OMON* pitted the central Government against the republics, which were seeking increased autonomy if not independence. In the end, the drive by many republics for increased political autonomy broke the center's hold over the administration of internal affairs. In Moldavia,[80] the Caucasus, and the Baltics, leaders of national movements took increasingly bold steps to assert control over their republics' MVD. Lithuania took the most dramatic stance by establishing its autonomy from Moscow in all areas of Government administration by early 1991. Latvia and Estonia[81] were not far behind. In Latvia, severe conflict developed after an MVD chief loyal to the Latvian popular front was appointed. Many of the Russian *militsiia* personnel in Latvia that were loyal to the central MVD protested this attempt to establish regional control.[82] But such appointments were merely a prelude to the autonomy that would be achieved in the Baltics after the failed coup attempt of August 1991.

While the central MVD was trying to maintain control over the crumbling Soviet empire, the MVD chief, Vadim Bakatin, was trying to force his subordinates into observing the rule of law. In the latter half of 1990, Bakatin was increasingly criticized by the conservatives for his failure to put an end to ethnic disorders. Gorbachev, in what proved to be a great political mistake, ousted Bakatin in December 1990, appointing the hardliner Boris Pugo, a former Latvian KGB chief, in his place. Pugo and his deputy, Boris Gromov, a foreign military commander,[83] attempted to shift the direction of the MVD. In the early months of 1991, they sought to expand the MVD's power to search private businesses and to control public demonstrations. Increasingly the *OMON* was deployed in the Baltics and other republics to quell unrest.[84]

By 1991, however, the changes in Soviet society were already too far advanced to revive traditional methods of rule. Unwilling to acknowledge that reality, Boris Pugo, along with military leaders, the head of the KGB, and leaders of the military industrial complex, initiated the coup in August.[85] This ill-conceived venture led within months to the collapse of the Soviet state and the transfer of policing power from the USSR MVD to the ministries of internal affairs of the successor states.[86]

Notes

1. M.N. Eropkin, *Razvitie organov militsii v sovetskom gosudarstve* (Moscow: Vysshaia shkola MOOP, 1967), p. 19.

2. Robert Conquest, *The Soviet Police System* (New York: Praeger, 1968), p. 30.

3. *Ibid.*, p. 20.

4. *Ibid.*, p. 44.

5. *Ibid.*, p. 16.

6. M. Fainsod, *How Russia Is Ruled*, revised edition (Cambridge, MA: Harvard University Press, 1970), pp. 452-53.

7. R. Conquest, *The Soviet Police System*, p. 18. The plan of the new Russian Government to merge the remnants of the KGB with the Interior Ministry raised concerns among many who remembered the awesome power of the combined police apparatus. The post-Stalinist resolve never to unite the two police forces has prevented their planned merger by Yeltsin. "Russian Constitutional Court Annuls KGB/MVD Merger," *RFE/RL Daily Report*, no. 9, 15 January 1992, p.1.

8. Merle Fainsod, *Smolensk under Soviet Rule* (Cambridge, MA: Harvard University Press, 1958), p. 73.

9. G.P. Shelud'ko, *Sovetskaia militsiia na strazhe obshchestvennogo poriadka* (Kiev: Vishcha shkola), 1982, p. 23.

10. Ronald Hingley, *The Russian Secret Police* (London: Hutchinson, 1970), p. 188.

11. *Ibid.*, p. 202.

12. *Ibid.*, p. 212.

13. Robert Conquest, *Power and Policy in the USSR* (New York: St. Martin's Press, 1961), pp. 212-217.

14. "Lavrentiy Beria's Crimes, Arrest Recounted," *FBIS Daily Report* 2 March 1988, p. 60; V. Nekrasov, "Lavrentii Beria," *Sovetskaia militsiia* , no. 4 (1990), pp. 43-45.

15. See P.J. Stead, *The Police of France* (New York: Macmillan, 1983), p. 43, as well as the discussion in O. Marenin, "Police Performance and State Rule: Control and Autonomy in the Exercise of Coercion," *Comparative Politics* (October 1985), pp. 106-107.

16. Statement of A.M. Iakovlev on the law of the Stalinist period in "Kakim dolzhno byt' pravovoe gosudarstvo?" *Literaturnaia gazeta*, 6 June 1988, p. 11.

17. "N.R. Mironov Reviews Reformation of Soviet Punitive Agencies; Stalin and Vyshinskiy Blamed for Past Abuses," *Survey of the Soviet Press*, 13 March 1964, no. 351, p. 10.

18. R. Conquest, *The Soviet Police System*, pp. 24-25.

19. "Brief Item Announces Abolition of Ministry of Internal Affairs USSR," *Survey of the Soviet Press*, 8 February 1960, no. 142, p. 8.

20. V. Nekrasov, "Vadim Tikunov," *Sovetskaia militsiia*, no. 8 (1990), p. 20.

21. "Ministry of Internal Affairs Renamed Ministry for Defense of Public Order RSFSR," *Survey of the Soviet Press*, 24 September 1962, no. 277, p. 15.

22. V. Nekrasov, "Vadim Tikunov," p. 30.

23. Amy W. Knight, *The KGB: Police and Politics in the Soviet Union* (Boston: Unwin Hyman, 1988), pp. 62-63.

24. "Polozhenie o sovetskoi militsii," adopted by the USSR Council of Ministers, 8 June 1973, no. 385, and published in *Svod zakonov SSSR*, vol. 10, pp. 236-47.

25. Amy Knight, "Soviet Politics and the KGB-MVD Relationship," *Soviet Union*, vol. 11, part 2, (1984), pp. 157-181.

26. "'Brezhnev's Special Favour' Protected Corrupt," SU/0144, 6 May 1988, p. B/1.

27. A. Vaksberg, "Kost' Mamonta," *Literaturnaia gazeta*, 18 May 1988, p. 13, and Paul Quinn-Judge, "Moscow exposé bodes ill for Kremlin hard-liners," *Christian Science Monitor*, 4 May 1988, p. 11, discuss the corruption surrounding Shchelokov.

28. A. Knight, *The KGB*, pp. 88-91.

29. "V Politburo TsK KPSS," *Pravda*, 11 December 1982, p. 1.

30. P. Kruzhin, "Political Organs Created in the MVD," *Radio Liberty Research*, 5/84, 30 December 1983.

31. *Radio Liberty Research*, 92/83, 21 February 1983, p. 9.

32. A. Knight, *The KGB*, p. 89.

33. "Vsesoiuznoe soveshchanie," *Pravda*, 26 January 1983, p. 2.

34. A. Vlasov, "Na strazhe pravoporiadka," *Kommunist*, no. 5 (1988), p. 47.

35. P. Kruzhin, "Political Organs Created in the MVD," p. 3.

36. *Ibid.*, pp. 6-7.

37. *Radio Liberty Research*, 6/85, 9 January 1985.

38. *Pravda*, 9 November 1984.

39. "Interior Minister Interviewed by Yugoslav Journal," *FBIS Political Affairs Report*, 1 July 1988, p. 1; V. Nekrasov, "Nikolai Shchelokov," *Sovetskaia militsiia*, no. 9 (1990), p. 22.

40. "Report on the KGB: In Good Shape and Getting Stronger Despite Some Setbacks," *Soviet/East European Report*, vol. viii, no. 14, 1 January 1991, p. 1.

41. A.E. Lunev, *Upravlenie v oblasti administrativno-politicheskoi deiatel'nosti* (Moscow: Iuridicheskaia literatura, 1979), p. 130.

42. I. Zeldes, "The History and Organization of Police in the USSR," paper presented at the Annual Meeting of the Academy of Criminal Justice Sciences, 4 April 1985.

43. A.E. Lunev, *Upravlenie v oblasti administrativno-politicheskoi deiatel'nosti*, p. 130.

44. *Ibid.*, pp. 128-129.

45. V. Rudnev and S. Mostovshchikov, "'K' upalo, 'G' propalo, kto ostalsiia v KGB?" *Izvestiia*, 29 December 1991, p. 1, and "Yeltsin Dismisses Security, Interior Officials," *FBIS Daily Report*, 21 January 1992, p. 49.

46. The responsibilities of the republic ministries were in many respects analogous to the USSR ministry, except for their smaller territorial reach. A.E. Lunev, *Upravlenie v oblasti administrativno-politicheskoi deiatel'nosti*, p. 131. The same applied to the autonomous regions, which were established to grant formal recognition to the smaller ethnic minorities. Beneath this level, however, the responsibilities of the organs of internal affairs were more limited. *Ibid.*, p. 132.

47. *Ibid.*, p. 69.

48. V. Yasmann, "The Power of the Soviet Internal Security Forces," *Report on the USSR*, 26 October 1990, p. 13.

49. *Sovetskoe administrativnoe pravo* (Moscow: Iuridicheskaia literatura, 1981), p. 390.

50. See the statute at their inception, *Polozhenie o vedomstvennoi militsii i instruksiia o poriadke ee organizatsii i deiatel'nosti* ed. I.F. Kiselev (Moscow, 1929).

51. N.A. Shchelokov, *Sovetskaia militsiia* (Moscow: Znanie, 1971), pp. 66-67.

52. M.I. Eropkin, *Upravlenie v oblasti okhrany obshchestvennogo poriadka* (Moscow: Iuridicheskaia literatura, 1965), p. 99.

53. Resolution of the Council of Ministers USSR, 18 February 1966, "Model Statute on Extra-Departmental Guards attached to the *militsiia*," in *Spravochnik po zakonodatel'stvu dlia rabotnikov prokuratury, suda i ministerstva vnutrennykh del*, vol. 2 (Moscow: Iuridicheskaia literatura, 1971), pp. 404-11. The guards are not bound to a single installation. They must inspect the work of the departmental guards, review the protective measures of consumer cooperatives and other rural organizations and provide them with technical assistance.

54. "Militia work in protecting property and combating theft of alcohol," *BBC Summary of World Broadcasts*, SU/0141, 3 May 1988, p. B/4.

55. V. Yasmann, "The Power of the Soviet Internal Security Forces," p. 14.

56. See, for example, "MVD Troops Role Viewed," *FBIS Daily Report*, 8 November 1990, pp. 80-81; "MVD General on Role of Internal Troops," *RFE/RL Daily Report*, no. 112, 14 June 1991, p. 6, and "Situation Tense at Latvia's Press Building," *RFE/RL Daily Report*, no. 245, 4 January 1991, p. 3.

57. "Internal Troops to Retain Central Command," *RFE/RL Daily Report*, no. 222, 23 November 1990, p. 6.

58. "Bakatin: OMON Directly Subordinate to Pugo," *RFE/RL Daily Report*, no. 109, 11 June 1991, p. 4.

59. V. Yasmann, "The Power of the Soviet Internal Security Forces," pp. 13-14.

60. "Black Berets Shoot Unarmed Civilians in Latvia," *RFE/RL Daily Report*, no. 12, 17 January 1991, p. 5.

61. "Black Berets Storm Latvian Interior Ministry," *RFE/RL Daily Report*, no. 294, 3 January 1991, p. 3.

62. "In Lithuania A Tense Peace as Soviet Military Harasses Citizenry," *Soviet/East European Report*, vol. viii, no. 35, 20 June 1991, p. 1.

63. "USSR OMON Units Sent to Moldavia," *RFE/RL Daily Report*, no. 108, 10 June 1991, p. 8.

64. "Pugo Defends Soviet Legality," and "Trubin Orders Probe of Omon Actions," in *RFE/RL Daily Report*, no. 102, 31 May 1991, p. 3.

65. A.E. Lunev, *Upravlenie v oblasti administrativno-politicheskoi deiatel'nosti*, p. 125.

66. H. Oda, "The Communist Party of the Soviet Union and the Procuracy," in *Law and the Gorbachev Era*, ed. Donald D. Barry (Dordrecht: Martinus Nijhoff, 1988), p. 131.

67. B.A. Viktorov, *Pravovye osnovy deiatel'nosti organov vnutrennykh del* (Moscow: Iuridicheskaia literatura, 1979), pp. 66-69.

68. "Vlasov Attends Meeting on MVD Political Organs," *FBIS Daily Report*, 27 April 1988, p. 42.

69. S.N. Imashev, "V stroi sozidatelei," *Sovetskaia militsiia*, no. 6 (1982), p. 16.

70. E. Teague, "Andropov Cleans up the Militia," *Radio Liberty Research*, 424/83, 9 November 1983, p. 3.

71. Amy Knight, "Soviet Politics and the KGB-MVD Relationship," pp. 157-181.

72. "Conference on Internal Political Organisation of the MVD," SU/0142, 4 May 1988, p. B/5.

73. "Internal Affairs Officer on Party Activity," *Joint Publications Research Service*, 20 June 1985, p. 54.

74. "Political Organs to be Disbanded in the MVD," *RFE/RL Daily Report*, no. 57, 21 March 1990, p. 3.

75. Aleksandr Gurov and Iurii Shchekochikhin, "Okhota na l'va ili boi s ten'iu," *Literaturnaia gazeta*, 23 May 1990, p. 12.

76. Leonid Miloslavsky, "Militia Initiative," *Moscow News*, no. 32 (1989), p. 5.

77. Mikhail Tsypkin, "Worker's Militia: Order Instead of Law," *RFE/RL Report on the USSR*, 17 November 1989, p. 14.

78. *Ibid.*, p. 15.

79. *Ibid.*, p. 16.

80. "Secession Proclaimed in Moldavia's Eastern Area," *RFE/RL Daily Report*, 4 September 1990, p. 6.

81. "Estonian MVD Chief on Ministry's Role," *FBIS Daily Report*, 13 August 1990, p. 79.

82. "New Latvian Minister of Internal Affairs," *RFE/RL Daily Report*, no. 92, 14 May 1990, p. 3.

83. Michael Dobbs, "Gorbachev Ousts Minister of Interior," *Washington Post*, 3 December 1990, pp. A1 and A21.

84. "More Military Units Sent into Moldavia," *RFE/RL Daily Report*, 15 March 1991, p. 5, and "Discussions Held, But Results Unclear," *RFE/RL Daily Report*, 4 January 1991, p. 3.

85. Bill Keller, "Old Guard's Last Grasp," *The New York Times*, 22 August 1991, p. A1.

86. This transfer of responsibilities from the USSR to the RSFSR MVD began well in advance of the formation of the Commonwealth of Independent States. On 20 October 1991, for example, President Yeltsin issued a decree ordering all troops of the internal security troops of the USSR MVD located on Russian territory to be transferred to the Russian jurisdiction. "O vnutrennykh voiskakh MVD RSFSR," *Vedomosti S"ezda narodnykh deputatov RSFSR i Verkhovnogo Soveta RSFSR*, no. 46 (1991), item 1564.

10

THE ADMINISTRATION OF JUSTICE: COURTS, PROCURACY, AND MINISTRY OF JUSTICE

Eugene Huskey

Disputes arise in all societies. The question for students of politics is how they are resolved. In modern Western history competing claims have been reconciled through three public mechanisms: the market, representative institutions, and the courts. Elaborate arrangements emerged to parcel out conflicts among these three arenas and to decide disputes within each. Not so in the Soviet Union. The Russian Revolution of October 1917 rejected the Western model of a plurality of remedies in favor of an administered society where the power to resolve disputes was concentrated in the hands of party and Government functionaries. In such a system, courts developed as little more than appendages of executive power.[1]

That legal institutions developed at all in the Soviet Union testifies to the compromises that political life frequently requires of political ideas. The Bolsheviks came to power intent on eliminating law and courts altogether. A socialist revolution, they reckoned, would remove the need for a legal system, which had served only to protect the property of the capitalists and to mystify the workers. Acting on these ideas in the weeks after the revolution, the Bolsheviks issued a decree designed to abolish the institutional pillars of the old legal order—the courts, the Procuracy, and the Bar. Revolutionary expediency (*tselesoobraznost'*) was to replace the "bourgeois" concepts of constitutionality and legality as the new standard of justice.

The nihilist, or eliminationist, approach to law apparent in these measures was soon tempered, however, by the recognition that a state without law denies itself legitimacy as well as an efficient means of imposing discipline on the bureaucracy and society. In a series of experiments that stretched over the first two decades of Soviet rule, the revolutionary government reluctantly revived and reshaped selected legal norms, procedures, and institutions from the old regime. By the end of the 1930s, the Soviet Union had laid the philosophical and institutional foundations of a new legal order in which politics was in command.

Three institutions assumed direct responsibility for the administration of justice in this new order. They were the courts, the Procuracy, and the People's Commissariat of Justice (renamed the Ministry of Justice in 1946). A part of Lenin's original cabinet, the Justice Commissariat exercised a broad range of functions in the early years of Soviet rule, from legislative drafting to the investigation of criminal cases. It was, in short, the central Government institution in the making and implementation of legal policy. In the 1930s, the Justice Commissariat lost its leading role in legal affairs to the Procuracy. Originally designed as the "eye of the tsar" in the prerevolutionary legal system, the Procuracy had operated as a division of the Justice Commissariat for a decade after its revival in 1922, prosecuting criminal cases and reviewing the legality of judicial and administrative decisions. But in 1933 the Procuracy gained a measure of organizational independence from the Justice Commissariat. Three years later, a new constitution completed the Procuracy's break with the Justice Commissariat and widened its powers considerably, again at the expense of the commissariat.[2]

Reasons for this reversal of institutional fortunes must be sought in the conflict between their respective leaders as well as in the services that each could offer to the ruling Communist Party. In the mid-1930s, as Stalin and the party leadership began to understand the uses of law as an instrument of rule, the head of the Procuracy, Andrei Vyshinsky, succeeded in portraying the commissar of justice, Nikolai Krylenko, as a legal nihilist intent on running down the legal system. Where Krylenko and the Justice Commissariat appeared inattentive to the role that law might play in advancing party policy in areas such as economic affairs, Vyshinsky mobilized the Procuracy behind each new party campaign.[3]

This responsiveness of the Procuracy to central party directives was due to structural as well as leadership differences between the Procuracy and the Justice Commissariat. The apparatus of the Justice Commissariat was subject to dual subordination (*dvoinoe podchinenie*), that is, at each territorial level commissariat officials answered vertically to their superiors in the commissariat as well as horizontally to local government. The Procuracy, on the other hand, operated after 1936 on principles of strict centralization, much like the Communist Party itself. It was therefore more insulated from local pressures than perhaps any Government institution except the secret police. In the Procuracy Stalin and subsequent Soviet leaders found a faithful executor of party policy. Indeed, given the role of party directives in defining the Procuracy's tasks and the frequent secondment of Procuracy officials to work in the party apparatus, it is only a slight exaggeration to regard the Procuracy as an institutional extension of the Communist Party in the legal system.

The authority of the Procuracy increased further in the post-Stalin era, in part as a counterweight to a newly-restrained secret police and in part as a tool in the political struggle between Khrushchev, the party leader, and Malenkov and his allies, whose institutional base was the Council of Ministers.   Khrushchev's consolidation of power in the 1950s resulted in an even higher profile for the party-linked Procuracy and yet another blow to the prestige and influence of the Ministry of Justice, which was a member of the Council of Ministers.   As part of a mass assault on Government institutions in 1956, Khrushchev abolished the central apparatus of the Ministry of Justice.   During the next few years he eliminated the ministry altogether, distributing its functions to the courts and to newly-created crime-fighting organs attached to the soviets.   Only in 1970 did the Brezhnev leadership re-establish the Ministry of Justice.

Compared to the Procuracy and the Ministry of Justice, courts in the Soviet Union played only a supporting role in the administration of justice.   The weakness of the judiciary had several sources.   The first was the regime's preference for administrative rather than judicial remedies, which limited the range of issues brought before the court.   The second was the tradition of mobilizing the courts behind the latest official campaign, a practice that turned judges into executors of policy rather than servants of the law.   The third was the composition of the bench.   Judges were, and remain even in the post-Soviet era, among the least qualified jurists.   The fourth, and most important, source of judicial weakness was the dependence of judges on party and Government institutions for their positions, their job evaluations and rewards, and their work conditions.   Where the Procuracy was empowered to monitor and protest "incorrect" judicial decisions,[4] the Ministry of Justice carried out the "organizational supervision" of Soviet courts, which included the tasks of nominating, reviewing, and disciplining judges and of furnishing the courts with buildings, equipment, and staff.[5]

Until the end of the 1980s, the Soviet Union maintained the convenient fiction that while courts as institutions were subject to external oversight,[6] judges in their courtrooms were independent and subordinate only to law.   Behind this carefully cultivated facade of judicial independence functioned a corps of judges who conformed to the expectations, and occasionally the explicit commands, of the Communist Party, the Procuracy, the Ministry of Justice, and even local soviets.   This subservience of the courts came under fierce attack from legal reformers in the wake of the XIX Communist Party conference in 1988, which encouraged a break with the legal traditions laid in the first decades of Soviet rule. At stake here was more than a proposed realignment of authority among institutions administering justice. A new movement to create a judiciary independent of all political and legal institutions posed a challenge not only to the Procuracy and the Ministry of Justice but to the monopoly of executive power in the Soviet political system. In the event, it was the formation of a competitively-elected legislature in 1989 that first broke the executive monopoly. But it was the rise of an independent judiciary that could have guaranteed the permanence of the progressive political and legal reforms unleashed by Gorbachev. The section below examines the attempts at the end of the Gorbachev era to transform subservient Soviet courts into a judicial branch (*sudebnaia vlast'*) that operated autonomously within its own realm of authority.

The Rise of Judicial Power

Independent courts are more difficult to create and nurture than representative institutions. Where new legislatures emerged almost full-grown in the Soviet Union in 1989 and 1990, the courts were just setting out on a long and tortuous path of establishing a new identity. The first, tentative step in judicial reform was taken at the end of 1988 with the adoption of new legislation on the selection of judges. Until that time, the Communist Party apparatus in each locale had nominated judges, who stood unopposed for election to a five-year term. In order to break the bond of judicial dependence on the local party apparatus, the new law expanded the judicial term to ten years and granted the soviets at the next higher territorial level responsibility for selecting a court's judges. Thus, whereas people's court judges in Moscow's thirty-two administrative districts (*raiony*) had previously run unopposed in direct, popular elections in each district, they were now chosen by the deputies of the Moscow city soviet. The responsibility for nominating candidates to the soviets shifted to the Ministry of Justice and to the courts' own "qualifying boards" (*kvalifikatsionnye kollegii*), new institutions intended to depoliticize further the selection of judges and, it was hoped by some reformists, to eventually replace the Ministry of Justice as the supervisory organ for the courts.[7]

The new legislation on the selection of judges was designed to lay the foundation for a protective wall around the courts.[8] The foundation was shored up by additional legislation outlawing interference in judicial decisionmaking and by the party's own campaign of self-restraint in legal affairs.[9] Except in some conservative provincial areas, party officials abandoned the practice of telephone justice (*telefonnoe pravo*), that is, the tradition of offering instructions to judges on how to decide cases.[10] The Communist Party refused, however, to close down its primary party organizations operating within the courts and other legal institutions. Virtually all Soviet judges were members of these party cells and as such were expected to participate in regular party meetings at their place of work and to faithfully implement directives from the party apparatus. Where telephone justice exposed judges to occasional interference in cases *sub judice*, the primary party organizations subjected judges to regular briefings (*instruktazh*) on the party's expectations regarding judicial behavior. These briefings encouraged judges to place party loyalty (*partiinost'*) above concerns for legality (*zakonnost'*).

In the summer of 1990, the renunciation of a one-party monopoly in the Soviet Union launched a vigorous debate over the future of primary party organizations. While the party establishment clung fiercely to one of its last remaining instruments of rule, reformists sought the immediate expulsion of party organizations from the workplace. An initial attempt in the fall of 1990 to legislate an end to the primary party organizations failed, but support for the closure grew among the population and jurists. In several regions judges and Procuracy officials either left the party or suspended their party membership to protest the continued presence of party organizations in legal institutions. The denouement came in the late summer of 1991 when Boris Yeltsin, two months after his direct election as president of the Russian Republic, issued a decree banning primary party organizations in the workplace throughout the republic.[11]

Party officials resisted the decree, but with only limited success. All the members of the RSFSR Supreme Court, for example, suspended their membership in the party.[12] The coup of 19 August 1991, inspired in part by Yeltsin's insistence on the depoliticization of the courts and legal institutions, accelerated the removal of party organizations in courts and other legal institutions. By the beginning of November the issue of depoliticization was rendered moot in the Russian Federation by the proscription of the Communist Party.[13]

Even before the August coup it appeared that the most serious challenge to the autonomy of the courts would not come from a collapsing Communist Party but from legislators, many of whom had been seeking to parlay their new role in the selection and recall[14] of judges into direct influence in the administration of justice.[15] At the beginning of 1991, a high-ranking jurist complained that "people's deputies, not having a clear sense of their own powers, try to influence directly court decisions [and] require courts to give account of their actions in specific cases."[16] Moreover, some soviets exceeded their authority by nominating as well as approving candidates for judicial office. These unwelcome and unintended consequences of political reform served as reminders that changes in legal structures and procedures had to be accompanied by equally far-reaching changes in legal culture.

The sources of judicial dependence lay traditionally in the manner of rewarding judges as well as in the method of selecting and recalling them. Soviet judges were especially vulnerable to cooptation by executive authority because they depended on the state to provide essential goods and services to themselves, their families, and their courts.[17] For the Western reader unfamiliar with the Soviet Union, an act of imagination is required to understand the exposed position of the judges. To obtain the most basic provisions—an apartment, day care for the children, an annual vacation, transportation to "visiting sessions" of the court, and heating and repair of the courtroom—the judges had to appeal to local political authorities for assistance.[18] Because of the low prestige of the judiciary, judges' appeals carried little weight. In Leningrad, a city where 40 percent of the judges lived in *kommunalki* (one-room apartments with common bath and kitchen), the local soviet made available to the judiciary only three or four self-contained apartments a year.[19] As the reformist jurist Valerii Savitskii noted, because the judiciary was "downtrodden and humiliated," any institution that took the trouble could order it about.[20]

The system of judicial pay and promotion also encouraged subservience toward other institutions. Unlike American judges, who receive a fixed salary that is adjusted upward at irregular intervals, Soviet judges received pay according to their service rank.[21] To obtain a promotion in rank judges had to satisfy the appointing authorities, which meant the party before 1989 and the legislature after that date. Promotion was traditionally based on the judges' political reliability, as measured in large part by quantitative indicators, such as the percentage of decisions upheld by superior courts, the number and type of private rulings (*chastnye opredeleniia*)[22] issued, and civic duties assumed. These indicators, compiled by the Ministry of Justice and the Procuracy, served to channel judicial behavior into narrowly prescribed bounds. For example, the chair of a people's court in the Tiumen region reported that at the beginning of the Gorbachev era the local division of the Ministry of Justice expected judges to imprison at least 70 percent of persons convicted of crimes. This judge considered imprisoning fewer persons, but in the end he adhered to the standard because of his fear of carrying "low percentages." "Things have improved," he admitted in 1990. "But the quality of the judiciary is still measured by the Ministry of Justice in terms of these percentages."[23]

To combat these external levers of influence over the court, the advocates of an independent judiciary proposed an array of radical reforms at the end of the 1980s, including the elimination of Ministry of Justice and Procuracy supervision, the removal of quantitative measures of judicial competence, and the granting of life tenure to judges. These proposals met with some success. The Procuracy closed its departments for supervising the courts and new legislation reduced the Ministry of Justice's responsibilities toward the court from "organizational supervision" to "guaranteeing the organizational independence" of the courts.[24] Although quantitative measures of judicial behavior did not disappear, they were taken less seriously by judges. It would be a mistake, however, to deny their continuing influence on judicial behavior right until the collapse of the Soviet Union and even beyond. The pattern of fluctuations in the rates of acquittals suggests that even if rigid numerical targets were no longer employed after 1990, judges still responded to shifts in party and Government policy toward crime.[25] Reform in the courts, as in other legal institutions, was at times in the Gorbachev era held hostage to the conservative backlash among elites and masses against the country's rising crime rate.[26]

Perhaps the most controversial reform proposal concerned the establishment of a judiciary with life tenure or, in most versions, tenure until age 65. As early as 1988 this proposal gained the support of many notable jurists, including the former chair of the USSR Supreme Court, Vladimir Terebilov. However, a coalition of conservative and reformist forces initially prevented its adoption. Where the conservatives feared a loss of influence over the judiciary, the reformers worried that life tenure would lock in place for a generation and more a poorly qualified and politically traditional corps of judges. It now appears that most of the successor states will adopt legislation granting judges tenure to judges until age 65 or beyond. In the fall of 1991, President Yeltsin of Russia declared himself to be "a firm supporter of permanent tenure (*nesmeniaemost'*) for judges."[27]

Both the quantity and quality of Soviet judges have impeded the rise of judicial power in the Soviet Union and its successor states. On 1 January 1988, there were 15,781 judges in the Soviet Union, approximately the same number as in the Federal Republic of Germany, a country with one-quarter the population of the USSR.[28] The small size of the Soviet judiciary imposed enormous case loads on the courts and thereby discouraged the thorough and careful consideration of legal disputes. Most reform-oriented jurists have favored a dramatic expansion in the judicial corps.[29] This goal will be difficult to achieve, however, at least over the short term, without a decline in the quality of judges. The campaign to professionalize Soviet legal personnel, begun at the end of the 1930s, required almost a half century to establish a university law degree as a minimum qualification for a legal career. And that was accomplished only by taking shortcuts. In late 1991, as a means of expediting the training of a new generation of qualified judges, Justice Minister Nikolai Fedorov of the Russian Federation began to open new law faculties (in the universities of Kabardino-Balkaria, Petrozavodsk [Karelia], Syktyvkar [Komi], Chechen-Ingushetia, and Cheliabinsk and in the polytechnic institute in Kursk) and to send hundreds of young Russian judges abroad for education and re-education in law.[30] Such measures were needed because a significant minority of sitting Soviet judges on the bench in December 1991 had received their legal education by correspondence, a course of study which the Ministry of Justice has been phasing out because of its abysmally low standards.

Set against the promise of a larger and weightier judiciary has been the reality of miserly pay, low status, and unpleasant working conditions, all of which have made it difficult to attract and retain judges when more promising careers beckon in the Procuracy, the MVD, and the rapidly expanding private sector. Thus, recruitment to the courts in the Soviet era was based on what one Soviet jurist called "the leftover principle."[31] By the 1980s, the problem of judicial recruitment had become a crisis. Between 1982 and 1987, more than one third of Soviet judges quit the bench, leaving behind a judicial corps increasingly young, female, and inexperienced.[32] In advance of judicial elections in 1989, judges in many areas threatened to resign en masse if measures were not taken to address their deteriorating working conditions and living standards.[33] Under the threat of the collapse of the court system, the USSR Supreme Soviet in the fall of 1989 introduced emergency legislation to raise judicial salaries by more than 50 percent, bringing average monthly pay for judges from just under 200 rubles to approximately 300 rubles. This step prevented a de facto strike by the country's judges, but it did little to alter the relative standing of the judiciary among legal institutions.

Where the Gorbachev era brought only a modest increase in the professional and personal autonomy of judges, it expanded generously the formal jurisdiction of the courts. In 1989 and 1990 more than 30 new laws created judicial remedies where previously no remedies, or only executive remedies, existed. For the first time, complaints concerning strikes, journalists' rights to government information, leaseholds on land, and the violation of citizens' rights by executive agencies could be directed to the court.[34] Whether citizens in the successor states to the Soviet Union will seek and receive judicial remedies in these and other areas remains an open question. The early evidence from cases brought under the law on the violation of citizens' rights in the last months of Soviet rule suggests that the population did not yet view the court as a reliable source of justice. Millions of citizens annually sent letters to the press, party, and Government complaining of violations of their rights by executive agencies, yet less than 4000 sought a redress of these grievances in court during 1990.[35] The gap between jurisdiction available and used could close quickly, however, if judicial remedies are forthcoming in the successor states.

Perhaps no area of expanded jurisdiction remains more problematic than that related to constitutional interpretation. As early as 1982 the regular court system began to rule for the first time on the legality of what in America would be called federal regulations, the substatutory acts issued by Government institutions.[36] At the end of 1989, the new Supreme Soviet took judicial review a step further by establishing a Committee of Constitutional Supervision to rule on the constitutionality of the highest acts of the state, those issued by the parliament, the Council of Ministers, and, after March 1990, the President. Like similar institutions in Western Europe, the Committee of Constitutional Supervision and its equivalent in the Russian Republic, the Constitutional Court, functioned parallel to the regular court system.

In its first year of existence, the Committee of Constitutional Supervision succeeded in disappointing both radicals and conservatives. Lacking the guns of the executive, the direct popular mandate of the legislature, or even the moral authority of a long-established constitutional court, the Committee understandably avoided issues and remedies that might have provoked a constitutional crisis in the volatile economic and political climate of the day. It was not, however, merely a handmaiden of Gorbachev or the political establishment. In pathbreaking rulings in 1990, the Committee, under the leadership of the reformist jurist Sergei Alekseev, struck down a presidential decree transferring jurisdiction of the central precinct of Moscow from local to all-union hands. It also ordered Government agencies to publish or eliminate all substatutory acts affecting the rights of citizens. Most dramatically, the Committee refused to accede to the unconstitutional seizure of power in August 1991, insisting that only the USSR Supreme Soviet was empowered to invoke emergency rule and to authorize a transfer of power from a duly elected president.

It is tempting to conclude that the emerging authority and prominence of constitutional courts will lead to a general rise in judicial power in the republics of the old Soviet Union. In November, 1991, the new Constitutional Court of the Russian Federation began operation with an impressive group of judges and with a bolder judicial philosophy than that evidenced by the Constitutional Review Committee. However, the diffusion of judicial functions among three discrete institutions—the constitutional courts, the regular courts, and economic (arbitrazh) courts—may complicate this development. As in earlier periods of Soviet history, when revolutionary tribunals, transport courts, and the infamous three-person "special sessions" compromised the regular courts' authority, the executive continues to discourage the establishment of an integrated judiciary. Where the constitutional courts resolve disputes on such fundamental questions as conflicts of laws and the rights of citizens before the state, the regular courts decide criminal cases and most civil suits.[37] Disputes between economic enterprises come before a newly-reformed system of arbitrazh courts.[38] Before the collapse of the Soviet Union, there also existed a little known network of special courts that heard in closed session cases involving workers in the many secret government factories and research institutes.[39] Soviet reformers fought unsuccessfully to eliminate these institutional remnants of Stalinism. It now appears that these special courts are being disbanded in the successor states.[40]

In terms of its size and jurisdiction, the central core of the judiciary at the end of the Soviet era remained more than 2000 regular courts, one in each of the country's political subdivisions. At the apex of this hierarchy was the USSR Supreme Court, with a total of 32 judges and 226 support staff servicing its three divisions (*kollegii*), civil, criminal, and military. The functions of the USSR Supreme Court have now been eliminated or transferred to the supreme courts in the republics. In the Russian Federation, for example, the Supreme Court had at the end of 1991 a staff of 414, including a chairman, a first deputy chairman, four deputy chairmen, and 100 justices. The Supreme *Arbitrazh* Court of the Russian Federation had a staff of 300, including a chairman, a first deputy chairman, four deputies, and 60 justices.[41]

At the base of the judiciary are the local people's courts, which hear more than 90 percent of all court cases. While the composition of the regular court varies, from three professional judges in appellate cases to a single professional judge in certain simplified proceedings, most cases are still decided by a three-person bench consisting of a professional judge and two lay assessors.[42] Introduced in the early days of the revolution, the three-person bench ensured that Soviet trials, unlike the jury trials in late Imperial Russia, would produce the desired verdict (*prigovor*).

Viewing the jury as one of the guarantors of judicial independence, legal reformers in the Gorbachev era unleashed a campaign to reintroduce the jury trial, and in 1989 new all-union legislation approved in principle the use of juries in cases where defendants faced the death penalty or a long prison term.[43] The struggle between legal reformists and legal conservatives continues, however, over legislation in the successor states that will set out in detail the role of juries in criminal cases. Central to the debate is whether the jury will sit as a separate body, deciding only questions of fact, or as part of the bench, deciding questions of law and fact together with the presiding professional judge.[44]

The limited and provisional nature of court reform suggests that it may still be premature to speak of the rise of judicial power as a relatively autonomous area of government.[45] The judiciary remains too divided, too beholden to other institutions for its welfare, and too uncertain of its own powers. It is no longer, however, an integral part of executive power. That was made clear in January 1992 when Russia's new Constitutional Court ruled invalid President Yeltsin's decree merging the secret and regular police into a new superministry of security, a merger that recalled for many the formation of the dreaded NKVD in 1934.

The Crisis of Executive Power in the Administration of Justice

The relative calm surrounding the Procuracy and the Ministry of Justice in the first years of perestroika gave way at the beginning of the 1990s to a crisis in their institutional mission and identity. The sources of this crisis lay in a changing division of labor between these institutions and the court, other executive agencies, and the market. For example, even the halting and as yet incomplete reform of the judiciary has virtually stripped the Procuracy and Ministry of Justice of their role as overseers of the courts. The Procuracy and the Ministry of Justice are now losing, or are threatened with the loss of, other functions that for decades had been accepted as integral to their mission.

Under challenge in the case of the Procuracy are all its duties save court prosecution.[46] In 1990, responsibility for coordinating the fight against crime and other legal campaigns shifted from the Procuracy to a newly-formed Committee on Coordinating the Activity of Law Enforcement Organs, attached to the USSR presidency. In the same year, another new institution, the Monitoring Agency (*kontrol'naia palata*), promised to displace the Procuracy as the primary inspector of executive agencies.[47] The tentative moves toward a market economy have also threatened to eliminate the need for Procuracy intrusion into what in the West would be regarded as business decisions, concerning such mundane matters as how the cows are fed and how farms prepare machinery for the winter.[48] Furthermore, the Procuracy is likely to lose its large corps of criminal investigators to a new investigative apparatus, which may be either fully independent or attached to the MVD, Council of Ministers, Justice Ministry, or courts of the successor states. This reform would be a major blow to the size and influence of the Procuracy, which investigates directly approximately 15 percent of all criminal cases and a large majority of serious criminal cases.[49]

The as yet unresolved debate surrounding the investigative organs is part of a broader campaign to eliminate the accusatorial bias that permeated Soviet criminal justice. This bias has been grounded in the extensive and largely unchecked powers of the Procuracy, which investigates criminal cases, oversees the legality of these investigations, issues indictments based on the investigative materials, prosecutes the cases in court, and then appeals the verdict if it disagrees with the decision of the court. For a generation, Soviet legal reformists argued that the concentration of these powers in the hands of a single institution undermined principles of adversariness and the presumption of innocence. A consensus finally emerged at the beginning of the 1990s that the right of the accused could not be guaranteed unless the incestuous relations among different divisions of the Procuracy ended. The Procuracy, it was argued, could not be both prosecutor and guardian of legality.[50] The question, then, was how many functions the Procuracy would abandon in criminal proceedings and to whom. While reformists sought the transfer of many of the Procuracy's functions to the judiciary, conservatives have wanted to shift some of the functions to other executive institutions, most notably the MVD. This continuing debate merits close scrutiny as an indicator of the evenness of the playing field for the two "sides," prosecution and defense, in the legal systems of the successor states.[51]

In spite of recent challenges to its authority and the closure of the USSR Procuracy in late 1991, the Procuracy remains a large and intricate bureaucracy in each of the new republics. The number of Procuracy personnel was scheduled to rise to 39,500 in 1992 in the Russian Federation alone.[52] Where the typical Procuracy office in a small rural district has a procurator (prokuror), an assistant procurator (pomoshchnik prokurora), and a criminal investigator (sledovatel'), the city Procuracy office in Moscow employs well over 100 persons in numerous specialized departments. Besides the usual internal housekeeping departments found in all executive agencies, the Procuracy has had departments monitoring legality in areas as diverse as state security and youth affairs. At the end of the 1980s, new departments were added for the monitoring of environmental affairs and citizens' rights, an obvious attempt to bring the institution into line with the politics of perestroika.[53] The last decade of Soviet rule witnessed an unchecked growth of supervisory personnel in higher-level Procuracy offices. In the Moscow city Procuracy office, for example, the number of department heads and deputy heads grew from 29 in 1979 to 41 in 1990. The expansion of supervisory personnel was even more marked in the USSR and RSFSR procuracies during this period.[54]

In addition to the familiar tasks of criminal investigation and prosecution, a major responsibility of the Procuracy has been the general supervision (obshchii nadzor) of legality, that is, ensuring that the actions of individuals and institutions were consistent with law.[55] In fulfilling this grand-sounding duty, the Procuracy did not wait until laws were violated before acting. It sought to pre-empt illegality by conducting routine inspections of Government departments and economic enterprises. In so doing, it duplicated the work of the Government's auditing agencies and disrupted the work of inspected institutions. At the end of the Soviet era, even the Procuracy's own leadership attacked the arrogation by the Procuracy of responsibilities "inappropriate to its mission."[56]

The makework character of much of this general supervision was rendered all the more pathetic by the Procuracy's traditional lack of enforcement authority. Even when illegalities were uncovered, the Procuracy could only protest them to the administrative superior of the offending institution, who then could ignore the Procuracy's protest without penalty. In 1987, new legislation authorized the Procuracy in urgent cases to suspend the actions of an offending institution. This right to issue injunctions (*predpisaniia*) was largely ignored, however, by the Procuracy as well as by agencies against which injunctions were issued. In June 1991, the legislative organs revised the powers of Procuracy protest yet again, this time by directing the Procuracy to submit urgent protests to the courts, which could then issue judicial sanctions against the offending institution.[57] This measure illustrated the emerging dependence of the Procuracy on the courts, an uncomfortable position indeed for an institution traditionally superior in influence to the judiciary.

The years of perestroika brought only modest changes in the personnel that comprised the Procuracy. Gorbachev's accession to power in 1985 swept a younger group of procurators into leadership posts at the regional level. By the late 1980s, however, the turnover of regional and republican procurators had slowed dramatically, except in the Muslim republics of Azerbaijan and Central Asia, which in 1989 and 1990 accounted for one half (36 of 68) of the new appointments to leading posts in regional and republican procuracies.[58] The relative stability of cadres at the apex of the Procuracy was finally disturbed in early 1991 with the rightward shift in legal policy. Appointed to replace Alexander Sukharev as USSR Procurator-General in January 1991, Nikolai Trubin offered to resign in late August of that year after he and other senior members of the Procuracy supported the coup. In the event, he continued in office until the collapse of the USSR.

The Procuracy has remained a male-dominated institution, with men accounting for approximately three-quarters of Procuracy personnel.[59] Men and women have always been distributed quite unevenly across occupational lines in the Procuracy, with men drawn disproportionately into criminal investigation work and women overrepresented among general supervision personnel, who spend much of their time examining documents. Unlike in earlier decades, the Procuracy in the late 1980s began to find it difficult to attract and retain personnel. Traditionally one of the most popular legal careers, the Procuracy lost many of its most talented staff to better-paying jobs in the Bar, economic enterprises, and new legal cooperatives. At the end of 1990, the procurator of the Leningrad region complained that because of such mid-career transfers, 25 of his 200 posts were vacant.[60] One can only imagine the difficulty of attracting and retaining personnel in more remote areas.

At the end of the 1980s, approximately 80 percent of Procuracy workers were members of the Communist Party, and many of the remaining 20 percent were young Komsomol members intent on joining the party. But three signal developments in Soviet politics in 1990 and 1991—the Communist Party's renunciation of one-party rule, Boris Yeltsin's ban on party organizations in Government institutions, and the unsuccessful August coup—prompted an exodus of Procuracy workers from the party. Indeed, on the day following the coup's collapse, the USSR Procuracy office closed down its party organization and declared itself "depoliticized." These developments further deepened the Procuracy's crisis of identity and mission. With the collapse of the Communist Party, the Procuracy lost its longstanding institutional master. Thus, the pressing tasks of the Procuracy in the successor states include not just the delineation of a new role but the discovery of a new institutional master.

In the final years of Soviet rule, the crisis of identity and mission was even more acute in the Ministry of Justice than in the Procuracy. Until the end of the 1980s, the major responsibilities of the Ministry of Justice had been the supervision of other legal insitutions, such as the courts, the Bar, the notariat, and the jurisconsults, who are in-house counsel in economic enterprises.[61] But the expanding independence of its two most important charges, the courts and the Bar, diminished considerably the standing and influence of the ministry among executive institutions.

The Bar's break with the Ministry of Justice was more dramatic and, it would appear, more complete than that of the court. After two years of bitter struggle with the Ministry of Justice, reform-minded advocates founded the country's first national Bar association, the Union of Advocates of the USSR, in February 1989. Although local-level Bar organizations, the colleges of advocates, remain in existence and under the nominal supervision of the Justice Ministry, the levers of ministerial influence over the Bar are rapidly disappearing. Where historically the income of advocates had been limited by an official ceiling and by a fee schedule approved by the Ministry of Justice, since the end of 1989 the ceiling has been removed and advocates have been able to arrange fees directly with clients. Further, the Ministry of Justice in the waning months of Soviet rule lifted the membership ceilings imposed on local colleges of advocates, which had kept the profession small in comparison to its Western counterparts. Finally, the cooperative movement launched in the late 1980s spawned new law firms, the legal cooperatives, which operated outside the jurisdiction of the Ministry of Justice. These legal cooperatives, originally spurned by the established Bar, are serving in the post-Soviet era as a model for legal practice in an expanding profession.[62] It appears that the traditional role of the republic ministries of justice as overseers of the Bar will soon be reduced to monitoring the provision of legal assistance to the poor as well as the education and membership standards of advocates.

The few administrative tasks performed directly by the Ministry of Justice also appear to be diminishing in scale and importance. Legislative drafting, once dominated by the ministry, is now shared among a host of institutions, including parliamentary committees.[63] Traditionally a major center of data collection and analysis in legal affairs, the USSR Ministry of Justice lost most of its research personnel and responsibilities to the research institute of the USSR Supreme Soviet presidium at the end of the 1980s. Although the ministry's All-Union Scientific Research Institute of Soviet Legislation remained a clearinghouse for legal information until the abolition of central ministry structures at the end of 1991, its size and prestige was dwarfed by the MVD Academy, the Procuracy Institute, and the Academy of Science's Institute of State and Law.

Set against these losses of responsibility was the addition of an important new task at the beginning of the 1990s, registering and monitoring political parties and associations that were formed pursuant to the October 1990 law on public organizations and subsequent legislation in the republics.[64] The collapse of party patronage power also gave local divisions of the Ministry of Justice increased responsibility in judicial nominations. Furthermore, the ministry has been seeking a higher profile in university legal education and in international trade and legal relations.[65]

But even with these additional or enhanced functions, the Ministry of Justice remained one of the smallest and least influential ministries at the end of the Soviet era. It operated with a skeleton staff—in the Brezhnev years the department for supervising the Bar had only two members—and with a leadership recruited almost exclusively from other legal institutions, most notably the Procuracy. In terms of pay and access to scarce goods, such as housing, the Ministry of Justice was in the bottom rank of Soviet ministries.[66] At the beginning of 1991, Fedor Burlatskii claimed that even the chair of the USSR Supreme Court was a more important figure than the USSR Minister of Justice.[67] In the view of Veniamin Yakovlev, the former minister of justice, the low standing in the USSR of a classic ministry (vechnoe ministerstvo) like justice "testifies first of all to the very small role that law plays in regulating social relations."[68]

One might anticipate a renascence of a vital Ministry of Justice if the society's reliance on law increases in the post-Soviet era. There are indeed signs, especially in the Russian Federation, that the Ministry of Justice is beginning to move into the front rank of ministries. Its young, progressive, and energetic justice minister, Nikolai Fedorov, is now competing successfully for scarce goods, such as photocopiers and housing space, with the more traditionally powerful ministries.[69] But the position of the Ministry of Justice continues to be weakened by its tortured relations with the Procuracy. Only the very boldest of legal reformers in the old Soviet Union dared to propose what seemed to the Western observer to be the inexorable logic of perestroika in the administration of justice—the re-absorption of the Procuracy into the Ministry of Justice. Separate institutions served the purposes of Stalin; they are inappropriate to a law-based state. This argument is at last being made by Fedorov, who noted that "as long as we don't resolve the place of the Procuracy in the state, in the legal system, there will not be real judicial power in Russia."[70] Fedorov's plea is unlikely to be heeded over the short term, however, since new Russian legislation makes the parliament the Procuracy's institutional master. The stage is now set for a fresh round of institutional conflict between the Ministry of Justice and Procuracy, as the former advances the interests of the reformist executive and the latter the interests of the more conservative legislature.

Challenges from Below

The administration of justice was highly centralized throughout Soviet history. In reviving the Procuracy in 1922, Lenin sought to guarantee that justice would be uniform "in Kaluga as well as in Kazan." In the ensuing decades, the political leadership in Moscow continued to insist on a single national legal policy, even if it was implemented with some variation through republican codes and institutions or compromised in places by corrupt local officials. But the twin forces of nationalism and democratization unleashed in the Gorbachev era encouraged the development of multiple legal policies and even multiple legal systems on the territory of the USSR. Radical political devolution realigned power within the courts, the Procuracy, and the Ministry of Justice as well as between these institutions.

Perhaps the most visible sign of struggle between center and periphery in legal affairs was the "war of laws" (*voina zakonov*) at the end of the Soviet era. The formation of independent, competitively-elected republican parliaments in 1990 led to the adoption of republican laws that were frequently in conflict with all-union statutes, provoking what in the West would be regarded as a constitutional crisis. Gorbachev and the leaders of a majority of the then 15 republics sought to overcome that crisis by drafting a new union treaty that would clearly delineate the jurisdictions of both central and republican laws and legal institutions and provide a mechanism for resolving jurisdictional conflicts. As we now know, that effort was abandoned by the republics themselves at the end of the 1991 with the formation of the Commonwealth of Independent States.

Some republics, notably those in the Baltics, had begun the establishment of a legal system wholly independent of the center without waiting for the collapse of the Soviet Union.   Such republican initiatives led for a time to the awkward, and dangerous, presence of competing legal institutions on the same territory. In Lithuania, for example, a Procuracy loyal to Moscow maintained a skeletal staff in the old republican Procuracy headquarters in Vilnius while a new Lithuanian Procuracy, loyal to the Government and parliament of independent Lithuania, exercised real procuratorial authority in the territory.

At least until late August 1991, most republics had not sought full sovereignty. But even the most politically traditional republics, such as those in Central Asia, demanded greater control over the administration of justice in their areas.   Their concern was not so much with the courts and the Ministry of Justice, which were already subject to republican authority before the August coup. Interviewed at the end of 1990, Justice Minister Fedorov reflected on his three years on the USSR Ministry of Justice staff in the 1980s.

> At that time ... you picked up the telephone, phoned the republic, any republic, and said what needed to be done. They answered "it will be done," and it was. Now when I meet former colleagues from the USSR Ministry of Justice, they complain that work has become very hard. You cannot command as before.[71]

The highly-centralized Procuracy, on the other hand, was much more resistant to the encroachment of republican authority.   In order to decentralize power in the Procuracy, in the declarations of sovereignty adopted by all Soviet republics in 1989 and 1990 the republics insisted that their legislatures approve, if not select outright, republican procurators, who had previously been appointed by the procurator-general of the USSR.[72]   Amendments to the USSR Constitution introduced in December 1990 granted the republican supreme soviets the right to appoint republican procurators, though with the agreement of (*po soglasovaniiu*) the USSR procurator-general.[73]   And for the first time, republican procurators received seats on the governing board of the USSR Procuracy.[74] The August coup hastened this reduction and decentralization of central procuratorial powers during the fall of 1991, and with the formation of the Commonwealth of Independent States in December, the remaining responsibilities of the USSR Procuracy were transferred to the republics.

The collapse of the Soviet state halted work in progress on the formation of an authentic federal legal system in the USSR.   Such a system promised to create federal courts and codes that were modest in scale but notable for the issues within their jurisdiction.   But by the beginning of 1992, the successor states had assumed sole responsibility for the development of legal norms and institutions on their territories.   The Russian Federation has now proposed the establishment of its own federal legal system, which would grant a degree of judicial autonomy to the non-Russian republics within the Federation, such as Tatarstan and Bashkiria. The Russians are also planning to revive a pre-revolutionary legal institution, the justice of the peace (*mirovoi sud'ia*), to function at the base of a new judiciary. At this writing, the other successor states are pursuing separate paths of legal development, though the example of the Russian Federation is certain at least to influence the direction of legal change in many of its neighboring states. A central question for the future is what legal traditions, whether indigenous or exogenous, European or Islamic, will shape the development of new legal norms and institutions in the Soviet successor states.

Whether the former Soviet republics emerge as wholly independent states with distinct political and legal systems depends in large measure on the interests of their governments in sustaining a single economic space. Put simply, a single economic space cannot exist without a single legal space, at least on commercial matters. And a single legal space will require the transfer of a degree of sovereignty from the successor states to Commonwealth-wide legal codes and institutions, which do not yet exist. Thus, while the successor states build new legal systems, they are likely to come under pressure from economic integrationists to cede some authority to superstate legal structures in order to facilitate trade throughout much, or all, of the territories of the former Soviet Union. The successor states will be pressured at the same time by local nationalists, such as the Tatars, to cede authority to substate legal institutions in order to satisfy the demands of ethnic minorities for home rule. Whatever the outcome of the current conflict over issues of sovereignty and statehood, the precise role of institutions in administering post-Soviet justice will take shape only gradually, amid the daily routine of citizens seeking remedies and of jurists working under the pressures of political, professional, and personal loyalties.

Notes

1. In the words of a legal scholar, and member of the Constitutional Court of Russia, Tamara G. Morshchakova: "Courts, like the entire justice system, have been an important part of the command system of leadership in the country." T. Morshchakova, *Sudebnaia reforma: sbornik obzorov* (Moscow: Institut nauchnoi informatsii po obshchestvennym naukam AN SSSR, 1990), p. 9. The idea of the court as an extension of the executive apparatus is so deeply ingrained that people's court judges, elected to their posts, began to be fired at the end of the 1980s as part of a general reduction of staff in the Government bureaucracy. A. Koblikov, "Neuvazhenie k sudu," *Sovetskaia iustitsiia*, no. 7 (1989), p. 13.

2. Until the creation of a USSR People's Commissariat of Justice in 1936, the justice commissariats functioned only at the republican level. There was a Procuracy at the all-union level as early as 1924, but it was attached to the USSR Supreme Court and had a narrow range of responsibilities.

3. On the Vyshinsky-Krylenko conflict, see E. Huskey, "Vyshinsky, Krylenko, and the Shaping of the Soviet Legal Order," *Slavic Review*, nos. 3-4 (1987), pp. 414-428. A history of the Procuracy may be found in G. Morgan, *Soviet Administrative Legality: The Role of the Attorney General's Office* (Stanford: Stanford University Press, 1962), pp.8-130, and *Sovetskaia prokuratura* (Moscow: Iuridicheskaia literatura, 1982).

4. On relations between courts and the Procuracy, see G. Ginsburgs, "The Soviet Judicial Elite: Is It?" *Review of Socialist Law*, no. 2 (1985), pp. 303-305, and G. Fletcher, "The Presumption of Innocence in the Soviet Union," *UCLA Law Review* (1968), pp. 1203-1225.

5. Executive supervision of the courts was institutionalized in the 1930s in response to the judiciary's unwillingness to adhere faithfully to the many twists and turns of party policy in legal affairs. A handbook prepared for local procurators in 1934 noted that "an indispensable duty for the district procurator is to struggle against all defects and distortions in the policy toward criminal justice adopted by the people's courts." N. Lagovier, *V pomoshch' raionnomu prokuroru i narodnomu sledovateliu. Prakticheskoe posobie* (Moscow, 1934), p. 126, quoted in V.N. Tochilovskii, "O kontseptsii prokurorskoi vlasti," *Sovetskoe gosudarstvo i pravo*, no. 9 (1990), p. 40.

6. That courts were formally a division of the Ministry of Justice is confirmed by the plaques that hung outside the entrance to all courts. They contained inscriptions such as: "Ministry of Justice RSFSR. People's Court. Lenin District." V. Vlasikhin, "Sniat' s suda 'ministerskuiu shapku'," *Argumenty i fakty*, no. 5 (1989), p. 3.

7. T. Morshchakova, *Sudebnaia reforma: sbornik obzorov* (Moscow: Institut nauchnoi informatsii po obshchestvennym naukam, 1990), pp. 70-71. At the beginning of 1990 more than 2000 judges were members of 189 qualifying boards. "Vsesoiuznoe soveshchanie rukovodiashchikh rabotnikov organov iustitsii, sudov i kollegii advokatov," *Biulleten' Verkhovnogo Suda SSSR*, no. 2 (1990), p. 4.

8. Initial changes were made to Article 152 of the USSR Constitution, "Ob izmeneniiakh i dopolneniiakh Konstitutsii (Osnovnogo zakona) SSSR," *Vedomosti Verkhovnogo Soveta SSSR*, no. 49 (1988), item 727. Detailed provisions on judicial elections followed in "O statuse sudei v SSSR," *Vedomosti S"ezda narodnykh deputatov SSSR i Verkhovnogo Soveta SSSR*, no. 9 (1989), item 223. See also, J. Henderson, "Law of the USSR: On the Status of Judges in the USSR," *Review of Socialist Law*, no. 3 (1990), pp. 307-326.

9. New legislation on the judiciary included "Ob otvetstvennosti za neuvazhenie k sudu," *Vedomosti S"ezda narodnykh deputatov SSSR i Verkhovnogo Soveta SSSR*, no. 22 (1989), item 418; "O poriadke obzhalovaniia v sud nepravomernyhk deistvii organov gosudarstvennogo upravleniia i dolzhnostnykh lits, ushchemliaiushchikh prava grazhdan," *Vedomosti S"ezda narodnykh deputatov SSSR i Verkhovnogo Soveta SSSR*, no. 22 (1989), item 417; "Osnovy zakonodatel'stva Soiuza SSR i soiuznykh respublik o sudoustroistve," *Vedomosti S"ezda narodnykh deputatov SSSR i Verkhovnogo Soveta SSSR*, no. 23 (1989),

item 441. On the outlines of judicial reform in the Russian Federation after the August 1991 coup, see "O Kontseptsii sudebnoi reforme v RSFSR," *Vedomosti S"ezda narodnykh deputatov RSFSR i Verkhovnogo Soveta RSFSR*, no. 44 (1991), item 1435.

10. Telephone justice was by no means the exclusive weapon of the party. A survey in 1989 of 250 people's court judges in the Sverdlovsk and Cheliabinsk regions revealed that pressure applied in cases *sub judice* came from numerous institutions. To the question "who applied pressure in specific cases?", 30 percent of the respondents identified the Communist Party, 25.5 percent the local soviet executive committee, 14.5 percent the local organs of the Procuracy, MVD, and KGB, and 7.8 percent the local department of justice. V. Zaitsev, "O nezavisimosti sudei," *Sovetskaia iustitsiia*, no. 11 (1990), pp. 6-7.

11. "O prekrashchenii deiatel'nosti organizatsionnykh struktur politicheskikh partii i massovykh obshchestvennykh dvizhenii v gosudarstvennykh organakh, uchrezhdeniiakh i organizatsiiakh RSFSR," *Argumenty i fakty*, no. 29 (1991), p. 2; "Ukaz o departizatsii vospriniat poraznomu," *Izvestiia*, 27 July 1991, p. 2. It should be noted that the decree did not apply to central institutions, such as the USSR Supreme Court, the USSR Procuracy, and the USSR KGB, though it did cover the subordinate institutions of central organizations located on the territory of the Russian republic. "Ukaz Prezidenta Rossii o departizatsii," *Izvestiia*, 22 July 1991, p. 1. The Constitutional Review Committee agreed at the end of July to rule on the constitutionality of the decree and asked that Yeltsin suspend the decree pending a ruling. Yeltsin refused. "Reshenie Komiteta konstitutsionnogo nadzora SSSR," *Izvestiia*, 29 July 1991, p. 2.

12. "Verkhovnyi Sud Rossii depolitizirovan," *Izvestiia*, 6 August 1991, p. 2.

13. "Ukaz Prezidenta Rossiiskoi Sovetskoi Federativnoi Sotsialisticheskoi Respubliki 'O deiatel'nosti KPSS i KP RSFSR'," *Rossiiskaia gazeta*, 9 November 1991, p. 2.

14. New laws made recall easier than in the past. Instead of holding a recall election, legislatures had only to vote a judge out of office. Reform-oriented jurists warned of the excessive influence that this gave to legislators over the judiciary. See, for example, T. Morshchakova, *Sudebnaia reforma: sbornik obzorov* (Moscow: Institut nauchnoi informatsii po obshchestvennym naukam, 1990), p. 32.

15. See, for example, K. Gutsenko, "O sudebnoi vlasti i sudeiskom korpuse," *Sovetskaia iustitsiia*, no. 2 (1990), pp. 2-4; and "Sudy i sovety: problemy i suzhdeniia," *Sovetskaia iustitsiia*, no. 19 (1990), pp. 5-7. More than 90 percent of judges polled in the RSFSR in 1990 believed that their selection by legislatures violated the independence of the judiciary. *Ibid.* Some commentators also expressed alarm about "megaphone law," the tendency of crowds to seek to intimidate judges in politically sensitive cases. See A.S. Koblikov, "Sudebnaia politika i sposoby ee realizatsii," *Sovetskoe gosudarstvo i pravo*, no. 6 (1991), p. 73.

16. K. Gutsenko, "O sudebnoi vlasti i sudeiskom korpuse," *Sovetskaia iustitsiia*, no. 2 (1990), p. 3. The law on the status of judges itself compromises judicial independence by having judges periodically report to the legislative body electing them. V. Savitskii, "Ne osudit', a rassudit'," *Izvestiia*, 18 July 1991, p. 3.

17. Legal reformists noted the irony of a money-making institution for the state that is itself starved of goods. Through the collection of fees, fines, and the reimbursement of

harm to the state, the courts brought in 800 million rubles annually to the Soviet budget. Only 160 million rubles was expended on the courts, approximately 40 million rubles less than was spent on the Procuracy. A. Borin, "Nishchaia iustitsiia, ili skol'ko stoit pravovoe gosudarstvo?" *Literaturnaia gazeta*, 23 August 1989, p. 10.

18. Unlike most powerful Government ministries, the judiciary does not have its own housing stock and other scarce goods to allocate to its officials.

19. "Sudy i sovety: problemy i suzhdeniia," *Sovetskaia iustitsiia*, no. 19 (1990), p. 6.

20. V. Savitskii, "Aspects of Judicial Reform in the USSR," *Coexistence*, vol. 28 (1991), p. 119.

21. For a description of judicial service ranks, see "Ob ustanovlenii dlia sudei sudov Soiuza SSR i soiuznykh respublik kvalifikatsionnykh klassov," *Biulleten' Verkhovnogo Suda SSSR*, no. 1 (1990), pp. 22-23.

22. For examples of private rulings issued by courts, see "Vynesenie sudami chastnykh opredelenii (postanovlenii) pri rassmotrenii ugolovnykh i grazhdanskikh del," *Biulleten' Verkhovnogo Suda SSSR*, no. 2 (1989), pp. 36-43. It should be noted that unlike contempt citations in American judicial practice, private rulings carry no penalty. In 1987, 45 percent of those targeted by private rulings did not respond to them. *Ibid.*

23. P. Mel'nikov, "Pravo sud'i na oshikbu?" *Sovetskaia iustitsiia*, no. 7 (1990), p. 5.

24. In many regions, of course, old traditions died hard. A report at the end of 1990 noted that many local justice departments were not adhering to USSR Ministry of Justice directives on new, and more distant, relations with the court. L. Simkin, "Organy iustitsii i sudy: novaia model' vzaimootnoshenii," *Sovetskaia iustitsiia*, no. 20 (1990), pp. 2-4. On resistance to reform within the USSR Ministry of Justice itself, see Iu. Severin, "Organizatsionnoe obespechenie deiatel'nosti sudov—na uroven' trebovanii sudebno-pravovoi reformy," *Sovetskaia iustitsiia*, no. 4 (1990), pp. 2-3. At the end of the 1980s, the Ministry of Justice imposed administrative punishment on as many as 700 judges a year (approximately five percent of all judges) for malfeasance in office. "Otchet o deiatel'nosti Verkhovnogo Suda SSSR," *Biulleten' Verkhovnogo Suda SSSR*, no. 4 (1988), p. 9. Some uncooperative judges have been subject to false criminal prosecutions. T. Morshchakova, *Sudebnaia reforma: sbornik obzorov*, pp. 63-63.

25. For acquittal rates and other judicial statistics, see "Verkhovnyi sud," *Ogonek*, no. 8 (1989), pp. 4-6; "Kto osudil sud'iu?" *Ogonek*, no. 14 (1989), pp. 26-27; "Vsesoiuznoe soveshchanie rukovodiashchikh rabotnikov organov iustitsii, sudov i kollegii advokatov," *Biulleten' Verkhovnogo Suda SSSR*, no. 2 (1990), p. 7; "Svidetel'stvuet sudebnaia statistika," *Narodnyi deputat*, no. 13 (1990), p. 89. As V. Savitskii points out, even with the rise in the incidence of acquittals, the Soviet Union acquitted .3 percent of its defendants compared to 10 percent in France. "Pravo i sila," *Moskovskii komsomolets*, 18 May 1991, p. 2.

26. For statistics on the changes in criminality in the USSR from 1979 to 1989, see Ia. Gilinskii, "Illiuzii—ne izbavlenie," *Narodnyi deputat*, no. 14 (1990), pp. 78-82.

27. "B. El'tsin, Prezident RSFSR: Nam nuzhen Sud, a ne ugodlivoe pravosudie," *Sovetskaia iustitsiia*, nos. 23-24 (1991), p. 2.

28. These figures are as of 1 January 1988. V. Terebilov, *Perestroika Demands Judicial Reform* (Moscow: Novosti, 1988), p. 21.

29. On the initiative of the Ministry of Justice of the Russian republic, there was a significant expansion in the number of judges in 1991. "V povestke dnia - pravovoe gosudarstvo," *Sovetskaia iustitsiia*, no. 4 (1990), p. 2.

30. N. Fedorov, *Sudebnaia vlast' v Rossiia* (unpublished manuscript, October 1991). I am grateful to Peter Solomon for sharing this source with me.

31. "Problemy sudebnoi reformy," *Sovetskaia iustitsiia*, no. 8 (1990), pp. 25-27.

32. "Komu vershit' pravosudie?" *Sovetskaia iustitsiia*, no. 7 (1990), p. 2. Slightly over 42 percent of Soviet judges were women in 1988, V. Terebilov, *Perestroika Demands Judicial Reform* (Moscow: Novosti, 1988), p. 21. The proportion had climbed to over 50 percent by 1990. "Komu vershit' pravosudie?" *Sovetskaia iustitsiia*, no. 7 (1990), p. 2. If in 1978 almost 42 percent of Soviet judges were under 40 years of age, the figure rose to more than 61 percent 1990. *Ibid.*

33. Like many segments of Soviet society, judges lived less well in the 1980s than in the 1970s. An indication of the drop in living standards may be found in the number of cars "distributed" to judges. In the early 1970s, the judiciary received 177 cars a year; at the end of the 1980s the number had dropped to 16. "Press-konferentsiia v Ministerstve iustitsii SSSR," *Sovetskaia iustitsiia*, no. 1 (1990), frontispiece.

34. V. Savitskii, "Ne osudit', a rassudit'," *Izvestiia*, 18 July 1991, p. 3.

35. Personal interview, Tamara Morshchakova, Moscow, 23 May 1991. 2869 such cases were brought in 1988. A. Borin, "Nishchaia iustitsiia, ili skol'ko stoit pravovoe gosudarstvo," *Literaturnaia gazeta*, 23 August 1989, p. 10.

36. P. Solomon, "The USSR Supreme Court: History, Role, and Future Prospects," *American Journal of Comparative Law*, no. 1 (1990), pp. 138-139. It appears likely that the courts will supersede the Procuracy as the organ responsible for ruling on the legality of ministerial instructions and the decisions of local soviets.

37. In recent years, however, the regular courts began to rule on the constitutionality of Soviet legislation. On 5 December 1990, the Moscow City Court refused to apply art. 88 of the RSFSR Criminal Code because it was unconstitutional. A.D. Boikov, "Problemy sudebnoi reformy," *Sovetskoe gosudarstvo i pravo*, no. 4 (1991), p. 15.

38. On the *arbitrazh* courts, see Iu. Feofanov, "Sud dlia rynka," *Izvestiia*, 20 June 1991, p. 2. The entire system of *arbitrazh* courts throughout the Russian Federation employed 4040 persons in early 1992. "Ov utverzhdenii obshchei chislennosti rabotnikov arbitrazhnykh sudov Rossiiskoi Federatsii," *Vedomosti S"ezda narodnykh deputatov RSFSR i Verkhovnogo Soveta RSFSR*, no. 8 (1992), item 375.

39. T. Morshchakova, *Sudebnaia reforma: sbornik obzorov* (Moscow: Institut nauchnoi informatsii po obshchestvennym naukim, 1990), p. 48. Special courts in the USSR were the subject of a working session attended by the author at the First International Andrei Sakharov Memorial Congress, Moscow, May 1991. The following secret decree on such courts, issued by the USSR Supreme Soviet presidium on 1 June 1979, was first made public in 1991: "O sudakh, prokurature, advokature, notariate i organakh vnutrennykh del, deistvuiushchikh na osobo rezhimnykh ob"ektakh," *Sotsialisticheskaia zakonnost'*, no. 7 (1991), pp. 45-47.

40. It was reported at the beginning of 1991 that the RSFSR Justice Minister, N. Fedorov, had "on his agenda" draft laws outlawing special courts. "V povestke dnia - pravovoe gosudarstvo," *Sovetskaia iustitsiia*, no. 4 (1991), pp. 2-3.

41. "O strukture i shtatnoi chislennosti apparata Verkhovnogo Suda SSSR," *Biulleten' Verkhovnogo Suda SSSR*, no. 2 (1990), p. 9. Eight of the judges on the USSR Supreme Court were in the military collegium, which was the capstone of a discrete hierarchy of military courts directly subordinated to the USSR Supreme Court. The USSR Supreme Court also had a Scientific-Consultative Council comprised of 49 scholars, a third of whom were drawn from research institutes in the Procuracy, the Ministry of Justice, the MVD, and the armed forces. "Plenum Verkhovnogo Suda SSSR," *Biulleten Verkhovnogo Suda SSSR*, no. 2 (1990), p. 9. For a history of the USSR Supreme Court see P. Solomon, "The USSR Supreme Court: History, Role, and Future Prospects," *American Journal of Comparative Law*, no. 1 (1990), pp. 127-142. The figures for the staffs of the courts is drawn from "O shtatnoi chislennosti apparata Verkhovnogo Suda RSFSR," *Vedomosti S"ezda narodnykh deputatov RSFSR i Verkhovnogo Soveta RSFSR*, no. 43 (1991), item 1388, and "O shtatnoi chislennosti apparata Vysshego Arbitrazhnogo Suda RSFSR," *Vedomosti S"ezda narodnykh deputatov RSFSR i Verkhovnogo Soveta RSFSR*, no. 43 (1991), item 1387.

42. In recent years it has become increasingly difficult to recruit lay assessors for service on the bench. Selected by their work or housing collective for a short stint on the bench, lay assessors are often exemplary workers that factory managers do not wish to lose to court service. Because the employer must continue to pay the salaries of lay assessors while they are on the bench, enterprises have been reluctant to allow even mediocre workers to serve. Shortages of lay assessors have been particularly acute in Moscow and St. Petersburg, and measures have recently been taken to force employers to release their workers for service as lay assessors. "Glavnaia problema - nezavisimost' sudei," *Sovetskaia iustitsiia*, no. 12 (1990), frontispiece.

43. "Osnovy zakonodatel'stva Soiuza SSR i soiuznykh respublik o sudoustroistve," *Vedomosti S'ezda narodnykh deputatov SSSR i Verkhovnogo Soveta SSSR*, no. 23 (1989), item 441. Fedor Burlatskii reported that the reintroduction of the jury trial was discussed by USSR Supreme Soviet staff in the early 1960s. "Interview with the Editor-in-Chief of Literaturnaia Gazeta, Fedor Burlatskii," *New Outlook*, no. 2 (1991), p. 39.

44. For some commentators, the question is whether the jury will be able to "sit" at all. In most courts there is not a spare room large enough for jury deliberations. It is easy for Western observers to overlook the changes in physical infrastructure required for a reformed judiciary. "Pravo i sila," *Moskovskii komsomolets*, 18 May 1991, p. 2.

45. See "Avgustovskii putch: posledstviia i uroki," *Sovetskoe gosudarstvo i pravo*, no. 10 (1991), pp. 16-17.

46. For a statistical portrait of the activities of the Procuracy at the end of the 1980s, see "Prokuratura v tsifrakh," *Sotsialisticheskaia zakonnost'*, no. 10 (1990), pp. 54-58.

47. "O kontrol'noi palate i arbitrazhnom sude," *Izvestiia*, 13 April 1991, pp. 1-2.

48. "O zadachakh organov prokuratury pri podgotovki narodnogo khoziaistva k rabote v zimnykh usloviiakh," Ukazanie no. 82/7, 23 okt. 1987 (Moscow: Prokuratura SSSR, 1987). This is one of a large number of internal directives of the USSR Procuracy made

available to the author in the Law Faculty of Moscow State University in late 1988. Even in the Procuracy itself there seems to be a consensus that market reforms will make Procuracy oversight of the economy redundant. Iu. Korenevskii, "Kakovy perspektivy?" *Sotsialisticheskaia zakonnost'*, no. 1 (1991), p. 33.

49. Its own institutional interests notwithstanding, the USSR Procuracy proposed in the 1970s the formation of an independent USSR Investigative Committee (*Sledstvennyi komitet SSSR*), to be staffed by the investigators of the MVD and Procuracy. Greeted favorably by the presidium of the USSR Supreme Soviet, the proposal lost support when Brezhnev replaced Nikolai Podgornyi in 1977 as chair of the presidium of the USSR Supreme Soviet.   S.I. Gusev, "Nekotorye problemy budushchei kontseptsii prokurorskogo nadzora v strane," *Sovetskoe gosudarstvo i pravo*, no. 9 (1990), p. 50.

50. I.L. Petrukhin, "Funktsii prokurora v sude," *Sovetskoe gosudarstvo i pravo*, no. 6 (1990), p. 81.

51. Reform-oriented jurists point out that one of the reasons for an uneven playing field is the court's own powers to initiate criminal cases and to continue with a criminal trial even if the prosecutor abandons the case.   V. Savitskii, "Ne osudit', a rassudit'," *Izvestiia*, 18 July 1991, p. 3.

52. "Ob obrazovanii edinoi sistemy organov prokuratory RSFSR," *Vedomosti S"ezda narodnykh deputatov RSFSR i Verkhovnogo Soveta RSFSR*, no. 48 (1991), item 1661. The new statute on the Procuracy in the Russian Federation brought only marginal change to the institution.   See "O prokurature Rossiiskoi Federatsii," *Vedomosti S"ezda narodnykh deputatov RSFSR i Verkhovnogo Soveta RSFSR*, no. 8 (1992), item 366.

53. The structure of the USSR Procuracy is set out in "O strukture Prokuratury Soiuza SSR," *Vedomosti Verkhovnogo Soveta SSSR*, no. 6 (1989), item 42.   For a detailed examination of the structure and functions of the Procuracy, see E. Huskey, "Careers in the Soviet Legal Bureaucracy: Recruitment Patterns and Professional Backgrounds of Procuracy Officials at the Regional, Republican, and All-Union Levels," Final Report to the National Council for Soviet and East European Research (1987) and G. Smith, *The Soviet Procuracy and the Supervision of Administration* (Alphen aan den Rijn: A.W. Sijthoff & Noordhoff, 1978).   Just as the USSR Supreme Court had a military division that was the capstone of a discrete hierarchy of military courts, the USSR Procuracy contained the Main Military Procuracy, which supervised a network of offices that operated in military administrative districts. There was also a separate hierarchy of transport Procuracy offices, which was organized by air, water, or rail transport districts or regions.   It is not yet known what will happen to the Main Military Procuracy in the Commonwealth of Independent States, which has a centralized army but no centralized Procuracy.

54. Iu. Semin, "Izmenit' struktury?" *Sotsialisticheskaia zakonnost'*, no. 3 (1991), p. 31.

55. Readers interested in quantitative indicators of criminal and general supervision activity by the contemporary Procuracy will find remarkably detailed tables in "Prokuratura v tsifrakh," *Sotsialisticheskaia zakonnost'*, no. 10 (1990), pp. 54-58.

56. At the beginning of 1991, for example, the newly-appointed procurator-general, N.S. Trubin, expressed his concern about the proliferation of Procuracy departments and

responsibilities. In 1987, the Procuracy divided its general supervision department into four sections, which were responsible for the rights of citizens, economic activity, administrative law violations, and the environment. Parallel with the formation of an environmental department in the USSR Procuracy was the creation of local Procuracy offices dealing exclusively with environmental affairs. By the beginning of 1990, 30 such offices existed at the regional and district level. K.F. Gutsenko, "Pravosudie i prokurorskii nadzor v usloviiakh formirovaniia pravovogo gosudarstva," *Vestnik MGU. Seriia 11 (Pravo)*, no. 4 (1990), pp. 12-21; N. Trubin, "Po tomu li puti idem? (o problemakh ogshchego nadzora," *Sotsialisticheskaia zakonnost'*, no. 11 (1990), pp. 9-13; N. Trubin, "Vremia idet, a dvizheniia v glavnom net," *Sotsialisticheskaia zakonnost'*, no. 1 (1991), pp. 21-23. And yet despite the rhetoric of reform, the Procuracy apparatus continued to operate much as before. At the end of 1990, for example, the monthly meeting of the USSR Procuracy's governing board (*kollegiia*) devoted most of its attention to improving the delivery of goods between enterprises. "V kollegii," *Sotsialisticheskaia zakonnost'*, no. 1 (1991), p. 76.

57. "O rassmotrenii sudom obrashcheniia prokurora o priznanii pravovogo akta nezakonnym i o vnesenii dopolnenii v Zakon SSSR 'O prokurature SSSR'," *Izvestiia*, 21 July 1991, p. 2.

58. The purge of procurators in these regions was apparently carried out in response to the localism and corruption observed first hand by special detachments from the USSR Procuracy investigating the interethnic bloodshed in Azerbaijan and Kirgizia and the cotton scandal in Uzbekistan.

59. *Sovetskaia prokuratura* (Moscow: Iuridicheskaia literatura, 1982), p. 209.

60. G. Porukov, "Rabotniki ukhodiat," *Sotsialisticheskaia zakonnost'*, no. 1 (1991), pp. 28-29.

61. For an introduction to the structure and functions of the Ministry of Justice at the end of the 1980s, see V.M. Semenov, *Pravookhranitel'nye organy v SSSR* (Moscow: Iuridicheskaia literatura, 1990), pp. 208-224.

62. On the rise of individual private practitioners in Russia, see A. Zhdankin, "Advokatskoe biuro Kuznetsova," *Rossiiskaia gazeta*, 12 September 1991, p. 2.

63. The department for legislative drafting remained, however, the largest employer in the ministry. "Nuzhna li sudu 'Ministerskaia shapka'?" *Chelovek i zakon*, no. 12 (1989), pp. 6-9.

64. "O poriadke registratsii ustavov politicheskikh partii, professional'nykh soiuzov i drugikh obshchestvennykh ob'edinenii v RSFSR," *Vedomosti S"ezda narodnykh deputatov RSFSR i Verkhovnogo Soveta RSFSR*, no. 2 (1991), item 15. It was the Ministry of Justice's power to revoke the registration of parties that Boris Yeltsin used to close down the Communist Party in the wake of the August coup.

65. Russian Federation Minister of Justice, N.V. Fedorov, proposed the creation of legal lycees and a transfer of responsibility for university legal education from the State Committee on Public Education to the Ministry of Justice. "Ministr iustitsii suverennoi Rossii," *Sovetskaia iustitsiia*, no. 16 (1990), p. 3.

66. At the end of the 1980s the average pay in the Ministry of Justice apparatus was 137 rubles a month, compared to 217 for the country as a whole. J. Henderson, "Law

of the USSR: On the Status of Judges in the USSR," *Review of Socialist Law*, no. 3 (1990), p. 312.

67. "Interview with Editor-in-Chief of Literaturnaia Gazeta, Fedor Burlatskii," *New Outlook*, no. 2 (1991), p. 40. The talented USSR Justice Minister, Veniamin Iakovlev, left his post in 1990 to become the chair of a newly-invigorated *arbitrazh* court, perhaps because of the declining prestige of the Ministry of Justice or perhaps because he was forced to make way for a more traditional minister, Sergei Lushchikov. Lushchikov's unreconstructed views were evident in "Interview with the USSR Minister of Justice, Sergei Lushchikov," *New Outlook*, no. 2 (1991), p. 37.

68. "Sil'naia iustitsiia-velenie vremeni," *Sotsialisticheskaia zakonnost'*, no. 4 (1990), p. 4.

69. N. Fedorov, *Sudebnaia vlast' v Rossii* (unpublished manuscript, October 1991), pp. 14-15. Now that the Ministry of Justice is emerging as a more influential patron, even independent-minded members of the judiciary may be rethinking their goal of full organizational autonomy from the ministry, at least over the short term. In 1991, the ministry managed to procure more than 1000 imported copiers for the courts. In previous years it had supplied only 10-20. *Ibid.*

70. "N. Fedorov, Ministr iustitsii RSFSR: Glavnoe—vopros o vlasti," *Sovetskaia iustitsiia*, nos. 23-24 (1991), p. 4.

71. "Ne predat' istinu," *Sotsialisticheskaia zakonnost'*, no. 1 (1991), p. 35.

72. See, for example, B. Kasymov, "Nuzhno li dvoinoe podchinenie prokurorov?" *Narodnyi deputat*, no. 11 (1990), p. 59.

73. "Ob izmeneniiakh i dopolneniiakh Konstitutsii (Osnovnogo zakona) SSSR v sviazi s sovershenstvovaniem sistemy gosudarstvennogo upravleniia," *Vedomosti S"ezda narodnykh deputatov SSSR i Verkhovnogo Soveta SSSR*, no. 1 (1991), item 3.

74. N. Trubin, "Prokuratura dolzhna zanimat'sia svoim delom," *Sotsialisticheskaia zakonnost'*, no. 3 (1991), p. 8.

THE STATE AND
THE FUTURE

11

THE REBIRTH OF THE RUSSIAN STATE

Eugene Huskey

Soviet history ended in a struggle between a decaying central state and incipient states rising in the republics. To borrow Hirschman's language, politics in the USSR moved from loyalty to voice to exit.[1] Nationalists and democrats, whose voices fell on increasingly unsympathetic ears in the central state, gradually abandoned Soviet politics in favor of republican politics. This change of political venue, which promised remedies unavailable from the Soviet state, created a dozen or more political communities arrayed against the center. By the beginning of the 1990s, the war of laws between the center and the republics had become a war of states.

In this war of states, the decisive battle was between the Soviet Union and Russia. The skirmishes in the Baltic, important as a test of Western foreign policies and as an indication of the political will of Mikhail Gorbachev, were nonetheless a sideshow when set against the challenges posed by Russia, with its vast territory and population, its bold and charismatic president, Boris Yeltsin, and its historic role as the hegemonic nation in the region. Shortly after the popular election of Yeltsin as Russia's first president in June 1991, the authority of the Russian state began to encroach rapidly on that of the Soviet state. In a move that struck at the heart of the Soviet state's repressive machinery, President Yeltsin in July outlawed Communist Party organizations in the armed forces, the KGB, the MVD, and other legal institutions. The Russian parliament also mandated the transfer of ownership of land and enterprises in the republic to the Russian state.

Understanding the threat to the integrity of the Soviet Union posed by Russia's actions and by a forthcoming union treaty, which was designed to shift political power from the center to the republics, a group of military, law enforcement, and economic leaders launched a coup to restore the authority of the Soviet state. The failure of this coup only accelerated the decline of Soviet institutions and the rise of Russian competitors. From September to November 1991, Russian ministries began to displace their Soviet counterparts. Among the first targets were the institutions of coercion. On 20 October, the Russian Government ordered the transfer of the internal security troops of the USSR MVD to the Russian MVD.[2] Shortly thereafter, the Russian Procuracy began to take over the facilities of the USSR Procuracy.[3] In early November 1991, the Russian Government closed down the Communist Party of the Soviet Union and seized its considerable funds and property.[4] A few days later, Yeltsin signed a decree transferring the assets of the USSR Ministry of Finance to Russia's Ministry of Economics and Finance.[5] Through this series of extraconstitutional seizures, Russia was draining the last life from the dying Soviet state.[6]

   Russia's final assault on the Soviet state came in December 1991. Although Yeltsin had appeared content to leave an emasculated central state in place, apparently to facilitate economic and military relations among the republics, he abandoned this approach in early December when Ukraine announced its intention to withdraw from the Soviet Union. The Russian state then moved quickly to complete its absorption of Soviet institutions. The Kremlin guard, the Alpha group, shifted its allegiance from Gorbachev to Yeltsin in mid-December. Russia claimed for itself, *inter alia*, the Soviet seat at the United Nations, Soviet embassies abroad, and the central radio and television service.[7] The ultimate symbol of the state in the late twentieth century, the nuclear button, passed from Gorbachev to Yeltsin on Christmas Day 1991, marking the death of the Soviet Union and the birth of a new political order, the Commonwealth of Independent States, which embraced 11 of the 15 former Soviet republics, including Russia.

   While the territory of the USSR was divided among 15 successor states, the Soviet state was transferred to one, the Russian Federation. As the de facto successor to the Soviet state, Russia assumed not just the assets but the liabilities of the old center: its foreign debts and entanglements, its personnel, and its awkward relations with the periphery. From the perspective of the non-Russian republics, the powers of the Russian state were formidable. It dominated communications, the money supply, and the military (formally a Commonwealth force, in reality under the control of Russia). Whether the actions of the permanent, extensive bureaucracies of Russia can be limited by a commonwealth of unequal states, which makes decisions through periodic summitry and lacks an enforcement mechanism, is doubtful at best. The Commonwealth of Independent States will survive over the long term only if it becomes a useful instrument for the Russian state in controlling its borderlands and facilitating trade with the other Soviet successor states.

Center versus Periphery in the Russian State

After devouring the Soviet state, Russia set out to build an efficient, legitimate, and democratic successor state. But as early as the spring of 1992, it was apparent that state building in Russia would be protracted and fraught with crises, which emerged along both the vertical and horizontal axes of the state. At stake was the distribution of power among institutions in the center and between the central government and governments in the locales.

As long as the Soviet state existed to block, or at least temper, economic and political reform, the friends of change supported the devolution of authority from the center to republican and local institutions. But as Russian politics began to displace Soviet politics, the forces surrounding Yeltsin moved to halt, and even reverse, political decentralization. The logic was simple. While a few local governments, such as those in Moscow and St. Petersburg, appeared committed to democratic reform, most local authorities—even after the August coup—remained in the hands of conservatives who were intent on preserving or restoring elements of the old regime.[8] Further, the governments of several autonomous republics and regions (renamed republics in late 1991) threatened the integrity of the Russian Federation with programs that demanded home rule, if not independence. Even regions that were not home to large ethnic minorities were insisting on more autonomy from Moscow. The Krasnoiarsk region (*krai*) threatened to restyle itself the Enisei Republic in order to claim the more expansive rights to property accorded to republics in the Russian Federation.[9]

Faced with the dual challenge from below of nationalism and conservatism, the Russian leadership took dramatic, and some would say undemocratic, steps in the last half of 1991 to reconcentrate political authority in the central Russian state. In the wake of the August coup, Yeltsin began to appoint personal representatives (*predstaviteli*) to each of the Russian Federation's 20 constituent republics and 55 regions.[10] Labelled *namestniki* by the Russian press, a reference to the medieval Russian prefects, these representatives were supposed to ensure the faithful implementation of Russian laws and decrees, which were increasingly ignored by provincial elites. Although these representatives (like party officials in the Soviet era[11]) were not formally authorized to interfere in the day-to-day administration of local government, some assumed a dominant role in local affairs. According to a source in Tomsk: "People used to run to the *obkom* [regional party committee], now they turn to the representatives of the President."[12] Even Yeltsin's man in charge of the representatives admitted that "they are being called on to fill the ideological and organizational vacuum [left] by the destruction of the former party and administrative structures."[13]

Table 11.1
Structure of Regional Government in Russia, January 1992

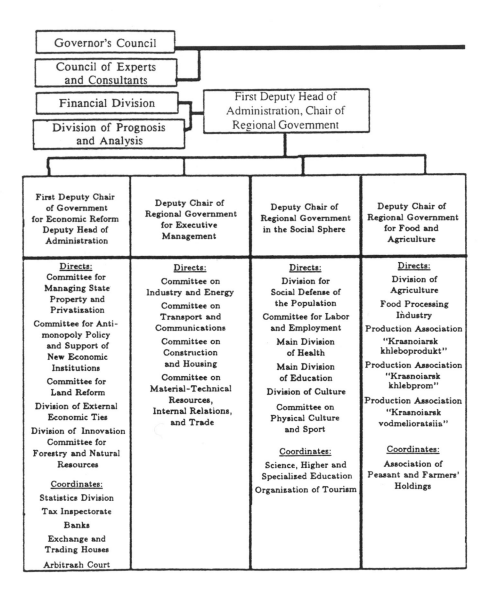

First Deputy Chair of Government for Economic Reform Deputy Head of Administration	Deputy Chair of Regional Government for Executive Management	Deputy Chair of Regional Government in the Social Sphere	Deputy Chair of Regional Government for Food and Agriculture
Directs: Committee for Managing State Property and Privatization Committee for Anti-monopoly Policy and Support of New Economic Institutions Committee for Land Reform Division of External Economic Ties Division of Innovation Committee for Forestry and Natural Resources	Directs: Committee on Industry and Energy Committee on Transport and Communications Committee on Construction and Housing Committee on Material-Technical Resources, Internal Relations, and Trade	Directs: Division for Social Defense of the Population Committee for Labor and Employment Main Division of Health Main Division of Education Division of Culture Committee on Physical Culture and Sport	Directs: Division of Agriculture Food Processing Industry Production Association "Krasnoiarsk khleboprodukt" Production Association "Krasnoiarsk khlebprom" Production Association "Krasnoiarsk vodmelioratsiia"
Coordinates: Statistics Division Tax Inspectorate Banks Exchange and Trading Houses Arbitrazh Court		Coordinates: Science, Higher and Specialized Education Organization of Tourism	Coordinates: Association of Peasant and Farmers' Holdings

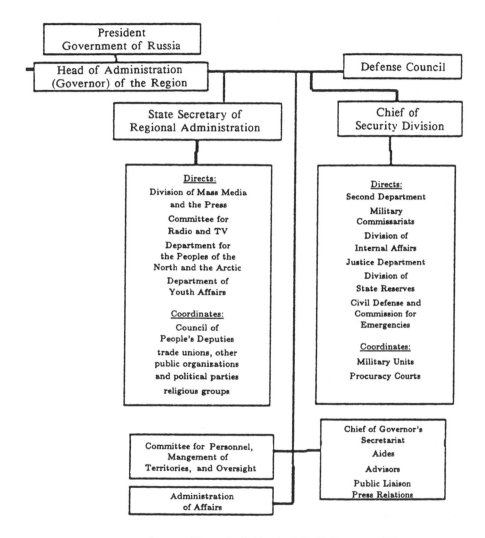

Source: *Krasnoiarksii rabochii*, 30 January 1992

In most regions, however, the leading political figure at the beginning of 1992 was the head of administration (*glava administratsii*), often referred to as governor in the Russian press (see Table 11.1).[14]   Created by the July 1991 law on local government as the successor to the old soviet executive committee chairman, the governor was granted sweeping patronage powers in his region by the new legislation.   Governors throughout the Russian Federation were scheduled to be directly elected to office on 8 December 1991.[15]   But in early November, President Yeltsin unexpectedly asked the Russian legislature to postpone the elections for a year.   After initial hesitation, the Congress of People's Deputies agreed, thus granting Yeltsin the power to appoint governors in the interim.   Yeltsin made full use of this authority by placing in office governors who were committed, at least publicly, to advance the reform program of the president.   According to the head of the president's Monitoring Department, to whom the governors reported, the most important qualification for a governor was his devotion to the cause of the Russian president.[16]

Even with these extraordinary patronage powers, the central state struggled to govern the vast and ethnically-diverse Russian Federation.   Powerful conservative elites in many local areas launched campaigns to resist centrally-imposed policies and to discredit the Yeltsin appointees, in some cases by setting the governors against the *namestniki*.   At times, Yeltsin's appointees in provinces played into the hands of the conservatives through their incompetence, arrogance, or complicity.[17]   There were numerous complaints by forces to the left and right of Yeltsin that the president selected ethically or politically compromised officials for these provincial sinecures.[18]   Whatever the validity of these claims, it is certainly true that both the governors and the representatives were drawn largely from the old *nomenklatura*.

If the Russian leadership is successful in rooting out the entrenched conservatives elites in the provinces, it still faces a nationalist challenge from the non-Russian areas of the Russian Federation (English, unfortunately, does not capture the distinction between *rossiiane*—all citizens of the *Rossiiskaia federatsiia*—and *russkie*—ethnic Russians).   It is worth recalling that the 20 non-Russian republics of the Federation differ in terms of size, the proportion of ethnic Russians to titular nationals (less than 10 percent Russians in Dagestan as opposed to 73 percent in Karelia), location (most republics are on the southern borders, though some, like Tatarstan and Bashkiria, are in the heartland), and the virulence of separatist sentiment.   In order to accomodate the national aspirations of the minority peoples of the Federation, the Russian leadership has attempted to develop a federal state structure that grants the 20 minority republics a degree of political autonomy from the center (see Table 11.2).   But

Table 11.2
Ethnic Republics in the Russian Federation
1989

Bashkiria		3,943,113	*Komi*			1,250,847
	Bashkir	863808 21.9%		Komi	291542	23.3%
	Russians	1548291 39.3%		Russians	721780	57.7%
	Tatars	1120702 28.4%		Ukrainian	104170	08.3%
Buriatia		1,035,252	*Mari*			749,332
	Buriat	249525 24.1%		Mari	324349	43.3%
	Russians	726165 70.1%		Russians	355973	47.5%
	Ukrainians	22868 02.2%		Tatars	43850	05.9%
Chechen-Ingushetia		1,270,429	*Mordva*			963,504
	Chechen	734501 57.8%		Mordvin	313420	32.5%
	Ingush	163762 12.9%		Russians	586147	60.8%
	Russians	293771 23.1%		Tatars	47328	04.9%
Chuvash		1,338,023	*Northern Ossetia*			632,428
	Chuvash	906922 67.8%		Ossetians	334876	53.0%
	Russians	357120 26.7%		Russians	189159	29.9%
	Tatars	35689 02.7%		Ingush	32783	05.2%
Dagestan		1,802,188	*Tatarstan*			3,641,742
	Avar	496077 27.5%		Tatars	1765404	48.5%
	Darghin	280431 15.6%		Russians	1575361	43.3%
	Kumyk	231805 12.9%		Chuvash	134221	03.7%
	Lezgin	204370 11.3%				
	Russians	165940 09.2%	*Tuva*			308,557
				Tuvin	198448	64.3%
Kabardino-Balkaria		753,531		Russians	98831	32.0%
	Kabardin	363494 48.2%		Khakass	2258	00.7%
	Balkar	70793 09.4%				
	Russians	249750 33.1%	*Udmurtia*			1,605,663
				Udmurts	496522	30.9%
Kalmykia		322,579		Russians	945216	58.9%
	Kalmyks	146316 45.4%		Tatars	110490	06.9%
	Russians	121531 37.7%				
	Darghin	12878 04.0%	*Yakutia*			1,094,065
				Yakuts	365236	33.4%
Karelia		790,150		Russians	550263	50.3%
	Karelians	70928 09.0%		Ukrainians	77114	07.0%
	Russians	581571 73.6%				
	Beloruss	55530 07.0%				

Source: *National'nyi sostav naseleniia SSSR (po dannym vsesoiuznoi perepisi naseleniia 1989 g.)* (Moscow: "Finansy i statistika," 1991), pp. 34-40.

while 18 republics signed a new federal accord in mid-March 1992, two republics—Tatarstan and Chechnia—postponed acceptance of the agreement.

The hesitation of Tatarstan has been especially troubling to the center because of its large population of Russians, its central location, and the claims for full independence advanced by some Tatar elites.[19] In a referendum ruled illegal by the Constitutional Court of Russia, the electorate of Tatarstan voted for independence by a margin of three to two. It is at this writing too early to say whether the Tatarstan leadership will use this mandate to seek separation from the Russian Federation or merely further concessions on republican autonomy. Regardless of the outcome of the current negotiations between Tatarstan and the center, Tatarstan serves as a reminder that the Russian Federation, much as the Soviet Union before it, has yet to create a single political community. And without a single political community, a single state cannot endure.

The New Russian Executive

State building is in part about how one divides political labor within the center itself as well as between the center and periphery. Since the summer of 1991, politicians in Moscow have been locked in a battle to define, and where possible to expand, the powers and jurisdictions of their respective institutions. These institutions include the presidency, the Government, the parliament, and the constitutional court.

For English or American observers, the institutional arrangements at the center of the Russian Federation appear awkward and unfamiliar. They would be immediately recognized by the French, who first developed the hybrid presidential/parliamentary model on which the Russian state is based. Yeltsin, much like de Gaulle at the beginning of the Fifth Republic, established an elected presidency that rules alongside as well as through the Government and its ministries. On certain matters, the president governs directly through the issuance of decrees. He sends other matters, which require the attention of the ministries or the parliament (the range of such matters is still in dispute), to the Government and its staff for disposition.[20]

One of the most remarkable features of the fledgling Russian state is the size of the presidential staff. From a small group of personal advisors in the summer of 1991, the presidential staff mushroomed by the beginning of 1992 into an intricate bureaucracy employing over 1000 persons. Attached to the president at the beginning of 1992 were 12 state counsellors and several state secretaries, each with responsibility for a particular area of policy.[21] An extensive staff assisted each of the secretaries and counsellors in developing and supervising policy. Within the office of the presidency there also functioned a secretariat, an administrator of affairs—akin to the chief of staff, a group of policy experts, and a Monitoring Department, charged with the oversight of executive institutions in the republics and regions of the Federation.[22] The establishment of a large presidential staff to monitor, and in some cases direct, the implementation of policy recalls earlier state-building episodes in Russian history, when tsars created their own chancellery and Soviet leaders developed a party apparatus parallel to state structures.[23]

As yet the office of the vice-president, occupied by General Alexander Rutskoi in the immediate post-Soviet era, has shown little sign of developing fixed responsibilities. At the end of 1991, the vice-president served as something of a minister without portfolio, assigned by the president to head numerous ad hoc committees that were of vital importance to economic reform and national defense.[24] Rutskoi's responsibilities were curtailed at the beginning of the 1992, however, after he began to advance an alternative reform program to that of the president. It was a measure of the growing political rift between president and vice-president that Yeltsin assigned Rutskoi the task of overseeing agricultural reform, a traditional albatross for politicians in the Soviet era. Despite the lack of an institutional base or firm responsibilities, the vice-president is next in line to succeed the president, and that function alone, given the health of Yeltsin and the role of the USSR vice-president in the August coup, makes the Russian vice-presidency worthy of scrutiny.[25]

To enhance the authority of the Government and to encourage smooth relations between the bureaucracies of the president and the Government during the rebirth of the Russian state, Yeltsin assumed the additional role of prime minister in November 1991. The day-to-day management of Government, however, fell to the first deputy prime minister, Gennadii Burbulis. A former professor of Marxism-Leninism from Yeltsin's home region of Sverdlovsk (now Ekaterinburg), Burbulis quickly amassed a large staff in the Government's secretariat and its office of administration of affairs. Working beneath Burbulis at the beginning of 1992 were several deputy prime ministers, each with responsibility for a particular branch of governmental affairs. These included Mikhail Poltoranin, who oversaw ministries in the press and cultural sector, Sergei Shakhrai, who supervised the legal affairs ministries, and Alexander Shokhin, who was in charge of ministries in the social sector.[26]

Perhaps the most visible, and politically vulnerable, deputy prime minister was Egor Gaidar, an academic economist who assumed direct control of the economic reform program launched in January 1992. Throughout the winter of 1991-92, Gaidar served as a lightning rod for critics of a market-oriented economic policy that dramatically increased inflation and unemployment. That Gaidar enjoyed the confidence of Yeltsin through these difficult first weeks of reform was indicated by his promotion to the post of first deputy prime minister (alongside Burbulis) at the beginning of March 1992. Following this reshuffling of the Government, Burbulis supervised the work of Shakhrai and Poltoranin while Gaidar oversaw the work of Shokhin and Valerii Makharadze, the latter a newcomer to the Government whose task was to act as the "chief communications officer" (*glavnyi dispatcher*) in economic affairs.[27]

A further reshuffling of the Government occurred at the beginning of April 1992, when Burbulis vacated his post as first deputy premier to return to full-time work in the presidential apparatus as state secretary. This move seemed designed to distance Burbulis, now out of the Government, from mounting legislative criticism rather than to change his area of responsibility. By attaching Burbulis to the presidential staff, Yeltsin signalled his intent to further decouple the executive from the legislature. Thus, the transfer of Burbulis, made on the eve of the first congress of people's deputies to meet since the collapse of the USSR, pushed Russia one step closer to a pure presidential system, in which the president would direct the ministers without a Government organically linked to parliament.

The Russian Government included, of course, not just a central management team but ministers and state committee chairmen with specific portfolios. In Russia, the ministries and state committees remained the organizations with direct responsibility for Government administration (though by the spring of 1992 there was apparently a move afoot to relabel some of them "departments" [*departamenty*]).[28]   Following the major reorganization of the Russian Government in the fall of 1991, the number of ministries and state committees declined from 46 to 23 (see Table 11.3). Thus, the Russian ministerial structure appeared lean compared to the over 100 ministries and state committees that had constituted the Soviet Council of Ministers a few years earlier. Yet this simplified structure did not necessarily signify a reduction in the size of the ministerial apparatus. The Russian Ministry of Industry, for example, absorbed into its operations 14 specialized industrial ministries from the former Soviet state.[29]   An indication of the scale of the ministerial apparatus in the new Russian state came in criticism levelled by deputies against the budget of Gaidar in January 1992. Where the budget allocated 78 million rubles to fund the Russian Supreme Soviet, 104 million rubles for the administration of the president, and 1.75 billion rubles for the entire apparatus of the Ministry of Health throughout the Federation, it earmarked more than 3 billion rubles to support the operations of central ministries and agencies.[30]

Constraints on Executive Power

Despite the existence of separate executive bureaucracies surrounding the president and Government, Yeltsin envisioned the development of what he termed a single executive power in the Russian Federation. Put simply, all executive institutions should work in concert toward common goals. Opposition has its place, but in parliament and society, not in the executive, a principle to which all modern democracies adhere (except France during periods of "cohabitation"). The depth of concern about the internal opposition within the executive was evident in remarks by the senior official in the Government, Gennadii Burbulis.

> Now it is rather well known where the Party nomenklatura at the territory, province, city and district level resettled. Within a month, the overwhelming majority of these people turned up in the structures of state executive power. Many of them remained in the Soviets. Where there were no positions for them, some were concocted. A large number of these people, dropping all camouflage, openly threw themselves into gangsterism at the working level.[31]

Having declared war on such executive opposition, would Yeltsin's revolution from above respect the opposition of "representative power" (the parliament) and its role in shaping, or at least limiting, executive power? Firm conclusions about executive-legislative relations in Russia must of course await the development of mature parties that will serve in parliament as the political base, or the political opposition, of the president and Government.[32] But the early evidence indicates that the Russian parliament has been willing to vigorously oppose the executive and that that opposition has at times modified and constrained executive behavior.[33] It is clear, however, that Yeltsin views the parliament's role as limited in the transition period. In response to the question, "What should Russia be—presidential or parliamentary?," Yeltsin responded:

> Given the current alignment of political forces, including in the parliament, ... the transition to a parliamentary form would be simply inadmissable .... In the conditions of crisis such a policy would be equivalent to suicide. I, as president, will never agree to such an option .... [I]n the current situation, for the next two-three years, one can only speak of a presidential republic.[34]

In the wake of the August coup, which brought the victory of Yeltsin and Russia over Gorbachev and the Soviet Union, the two legislative institutions in

Table 11.3
Ministries and State Committees
in the Russian Federation
December 1991

Ministries	State Committees
Agriculture	Agency of Federal Security
Architecture, Construction, and Housing	Antimonopoly Policy and Support of New Economic Structures
Communications	
Culture	Customs Committee
Ecology and Natural Resources	Defense Questions
Economics and Finance	Management of State Property
Education	Nationality Policy
Foreign Affairs	Protection of Persons and Rehabilitation of Territory Suffering from Chernobyl
Fuel and Energy	
Health	
Industry	Social and Economic Development of the North
Internal Affairs	
Justice	Tax Service
Labor and Employment	
Press and Information	
Science, Higher Schools, and Technical Policy	
Social Protection of the Population	
Trade and Material Resources	
Transport	

Source: "O reorganizatsii tsentral'nykh organov gosudarstvennogo upravleniia RSFSR," *Vedomosti S"ezda narodnykh deputatov RSFSR i Verkhovnogo Soveta RSFSR*, no. 48 (1991), item 1696.

Russia (the large, popularly-elected Congress of People's Deputies and the smaller, indirectly-elected parliament) rallied behind the president. As the decisive winter of 1991-1992 approached, the legislature acceded to Yeltsin's request for extraordinary powers to govern the country in what was certain to be a period of crisis. The November session of the Congress of People's Deputies authorized the president to reorganize executive institutions without legislative approval and to issue legislation on economic affairs. This voluntary transfer of legislative authority to the president, reminiscent of a measure adopted by the USSR legislature a year earlier, was tempered by the requirement that all presidential decrees on the economy first pass through an expedited parliamentary review and by the legislature's right to veto such decrees within a week of their enactment. The ground was laid for an executive-legislative condominium on economic policy.[35]

Relations between the Russian executive and legislature steadily deteriorated, however, at the end of 1991 and the beginning of 1992.[36] The first clear evidence of this rift came in mid-November 1991, when the parliament annulled Yeltsin's hastily-prepared declaration of emergency rule in the southern republic of Chechen-Ingushetia. The Russian president was forced to withdraw troops from the region only three days after sending them in.[37] A more serious and protracted dispute between executive and legislature arose over economic reform. In its harsh criticism of the economic shock therapy administered by the executive in January 1992, the legislature gave voice to the discontent of the population and to its own ideological misgivings about the marketization of the Russian economy.[38] The chair of the parliament, Ruslan Khasbulatov, known popularly as the speaker, was the most visible, and one of the most acerbic, critics of the executive's handling of the economy. According to Khasbulatov, the members of Yeltsin's Government "are there by chance (*sluchainimi liudmi*). They are poor professionals who ... do not have a clue about macro-economics."[39]

The heightened tension between the Russian executive and legislature had its roots in the dramatic rise of presidential power in late 1991, in the personal competition between the technocratic "Young Turks" in Yeltsin's Government[40] and the more traditional politicians in the legislature, and in the widening gap between the cautious reformism of the legislature and the radical policies of the executive. When elected at the beginning of 1990, the Russian Congress of People's Deputies and the parliament selected from within it were agents of change. They became barriers to reform by the end of 1991, having been leapfrogged politically by a president with a more recent, and more radical, mandate. As late as the end of October 1991, for example, the Congress of People's Deputies blocked attempts by the executive to privatize land.[41]

It is uncertain whether a constitutional crisis in relations between executive and legislature can be avoided. Complaining that Government officials are treating the legislature as merely "one of the elements in the structure of presidential power," Khasbulatov began to boldly assert legislative prerogatives by the end of 1991. Vowing that "[w]e are not going to just sit and watch what the President and the Government do,"[42] in February 1992 Khasbulatov appointed the first legislative representatives in the provinces to shadow Yeltsin's *namestniki*.[43] He also demanded that Yeltsin resign his post as prime minister, thereby making it easier for the parliament to express its lack of confidence in a head of Government. In exchange for this resignation, Khasbulatov offered to ensure the passage of a new Russian Federation constitution desired by Yeltsin at the April 1992 meeting of the Congress of People's Deputies.[44]

At the April Congress of People's Deputies, the legislature sought to claw back some of the authority for economic decisionmaking that it had granted earlier to the executive. The Government, now under the leadership of Gaidar, responded by tendering its resignation to Yeltsin (it was refused by the president). This move, designed to signal alarm in the country and the West about the ungovernability of Russia without strong and unchallenged executive leadership, prompted angry exchanges on the floor of the Congress. Hearing his Government described by Speaker Khasbulatov as "fellows who had lost their heads," Gaidar and his deputies stalked out of the Congress session.[45]

Such posturing for advantage by both legislative and executive officials seems destined to continue as long as the Government lacks a working majority in the Congress and parliament. Unlike de Gaulle at the beginning of the Fifth Republic, or even the president of post-Soviet Kyrgyzstan, Askar Akaev, Boris Yeltsin has not succeeded in building a presidential coalition in the legislature.[46] The parliamentary support he does enjoy, concentrated in groups such as Democratic Russia, has been limited and transient.[47] For the efficient and democratic functioning of the Russian state, it is essential that the executive at some point secure a loyal majority in parliament. In the current conditions, however, Yeltsin has little hope of achieving such a majority through new parliamentary elections.[48] Over the short term, then, he appears to face a Hobson's choice: to cohabit with an often obstructionist parliament or provoke a constitutional crisis by suspending the legislature temporarily. Rumors of such a suspension—akin to the "autocoups" of Latin American politics—were circulating in March 1992 and may well have been the work of a frustrated executive seeking to encourage parliamentary quiescence.[49]

The new Constitutional Court has also constrained the Russian executive. Within weeks of its formation in November 1991, the Constitutional Court of the Russian Federation had asserted its right to review the constitutionality of what appeared to many to be a routine executive decision. In January 1992, the Court ruled unconstitutional the merger of the ordinary and security police into a new superministry, reminiscent of Stalin's NKVD. When Yeltsin's spokesman on legal affairs, Shakhrai, complained publicly that the Constitutional Court had reached a political and not a legal decision, the chairman of the Court, Valerii Zorkin, threatened to remove Shakhrai from office. As it happened, Yeltsin agreed to respect the Court's ruling.[50]

In the coming months, the Court will undoubtedly be faced with politically explosive cases on federalism and administrative law. It is as yet uncertain whether the Constitutional Court will be able to establish its authority quickly enough to rule decisively in such disputes. But at least a symbolic measure of the new respect given to the judiciary is the salary of the chair of the Constitutional Court, which is equal to that of the heads of the other two "branches," the president and the speaker of parliament.[51]

In the spring of 1992, Russia was on the eve of the enactment of a new constitution, which promised to clarify the formal relations among institutions and administrative levels and to invest the Russian political system with added authority. As we know from Soviet history, however, adopting a constitution does not signal the introduction of constitutionalism. Establishing a clear division of political labor and a respect for law and procedure is a formidable, and time-consuming, assignment, which for most countries has remained unfulfilled. It is perhaps worth reminding ourselves that Russia at its rebirth in the early 1990s faced two daunting tasks: building a constitutional state and governing a society in crisis. Ernest Gellner has captured the enormity of this challenge:

> What the Russians and the other members of the new [Commonwealth] ... are attempting is, all at once, to dismantle an Empire, to operate an economic miracle, to transform a moral and economic climate, to turn a gulag state into a nightwatchman, to settle old national border and other disputes, and to revive a culture. If any significant part of this agenda is achieved, we shall indeed be able, and obliged, to salute a miracle.[52]

Notes

The author wishes to thank Thomas Remington of Emory University and Paul Steeves of Stetson University for their comments on an earlier version of this chapter, Tim Heleniak of the United States Census Bureau for providing census figures, and Igor Filippov of the Russian State Library for bibliographic assistance.

1. Albert Hirschman, *Exit, Voice, and Loyalty: Responses to Decline in Firms, Organizations, and States* (Cambridge, MA: Harvard University Press, 1970).

2. "O vnutrennykh voiskakh MVD RSFSR," *Vedomosti S"ezda narodnykh deputatov RSFSR i Verkhovnogo Soveta RSFSR*, no. 46 (1991), item 1564.

3. V. Rudnev, "The Union Prosecutor's Office is Ordered to Surrender Everything," *Izvestiia*, 18 November 1991, p. 2, translated in *Current Digest of the Soviet Press*, no. 46 (1991), p. 23.

4. "O deiatel'nosti KPSS i KP RSFSR," *Vedomosti S"ezda narodnykh deputatov RSFSR i Verkhovnogo Soveta RSFSR*, no. 45 (1991), item 1537.

5. S. Razin, "Boris Yeltsin's Autumn 'Putsch'," *Komsomolskaia pravda*, 19 November 1991, p. 1, translated in *Current Digest of the Soviet Press*, no. 46 (1991), p. 1.

6. By 26 November 1991, the Russian Ministry of Justice had taken over the publication of the USSR Justice Ministry's bulletin of normative acts, a measure "linked to the liquidation of Union structures of management and economics, including USSR ministries and agencies." *Biulleten' normativnykh aktov*, no. 1 (1992), p. 3. This move was just one small part of the massive seizure of the personnel, property, and finances of USSR ministries by RSFSR ministries. For a list of USSR ministries and their new institutional homes in Russia, see "O reorganizatsii tsentral'nykh organov gosudarstvennogo upravleniia RSFSR," *Vedomosti S"ezda narodnykh deputatov RSFSR i Verkhovnogo Soveta RSFSR*, no. 48 (1991), item 1696.

7. See the several articles translated by *Current Digest of the Soviet Press*, no. 52 (1991), pp. 5-6 under the rubric "Kremlin Power Formally Shifts to Yeltsin," and S. Semendyayev, "Ministry of Foreign Affairs is 'Absorbing' Ministry of Foreign Relations and Moving to Skyscraper on Smolensk-Sennaya Square," *Rossiiskaia gazeta*, 26 December 1991, p. 7, translated in *Current Digest of the Soviet Press*, no. 51 (1991), p. 9.

8. Even in the spring of 1992, many official regional newspapers in Russia had not removed Soviet emblems from their mastheads. See, for example, *Ulianovskaia pravda* and *Krasnoe znamia* (Komi). The Supreme Soviet in Komi was still referring to the territory as the Komi Soviet Socialist Republic in February 1992. "Postanovlenie Verkhovnogo Soveta Komi SSR," *Krasnoe znamie*, 19 February 1992, p. 1.

9. V. Pavlovskii, "Daesh prava respubliki?" *Krasnoiarskii rabochii*, 28 January 1992, p. 2.

10. That the appointment of such representatives was envisioned even before the coup, see V. Kornev, "Predstaviteli Prezidenta Rossii vidiat svoi dolg v tom, chtoby mestnye administratsii byli deesposobnymi," *Izvestiia*, 12 September 1991, p. 3. Yeltsin's example was followed by several other republics, notably Kazakhstan. "Glavy administratsii—'gvardiia partapparata'," *Izvestiia*, 18 February 1992, p. 2.

11. The representatives are somewhat akin to zonal instructors in the old apparatus of the Central Committee of the Communist Party, except that they are based in the region instead of Moscow. The governors, discussed below, are reminiscent of the regional first party secretaries.

12. V. Vyzhutovich, "Namestnik. Novaia rol' na politicheskoi stsene: predstavitel' Prezidenta RSFSR," *Izvestiia*, 25 November 1991, p. 4.

13. "Rossiia: Institut doverennykh lits prezidenta protiv paralicha vlasti i upravleniia," *Izvestiia*, 1 November 1991, p. 2. The official interviewed here was Valerii Makharadze, head of the Monitoring Department of the president.

14. On the role of the governor in one provincial area, see J. Hahn, "Local Politics and Political Power in Russia: The Case of Yaroslavl'," *Soviet Economy*, no. 4 (1991). For more on the governor's difficulties in Yaroslavl, see M. Ovcharov, "Upravlentsy raspushcheny. Novykh naberut po kontraktu," *Izvestiia*, 7 December 1991, p. 2.

15. "O mestnom samoupravlenii v RSFSR," *Vedomosti S"ezda narodnykh deputatov RSFSR i Verkhovnogo Soveta RSFSR*, no. 29 (1991), item 1010; "O vyborakh glavy administratsii," *Vedomosti S"ezda narodnykh deputatov RSFSR i Verkhovnogo Soveta RSFSR*, no. 45 (1991), item 1491; and "O poriadke naznachenii glav administratsii," *Vedomosti S"ezda narodnykh deputatov i Verkhovnogo Soveta RSFSR*, no. 48 (1991), item 1677.

16. J. Wishnevsky, "Russia: Liberal Media Criticize Democrats in Power," *RFE/RF Research Report*, 10 January 1992, p. 8.

17. See, for example, V. Shchepotkin, "Ochen' predan. Delu ili litsu? Kak voznikaiut konflikty v khode reformy mestnoi vlasti v Rossii," *Izvestiia*, 5 November 1991, p. 2, and "Pravitel'stvu nuzhna podderzhka," *Izvestiia*, 2 March 1992, p. 1.

18. "According to figures from the Monitoring Department of the Administration of the RSFSR President, [executive] power in the provinces is represented primarily by former party officials at the rank of district first secretary or higher. In the Ulianovsk region there are 31 of them [in executive posts], in Penzen 23, in Kirov 22, in Cheliabinsk 11 and in Rostov 10." V. Vyzhutovich, "Namestnik. Novaia rol' na politicheskoi stsene: predstavitel' Prezidenta RSFSR," *Izvestiia*, 25 November 1991, p. 4.

19. On the separatist movement in Tatarstan, see G. Kovalskaya, "Have we to take Kazan?" *New Times*, no. 9 (1992), pp. 6-7.

20. On the responsibilities of the Government (Council of Ministers), see "O roli Soveta ministrov RSFSR v sisteme ispolnitel'noi vlasti Rossiiskoi Federatsii," *Vedomosti S"ezda narodnykh deputatov RSFSR i Verkhovnogo Soveta RSFSR*, no. 37 (1991), item 1200; "Ob organizatsii raboty Pravitel'stvo RSFSR v usloviiakh ekonomicheskoi reformy," *Vedomosti S"ezda narodnykh deputatov RSFSR i Verkhovnogo Soveta RSFSR*, no. 45 (1991), item 1538. This last presidential decree envisioned the formation within the Government of a board (*kollegiia*) for urgent policy matters, which is to include as members the president, the vice-president, the prime minister and deputy prime ministers, the minister of foreign affairs, the minister of press and information, and the head of the KGB. The state secretary for legal affairs and the head of the state bank are to have consultative voices on the board. It is not known if this institution has met.

21. These secretaries and counsellors, apparently directly subordinate to the president, had been part of a state council until the last weeks of 1991, when the council was disbanded. Initial appointments to the posts of state counsellor from July 1991 through January 1992 included: legal policy, Shakhrai, Sergei Mikhailovich (19 Jul 1991); development of proposals on status, structure, and form of activity of Security Council RSFSR, Skokov, Iurii Vladimirovich (12 Sep 1991); issues of federation and territories (first occupant unknown); questions of conversion, Malei, Mikhail Dmitrievich (20 Nov 1991); questions of mother and child, Lakhova, Ekaterina Filippovna (20 Nov 1991); questions of science and higher schools, Malyshev, Nikolai Grigor'evich (12 Nov 1991); questions of economic cooperation and interrepublican relations, Granberg, Aleksandr

Grigor'evich (22 Oct 1991); questions of defense and its Services, Kobets, Konstantin Ivanovich (10 Sep 1991), replacing Volkogonov, Dmitrii Antonovich (20 Jul 1991); questions of interethnic relations, Starovoitova, Galina Vasil'evna (20 Jul 1991); questions of ecology and health and its Services (first occupant unknown); relations with social organizations, Stankevich, Sergei Borisovich (27 Jul 1991); foreign policy questions, Vorontsov, Iulii Mikhailovich (23 Jan 1992). These appointments are found in the *Vedomosti S"ezda narodnykh deputatov RSFSR i Verkhovnogo Soveta RSFSR*, July 1991 through January 1992. By early April 1992, only one state secretary, Burbulis, remained in place. See "Key Officials in the Russian Federation: Executive Branch," *RFE/RL Research Report*, no. 15 (1992), pp. 47-51.

22. On the various subdivisions of the presidency, see *Vedomosti S"ezda narodnykh deputatov RSFSR i Verkhovnogo Soveta RSFSR*, no. 46 (1991), items 1627 and *passim*.

23. For accusations by critics on the left of Yeltsin that he is restoring party-style structures, see J. Wishnevsky, "Russia: Liberal Media Criticize Democrats in Power," *RFE/RL Research Report*, 10 January 1992, pp. 6-9.

24. The number of committees entrusted to Rutskoi was astounding. See the *rasporiazhenie* of the president, "Ob obiazannostiakh vits-prezidenta RSFSR," *Vedomosti S"ezda narodnykh deputatov RSFSR i Verkhovnogo Soveta RSFSR*, no. 48 (1991), item 1674.

25. For an excellent summary of the Yeltsin-Rutskoi relationship and of institutional relations more generally at the apex of the Russian state, see A. Rahr, "Challenges to Yeltsin's Government," *RFE/RL Research Report*, 28 February 1992, pp. 1-5.

26. For a list of ministries overseen by Gaidar and Shokhin in late 1991, see "O raspredelenii obiazannostei mezhdu zamestiteliami Predsedatelia Pravitel'stva RSFSR," *Vedomosti S"ezda narodnykh deputatov RSFSR i Verkhovnogo Soveta RSFSR*, no. 46 (1991), item 1580. A list of leading officials in the executive and legislative branches of Russian Government as of 3 April 1992 may be found in *RFE/RL Research Report*, no. 15 (1992), pp. 47-55.

27. "G. Burbulis i E. Gaidar teper' budut delit' otvetstvennost'," *Izvestiia*, 3 March 1992, p. 2. One has the sense that Makharadze was appointed to "put out fires" in economic affairs, a task that had distracted Gaidar from the broader policy questions associated with the reform. See "Our Defeat Will Amount to More than Personal Failure .... " *Moscow News*, no. 2 (1992), p. 9. Makharadze had been head of the Monitoring Department of the president. For brief biographies of Yeltin's "team," see "Kto est' kto v 'komande' El'tsina," *Izvestiia*, 22 November 1991, p. 2.

28. "Veriu v zdravyi smysl' i zakony rynochnoi ekonomiki," *Krasnoiarskii rabochii*, 21 January 1992, pp. 1-2. In Krasnoiarsk, the introduction of *departamenty* signified the abolition of the old collegial system used in both Imperial Russian and Soviet ministries in favor of one-man management. *Ibid.*

29. "O reorganizatsii tsentral'nykh organov gosudarstvennogo upravleniia RSFSR," *Vedomosti S"ezda narodnykh deputatov RSFSR i Verkhovnogo Soveta RSFSR*, no. 48 (1991), item 1696.

30. "Zatianut' poiasa ili narastit' .... ," *Rossiiskaia gazeta*, 25 January 1992, p. 1. The figures for the operation of the central ministries include, *inter alia*, embassies abroad

(348 million rubles). "O biudzhetnoi sisteme Rossiiskoi Federatsii na I kvartal 1992 goda," *Vedomosti S"ezda narodnykh deputatov RSFSR i Verkhovnogo Soveta RSFSR*, no. 9 (1992), item 392. This budgetary law should be essential reading for all students of Russian government and politics.

31. "Will We Finally Get Moving?" *Literaturnaia gazeta*, 13 November 1991, p. 5, translated in *Current Digest of the Soviet Press*, no. 46 (1991), p. 5. One of the most difficult tasks facing the Yeltsin Government, and any democratically-oriented successor Government, is training a new generation of officials to replace the *nomenklatura*. To provide this training, the Government established in early March 1992 the Main Administration for the Preparation of Personnel for Government Service (*Glavnoe upravlenie po podgotovke kadrov dlia gosudarstvennoi sluzhby*), which will operate regional training centers based on the old higher party schools in Novosibirsk, Ekaterinburg, Khabarovsk, Rostov-on-Don, Nizhnii Novgorod, Saratov, and St. Petersburg. "Rezerv dlia pravitel'stva," *Izvestiia*, 5 March 1992, p. 3.

32. One of the traditional mechanisms of parliamentary oversight of the executive, question time, was in place in Russia at the beginning of 1992. It takes places at 3 p.m. on Tuesday afternoons when members of the Government appear before parliament. "Prishla pora delit' biudzhetnyi pirog," *Rossiiskaia gazeta*, 22 January 1992, p. 1.

33. It has certainly been an active law-making institution, enacting 38 laws and approximately 100 *postanovleniia* from September through December, 1991. O. Burkaleva, "Pokoi deputatov i ne snitsia," *Rossiiskaia gazeta*, 31 December 1991, p. 2.

34. "Boris El'tsin: my obustraivaem velikiiu Rossiiu, nas mnogo, i u nas dostatochno dlia etogo sil," *Izvestiia*, 6 April 1992, p. 1.

35. "O nekotorykh voprosakh primeneniia Postanovleniia S"ezda narodnykh deputatov RSFSR 'O pravovom obespechenii ekonomicheskoi reformy'," *Vedomosti S"ezda narodnykh deputatov RSFSR i Verkhovnogo Soveta RSFSR*, no. 47 (1991), item 1593, and "O Komissii zakonodatel'nogo obespechenii ukazov Prezidenta RSFSR," *Vedomosti S"ezda narodnykh deputatov RSFSR i Verkhovnogo Soveta RSFSR*, no. 48 (1991), item 1678. For a perceptive analysis of why the deputies agreed to lessen their own authority vis-a-vis the president, see I. Yelistratov, "It Was Not For Nothing That Khasbulatov Called the Congress Historic," *Izvestiia*, 4 November 1991, p. 1, translated in *Current Digest of the Soviet Press*, no. 44 (1991), p. 8.

36. In an article in December 1991, Olga Bychkov argues that "the first stirrings of a conflict between Yeltsin and the Supreme Soviet did not begin a fortnight ago with the defeat of three out of four presidential proposals on economic reform. The argument about who's more important started during the January [1991] crisis in the Baltics." "The Russian parliament: a melting pot," *Moscow News*, no. 50 (1991), p. 5.

37. Rutskoi argued before the parliament that he was to blame for initiating the emergency decree that Yeltsin signed on Chechen-Ingushetia. I. Muravyova and R. Minasov, "A Step Dictated by the Logic of Events," *Rossiiskaia gazeta*, 12 November 1991, p. 1, translated in *Current Digest of the Soviet Press*, no. 45 (1991), p. 14.

38. The conservative position on economic reform was nicely summarized by an anti-reform newspaper in late 1991: "There exist fundamental national traditions that do not change even under the influence of the most desperate propaganda; yet this policy course

[of Yeltsin's toward privatization and economic liberalization] ignores our traditions of sympathy and compassion in order to favor the enterpreneur, who over the past six years has already demonstrated his ability to flout both law and morality." E. Volodin, "The Right Step, But Toward What?" *Sovetskaia Rossiia*, 5 November 1991, p. 2, translated in *Current Digest of the Soviet Press*, no. 45 (1991), p. 13.

39. "Spiker rossiiskogo parlamenta predlagaet prezidenta konstitutsiiu v obmen na otkaz ot posta prem'era," *Izvestiia*, 13 March 1992, p. 2. For students of executive-legislative relations in the West, one of the most unusual, and troubling, features of the Soviet and now Russian parliament has been the presidium, a kind of parliamentary cabinet that functions as the organizer of legislative activity, law-giver, and, in some respects, executive. The chair of the Constitutional Court complained at the end of 1991 that "in its activity the Presidium of the Russian Federation Supreme Soviet frequently goes beyond its constitutional powers, usurping the powers of legislative and executive authorities." O. Burkaleva, "The Deputies Didn't Even Dream of Peace and Quiet," *Rossiiskaia gazeta*, 25 December 1991, p. 6, translated in *Current Digest of the Soviet Press*, no. 52 (1991), p. 16.

40. As Alexander Rahr points out, there are tensions within the executive on generational (and ideological) grounds as well as between the executive and legislature. "Russian's 'Young Turks' in Power," *Report on the USSR*, 22 November 1991, pp. 20-23. This article also discusses the conservative role played within Yeltsin's inner by Iurii Petrov, the president's administrator of affairs. For more on Petrov and the "conservatives" in Yeltsin's entourage, see "The Nomenklatura Underground is Taking Control of the President's Staff," *Nezavisimaia gazeta*, 24 January 1992, translated in *Current Digest of the Soviet Press*, no. 4 (1992), pp. 6-7. According to this article, there was a transfer en masse of personnel from the Communist Party Central Committee apparatus to Russian executive institutions after the coup. The claim is that now many of these officials, working under Petrov in the president's office of administration of affairs, are serving as "a unified antigovernment mechanism." *Ibid.*

41. I. Elistratov, "El'tsin poluchaet novye polnomochiia," *Izvestiia*, 1 November 1991, p. 2.

42. S. Chugayev, "Reforms Must be Done by a Team, not by Freelancers," *Izvestiia*, 14 January 1992, p. 1, translated in *Current Digest of the Soviet Press*, no. 2 (1992), p. 7.

43. S. Chugayev, "Parliament Appoints Commissars in the Provinces," *Izvestiia*, 11 January 1992, p. 2, translated in *Current Digest of the Soviet Press*, no. 2 (1992), pp. 22-23.

44. "Spiker rossiiskogo parlamenta predlagaet prezidentu konstitutsiiu v obmen na otkaz ot posta prem'era," *Izvestiia*, 13 March 1992, p. 2.

45. *Novosti* (Russian Television One), 1815 GMT, 12 April 1992.

46. On the attempts of Akaev to develop a presidential party from among reform-oriented state and party officials and democratic elements in Kirgiz society, see E. Huskey, "Kyrgyzstan: The Politics of Demographic and Economic Frustration," in *Nations and Politics in the Soviet Successor States*, ed. Ian Bremmer and Raymond Taras (Cambridge: Cambridge University Press, 1992).

47. A. Dubnov, "Will the Democratic Russia movement become a presidential party," *New Times*, no. 10 (1992), pp. 9-11, and M. Urban, "Boris El'tsin, Democratic Russia and the Campaign for the Russian Presidency," *Soviet Studies*, no. 2 (1992), pp. 187-207. Burbulis described the parliament as a "bailiwick of the totalitarian system." TASS, 14 January 1992, cited in *RFE/RL Research Report*, 24 January 1992, p. 68.

48. As one local governor noted with regard to the legislature in his region, "since it's impossible to elect a new regional soviet soon ... the key to the resolution of the problem [of reform] lies in the executive vertical." S. Sulakshin, "Neprosty prostye resheniia. Razmyshleniia predstavetelia Prezidenta RSFSR o demokratii i vlasti," *Izvestiia*, 4 October 1991, p. 2.

49. "Spiker rossiiskogo parlamenta predlagaet prezidentu konstitutsiiu v obmen na otkaz ot posta prem'era," *Izvestiia*, 13 March 1992, p. 2.

50. V. Rudnev, "The Decision is Final. It Cannot be Appealed," *Izvestiia*, 15 January 1992, pp. 1,3, translated in *Current Digest of the Soviet Press*, no. 3 (1992), pp. 13-14.

51. On the next lower salary level are the prime minister, the vice-president, the first deputy chair of the Supreme Soviet, the chairs of the Supreme Court and the Supreme *Arbitrazh* Court, and the Procurator General. The highest state salary is to be no more than 21 times that of the lowest. "O dolzhnostom sootvetstvii v oplate truda v strukturakh vysshikh organov zakonodatel'noi, ispolnitel'noi i sudebnoi vlasti v RSFSR," *Vedomosti S"ezda narodnykh deputatov RSFSR i Verkhovnogo Soveta RSFSR*, no. 47 (1991), item 1591.

52. E. Gellner, "From the ruins of the Great Contest. Civil society, nationalism, and Islam," *Times Literary Supplement*, 13 March 1992, p. 10.

INDEX

Adams, Jan, 59
Administrative-Financial Commission, 18–19
Agencies, types of, 182
Agrarian Questions and Food, USSR
  Supreme Soviet Committee on,
  169–71
Agricultural Academy, All-Union, 165
Agricultural Commission (Central
  Committee), 62, 73
Agricultural Department (Central
  Committee), 170–71
Agricultural ministries, 161–72
  administrative decentralization, 166–71
  creation of *Gosagroprom* USSR, 163–66
  final attempts at improvement, 171–72
  before Gorbachev, 162–63
Agriculture, Ministry of, 162
Agriculture, People's Commissariat for,
  16, 23, 162
Agriculture and Food, Ministry of, 171
Agroindustrial associations, 163
Agroindustrial Bank, 170
Akaev, Askar, 116, 262
Alekseev, Sergei, 102*n. 48*, 229
Alexander I, 3–4
Alexander II, 4–5
Alexander III, 5
Aliev, Gaidar A., 34
Alksnis, Viktor, 193
"All Power to the Soviets" (slogan), 84
All-union ministries, 112, 182
Alpha group, 250
Andropov, Iurii, 36, 52, 207–8, 213
Animal Industry Machine Building,
  Ministry for, 152
Anti-alcohol campaign, 139
Arakcheev, A.A., 4
Argumenty i fakty, 94
Arkhipov, Ivan V., 34

Armed Forces, People's Commissariat for,
  183
Armed Forces, USSR, 185
Armenia, 194
Automobile and Agricultural Machine
  Building, Ministry of, 156
Avtosel'khozmash-Kholding (joint-stock
  company), 156
Azerbaijan, 116, 194

Bakatin, Vadim, 74, 76, 115, 124*n. 45*,
  215–16
Baltic states, 77
  after coup attempt, 121
  currencies, 138–39
  establishment of independent legal
  system in, 237
Bank for Foreign Economic Relations,
  USSR, 121
Belorussia, 15, 117–18
Belorussian Military District, 186
Belozertsev, S., 104*n. 67*
Beria, Lavrentii P., 24, 28–30, 36, 204–5
Bessmertnykh, Aleksandr, 115, 124*n. 45*
Biriukova, Alexandra, 87
BKHSS, 209–10
Black Sea Fleet, 194
Boards (*kollegii*), 3, 153
  commissariats, 22
  courts, 224
  defense ministry, 185
  internal affairs ministry, 209
  military, 196
Bolsheviks, 3
  executive-legislative relations under, 84
  finance ministry under, 130–31
  reliance on structures and processes of
  Provisional and Imperial
  governments, 7

Revolutionary government, 10–12
in Sovnarkom, 8
use of tsarist military officers in Civl
War, 189
Bonch-Bruevich, Vladimir D., 8, 10
Brezhnev, Leonid, 52
agricultural management, 163
Council of Ministers under, 34–35
industrial ministries under, 147, 152
internal ministry, 206–7
police leaders after death of, 205
state bureaucracy under, 58
Brooks, Karen M., 167
Budget, Union, 137
Bulganin, N.A., 29, 30, 31, 44n. 63
Burbulis, Gennadii, 257–58
Bureaucracy
Gorbachev economic reforms and
resistance from, 61
official Soviet explanation of
bureaucratism, 143
party-state relations and, 58–59
Burlatskii, Fedor, 235

Cabinet of Ministers, 76, 89, 94
coup attempt and, 120–21
presidential power and, 110–16
republics and, 118–19
Candidate membership (Central
Committee), 52
Capital investment, 149
Carr, E.H., 15
CEC. See Central Executive Committee
Central Auditing Committee, 52–53
Central Committee, 146, 167
Agricultural Commission of, 62, 73
Agricultural Department of, 170–71
under Brezhnev, 32, 35–38
candidate membership in, 52
housing policy, 58
interlocking membership with state
bodies, 52, 54–55
International Department of, 59, 64
members in state institutions (1990)
(table), 69
new departments (October 1990), 71–72
Presidium of, 27, 29, 31–32
restructuring of, after 19th Party
Conference, 62–64
separation of party and government
following Khrushchev, 32

Central Committee (continued)
under Stalin, 25–26
weakening of, under Gorbachev, 57
Yeltsin on duplication of minsterial work
by, 60
Central Committee plenums
July 1988, 62, 63
March 1989, 166
October 1990, 70, 73, 74–76
September 1988, 62
Central Control Commission, 16
Central Executive Committee (CEC),
11–12, 14, 17–20
Centralism/centralization, 49, 182
Central Statistical Directorate, 15–16
Chancellery, 9–10
Chazov, Evgenii, 86
Chechen-Ingushetia, 261
Chechnia, 256
Cheka. See Extraordinary Commission for
Combating Counter-Revolution,
Speculation and Sabotage, All-Union
Chernavin, Vladimir N., 181, 192
Chernenko, Konstantin, 52, 208
Chernobyl' accident (1986), 170
Chernoivanov, Viacheslav I., 169, 171
Chubar', Vlas Ia., 17
Churbanov, Yurii, 207–8
Civil War, 9, 12
Bolshevik use of tsarist military officers
during, 189
Supreme Economic Council and, 144–45
Collectivization, 16
Commissariat boards, 22
Commissariats. See People's commissariats
Committee of Ministers (Tsarsist Russia),
4, 6
Commonwealth Command, 181
Commonwealth General Purpose Forces,
196
Commonwealth of Independent States, xii,
78, 250
agricultural policy, 172
armed forces, 193–96
food shortages, 161
formation, 181
industrial ministries, 157
internal ministry troops, 202
legal codes, 238
monetary policy, 139–40
Communications, Ministry of, 112–13

Communist Party. *See also* Central Committee; Party-state relations; Secretariat
accountability of Government and, 85
agricultural policy, 161–62
control over MVD, 212–14
defense ministry and, 182
dissolution, 78
judiciary and, 223–25
military policy, 188–90
Procuracy and, 234
under Stalin, 21
structure (January 1991) (table), 72
structure (1986) (table), 50
Communist Party conference (19th, 1988), 56, 61–63, 223
Communist Party Congress (23rd, 1966), 32
Communist Party Congress (27th, 1986), 60
Communist Party Congress (14th, 1925), 21
Communist Party Congress (28th, 1991), 68–69, 73–74
Communist Party Congress (11th, 1922), 13
Communist Party Congress (19th, 1952), 27
Communist Party plenum (June 1987), 92
Congress of People's Deputies, 64, 97, 260–62
agricultural policy, 171
dissolution, 78
failure of, 83
formation, 61
Constitution, USSR
Brezhnev constitution (1977), 35, 39, 50, 93, 182–83
first (1918), 11
Stalin constitution (1936), 22, 182
Constitutional Court of the Russian Federation, 229–31, 262–63
Constitutional interpretation, 228–29
Constitutional Review Committee, 92–93
Conventional Forces in Europe, 193
Coordinating the Activity of Law Enforcement Organs, Committee on, 231
Coordination Agency for the Supervision of Law and Order, 76
Corrective Labor Administration (MVD), 211

Council of Foreign Ministers of the USSR and Union Republics, 119
Council of Ministers, USSR, 7, 84, 146, 147, 167. *See also* Cabinet of Ministers
under Brezhnev, 32–38
Cabinet of Ministers compared with, 111–12
careerism in, 59
interlocking membership with party bodies, 52–54
under Khrushchev, 29–32
party officials in, 80*n. 18*
post-Stalin period, 27–29
presidium of, 26, 31, 32–38
under Stalin, 25–26
Council of Ministers of Culture, 119
Council of Ministers (Tsarsist Russia), 4–6
Council of Nationalities, 55
Council of People's Commissars (Sovnarkom), 7–20, 42*n. 34*, 42*n. 43*, 84, 146
under Stalin, 20–25
Council of the Union, 55
Coup attempt (August 1991), xi-xii, 77, 225
MVD and, 214
political divisions within officer corps and, 193
presidency and, 120–21
scarcity of affordable food and, 161
Yazov and, 188
Courts, 223, 230
Credit, provision of, 150
Crimea, 194
Currency, 138–40
Current Affairs, Commission on, 31, 33

Defense, Ministry of, 181–96
civil-military relations in Soviet era, 187–90
Gorbachev reforms and, 190–93
management of armed forces, 185–87
post-Soviet era, 193–96
Soviet federal structure and, 181–83
structure in Soviet era, 183–85
Defense, People's Commissariat of, 183
Defense Council, 9, 115–16, 185, 188
Defense Minister, 185
Defense of Public Order, Ministry for (MOOP), 206

Demichev, Petr N., 38
"Democratic centralism," 61
Demokratizatsiia, xi
Departmentalism, 94, 146, 148, 152
Department for Ties with Socio-Political
    Organizations (Central Committee),
    71–72
Department of Administrative Organs
    (Central Committee), 212
Department of Economics and Finance
    (Interrepublican Economic
    Committee), 146
Department of Organizational Party Work
    (Central Committee), 52
Department of State and Law (Central
    Committee), 215
Department on Legislative Initiatives and
    Questions of Law (CPSU), 70
Destatization, 157
Dobrynin, Anatolii, 55
Dolgikh, Vladimir I., 35
Domestic Trade, People's Commissariat,
    15
Draft treaty on economic union
    (September 1991), 139
Duma
    Alexander I, 4
    following revolution of 1905, 6
Dzasokhov, Alexander, 73
Dzerzhinsky, Felix, 17

Economic Council, 23
Economic Reform of the USSR Council of
    Ministers, State Commission for,
    170
Economic reform under Gorbachev, 61
Efremov, D.V., 46*n. 93*
Elections, military officers in, 192
Enisei Republic, 251
Environment Ministry, 89
Estonia, 75, 77, 121
Execution Commission, 22
Executive branch (Russian Federation),
    256–63
Executive-legislative relations, 83–98
    lawmaking, 91–95
    legislative oversight of executive, 95–97
    legislative powers over executive
        appointments, 85–91
    Soviet history, 84–85
Extra-departmental guard (MVD), 210–11

Extraordinary Commission for Combating
    Counter-Revolution, Speculation and
    Sabotage, All-Union (Cheka), 10, 12,
    15, 16

Federation Council, 76, 108–9, 111
    repbulics and, 118, 120
Fedorchuk, Vitalii, 207–8
Fedorov, Nikolai, 227, 235–36, 237
Filatov, Alexander, 87
Finance, Ministry of, 129–40, 170
    future trends, 135–40
    historical overview, 129–30
    Russian Republic takeover (1990),
        133–34
Finance, People's Commissariat of,
    130
Fire guards (MVD), 211
"500 day plan," 75, 138
Food and Purchasing, State Commission
    for, 166–71
Food Processing, Ministry of, 152
Food Program, 163
Food Supplies, People's Commissariat for,
    15
Foreign Affairs, Ministry of, 59, 119
Foreign and Domestic Trade, People's
    Commissariat of, 15
"Foreign currency plan," 138
Foreign Economic Commission, 88
Foreign policy, 59
Forestry, Ministry of, 150
Fotieva, Lidia, 10
Fundamental Laws (1906), 6
Furtseva, Elena A., 35

Gaidar, Egor, 257–58
GAI (State Automobile Inspectorate),
    209–10
Gamsakhurdia, Zviad, 116
Gaulle, Charles de, 90, 256, 262
Gellner, Ernest, 263
General secretary, 49–50
General Staff (Defense Ministry), 185–87
Georgadze, 47*n. 101*
Georgia, 118, 165
GKNT. *See* Science and Technology,
    State Committee for
GKO. *See* State Defense Committee
Glasnost, xi, 214
Glavki, 144–45, 153–54

Gorbachev, Mikhail S., xi, 35, 52, 147, 169
  agricultural reforms, 166–67, 172
  Cabinet of Ministers and, 110, 113–16
  creation of presidency by, 106–10
  erosion of parliamentary power and, 94–95
  executive appointments and, 85, 88–90
  industrial management under, 151–52
  military reforms, 190–93
  party-state relations under, 60–75
  weakening of Central Committee under, 57
Gorbunov, Nikolai P., 19
Gorkii, 215
Gosagroprom. See Scientific Research
  Institute for the Processing of Fruits
  and Vegetables, All-Union
Gosbank. See State Bank
Gosplan. See State Planning Commission
Gossnab. See State Supply Committee
Gosstrakh, 138
Gostsen. See Prices, State Committee on
Government structure
  January 1991 (table), 72
  1986 (table), 50
GPU, 16–17
Grechko, Andrei A., 36, 188
Gromov, Boris, 192, 216
Gromyko, Andrei A., 34, 36, 38
Gusev, Sergei, 87

Health, Ministry of (Russian Federation), 258
Heavy industry commissariats, 23, 146
High Commands of Forces, 187
Holding companies, 156
Hough, Jerry, 57–58

Iakovlev, Veniamin, 246*n. 67*
Ievlev, Alexander I., 164
Industrial ministries, 143–57
  budget formation, 150
  capital investment, 149
  functions, 147–53
  historical overview, 143–47
  material-technical supplies, 149–50
  personnel, 151
  plan formulation, 147–48
  plan fulfillment, 148–49
  reforms and reorganizations, 154–57
  science and technology, 151–52
  staff and structure, 152–54
Industry, Ministry of (Russian Federation),
  258

Industry councils, 23
Inflation under Gorbachev, 139
Information, control over, xii
Institutes, research, 151
"Institutional pluralist" model of Soviet
  politics, 57
Integrated Fund for the Development of
  Science and Technology, 151
Interior Ministry (Tsarist Russia), 3
Internal Affairs, Ministry of (MVD), 186,
  202–16
  control and coordination, 212–14
  historical development, 203–4
  judicial system and, 231–32
  Perestroika and, 214–16
  Russian Republic, 250
  structure, 209–12
Internal Affairs, People's Commissariat of
  (NKVD), 203–5
International Department (Central
  Committee), 59, 64
Interrepublican Economic Committee, 78,
  119–20, 146
Investigative Committee, USSR, 244*n. 49*
Ivan IV, 3
Ivashko, Vladimir, 73–76, 82*n. 39*

Joint-stock companies, 156
Judges, 223, 226–28
Justice, administration of, 221–38
  challenges from below, 236–38
  crisis of executive power and, 231–36
  historical background, 221–24
  rise of judicial power, 224–31
Justice, Ministry of, 231–36
Justice, People's Commissariat of, 222

Kaganovich, Lazar M., 24
Kamenev, Lev B., 13, 17–18
Kazakhstan, 117, 157
KGB. *See* State Security, Committee for
Khasbulatov, Ruslan, 261
Khlystov, Aleksandr, 126*n. 79*
Khrushchev, Nikita, 26, 52
  agricultural reorganization, 163
  government under, 29
  industrial ministries, 146–47
  Procuracy and, 223
Kirilenko, Andrei P., 34–35
Kirov oblast, 165
Kolbin, Gennadii, 85–86

Kolkhozy, 163
Kollegii. See Boards
Komsomol, 190
Kosygin, Alexei N., 25, 30, 33, 35, 44*n. 63*
  government under, 32–35
Krasnoiarsk region, 251
Kriuchkov, Vladimir, xi, 87–88, 113, 115,
  124*n. 45*
Krylenko, Nikolai, 222
Kuibyshev, Valerian V., 16, 20
Kuptsov, V., 71
Kuriachev, Mikhail, 126*n. 79*
Kyrgystan, 116–17

Labor and Defense Council (STO), 9,
  11–13, 17, 18–19, 22, 42*n. 34*
Laird, Betty, 161
Laird, Roy, 161
Lane, David, 55
Latvia, 121
  crackdown (January 1991), 77
  MVD and, 212, 215
Law on the Basic Foundations of the
  Destatization and Privatization of
  Enterprises (1991), 156
Law on the Cabinet, 111–12, 119
Law on the Council of Ministers (1978),
  33–34
Law on the Enterprise (1990), 93, 154–55
Law on Foreign Investments
  (Kasakhstan), 135
Law on Foreign Investments (Russian
  Republic), 135
Law on Privatization of State and
  Municipal Enterprises (Russian
  Republic), 135
Law on Privatization (RSFSR), 157
Law on the State Bank (1990), 138
Lay assessors, 243*n. 42*
Lazarev, Igor', 126*n. 79*
Left Communists, 11
Left Socialist-Revolutionaries, 8
Legislation and Legality, Committee on, 87
Legislative Proposals Commission, 18–19
Lenin, Vladimir
  forced confiscation from State Bank and,
    131–32
  government under, 7–13
  judicial system and, 236
  "tsarist hangovers" and, 143–44
Leningrad, 226

Leplevskii, G.M., 18
Leroy-Beaulieu, Anatole, 5
Ligachev, Egor, 55, 61–62
Lipitskii, V.S., 70–71
Lithuania, 74–75, 121, 215
  Procuracy in, 237
Little Sovnarkom, 9, 12, 13, 18–19
Local government under Gorbachev,
  117–18
Loris-Melikov, M.T., 5
Lukianov, Anatolii, 90, 93–94, 98, 104*n.
  71*
Lushchikov, Sergei, 246*n. 67*

Machine-Tool Industry and Instruments,
  Ministry of, 155
Main Politcal Administration (MPA), 190
Main Tax Inspectorate (USSR Ministry of
  Finance), 132
Makashov, Albert, 192
Makharadze, Valerii, 258
Malenkov, Georgii M., 24, 27–29, 30
Malyshev, Viacheslav A., 30, 44*n. 63*
Mangazaev, Valerii, 126*n. 79*
Material-technical supplies (MTS), 149–50
Matveev, Yurii, 85
Mazurov, Kirill T., 34
Meat and Milk Industry, USSR Ministry
  of, 164
Medvedev, Roy, 86
Medvedev, Vadim, 63
Medvedev, Zhores, 52
Mensheviks, 14
Merkulov, Vsevolod N., 204
MGB, 205
Micro-management, 60, 148–49
Mikoian, Anastas I., 24, 30
Military Affairs, People's Commissariat
  for, 183
Military and Naval Affairs, People's
  Commissariat for, 183
Military commissars, 189
Military districts, 186–87
Military Industrial Commission, 33
Military Revolutionary Committee, 8
Militsiia, 209–11
Miliutin, Vladimir P., 162
Ministries, 112–13. *See also* under specific
  areas, e.g.: Defense, Ministry of
Moisseev, Mikhail, 192
Moldavia, 75

Molotov, Viacheslav M., 20–22, 30
MOOP. *See* Ministry for Defense of
    Public Order
Morozov, 194
Moscow
    city soviet, 75
    people's court judges in, 224
    police, 203
    Procuracy in, 232
    reorganization of city government, 117
MPA. *See* Main Politcal Administration
MTS. *See* Material-technical supplies
Murakhovskii, Vsevolod S., 164–65, 169
Muscovy, 3
MVD. *See* Internal Affairs, Ministry of

Nagorno-Karabakh, 194, 211, 215
Namestniki, 251, 254, 262
Napoleon, 4
Narkomtiazhprom, 146
National Economic Council, 14
Nationalities, People's Commissariat for,
    10
Navy, 183
Nazarbaev, Nursultan, 117, 157
NEP. *See* New Economic Policy
New Economic Policy (NEP), 12, 15, 145
Nicholas II, 6
Nihilists, 5
Nikitin, Vladilen V., 168–69
NKGB. *See* State Security, People's
    Commissariat for
NKVD. *See* Internal Affairs, People's
    Commissariat of
Nomenklatura, 51–52, 61, 151, 254
    military appointments, 189
    NKVD and, 204
Noren, James H., 161

October Revolution (1917), 7
OGPU. *See* Unified State Political
    Administration
OMON. *See* Special Purpose Security
    Detachments
One-man management (*edinonachalie*),
    152
Operational Administration of the
    Economy, Committee for the, 78,
    137, 172
Operative Questions, Commission on, 33
Orakhelashvili, Ivan D., 17

Ordzhonikidze, Grigorii K., 16, 20
Organization Bureau (Orgburo), 12
Orgburo. *See* Organization Bureau
OVIR, 209
Owners, enterprise, 155

Paris commune, 8
"Party factions," 70
Party of Communists, 78
Party-state relations, 49–79
    fall of Gorbachev and, 75–79
    under Gorbachev, 60–75
    overview, 51–59
Patronage, 151
Pavlov, Valentin, xi, 76–77, 87, 88, 95,
    113–15, 120, 124*n. 45*, 129
People's commissariats. *See also* specific
    areas, e.g.: Agriculture, People's
    Commissariat for
    November 1923 (table), 16
    under Stalin, 23
People's commissars, 7
Perbukhin, 35
Perestroika, 38
    crisis in judicial system and, 231–36
    MVD and, 211, 214–16
Personnel, enterprise, 151
Pervukhin, Mikhail G., 30–31, 44*n. 63*
Peter the Great, 3, 39–40*n. 2*
Plan formulation, 147–48
Plan fulfillment, 148–49
Pobedonostsev, K.P., 5
Podmena, 56, 60–61
Polianskii, Dmitrii S., 34
Police, 77
Politburo, 14, 50, 147
    establishment of, 12–13
    Lenin's authority and, 19
    membership (October 1990) (table), 66
    membership (1986) (table), 53
    military policy, 188
    reorganization of centrral economic
        institutions by, 166
    under Stalin, 26
    28th Party Congress, 68
Poltoranin, Mikhail, 257–58
Popov, Gavriil, 117
Popular Democratic Party of Uzbekistan,
    78
Poshkus, B.I., 168
Postanovleniia, 111

PPOs. *See* Primary party organizations
Pravda, 68
Pravitel'stvo, xi
Prepatory Commission, 19, 22
Presidency, 106–21
  Cabinet of Ministers and, 110–16
  coup attempt and, 120–21
  creation of, 65–66, 89–90
  departmentalism and, 94
  early reforms under Gorbachev, 106–10
  effect of creation of, 90–91, 98
  reforming of republican and local
    government and, 116–18
  relations between center and periphery
    and, 118–20
  Russian Federation, 256–57
Presidential Council, 66, 76, 108
  membership (October 1990) (table),
    65
Price policy, 88
Prices, State Committee on (*Gostsen*),
  112, 137, 147
Primakov, Evgenii, 115
Primary party organizations (PPOs),
  55–57, 73–75
Prime minister, 49–50
  creation of office of, 113
  Russian Republic, 257
Procuracy
  collapse of Soviet Union and, 237
  independent judiciary and, 226–27
  nominations to, 87–88
  perestroika and, 231–36
  post-Stalin era, 223
  Russian Republic, 250
  under Stalin, 222–23
Profits, enterprise, 150
Properties of the Republic, People's
  Commissariat for, 10
Pugo, Boris, xi, 74, 76, 113, 115, 124*n.*
  45, 216
Purchases of Food Resources, State
  Committee for, 171–72
Putnam, Robert, 58

Rabkrin. See Worker-Peasant Inspection,
  People's Commissariat for
Rails, Ministry of, 88–89
Rasporiazheniia, 111
Rasputin, Valentin, 108
Razumovskii, Georgii, 55–56

Republics
  government reform under Gorbachev, 116
  ministries, 182
  sovnarkoms, 15
Research and development, 151–52
Revolutionary-Military Council, 9
Revolution of 1905, 6
Right Opposition, 145
Rozenova, Lira, 87–88
Rudzutak, E., 17, 20
Russian Federation, 121, 249–63
  appropriation of enterprises, 157
  armed forces, 194–96
  center versus periphery in, 251–56
  ethnic republics (1989) (table), 255
  executive in, 256–63
  judicial system, 237–38
  ministries and state committees (table), 260
  Procuracy in, 232
  structure of regional government (table),
    252
  Yeltsin and establishment of, 249–50
Russian Republic
  financial assets of USSR and, 133–34
  foreign investments, 135
  Yeltsin's rise to president, 116
Rust incident (May 1987), 188
Rutskoi, Alexander, 192, 257
Rykov, Alexei Ivanovich, 13, 43*n. 52*
  government under, 14–20
Ryzhkov, Nikolai, 64–65, 76, 110, 113,
  166, 192
  executive appointments and, 85–90

Saburov, Maksim Z., 30, 35
Saltykov, N.I., 4
Savitskii, Valerii, 226
Science and technology, 151–52
Science and Technology, State Committee
  for (GKNT), 112, 147
Scientific Research Institute for the
  Processing of Fruits and Vegetables,
  All-Union (*Gosagroprom*), 163–69,
  165, 171
Scientific-Technical Council, 151
Secretariat
  careerism in, 59
  departments of (table), 51
  Gorbachev and, 62, 73–74
  membership (October 1990) (table), 67
  28th party congress, 68

Security Council, USSR, 76, 115
Semenova, Galina, 82n. 39
Shakhrai, Sergei, 257–58, 262–63
Shaposhnikov, Evgenii, 181, 193–95
Shatalin, 75
Shchelokov, Nikolai, 207–8
Shelepin, Alexander, 206
Shevardnadze, Eduard, 76, 87
Shmidt, Vasilii V., 17
Shokhin, Alexander, 257–58
Siberian miners' strike, 213–14
Sidorenko, N., 168
Sizenko, Evgenii I., 164
Smolensk archives, 204
Smolentsev, Evgenii, 85
SNK. See Sovnarkom
Socialist legality, 15
Socialist Revolutionaries, 162
Soiuz (coalition), 193
Sokolov, Sergei, 188
Solomon, Peter, 97
Sovkhozy, 163
Sovnarkhozy
  Bolshevik period, 30–31, 144
  under Khrushchev, 146
Sovnarkom. See Council of People's
  Commissars
Special Purpose Security Detachments
  (OMON), 211–12, 215
Speransky, Mikhail, 3–4
Stalin, Iosif, 8, 10, 12, 52
  government under, 20–27
  industrialization under, 145–46
  internal affairs, 203–5
  judicial system under, 236
  law and, 222
  Rabkin under, 16
Starovoitova, Galina, 97
State and Law Department (Central
  Committee), 64, 212
"State and Revolution" (Vladimir Lenin), 8
State Bank (Gosbank), 121
  finance ministry and, 137–39
State committee, 112
State Council (Tsarist Russia), 4–6
State Council (USSR), 78, 161
  agricultural policy, 172
State Defense Committee (GKO), 24–26
State Economic Commission, 31
State Joint-Stock Association, 155–56
State order (goszakaz), 165

State Planning Commission (Gosplan), 17,
  31, 147, 165, 166
State Procurements, Ministry of, 162
State Security, Committee for (KGB), 36,
  77, 130, 190, 205, 207
State Security, People's Commissariat for
  (NKGB), 204–5
State Supply Committee (Gossnab), 147,
  149–50
STO. See Labor and Defense Council
Stolypin, Petr, 9
Strategic Deterrence Force, 185
Sukharev, Alexander, 85, 99n. 11, 233
Sununu, John, 108
Supply, People's Commissariat for, 23
Supply Administration, 152
Supreme Commission (Tsarist Russia), 5
Supreme Court (RSFSR), 225
Supreme Court (USSR), 230, 235, 243n.
  41
  judicial salaries and, 228
  nominations to, 87–88
Supreme Economic Council (Vesenkha,
  VSNKh), 10–11, 23, 144–46
  under Khrushchev, 31
Supreme Soviet, 152
  after 1991 coup attempt, 78
  executive appointments, 87–90
  executive appointments in reformed,
    85–91
  failure of reformed, 83
  Gorbachev's presidency proposal and,
    107, 109
  judicial review and, 229
  as lawmaking institution, 91–92, 93–95
  new powers under Gorbachev, 64
  overlapping membership between party
    institutions, 53, 55
  oversight of executive, 95–97
  Presidium of, 53, 55, 98, 167
  under Stalin, 27
Sverdlov, Iakov, 11
Sydicates, 145

Tadzhik SSR, 15
Tajikistan, 118
Tatars, 3, 238
Tatarstan, 256
Taxation, financing by, 132
Technical Administration, 151, 152
Telegin, Valerii, 126n. 79

"Telephone justice," 224
Teodorovich, Ivan A., 162
Terebilov, Vladimir, 227
Tevosian, Ivan F., 30
Third World, 59
Tikhomirnov, Robert, 87
Tikhonov, Nikolai A.
  government under, 34–36, 38
Tikhonov, Vladimir A., 165–66
Tikunov, Vadim S., 206
Timber Industry, Ministry of, 88
Tiumen region, 226
Tiziakov, Aleksandr, 126n. 77
Totalitarian model of Soviet politics, 57
Tractors and Agricultural Machinery,
  Ministry of, 153
Transcaucasian Soviet Federated Socialist
  Republic, 15
Trotsky, Lev D., 8–9, 12–13
Trubin, Nikolai, 212, 233, 244–45n. 56
Trusts, 145
Tsarist Russia, 3–7
  finance ministry, 129–30
  industrial ministries, 143–44
Tsiurupa, Alexander D., 13, 17
Tsypkin, Michael, 96
Turkmen SSR, 15

Ukraine, 15, 77, 168, 250
  prime ministership in, 117
  split in military and, 193–95
Unified State Political Administration
  (OGPU), 16, 204
Union ministries, 182
Union-republic ministries, 112–13, 182
United Nations, 250
United States, finance policy compared to,
  136
Ustinov, Dmitirii, 188–89
Uzbek SSR, 15
Uzun, Vasilii, 166

Varennikov, Valentin I., 192
Vasiliev, Aleksei, 87
Vesenkha. See Supreme Economic Council
Vice-presidency, 94, 110, 113
  Russian Republic, 257
Volskii, Arkadii, 126n. 80
Voroshilov, Kliment E., 20, 24, 30, 45n. 75

Voznesenskii, Nikolai A., 24, 44n. 63,
  44n. 67
VSNKh. See Supreme Economic Council
VTsIK. See Central Executive Committee
Vydvizhenie movement, 145
Vyshinsky, Andrei, 222

"War of laws" (voina zakonov), 236
Women, Procuracy and, 233
Worker-Peasant Inspection, People's
  Commissariat for (Rabkrin), 16, 22
Workers' Detachments to Support the
  Militia, 215
Workers' Opposition, 145

Yagoda, Genrikh, 204
Yakovlev, Alexander Nikolaevich, 108
Yakovlev, A.M., 96
Yakovlev, Jeniamin, 235
Yanaev, Gennadii, xi, 76–77, 113–15,
  124n. 45
Yazov, Dmitrii, xi, 88, 113, 115, 188
Yeltsin, Boris, 165, 214, 220
  ban on primary party organizations in the
    workplace, 225
  Cabinet of Ministers and, 121
  as candidate for People's Control
    Committee, 86
  consolidation of Russian power under,
    249–51, 254
  Constitutional Court and, 230–31
  on duplication of minsterial work by
    Central Committee, 60
  emergence as dominant political leader,
    78
  executive powers and, 256–63
  justice system and, 227
  military and, 192–93, 195
  as Russian Republic president, 116
Yermin, Lev B., 168
Yezhov, Nikolai, 204

Zakharova, Alla, 126n. 79
Zaprosy, 96
Zhukov, 36
Zorkin, Valerii, 263
Zverev, A.G., 130
Zverev, Andrei, 126n. 79

CONTRIBUTORS

James H. Brusstar is a senior fellow in the Institute for National Strategic Studies at the National Defense University. His past areas of research include Soviet military doctrine and strategy. He is currently working on a study of national security policymaking in Russia.

Barbara Ann Chotiner is Associate Professor of Political Science at the University of Alabama. She is the author of *Khrushchev's Party Reform* as well as shorter studies of the Soviet policy process and the role of the Communist Party in the Soviet economy.

Stephen Fortescue has worked at the Australian National University and the Center for Russian and East European Studies at the University of Birmingham. He currently teaches political science at the University of New South Wales. Fortescue is the author of *The Communist Party and Soviet Science, Science Policy in the Soviet Union*, and articles on Soviet science policy and administrative structures.

Brenda Horrigan is a Ph.D. candidate at the University of Denver's Graduate School of International Studies. A former Soviet affairs analyst for U.S. Government agencies and Science Applications International, she has specialized in questions of arms control and defense industries in the USSR.

Eugene Huskey has taught at Colgate University, Bowdoin College, and Stetson University, where he is currently Associate Professor of Political Science. He is the author of *Russian Lawyers and the Soviet State* as well as numerous articles on Soviet law and government. He has also written on politics in the Central Asian republic of Kyrgyzstan.

Ellen Jones is a senior researcher specializing in Russian military affairs at the Defense Intelligence Agency. She has written widely on Soviet military manpower policy, political institutions, and social trends. Her current research is on the emerging defense policies and structures of the Soviet successor states.

Theodore Karasik is a staff member of the International Policy Department at RAND and the editor of *Facts and Figures Annual*. He has just completed a study of the Communist Party of the Soviet Union.

Peter B. Maggs is Corman Professor of Law at the University of Illinois, Champaign-Urbana. He has published widely in the field of Soviet law. Among his books are *Soviet Law in Theory and Practice* (with O.S. Ioffe) and *Disarmament Inspection under Soviet Law* (with Harold J. Berman).

T.H. Rigby is Professorial Fellow in Political Science at the Australian National University. His many works include *Communist Party Membership in the USSR, 1917-1967, Lenin's Government: Sovnarkom, 1917-1922, The Changing Soviet System: Mono-organizational Socialism from its Origins to Gorbachev's Restructuring*, and *Political Elites in the USSR: Central Leaders and Local Cadres from Lenin to Gorbachev*.

Cameron Ross is Assistant Professor of Government at Oberlin College. He taught previously at Cambridge University and the College of William and Mary. Among his works is *Local Government in the Soviet Union*. His current research focuses on Soviet and post-Soviet political elites.

Louise Shelley is Professor and Chair in the Department of Justice, Law, and Society of The American University, Washington, D.C. She is the author of *Lawyers in Soviet Work Life* and a forthcoming book on the Soviet Ministry of Internal Affairs. She has also contributed numerous articles on criminology and the politics of Soviet law to journals of law, sociology, and Soviet affairs.